EUROPE AND ECONOMIC REFORM IN AFRICA

The relationship between Europe and the African, Caribbean and Pacific (ACP) states has always fascinated economists, political scientists and development experts.

This book analyses the economics and politics of the European Community's relations with Africa with a central focus on the questions of aid, structural adjustment and development policy since the early 1970s. It concludes that EC development policy in Africa is at best a moderate success and suggests that if African states are to avoid marginalization in the emerging world order they must rise to the challenge of global competitiveness.

Topics covered include:

- the origins of EC–African diplomacy in the Rome Treaty
- the Yaoundé conventions
- the Lomé agreements
- EC responses to the new politics of debt and structural adjustment
- the EC experience in Zambia.

Obadiah Mailafia studied Economics and Law in Paris and completed his doctorate at Oxford University. He has been a consultant to the United Nations and an Associate of the Centre for Policy Management, Queen Elizabeth House, Oxford. He is currently Lecturer in International Finance, Richmond Business School, the American University in London.

ROUTLEDGE STUDIES IN DEVELOPMENT ECONOMICS

1 **Economic Development in the Middle East**
Rodney Wilson

2 **Monetary and Financial Policies in Developing Countries**
Akhtar Hossain and Anis Chowdhury

3 **New Directions in Development Economics (Growth, Environmental Concerns and Government in the 1990s)**
Edited by Mats Lindahl and Benno J. Ndulu

4 **Financial Liberalization and Investment**
Kanhaya L. Gupta and Robert Lensink

5 **Liberalization in the Developing World**
Institutional and economic changes in Latin America, Africa and Asia
Edited by Alex E. Fernández Jilberto and André Mommen

6 **Financial Development and Economic Growth**
Theory and experiences from developing countries
Edited by Niels Hermes and Robert Lensink

7 **The South African Economy**
Macroeconomic prospects for the medium term
Finn Tarp and Peter Brixen

8 **Public Sector Pay and Adjustment**
Lessons from five countries
Edited by Christopher Colclough

9 **Europe and Economic Reform in Africa**
Structural adjustment and economic diplomacy
Obadiah Mailafia

EUROPE AND ECONOMIC REFORM IN AFRICA

Structural adjustment and economic diplomacy

Obadiah Mailafia

ROUTLEDGE

London and New York

First published 1997
by Routledge
11 New Fetter Lane, London EC4P 4EE

Simultaneously published in the USA and Canada
by Routledge
29 West 35th Street, New York, NY 10001

Typeset in Garamond by J&L Composition Ltd, Filey, North Yorkshire

Printed and bound in Great Britain by Biddles Ltd, Guildford and King's Lynn

British Library Cataloguing in Publication Data
A catalogue record for this book is available from the British Library

Library of Congress Cataloguing in Publication Data
Mailafia, Obadiah
Europe and economic reform in Africa : structural adjustment and economic diplomacy / Obadiah Mailafia.
(Routledge studies in development economics, ISSN 1359–7884)
Includes bibliographical references and index.
1. Economic assistance, European—Africa. 2. Structural adjustment (Economic policy)—Africa. I. Title. II. Series.
HC800.M338 1997
338.9′1406—dc20 96–2257 CIP

ISBN 0–415–14825–1

For Margaret,
Emmanuel and Samora

CONTENTS

List of figures x
List of tables xi
List of abbreviations and acronyms xiii
Preface xvii

1 INTRODUCTION 1
The general policy context 2
Aid, structural adjustment and international economic relations 4
Power, influence and social exchange 6
The triangle of development diplomacy 12

2 AFRICA AND THE NEW INTERNATIONAL AID REGIME 14
From the Monrovia Strategy to the Berg Report 14
IMF and World Bank Involvement in Africa 16
The critique of Structural Adjustment Programmes 17
African Attitudes to the IMF and World Bank programmes 23
Conclusion 33

3 THE ORIGINS OF EC–AFRICAN DIPLOMACY, 1957–71 35
Eurafrica and the geopolitics of empire 36
The Rome Treaty and the emergence of association 38
The Yaoundé Conventions 46
The Anglo-African Commonwealth and Association 51
Conclusion 60

4 THE EMERGENCE OF LOMÉ AND ITS INSTITUTIONS, 1973–78 61
Forging a Common African Front 65
The main provisions of Lomé 68
The institutional framework of Lomé 71
Lomé and development policy 80
Conclusion 84

5 LOMÉ, POLICY DIALOGUE AND STRUCTURAL ADJUSTMENT 85
The Pisani Memorandum on development policy 87
Policy dialogue and Lomé III 88
The EC Council resolution on structural adjustment in Africa 94
Lomé IV and structural adjustment 96
Conclusion 112

6 EUROPE AND THE AFRICAN EXTERNAL DEBT BURDEN 113
The African debt in international perspective 113
International responses 124
European Community responses 130
Conclusion 144

7 ECONOMIC DECLINE AND POLICY CHOICE IN ZAMBIA 146
Colonial policy and underdevelopment 146
The rise of the single-party state 147
Mineral dependence and development policy 150
The path to economic decline 153
The IMF extended programme, 1981–83 159
The Interim National Development Programme 173
The Fourth National Development Plan, 1989–93 175
Return to multi-party democracy 176
Conclusion 178

8 ZAMBIA AND LOMÉ AID DIPLOMACY 181
The first EEC mission to Zambia 182
Aid programming for Lomé I 183
Lomé II programming and the Foley mission 186
Lomé III programming and the food question 189
Lomé IV programming and the road to adjustment 191
EC food strategy dialogue in Zambia 192
Import support and the Special Action Programme 198
Sysmin and the mining sector 200
The rural smallholder project 207
Germany and the cobalt question 208
Problems of development aid management 210
Conclusion 215

9 THE EC AND ECONOMIC REFORM IN ZAMBIA 217
Liberals, moderates and hard-liners 219
European Community responses 222
Import financing and the foreign exchange gap 226
The EC foreign exchange facility 228

The EC Structural Adjustment Facility 230
The social dimensions of adjustment 233
Export promotion and economic diversification 247
Conclusion 251

10 EUROPE AND AFRICA IN A CHANGING WORLD 252
The prospects of Lomé in a changing world 255
Africa facing the twenty-first century 259

Notes 263
References 312
Index 338

FIGURES

1.1	The mechanism of influence in conditionality-based aid	11
1.2	The triangle of development diplomacy	12
3.1	EEC tariffs on selected products	47
3.2	Volume of the first three EDFs	56
3.3	Volume of first three EDFs by country	58
4.1	EDF aid under Lomé I and II	67
4.2	The institutional framework of Lomé	72
4.3	Organizational structure of the ACP Secretariat	78
4.4	The Lomé aid programming and implementation cycle	83
5.1	EC financial aid resources, Lomé I–III	93
5.2	Structural Adjustment Funds under Lomé IV	108
6.1	SSA external debt in comparison with other LDCs, 1988	114
6.2a	External debts of sub-Saharan Africa, 1970–87	115
6.2b	SSA debts in relation to total LDC debts	116
6.3	Growth of SSA debt burden, 1982–90	118
6.4	SSA debt service payments in 1989	119
6.5	Africa's major debtors, 1983–90	122
6.6	SSA debt restructuring, 1985–89	127
6.7	ACP debt to the European Community, 1963–90	131
7.1	Structure of government participation in the Zambian economy, 1971	151
7.2	Evolution of Zambia's Terms of Trade, 1970–82	153
7.3	Trends in Zambia's GDP, 1970–90	155
7.4	Zambia: public expenditure on subsidies, 1980–89	167
7.5	Zambia: external debt, December 1991	178
7.6	Zambia: debt arrears, December 1991	179
9.1	Administrative structure of the EC/World Bank Micro-Projects Unit	236
9.2	Zambia: expenditure on health and education, 1981–91	238
9.3	Structure of local government in Zambia, December 1990	240
9.4	Development financing and the mechanism of rural power in Zambia	243
9.5	Zambia: main non-traditional exports, 1987–89	250

TABLES

2.1 Typology of stabilization and structural adjustment 18
3.1 Volume of French investments in the African colonies: 1900–40 41
3.2 Total exports of French West Africa and Equatorial Africa in 1959 43
3.3 Contributions and allocations of EDF funds, 1958 46
3.4 Common external tariff rates applied to non-associated third countries by the EEC 47
3.5 EEC–AASM trade, annual rates of change, 1958–71 54
3.6 AASM exports to the EEC, annual rates of change, 1958–71 55
3.7 EEC exports to the AASM and other LDCS, 1958–71 56
3.8 Bilateral and multilateral aid to the AASM, 1962–73 57
3.9 Breakdown of EDF aid by country, December 1973 57
4.1 Comparison of financial aid under Lomé I and II 67
4.2 Summary of principal exports covered by Stabex in 1975 70
4.3 EEC–ACP trade balance, 1975–79 80
4.4 Stabex transfers by product, 1975–89 81
5.1 Price changes for ten selected ACP commodities between 1980 and August 1983 89
5.2 Lomé III funds as compared to Lomé I and II 92
5.3 Financial resources under Lomé IV 101
5.4 The structure of World Bank conditionality 106
5.5 Adjustment resources under Lomé IV, 1991–93 108
6.1 External debts of sub-Saharan Africa, 1970–87 115
6.2 Sub-Saharan Africa's external debt as a share of total developing country debt, 1986 117
6.3 Growth of the sub-Saharan African debt burden, 1982–90 117
6.4 Scheduled and actual debt service payments of sub-Saharan Africa, 1989 119
6.5 SSA debt burden relative to GNP and export capacity, 1991 120
6.6 United States bank claims and exposure to sub-Saharan Africa, 1987 120

6.7 SSA interest arrears in selected years, 1983–90 124
6.8 SSA debt restructurings, 1985–89 126
6.9 ACP debt to the European Community, 1990 132
6.10 Estimated global debt services due to the EC 132
6.11 Classification of EC import programmes, 1987–90 138
6.12 Financial disbursements under the EC Special Programme of Assistance, 1992 139
7.1 Zambia: Terms of Trade Index, 1970–82 152
7.2 Zambia: population and labour force 154
7.3 Long-term trends in Zambia's GDP in selected years, 1970–90 154
7.4 Zambia's transactions with the IMF 160
7.5 Chronology of important policy events, 1983–91 162
7.6 Zambia's balance of payments, 1982–85 163
7.7 Sources of foreign exchange in Zambia, 1986–89 166
7.8 Zambian government expenditure on subsidies, 1980–89 168
7.9 Criteria for selection and prioritization of externally aided projects in Zambia, 1989 174
7.10 Annual rates of inflation in Zambia, 1986–91 175
8.1 Economic aid of the DAC countries and international organizations, Zambia, 1971–80 181
8.2 EEC aid programme to Zambia under Lomé I, 1986 185
8.3 Sysmin allocations under Lomé II 202
8.4 Zambia: copper exports, 1980–90 206
8.5 Utilization of EDF funds from Lomé I to III 210
9.1 ECFF successful applications by sector and economic agents, 1988 229
9.2 Summary of ECFF successful applications by type of product, 1988 230
9.3 Disbursement of EC/GRZ countervalue funds in 1989–90 232
9.4 Cost estimates for disbursement of EC/GRZ countervalue funds during 1992/3 and 1993/4 232
9.5 Real expenditure on health and education in Zambia, 1981–91 237
9.6 Sectoral distribution of completed EC micro-projects, 1990 239
9.7 Spatial distribution of completed EC micro-projects 240
9.8 Existing financial arrangement of the Micro-projects Programme 244
9.9 Zambia: non-traditional exports, 1987–89 248
9.10 Zambia: value of non-traditional exports by sector, 1987–89 249
10.1 Potential external effects of Europe 1992 on developing countries 256
10.2 Potential dangers of 1992 for different LDCs 256
10.3 African and total overseas manufacturing investment by British companies, 1987–92 257
10.4 Gross portfolio equity flows to developing countries by region 258

ABBREVIATIONS AND ACRONYMS

AASM	Associated States of Africa and Madagascar
ACP	African, Caribbean and Pacific Group
AIISP	Agricultural Input Import Support Programme
APPER	African Priority Programme for Economic Recovery
BSAC	British South Africa Company
CAP	Common Agricultural Policy
CEDAF	Centre D'Étude et de Documentations Africaines
CET	Common External Tariff
CIPEC	Conseil Intergouvernemental des Pays Exportateurs de Cuivre
CODESRIA	Council for the Development of Economic and Social Research in Africa
COREPER	Comité des Représentants Permanents
CVF	Countervalue Funds
DAC	Development Assistance Committee
EBRD	European Bank for Reconstruction and Development
EC	European Community
ECA	European Commission for Africa
ECFF	European Community Foreign Exchange Facility
ECU	European Currency Unit
EDF	European Development Fund
EEC	European Economic Community
EIB	European Investment Bank
ESAF	Extended Structural Adjustment Facility
FAL	Final Act of Lagos
FEMAC	Foreign Exchange Management Committee
FIDES	Fonds d'Investissement pour le Développement Économique et Social
FINNIDA	Finnish International Development Agency
Forex	Foreign Exchange
GATT	General Agreement on Tariffs and Trade
GIP	General Import Programme

GRZ	Government of the Republic of Zambia
GSP	Generalized System of Preferences
IDA	International Development Association
IFI	International Finance Institution
IMF	International Monetary Fund
INDECO	Industrial Development Company
INDP	Interim National Development Programme
JMC	Joint Monitoring Committee
LEPP	Lomé Export Promotion Programme
LME	London Metal Exchange
LPA	Lagos Plan of Action
MINDECO	The Mining Development Corporation
MMD	Movement for Multi-Party Democracy
MPP	Micro-Projects Programme
MPU	Micro-Projects Unit
MYRA	Multi-Year Rescheduling Agreement
Namboard	National Agricultural Marketing Board
NATCAP	National Technical Coordination Action Programme
NCCM	Nchanga Consolidated Copper Mines
NCDP	National Commission for Development Planning
NCZ	Nitrogen Company of Zambia
NERP	National Economic Recovery Programme
NGO	Non-Governmental Organization
NIC	Newly Industrializing Country
NIEO	New International Economic Order
NIP	National Indicative Programme
NORAD	Norwegian International Development Agency
NTB	Non-Tariff Barrier
OAU	Organization for African Unity
OCAM	Organisation Commun de l'Afrique et Malgache
ODI	Overseas Development Institute
OECD	Organization for Economic Cooperation and Development
OEOA	Office for Emergency Operations in Africa
OFP	Operation Food Production Programme
OGL	Open General Licensing System
OPEC	Organization of Petroleum Exporting Countries
PAMSCAD	Programme of Action to Mitigate the Social Costs of Adjustment
PCU	Provincial Cooperative Union
PTA	Preferential Trading Area
RCM	Roan Consolidated Copper Mines
SAATA	Structural Adjustment Advisory Team for Africa

SADDC	Southern African Development and Coordination Committee
SAF	Structural Adjustment Facility
SAL	Structural Adjustment Loan
SAP	Social Action Programme
SDR	Special Drawing Rights
SIDA	Swedish International Development Agency
SILIC	Severely Indebted Low-Income Country
SIMIC	Severely Indebted Middle-Income Country
SIP	Sectoral Import Programme
SPA	Special Programme of Assistance
SPAH	Special Programme of Action against Hunger
Stabex	Stabilization of Exports
SWAPO	South West Africa People's Organization
Sysmin	System of Mineral Exports Stabilization
UDP	United Democratic Company
UNCTAD	United Nations Conference on Trade and Development
UNDP	United Nations Development Programme
UNICEF	United Nations International Children's Emergency Fund
UNIP	United National Independence Party
UNO	United Nations Organization
UNPAAERD	United Nations Programme of Action for African Economic Recovery and Development
USAID	United States Agency for International Development
WIDER	World Institute for the Development of Economic Research
ZCCM	Zambia Consolidated Copper Mines
ZCF	Zambia Cooperative Federation
ZCTU	Zambia Congress of Trade Unions

PREFACE

I once found myself in the debating chamber of the Oxford Union listening to a lecture by former American Secretary of State, Henry Kissinger. With magisterial eloquence, Kissinger was painting the broad canvas of the emerging post-Cold War international order, touching on the problems of every major region of the world with the exception of Africa. In Kissinger's world, it seemed, Africa, the second largest continent in the world, did not merit any attention. To many observers the enormity of the region's problems – poverty, ignorance, disease, war and its Byzantine governments – almost put it outside the framework of civilized discourse. I began this work in an attempt to understand the nature and causes of Africa's structural underdevelopment. In terms of orientation, I hasten to say that I am among those who have felt unease with much of what goes under the name of "development studies". Although I do not share their political assumptions, I believe with Lord Bauer, Deepak Lall, Paul Collier and others that there cannot be but one universal economic science, with the same standards of theoretical rigour applied to developing societies as to the advanced industrial world. Having received my formal academic training in economics, political science and public administration, it became clear to me that only a critical, multidisciplinary approach could hope to do justice to the complexity of structural underdevelopment.

What has come to be known as the discipline of "political economy" seeks to integrate the insights of political science with the rigour of economic theory. It may be viewed as one of the traditions within the general attempt to construct a "unified field theory" of the human sciences which has preoccupied scholars from Wilhelm Dilthey to Fernand Braudel, Michel Foucault and Immanuel Wallerstein. Political economy is clearly still in its infancy, with yet more room for growth in terms of methodological sophistication and disciplinary self-understanding in the sense in which Thomas Kuhn understood it. The work of Friedrich von Hayek, perhaps more than any other in this century, embodies this tradition of scholarship. In contemporary England, Lord Skidelsky and Susan Strange have been among the leading lights in the field. In the United States, the greatest theoretical advances have been made in the area of "public choice" theory, with the award of the Nobel Prize to James M. Buchanan in 1986 marking an important recognition for a growing and exciting field. This book is aimed at decision-makers in the development field, students of economics, political science and international affairs, and the general public at large. Much as I am interested in econometrics and in mathematical analysis, I did not consider such methods particularly germane to the object of the present inquiry.

This is a study of the politics and economics of EC–African relations between 1973 and 1991, with a focus on the key issues of development aid, debt and structural adjustment. Drawing inspiration from the neo-realist paradigm, the study considers EC–African diplomacy from the viewpoint of power, influence and social exchange. Chapter 1 considers the historical and policy context of the study and the key conceptual issues of power, influence, aid and structural adjustment. The North–South aid relationship is characterized as a power or influence relationship based on "social exchange". Chapter 2 discusses the emergence of structural adjustment as the new idiom of development diplomacy, considering the role of the key international institutions and the ensuing political responses by African governments. Chapter 3 traces the evolution of EC–African relations from colonial times to the founding of the association regime under the Rome Treaty in 1957. This period is characterized as being essentially the continuation of the colonial pattern of development. Chapter 4 looks at the emergence of the Lomé regime in 1975 and its key operational institutions. I have argued that the uncertainties following the collapse of the Bretton Woods system, Western insecurity with regard to raw materials following the OPEC crisis, and the accompanying challenge by the South for a more equitable international economic system, contributed to Europe's willingness to negotiate a new multilateral agreement with the ACP. We argued that Lomé was essentially Europe's answer to the challenge of the New International Economic Order (NIEO). Chapter 5 considers the dynamic of EC–ACP relations in the 1980s, when "policy dialogue" was gradually becoming the focal point of EC aid strategy. The EC's involvement with the new politics of structural adjustment and conditionality can be situated within the changed international economic environment of the 1980s: in particular, the internationalization of capital, the imperatives of global liberalization and the international debt crisis. Chapter 6 examines the origin and structure of the African debt and its role in the transformation of European development policy. Chapter 7 examines the specific experience of Zambia, tracing its pattern of post-colonial development, the role of the state in its underdevelopment, and the achievements and failures of its structural reform programme. Chapter 8 considers the role of Community aid in Zambia, in particular, aid diplomacy, the food dialogue strategy and support for the mining sector. Chapter 9 focuses on the EC response to the challenge of structural reform in Zambia, paying attention to the social dimensions of adjustment, micro-projects development, import support for structural adjustment, and the drive towards export diversification. Chapter 10 discusses the main findings and considers the prospects of EC–African diplomacy in a changing world. The study notes the changing economic and political landscape in Europe itself, the relative decline of the importance of Lomé in European policy, and the current trend towards disinvestment from sub-Saharan Africa. The view taken here is that adjustment is unavoidable. But it has to take account of the specificity of local conditions; it has to be "home-grown" and its implementation must seek a delicate balance between economic efficiency and the societal imperatives of order and equity. If African states are to avoid marginalization in the emerging world order, they have little choice but to rise to the challenge of global competitiveness.

This book grew out of my doctoral dissertation at Oriel College, Oxford University, which was submitted in the trinity term of 1994. Much of the library work was undertaken in Oxford and London, and in documentation centres in Brussels, Lusaka, and Uppsala, Sweden. Field work was carried out in Zambia and Brussels during several trips between 1990 and 1992. My interest in international economic relations began during my student days at the Sorbonne and the Institut International d'Administration Publique, Paris. I would like to thank Fatima Bensalem, Mario Bettati, Dominique Carreau, Alexandre Lazareff, Aléth Manin, Max Péyrard and Gérard Timsit, who inspired my interests. When I returned from France to my home country of Nigeria in 1986, I was appointed Research Fellow at the National Institute for Policy and Strategic Studies, Nigeria's pre-eminent policy think-tank. Much of my work at the Institute involved applied policy research, with all the attendant challenges of advising government in a declining oil-rich economy. My earliest work was on the reform of local government and its impact on local-level development. I subsequently worked on the World Bank-financed integrated development project in Plateau State, which was a real eye-opener. My interest in public-sector management led me into collaboration with Dotun Philips and Eghosa Osagie in a major study of the sectoral impact of Nigeria's structural adjustment experience. In the year preceding my going up to Oxford I was appointed coordinator of an enterprise development project mainly targeted at unemployed graduates to help them explore entrepreneurial opportunities opened up by the country's privatization programme. I was thus placed at a vantage position to appreciate the dilemmas of decision-makers as well as the despair of ordinary citizens who were at the receiving end of the adjustment pill. I witnessed the despair of youth who faced a bleak future, malnourished children, patients left to die unattended in clinics because they could not afford the newly introduced medical charges. There was also the reappearance of long-forgotten diseases such as kwashiorkor and meningitis, and the all-pervading atmosphere of hopelessness. It was for me an object lesson on how a decadent political order run by a destructive military oligarchy and with the support of misguided policies, could drive a once prosperous nation to the verge of bankruptcy. At the Institute it was my good fortune to have worked with outstanding scholars who advised and guided me in my academic career. I would like to mention in particular Eme Awa, Eghosa Osagie, Adedotun Philips and Ukwu I. Ukwu.

In the process of researching and writing this book, I have incurred the debt of several individuals. First and foremost, to my parents, I say a big thank you for their love, sacrifices and support. Thinking of them, I am forced into silence, realizing that I can never fully repay them. Thank you, mother, for being you; thank you, father, for being such an exemplar of the Platonic Ideal. Thanks also to Uncle J. A. Anche for his support throughout my school days. My earliest intellectual curiosity was awakened by my maternal grandfather, Mallam Anche Ogah Mukama, a self-taught thinker and a towering presence. My paternal grandfather, Baba Gambo Galadima, taught me to be courageous in adversity and to cherish our cultural heritage. Ayya Celia, my beloved grandmother, was the kindest and gentlest person I have ever met. All three went to join the ancestors while the quest for knowledge took me away from our humble village to Vichy, Paris, Ottawa, Oxford, Uppsala, Bergen, Helsinki, Brussels and Lusaka. They probably never understood my interminable absences, but I hope that they would have approved of the end result.

When I began graduate work at Oxford my joint supervisors were Professor Robert Cassen and Dr Christopher Stevens. I am most appreciative of their wise counsel and guidance. Mr Gavin Williams and Dr Andrew Wyatt Walter took over the task of supervision at a critical period in my work. They performed their role with thoroughness and understanding, to my eternal gratitude. Drs Frances Stewart, Loukas Tsoukalis, William Wallace, Marc Williams and two anonymous referees have also made useful suggestions for improving the work. Sir Zelman Cowen, former Governor-General of Australia and outgoing Provost of Oriel, helped me to settle quickly into College by his fatherly good cheer. Sir Zelman and Lady Cowen showed much interest in my academic career, often inviting me to tea to talk about my work and future plans. I shall always remember them kindly. Professors Adam Roberts and Terence Ranger, Dr Andrew Hurrell, and Mr Tony Kirk-Greene have also represented for me the Oxford tradition of excellence, intellectual independence and enlightened humaneness in an age when ethics and integrity seem to count for little, even in the hallowed walls of academia. Special thanks to my mentor and friend, Michael Blades, Principal of Plater College, Oxford, where I was a visiting lecturer in Economic Development for three years – an invaluable experience indeed. The unrelenting questioning of my students at Plater College compelled me to clarify some of my ideas. Food Studies Group at Queen Elizabeth House also gave me a "D.Phil associateship", for which I am especially grateful to the Director, Dr Roger Hay. I shall not forget the kindness and generosity of Ambassador Lawrence Agubuzu, Nigeria's High Commissioner in Lusaka, who provided me with free lodgings during field work in Zambia. Special thanks also to Cecilia Makota, Yoliswa and David Siyolwe, Abdul Badawi and my guide, Gorki. I am appreciative of the assistance given by several government and international officials in London, Brussels and Lusaka, who must remain anonymous. I am thankful for the editorial expertise of Sandra Jones, which has been crucial in bringing this book to its present shape. After Oxford I could not return to my fellowship at the Institute owing to unpropitious political developments in my country.

Although I have tried to maintain a level of detachment, a quality which is required of any work aspiring to scientific merit, as an African I cannot claim to be indifferent to the tragedies of our time. I too have been haunted by the images of the starving children of Somalia and Ethiopia, and the descent into barbarism in Rwanda, Liberia and Sierra Leone. Europe does and perhaps will continue to play an influential role in African affairs. Being an internationalist, I am sympathetic towards the idea of Euro-African cooperation, in spite of the many sceptics who point to the gap between Europe's noblest ideals and the savagery with which it has treated Africa in the past. But it is my view that Europe can play a constructive role in Africa only on the basis of equality and respect for African independence and sovereignty. The task of economic emancipation ultimately has to be the responsibility of Africans themselves.

Finally, it seems to me that authors often acknowledge the contributions of their families merely as a form of literary etiquette. In my own case, I can truly say that Margaret, Emmanuel and Samora have been a part of this project from its very inception. I would therefore prefer to see this as *our* book rather than mine. Although neither they nor anyone other than myself is responsible for any errors of fact or judgement which may be found herein, it is to them that it is dedicated, with the affection, joy, tears and smiles of all my life.

Obadiah Mailafia
Arundel, West Sussex
Lent 1996

1

INTRODUCTION

In our epoch of quantum leaps in human affairs, the North–South divide remains one of the enduring features of international economic relations. The major paradox of an integrated world economy is the phenomenon of hemispheric polarization, as zones of affluence are disengaging from a nascent global ghetto of economic and social deprivation. American industry secretary, Robert Reich – himself a keen student of political economy – observes that the wealthy regions are uncoupling from the rest of the world, "while much of what remains behind is sinking precipitously into hopeless poverty".[1] More than two decades ago the French political thinker, Maurice Duverger, reminded us: "Two worlds now confront each other; one rich, the other poor. . . .While the former sees on the horizon the society of abundance, the latter remains close to the Middle Ages, with its famines, epidemics and human misery."[2]

In the case of sub-Saharan Africa (SSA), a human drama akin to Dante's inferno has been unfolding over the last decade and a half. The collapse of national economies, the breakdown of civil society, the Hobbesian spectacle of war, famine and desperate misery have become the visible symptoms of structural underdevelopment and political decay.[3] During the euphoria of independence, there was much optimism that political freedom would sooner or later translate into social and economic advancement.[4] Ambitious development plans were launched, with the support of the industrialized nations and the international agencies, notably the United Nations and the International Bank for Reconstruction and Development, popularly known as the World Bank. The disappointing results of the first two decades of independence were soon to give way to disillusionment.[5]

In the 1970s the rise of OPEC and the cyclical upturn in raw material prices led to the elevation of the development question from the status of "low politics" to one of high international politics and diplomacy.[6] When the first Lomé Convention between the European Community (EC) and the African, Caribbean and Pacific (ACP) States was signed in 1975, its wide-ranging, contractual approach to the development question was widely acclaimed as a remarkable breakthrough in international cooperation, "a symbol of hope in a divided world",[7] coming as it did at a time when developing countries were demanding a "New International Economic Order" which was being upheld as a beacon of hope in dark times.[8] While it has been a predictable source of financial aid for ACP states, doubts have been raised about its relevance to the structural problems of underdevelopment and poverty.[9] Less generous critics have dismissed the entire scheme as a neo-imperial design aimed at preserving Africa's status in the international division of labour.[10] Sir Shridath Ramphal, former Secretary-General of the Commonwealth, put the matter more decorously when he observed that "the spirit of Lomé has not always burned brightly in the Council chambers of Brussels".[11]

THE GENERAL POLICY CONTEXT

The global context of this study is the "development crisis" of the 1980s and the problems of indebtedness and destitution which afflicted much of the African continent and sub-Saharan Africa (SSA) in particular. Linked to this is the ensuing response by external aid donors and the international finance institutions (IFIs) in the context of global liberalization. In 1991, thirty out of the forty-five countries officially classified as low-income (i.e. those with an annual per capita income lower than US$425) were from sub-Saharan Africa. The World Bank estimates that during 1970–80, the annual growth rate of food and agricultural production averaged 1.5 per cent and improved only marginally to 1.8 per cent during 1980–91, as compared to an average demographic increase of 3 per cent per annum. In the domain of international trade, Africa's share of the world market for non-oil commodity exports fell from 7 per cent in 1960 to less than 2 per cent in 1987/88.[12] For most Africans, living standards have fallen well below those of the 1960s, while the debt burden for the region has risen from a relatively low figure of US$6 billion in 1970 to more than US$150 billion in 1991.[13]

In this book I intend to address a set of interrelated questions:

- In what ways has Lomé responded to the changes in the international aid regime since the 1980s?
- How does the Lomé approach compare with the orthodox model of the Bretton Woods institutions?
- Does Europe have a different or "unique" approach to adjustment as it has often claimed?

In addressing these questions we shall first analyse the changes in Lomé development policy from its earlier, traditional "aid" orientation to its current emphasis on adjustment and policy reform and then examine the politics of EC aid in Zambia and its influence on the country's structural reform process. The central question to be considered is the claim that the

EC has a different or "unique" approach to adjustment and conditionality, as compared to the orthodox model of the IMF and the World Bank.

The choice of Zambia as a country case-study requires some justification. Zambia's post-independence development experience makes her almost a perfect model of African economic decline.[14] At independence in 1964, she enjoyed one of the highest living standards in the region. In the early 1970s, however, with the collapse of world copper prices, the government resorted to massive external borrowing to finance a worsening external deficit. Zambia's promise at independence remains a record of unfulfilled dreams: an impoverished country, saddled with external deficits, negative growth, indebtedness, malnutrition, and a general deterioration in living standards. With a per capita GDP estimated at US$156 (at 1989 prices), for a population of 7.5 million people (1988 estimates), its external debt of US$7 billion and debt service ratio averaging 83 per cent of export receipts, put Zambia within the ranks of highly indebted, low-income countries. Zambia's case is all the more interesting as a country which has had a long and chequered history of relations with the IFIs (International Finance Institutions) as well as being a major beneficiary of EC aid, from the Sysmin scheme for minerals to the Food Strategy Programme and the more recent Structural Adjustment Facility (SAF). The Zambian case should therefore serve to illustrate the evolving framework of EC–African aid diplomacy and, in particular, EC responses to the politics of structural adjustment and policy reform, in relation to a significant, if not necessarily typical, African country.

The policy context of this study is the emergence of the neo-liberal economic reform agenda in the politics of international development. In the 1970s development cooperation centred on the politics of "basic needs" and the North–South dialogue. According to Stephen Krasner, less-developed countries (LDCs) manifested a preference for principles and norms based on "authoritative allocation" and state intervention.[15] The 1980s witnessed a paradigmatic shift in world development thinking.[16] The neo-liberal monetarist orthodoxy which emerged put its emphasis on private enterprise and market solutions.[17] Adjustment programmes have had a profound impact, for better or worse, on the economies and polities of reforming countries. Even more interesting, for the student of political economy, is their meaning for the political relations between North and South, and the patterns of influence and power between rich and poor nations.[18] As a major actor in the international aid scene, the EC's role is worth studying in its own right. Europe is also undergoing transformation, from "the second enlargement" to the passing of the Single Act in 1985, and more recently, the Maastricht Treaty.[19] With the collapse of the Soviet empire and the opening up of the Eastern frontier, with its greater attractions for global investment capital, it is widely believed that Africa will suffer marginalization in the emerging world order.

Our main concern is with the politics and economics of structural reform and in the context of EC–African cooperation between 1973 and 1991. The central focus is on the politics and diplomacy of adjustment within the Lomé aid "regime".[20] This is neither a comprehensive history nor an evaluative account of the entire Lomé process. Rather, it is a political study of aid and economic diplomacy[21] as it relates to structural adjustment, "policy dialogue" and external debts. It would be legitimate to argue that Lomé is both an aid and a trade regime, and that abstracting the adjustment and development policy aspects from the commercial provisions is likely to give an incomplete picture. However, it is our considered view that inclusion of the trade aspect would have widened the scope of the study to perhaps unmanageable proportions. Given that our focus is on the broad dynamics of economic and political interactions, we are not chiefly concerned with micro-level issues of project performance.[22] It should also be added that this study is not concerned with the economic impact of adjustment as such, interesting as this would have been.

AID, STRUCTURAL ADJUSTMENT AND INTERNATIONAL ECONOMIC RELATIONS

The concept of "aid" appears at first sight to be a very simple one. Ordinary usage would see it in terms of all kinds of help or assistance which are offered by rich countries to less privileged ones. However, as former United States Under-Secretary of State George Ball observed, foreign aid is "a deceptive phrase that comprehends programmes and policies dissimilar in motive and effect".[23] While the liberal view sees aid as an important and critical input in the development process, neo-conservative as well as radical analysts have tended to question its utility. Radical critics such as Teresa Hayter view aid as a form of imperialism, while neo-conservatives such as Lord Bauer see it as a misplacement of scarce capital, given that it allegedly never reaches the poor for whom it is intended and also because it is no substitute for enterprise, discipline and hard work, which alone can bring about development.[24]

The Development Assistance Committee (DAC) has defined aid as any material or non-material input which is (a) undertaken by official agencies; (b) has the promotion of economic development and welfare as its prime objective; and (c) has a grant element of 25 per cent or more.[25] Professor Robert Cassen defines aid as "a transfer of resources on concessional terms – on terms, that is, more generous or 'softer' than loans obtainable in the world's capital markets".[26] In this study we shall understand aid to mean all the official and private transfers of resources and skills which are given either as grants or as loans on concessional terms to developing countries, with the aim of promoting economic development and human welfare.

"aid"

In its original usage by economists, the term *adjustment* referred to measures taken by countries to reduce or eliminate their balance of payments disequilibria with the support of IMF standby facilities. *Structural adjustment*, on the other hand, referred to policy packages introduced by the World Bank towards the end of the 1970s to redress the macroeconomic imbalances caused by the second oil shock. Such measures often entailed introduction of medium-term supply-side remedies, normally accompanied by long-term concessional loans. The World Bank officially distinguishes between *adjustment*, which is defined as "policies to achieve changes in internal and external balances . . . in the structure of incentives and institutions", and *structural adjustment*, which it defines as reforms of policies and institutions, involving both microeconomic aspects such as taxes and incentives and macroeconomic policies such as fiscal imbalances and public sector performance.[27]

Tony Killick has argued against too narrow a definition of adjustment, which seems to give it a "somewhat arbitrary character, influenced alike by donor ideology . . . and by simple fashion".[28] He calls for its replacement by the concept of *adaptation*, which he defines as "a subset of the adaptation of economies to changing circumstances and opportunities . . . continuous and intrinsic to the process of economic development".[29] Similarly, Paul Streeten has located the adjustment paradigm within the framework of development and societal change in general, involving rich and poor countries alike, as they strive to adapt their economies, societies and policy systems to changing circumstances. He defines adjustment as "adaptation to sudden or large, often unexpected, changes, which may be favourable or unfavourable to the set of objectives pursued by the government".[30] Seen in these broad terms, structural adjustment can be regarded as part of the wider process by which societies come to terms with disequilibria resulting from economic, social or technological changes. As Robert Gilpin explains:

> In every international system there are continual occurrences of political, economic and technological changes that promise gains and losses for one or another actor. . . . In every system, therefore, a process of disequilibrium and adjustment is constantly taking place.[31]

For James Rosenau, adaptation is a universal phenomenon, given that all countries have to adapt to changing demands in their internal and external environments.[32] Rosenau sees the adaptive process as being particularly crucial to the survival of developing polities, given that they are: "still in a process of evolving, still subject to redirection and fragmentation . . . with their essentiality still in question".[33] For him, successful adaptation is a factor of history, culture and the "capabilities of each organism" to attain equilibrium within the external environment.

POWER, INFLUENCE AND SOCIAL EXCHANGE

The conceptual approach in this study is based on an analysis of EC–African diplomacy from the viewpoint of power and influence.[34] Power is generally regarded as the most important feature of political life. This is particularly so in the case of the realist paradigm in international relations, an intellectual tradition which dates back from Thucydides and Herodotus to Machiavelli, Morgenthau and Kissinger.[35] According to Hans Morgenthau, power is "man's control over the minds and actions of other men".[36] For Kenneth Organski, power is the capacity to exert influence on "the behaviour of others" in pursuit of one's own ends; while for Karl Deutsch, it is simply "the ability to prevail in conflict and overcome obstacles".[37] Reviewing the vast literature on power, Steven Lukes concludes that a single comprehensive definition is impossible, given the diversity of interests in people's minds when they approach the question. According to him, "what unites the various views of power is too thin and formal to provide a generally satisfying definition, applicable in all cases".[38] Lukes underlines *interest*, *intention* and *will* as the crucial elements in the power equation. Thus, for him, "*[P]* exercises power over *[R]* when *[P]* affects *[R]* in a manner contrary to *[R's]* interests".[39] He proceeds to conceptualize power as a resource which actors utilize to effect desired outcomes. According to Lukes, ". . . to have power is to be able to make a difference in the world. Those interested in power are interested in two questions: in the difference that is made, and in the making of that difference".[40] Felix Oppenheim has argued that we need to go beyond the emphasis on interests and preferences and to focus, instead, on the actual or potential actions that underlie power relations. His own approach focuses on the resources which enhance (a) *persuasion* (rational or deceptive), (b) *inducement* and (c) *deterrence*.[41]

Part of the elusiveness of the concept of power has to do with the problem of its measurement.[42] Joseph Nye likens power to love, which is "easier to experience than to define or measure".[43] While it is possible to evolve common criteria of measurement for factors such as GNP, military capability, geographical position and population, it is much harder to measure factors such as national morale or societal cohesion.[44] A comprehensive notion of power will need to include the following elements:

1 power for whom;
2 entities or persons to which it is directed;
3 the nature of the power resources available;
4 the goals or intentions of the power exercised;
5 actions undertaken;
6 the whole range of structures, incentives and constraints involved, whether these are "normative [or] material, actual or potential, anticipated or unanticipated".[45]

Power, according to Klaus Knorr, may be seen as both a *means* and an *effect.* The first he terms "putative" power and the second, "actualized" power. As means, it relates to the ability of the power-wielder to "make effective threats"; while as an effect, it is measurable in terms of the actual amount of influence that an actor has achieved in a given situation.[46] The structural dimensions of power exist when the economic structure and capabilities of a country are arranged in such a way that (a) it exports goods that are in urgent demand by others and imports other products for which its own internal demand is elastic, and (b) it has monopoly control over goods required by other countries while having a monopsony control on items exported by others.[47]

A core element in the analysis of power in North–South relations is the unequal distribution of resources such as technology, production, finance and wealth in the world economy.[48] The structural analysis of power emphasizes the role of the state as the basic actor in the international system, with the behaviour of other major actors such as transnational corporations (TNCs) and international organizations mediated by state power and the interests of sovereign governments. All states, according to Stephen Krasner;

> . . . share the same minimalist objectives of preserving territorial and political integrity. The particular strategies adopted by a given state will be constrained by structural considerations – the distribution of power in the international system as a whole, and the place of a given state in that distribution. Within these structural constraints, strategies will also be affected by domestic attributes such as ideology, interest groups, and state–society relations.[49]

The key concept here is the notion of structure, which has been defined as "the parts of an economic whole which, over a period of time, appear relatively stable alongside others".[50] Structures determine the framework of constraints and opportunities within which international actors operate. As a major objective, states seek to change the structures that constrain the range of their external ambitions; they also seek the preservation and continuance of those structures that enhance their relative position within the global hierarchy of wealth and power. Developing countries, for example, may pursue policies aimed at changing the trade, finance and production structures which are seen as impediments to their economic performance.[51] Neo-Marxist analyses of structural power have often tended to be more illuminating in their insights into those aspects of power which are neglected by mainstream economics and political science.[52] For Stephen Gill, structural power is synonymous with the *hegemony* which is exercised by a dominant state or by a "condominium of states".[53] For Robert Cox, the point of departure is the interaction between production, institutions and social forces, which create "historic blocs" and shape forms

Struct power

of world order.[54] In terms of North–South relations, the asymmetry in power relations is illustrated by the deficiencies of the LDCs in technology, industrial capacity, financial capital and unequal trade relations. Needing foreign exchange to finance essential imports, they have to export primary commodities, even as commodity prices continue to fall. In place of the military force or "gunboat diplomacy" which prevailed in the era of "primitive accumulation", the North uses "market discipline" and the coercive power of global institutions to compel reform measures in the South:

> Market discipline and market necessity mean that [the South has] . . . very little or no alternative. Developing countries have to sell their products in international markets, and normally this involves competition between themselves, and also with some developed countries. These market pressures may lead some countries to increase, rather than reduce their supply of certain primary products, even when their price falls.[55]

Christopher Chase-Dunn has argued that "structural power" relates not only to material factors such as technology, production and finance; it includes the transmission of norms and cultural values from the North which serves to create "patterns of incentives" which conduce to dominance by the North.[56]

The constraints dictated by the market are reinforced by the cultural or normative aspects of structural weakness. This is informed by the cultural tastes and ideological outlook of ruling elites in the South, who come to identify with the aspirations of the metropolitan culture. Mass culture in the South tends to emulate the behavioural and consumption patterns of transnational capitalist culture, thereby narrowing the margins of what is defined as politically possible and giving automatic legitimation to reform agendas set by international finance institutions and their dominant shareholders. According to Gill and Law:

> the most skilful use of direct, coercive power requires a vision of self-reproducing structural power, both economic and ideological. Such use of direct power implies a hegemonic, long-term strategy. With time, the coercive use of power may become less necessary and also less obvious as consensus builds up . . . [and] a hegemonic structure of thought emerges, one which militates against the raising, or even conception of alternative types of political, economic and social arrangements.[57]

Any critical analysis of North–South relations and development diplomacy will have to take account of these insights. The "development problematic" and the manifold problems which poor countries face will have to be viewed within a broader framework of their relative position in the hierarchical structure of global power and wealth. The structural power of the North may be viewed in terms of their capacity to exercise dominance and control in the world political economy, while the relative weakness of the South may be said to be reflected in their inability to exert any control over markets, capital and decision-making. Structural weakness is underlined by a heightened sense of economic and political insecurity. Developing countries, as Caroline Thomas has explained, "suffer from an acute lack of control over the international environment in which they must function, and of all the world's states, they are the ones for whom the economic alternatives of survive or perish are the most pressing".[58]

Developing countries seek not only social and economic advancement; they want to decrease their vulnerability on the international environment. Indeed, their search for economic well-being is inseparable from their quest for political autonomy and freedom from external coercion and control. Their quest for economic security includes the desire to live in a less turbulent international economic environment; to have some control over the prices of national exports; and to have access to financial capital and markets for their products. The need for economic security implies a desire for freedom from undue influence and coercion, especially when it comes to the political choices which impinge on a country's long-term economic future. Much of the debate on the conditionality question is in part a reflection of this fundamental concern.

Our own analysis derives from an understanding of power as a category of influence. The work of Russett and Starr is particularly helpful in explaining the relationship between power and influence in international relations:

> Power means getting one's way. Influence is one method by which people and states get their own way. . . . getting others to do the things you want them to do. It is the ability to affect the behaviour of others. . . . If power is the general ability to overcome obstacles and prevail in some situation, influence is one way – in fact the dominant way – that international actors accomplish this.[59]

Russett and Starr distinguish between three forms of influence: First, we have *compellence*, which is the ability to induce a change of behaviour or reverse a course of policy. A good example of compellence would be the ability of the IMF to get a developing country to remove subsidies on agricultural produce or to follow some other policy which it would not otherwise have followed. Second, we have *deterrence*, which is the ability to influence other actors "to continue not to do something", i.e., being able to forestall a preferred course of action before it is undertaken. Third, we have *potential influence*, which relates to the prevailing perceptions and psychological conditioning as to the power resources of a given actor. Such awareness of the expected responses of a given actor may act as a barrier, for example, on the attempt by a small developing country to nationalize the assets of the subsidiary of a giant multinational.

The means of attaining influence range from the outright use of force to bargaining, offer of rewards, threats and non-violent punishment. The term *leverage* is often used to embrace "whatever means are used by one negotiator to influence, persuade, coerce, or force another negotiator to accept a particular bargain".[60] Influence may also derive from "political investment", i.e., improving one's asset position as a future resource which may be called upon. Does the Lomé "partnership" represent a form of "community building" which enables the EC to build a sense of "kinship" with the ACP states?

In this study we shall approach power in terms of influence and social exchange. This is especially apposite in relationships involving cooperation, in which influence is the preferred way of securing agreement.[61] As Jeffrey Hart explains, defining power as influence "permits the analyst to recognise the ranges of power existing outside the realm of coercion or control".[62] Although power and influence are used almost interchangeably, some analysts maintain a distinction between the two.[63] The understanding of power in terms of influence captures the *dynamic* element of power relationships, focusing as it does on the interactive processes in the relations between states.[64]

How does this discussion about influence relate to the international policies of multilateral organizations, and especially the EC? This question has normally been approached through consideration of the capabilities of the constituent members together with the resources available to the organization in question.[65] Cheryl Payer, for example, in her well-known study of the World Bank, explained the Bank's power in terms of the influence and *leverage* which it is able to wield in LDCs by virtue of the size of its annual budget, its intellectual and technical leadership in development economics, and its pre-eminence in project co-financing and aid coordination.[66] According to Russett and Starr: "If power is the general ability to overcome obstacles and prevail in some situation, influence is one way – in fact the dominant way – that international actors accomplish this."[67] From the viewpoint of social exchange and reciprocity, relations between the EC and the ACP are not regarded as zero-sum games, in which all power and influence reside exclusively in the Community. Rather, they are characterized by reciprocal, albeit asymmetrical influences.[68] Social exchange theory, according to David Baldwin, sees foreign aid as being "very much an ordinary commercial transaction, in that one party uses economic resources to get another party to change his behaviour".[69]

Social exchange theory provides an alternative way of thinking about foreign aid transactions. This approach depicts ordinary economic exchange as a subcategory of a broader range of social phenomena in

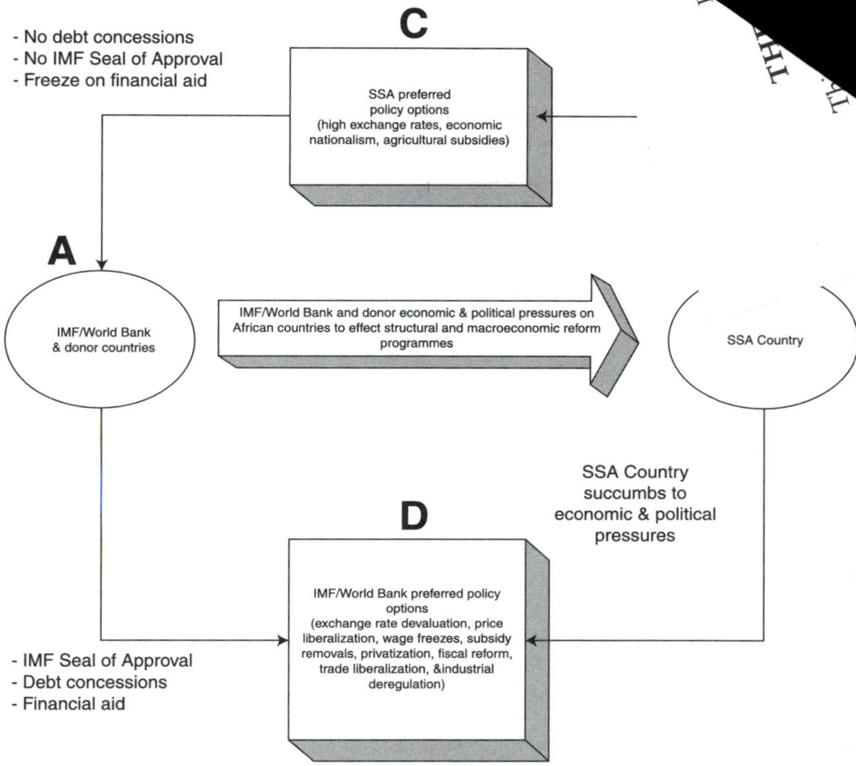

Figure 1.1 The mechanism of influence in conditionality-based aid

which people reward others in the expectation that the favour will be reciprocated.[70]

In the light of the preceding discussion, Lomé aid diplomacy can be analysed as a social exchange system in which patterns of international influence operate.[71] In the context of structural adjustment, EC aid diplomacy can be seen as an "influence attempt", by which the Community tries to get African countries to reform their economies in exchange for financial aid, debt forgiveness or reprieve, and other forms of development assistance (see Figure 1.1). Influence will be understood to mean any reciprocal relationship in which power resources are utilized to induce, deter or persuade an actor to a course of action which is preferred by the dominant partner. To find out what influence the EC had on a given issue-area, we might proceed by asking: What did the SSA country want? What were the preferred options of the Community? Whose preferences were reflected in the outcomes? What power resources were employed in the exercise of such influence?

THE TRIANGLE OF DEVELOPMENT DIPLOMACY

This is a study of "development diplomacy", which has been defined by one scholar as "the process whereby Third World countries attempt to negotiate improvements in their position in the international political economy . . . [through] bargaining with Western industrialised countries".[72] Development diplomacy, according to this view, is characterized by three features:

1 There is the asymmetry in power relations between North and South, underlined by the dominance of the industrialized countries as contrasted with the structural weakness of the underdeveloped countries.
2 Both sides entertain different "world models" of the past, present and future of the international economy.
3 The nature of "coalitional politics" between the two blocs entails an in-built structural limitation on the possibilities of fundamental changes in the prevailing system.[73]

We have characterized the matrix of EC–African diplomacy in terms of a triangular relationship between three clusters of actors: the EC, the ACPs and the IFIs. The *[A]* dimension constitutes the Lomé aid relationship, in which there exists an asymmetrical relationship of power and influence. The *[B]* dimension is the relationship between the EC and the Bretton Woods institutions. This relationship is more complex in the sense that EC

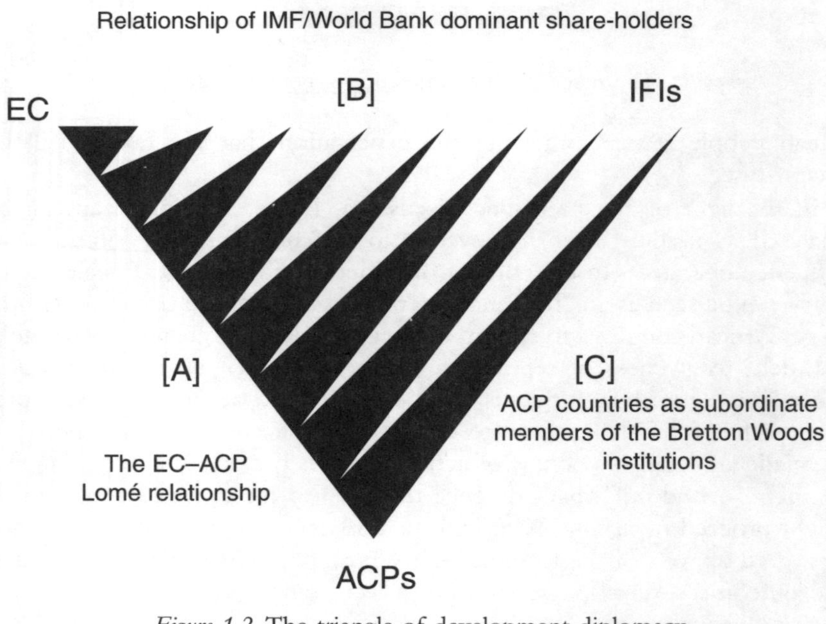

Figure 1.2 The triangle of development diplomacy

members are also prominent actors in the IFIs, with Germany, France and Britain having a combined vote of 16.99 per cent of the total votes in the Executive Board of the IMF.[74] The combined votes of the five dominant actors – the United States, the United Kingdom, Germany, France and Japan – constitute 40.32 per cent of the total votes within the Fund. This is an obvious indication of enormous decision-making powers and influence by the Big Five within the IMF. Both the EC Commission and the IFIs have sought to coordinate their policies on debt and adjustment and in the co-financing of development projects. The third aspect is the *[C]* dimension, the relationship between the ACPs and the IFIs. Like *[A]*, it is also an asymmetrical relationship, given the increasingly influential role of the IFIs in macroeconomic reforms in ACP countries. The main emphasis in this study is on the *[A]* dimension of the triangle, although we shall also consider certain important aspects of both *[B]* and *[C]* as they impinge on the *[A]* relationship.

In terms of a general perspective, this study draws on Stephen Krasner's "modified structural realism".[75] This approach accords a central role to power in international economic relations, especially in the asymmetry which underlies North–South relations. Whilst we do not share the classic realist assumption about the unqualified primacy of the state in international politics, we subscribe to the view that all states seek to preserve their autonomy and territorial integrity, and that their policies are constrained by the distribution of power in the international system and the position of a given actor in that structure.[76] Within these structural constraints, strategies will also be affected by domestic attributes such as ideology, interest groups, and state–society relations.[77] The economics and politics of aid are therefore not to be analysed from the viewpoint of charity but as elements within the general matrix of power and interest in North–South relations. The agenda of macroeconomic reform and structural adjustment may be said to reflect the long-term interests of the dominant partners in the aid relationship. The prospects for economic development in LDCs will thus be largely determined by structural constraints, both at the level of the global economy and in the configuration of classes, groups, interests and structures within the domestic economy.

2

AFRICA AND THE NEW INTERNATIONAL AID REGIME

By "the new international aid regime", I am referring to the neo-liberal ascendance in development policy which replaced the prevailing traditional consensus of the 1960s.[1] The so-called "neo-classical resurgence" in development theory and practice has marked a significant change in the character of the global "welfare regime"[2] and in the balance of power between North and South.[3] An understanding of the new international aid regime is critical to understanding recent initiatives in European development policy in Africa. In this chapter I shall examine how these changes have influenced the contemporary discourse on the politics and economics of African development. I shall discuss the evolution of IMF and World Bank intervention in Africa and, in particular, how African states have responded to the imperatives of adjustment under tutelage of the Bretton Woods institutions. We shall discuss the critique of structural reform policies and the more recent developments with regard to "governance" and political conditionality. Such a broad analysis will set the international context within which to understand the new politics of adjustment in general and European development policy in Africa in particular.

FROM THE MONROVIA STRATEGY TO THE BERG REPORT

In July 1979 African leaders launched the Monrovia Strategy: a programme of joint action within the auspices of the Organization of African Unity (OAU) to promote African economic recovery and development. This programme led to the Lagos Plan of Action (LPA) and the Final Act of Lagos (FAL), both of which were adopted by the OAU Summit of Heads of State and Government in Lagos in April 1980. Launched with much fanfare and ceremony, the Monrovia Strategy was essentially an ambitious blueprint for rapid economic transformation of the continent through regional cooperation and self-reliant development strategies.[4] Considering the generally poor record of Africa-wide collective efforts, it was in many ways a significant achievement for the OAU.

In 1981, one year after the LPA was adopted, the World Bank published its official study on Africa under the chairmanship of an American economist, Professor Elliot Berg.[5] The key assumption underlying the World Bank position was Africa's comparative advantage in agriculture and raw material exports. In contrast with the LPA's call for self-reliance and delinkage strategies, the Berg Report stressed the importance of policy reform, market solutions, and greater integration into the international economy.[6] The Berg Report maintained what many in African leadership and academic circles came to regard as an ominous silence on the African continental programme.[7]

Three explanations have been suggested for the World Bank's attitude: first, it was possibly viewed as being so unrealistic and impractical as to be unworthy of attention; second, it was perceived as being very much in conflict with the Bank's development philosophy and understanding of the world economy; third, it was seen as having little chance of receiving political support from African governments themselves as to warrant being overlooked.[8] The real reasons will perhaps remain known only within the precincts of the Washington institutions. What is obvious is that, with its traditional conservative neo-classical approach, the Bank could not have been in sympathy with the dependency assumptions of the LPA. Politically, it could also be inferred that the Bank was anxious to defend its traditional role as the mainspring of development policy in Africa and elsewhere, and therefore saw the LPA as an encroachment on its traditional prerogative.

In 1985 African states launched yet another joint programme of action, spelling out regional priorities for economic recovery. The African Priority Programme for Economic Recovery (APPER) was adopted in July 1985 by the OAU Heads of State and Government. According to Dr Adebayo Adedeji, the Executive Secretary of the UN Economic Commission for Africa (ECA), through the APPER African leaders were committing themselves to the implementation of a practical programme "with a view to laying the foundation for durable structural changes".[9] Coming at a time when the costs of adjustment were beginning to be felt in several SSA countries, the APPER was an attempt to ensure that such programmes conformed to the requirements of growth and long-term development.

The UN Special Session on Africa

Within the United Nations, international concern was also beginning to focus on the worsening African situation. In 1984 the General Assembly adopted a "Declaration on the Critical Economic Situation in Africa".[10] An urgent call was made for massive emergency relief assistance as well as support for economic recovery and rehabilitation efforts. The Office for Emergency Operations in Africa (OEOA) was established by Secretary-General Javier Perez de Cuellar. However, African states continued to lobby for a special session of the General Assembly to address their immediate and long-term development problems. A preparatory committee was set up under General Assembly Resolution 40/40 to do the necessary groundwork.[11] The UN "Special Session on Africa" was held in New York in May 1986. Its outcome was the United Nations Programme of Action for African Economic Recovery and Development (UNPAAERD).[12] Although it did not result in any firm financial commitments from the developed countries, it did lead to a "consensus of understanding" on African development challenges. From this viewpoint the session was a political success for the African Group, given that it was the first time that the world body would devote an entire session to the economic predicaments of a single region.[13] The international community pledged their support for APPER and for increased financial support both in terms of official development assistance (ODA) and replenishment of International Development Association (IDA) resources. It was also agreed that steps should be taken to repeal official debts for the most impoverished countries while supporting economic recovery and structural adjustment efforts.

Progress in the implementation of UNPAAERD was hampered largely by lack of financial support from the North.[14] Within the Group of 77, some critics argued that a special programme specifically designed for Africa might prove to be inimical to collective Southern solidarity. Outside the official negotiating forum, there was much scepticism about the prospects for the programme itself and of the preparedness of SSA countries to implement it.[15] During its final review in New York in September 1991, there was little enthusiasm for the Programme, with donors insisting that additional finance would be made available only to countries which were prepared to undertake democratic reforms.[16] The UN initiative served to publicize the problems of the African region but could not mobilize the required financial resources and political backing to ensure that it succeeded.

IMF AND WORLD BANK INVOLVEMENT IN AFRICA

After the publication of the Berg Report, it was clear that the Bretton Woods institutions were resolved to chart a new course with regard to African development.[17] Its proposals were hardly novel: what it was offering was "more of the same", i.e., more exports of raw materials, encouragement of foreign direct investment, and a reduced role for the state in the economy. The "Special Facility for Sub-Saharan Africa" was established by the Bank as a temporary financing scheme for African countries. The Bank also officially undertook to make half of all its new concessional loans from the Eighth IDA Replenishment available specifically to Africa. The Fund, for its part, had begun by 1979 to devote a greater proportion of its financing facilities to the region.[18] It has been estimated that during 1979 and 1980, some 30 per cent of the Fund's conditional credit went to Africa, in contrast to a mere 3 per cent during 1970–78.[19] By March 1986, the Fund had set up the Structural Adjustment Facility (SAF) to make long-term concessional loans to countries facing protracted balance of payments problems, of which two-thirds of the resources were earmarked for sub-Saharan Africa.

This activist role which the IFIs have found themselves exercising in Africa is reflective of their transformed role in the international economy. The original architects of Bretton Woods would probably never have imagined that the Bank and Fund would come to occupy such a pre-eminent profile in the affairs of the developing world. In the case of the Bank, the massive American aid programme under the Marshall Plan during 1945–50 had virtually rendered the Bank's existence superfluous. It thus had little choice but to reorient its mission to the developing countries.[20] The Bank has financed projects in infrastructures and rural development, and has been historically a prominent actor in African agricultural policy-making.[21] After the revocation of the gold–dollar standard by President Nixon in the summer of 1971, the role of the Fund had clearly become quite marginal to the control and management of international finance.[22] The Fund consequently turned its attention more towards provision of balance of payments financing to developing countries.[23] John Loxley has rightly observed that "there is no historical precedent for the extent and degree of overt policy leverage now being exercised by multilateral agencies on African governments".[24] Typical IMF/World Bank reform programmes, according to Thomas Biersteker, entail currency devaluation, restriction of the money supply, price and trade liberalization, privatization of public enterprises, fiscal adjustment, and removal of subsidies (see Table 2.1).[25] It is not only this new role which has come under intense controversy but also the socioeconomic impact and political implications of the kinds of policies which they have encouraged in the developing world.[26]

THE CRITIQUE OF STRUCTURAL ADJUSTMENT PROGRAMMES

Does structural adjustment work? Has it been effective in addressing the long-term needs of underdeveloped countries? Whose interests does it serve? Who are the losers and who are the winners? What are the implications of conditionality for political sovereignty and the independence of states? These rather uncomfortable questions often evoke defensive posturing and *argumentum ad hominem* rather than sober intellectual dialogue. I

Table 2.1 Typology of stabilization and structural adjustment

Typical IMF stabilization measures

1 Devalue currency
2 Restrict Money Supply
3 Pursue fiscal adjustment (in particular, cut government spending)
4 Pursue liberalization
  a of trade
  b of exchange regime
5 Adjust incomes policy (in particular, restrain wages)

Typical World Bank structural adjustment measures

1 Institutionalize real exchange rate adjustment
  a establish currency auction
  b introduce crawling peg
  c unify multiple rates
2 pursue fiscal policy reform
  a reduce or constrain the rate of growth of government spending
  b reform the tax structure
  c rationalize expenditures
  d phase out or reduce government subsidies
  e improve the efficiency of public investment
3 Liberalize trade
  a maintain exchange rate flexibility (1 above)
  b eliminate trade licensing
  c replace quantitative restrictions with tariffs
  d gradually lower tariff levels
4 Pursue financial reform
  a liberalize foreign exchange controls
  b reduce or eliminate subsidized credit
5 Proceed with other policy reform measures
  a reduce price controls
  b end or reduce price subsidies
  c adjust agricultural prices
  d eliminate state marketing boards
  e limit wage indexation
  f pursue privatization

Source: Biersteker, *Dealing With Debt*, Boulder, Col.: Westview Press, 1993, p. 13

shall attempt to paint the broad contours of the critique of adjustment policies as a prelude to examining African political attitudes to such programmes. The critique of adjustment policies may be categorized into five schools of analysis, namely: the humanitarian, the neo-conservative, the neo-Keynesian, the structuralist and the neo-Marxist.

By the humanitarian critique, I am referring to the school of thought which is chiefly preoccupied with the human impact of adjustment programmes. A number of Western NGOs, notably Oxfam, have been prominent in drawing attention to the human effects of adjustment policies, particularly on poor rural and urban families.[27] The study by Cornia, Jolly and Stewart under the auspices of UNICEF was especially significant in launching this critique.[28] The central concern of the study was with the human dimensions of adjustment, i.e., its effects on the welfare of children, women, the elderly and other "vulnerable groups". Whilst affirming the necessity for adjustment and absolving the reform programmes for the deteriorating social conditions in adjusting countries, the UNICEF study acknowledged the unsatisfactory approach to the adjustment problem, in particular, the deflationary element, with its negative impact on employment and real incomes; and policies such as exchange rates, subsidy cuts and producer prices, which affect the urban poor. Some of the inherent problems with adjustment were listed as: their short-term horizon; over-emphasis on macroeconomic aspects to the neglect of sectoral policy, and lack of any consideration for the distributional or equity question. The UNICEF study concluded by calling for "adjustment with a human face", to give a "poverty alleviation dimension" to adjustment in much the same way as "redistribution with growth" and "basic needs" added such a dimension to the debate on growth.[29]

The central element of the neo-conservative critique is that the IFIs are not radical enough in carrying out the task of supervising orthodox reform programmes in developing countries. Neo-conservatives argue that structural adjustment is not only necessary and unavoidable, but the only viable option for survival in a changed global economic environment. They question not the rationale behind adjustment programmes but the ineffectiveness and irresolution of the Washington institutions in ensuring that they are followed. The Reagan administration, for example, criticized the Fund in the early 1980s for allegedly over-extending itself in its issuance of structural adjustment loans, especially to countries that could have borrowed instead from commercial banks. The Fund was also accused of having "gone soft" on certain aspects of its adjustment programmes, thereby devaluing its authority and "seal of approval".[30] Thus, conditionalities are thought to be so soft that they are easily ignored with impunity by recipient countries. Some of those on the Right who pillory the Fund support the idea of starving it of funds in order to force it to ration its resources and to exert more pressures on adjusting countries.[31]

The neo-Keynesian critique derives from dissatisfaction by some of the adherents of the neo-classical economics tradition with the design and implementation of adjustment programmes. It is essential to note that what they criticize is not the underlying assumptions of such programmes – which they regard as theoretically unassailable – but the manner in which they are designed and implemented. For Robert Cassen, the main problem with adjustment in Africa has been its short-term horizon. According to him, this failing itself derives from the faulty design of programmes, errors of judgement and estimation, emphasis on demand rather than supply issues, and also the terms and volume of financial resources which are made available to adjusting countries.[32] A mild revisionism against neo-liberalism is embodied in the work of Tony Killick, which echoes the earlier doubts of Kaldor, Hendry and Ericsson.[33]

Given the realities of certain constraints – market imperfections, externalities, information failures, monopolies and distributional inequities – there is a need for "more caution and modesty" in imposing market solutions. Killick's main critique centres on what he describes as "the dangers of overkill, of overall reliance on simplistic . . . solutions", including repudiation of the state even in such vital areas as agricultural research, rural extension services and infrastructures.[34] He envisions the "impending decline" of neo-liberalism, given that some "lessons" have been learned and that past development follies are unlikely to be repeated.[35] While Killick's analysis is highly perceptive, his generous conclusions are inspired more by hope than by the lessons of experience.

The structuralist critique is derived from the work of economists who see inflation in LDCs as deriving not so much from the money supply problem as from market structures and the economic contest between different socioeconomic groups. When there is a decline in the income of a particular economically powerful group, for example, they could seek to protect themselves by driving up nominal prices in those sectors over which they exercise some control. The MIT economist Lance Taylor, for example, argues that the monetarist model of inflation is valid only where you have price-clearing markets, a situation which does not apply to "the parallel transactions and urban subsistence activities" in much of Africa.[36] Taylor and the WIDER Group[37] argue that there cannot be one universal remedy applied to all countries and that the design of programmes should therefore take account of the institutional and structural characteristics of particular LDCs.[38] The WIDER Group have also argued that, contrary to the Fund's assumptions, devaluation often does lead to stagflation unless it is used as a complement to other policy inputs such as public investment, sector-specific interventions, import tariff holidays for exporters, and agricultural research and technical assistance. There is also the paradox of capital flight, which follows trade liberalization measures intended to boost capital inflows.

Another group of structuralists, mainly associated with the Sussex Institute of Development Studies (IDS), have criticized neo-liberal economics from both the standpoint of theory and policy.[39] They have questioned the intellectual basis and selective use of evidence on which the neo-liberals have drawn some of their policy prescriptions. On trading regimes, for example, they have noted how fragile the evidence was upon which the notions of export-led growth and outward-oriented development strategies were raised to the status of infallible maxims.[40] John Toye has criticized in particular the concept of the state which underpins neo-liberal economic theory, in which the political process is perceived in purely rent-seeking terms:

> To say . . . that people in political positions are typically motivated *only* by individual self-interest is, and should be, shocking. It is shocking because it denies and disparages all the norms and values of political life no less dramatically than those ancient philosophers who pretended they were dogs in order to demonstrate their scorn for the ideals of the Greek *Polis.*[41]

The point of departure for the neo-Marxist critique is Marx's law of value as it relates to capital accumulation on the world scale. Such accumulation is understood to be necessarily based on unequal exchange, exploitative class relations and the peripheralization of underdeveloped social formations. The Egyptian economist Samir Amin sees structural adjustment as yet another stage in the subordination of Africa and other LDCs, a process which is bound to lead to greater impoverishment and social strife in the South. Amin sees the history of North–South relations as a process in which the poorer regions of the periphery have been continually adjusting to the needs of international capital, leading to:

> a contrast between centre and periphery that was immanent in actually existing capitalism. In this sense then, the development of the periphery has always entailed a never-ending "adjustment" to the demands and constraints of the dominant capital. The centres are "restructured", the peripheries are "adjusted" to this restructuring. Never the reverse.[42]

Problem of power in cooperative agreements of North–South

Structural Adjustment Programmes are viewed as favouring the alliance between the domestic and international bourgeoisie against the interest of workers and peasants. It represents in essence the internationalization of class struggles and a capital lesson on the impossibility of independent accumulation in the periphery.[43] The only viable alternative for LDCs is posed in terms of "delinking" away from international capital. Amin advocates that popular groups, in alliance with the "organic intellectuals" would seize control of state power. The problem with this view, besides its dogmatism, is that, pending the revolution, it offers no real alternatives in the medium term. It also lacks a clear strategy as to what aspects of international economic relations are to be delinked and whether there is to be selectivity in delinking and a rank-ordering of priority sectors where such action should take place.

It is evident that scholars will never agree on the ultimate verdict of the neo-liberal reform model of development. The relative success of countries such as Ghana, Mexico, Chile and Argentina will have to be weighed against the general poor record of such programmes in the South developing countries. Regardless of one's perspective, the economic indicators associated with adjustment have not been unassailably impressive.

Conditionality and the sovereignty question

Sovereignty refers to the capacity of a state to exercise its will within its territorial jurisdiction, and to do so without having to look constantly over its shoulder. From the point of view of international law, sovereignty is a fundamental requirement of modern statehood.[44] In the hard realities of international politics, however, there is often a divergence between sovereignty in fact and sovereignty in law.[45] While realist writers may see the concept as a fiction devised to fit with the tidy logic of international lawyers, it has to be recognized that sovereignty is nevertheless an essential part of the grammar of contemporary world politics.[46] In the sense understood here, state sovereignty extends to the ability of a state to formulate its own economic policies in accordance with its own defined objectives and priorities, and to do so without constant reference to external agencies and powers.

What are the implications of adjustment programmes for the principle of sovereignty? To what extent do macroeconomic conditionalities encroach on the sovereignty of recipient states?

A major element in the critique of adjustment policies is the allegedly unilateral manner in which the programmes are devised and imposed on developing countries.[47] Writing in the influential journal, *Foreign Affairs*, an American journalist, Marguerite Michaels, observes that "Africa has become a research lab for economic reform experimentation – much of it dictated by the terms of international lenders", and with a style that "has been a powerful combination of arrogance, ignorance and absolute, unchecked power. . . . If a country loses the bank's imprimatur, it loses aid from Western donors too. African economists are rarely invited to help design bank policies".[48]

It seems fairly obvious that structural adjustment has increased the degree of dependence of SSA countries on the Bretton Woods institutions. The single-country approach to the negotiations of such programmes ensures that LDCs cannot mobilize their collective bargaining leverage. Whilst there is little dispute over the rationale for conditionality, the manner in which it is often framed leaves the poorest developing countries with little or no room for manoeuvre. A study on decision-making on IMF conditionality by Kendall Stiles has posited three alternative explanations:

- bureaucratic expertise and authority by IMF officials;
- dominance of political interests of the major shareholders of the Fund;
- bargaining and compromise among Fund officials and between the latter and recipient LDCs.[49]

Based on evidence from interviews with Fund staff and on the basis of case-studies from Zaire, Sudan, Argentina, India, Jamaica, Turkey and the

United Kingdom, Stiles reached the dubious conclusion that the bargaining model is the most important explanation of IMF decision-making.[50]

It is clear that governments turn to the Fund often as a "lender of last resort"; indeed in some cases, as the sole lender. And with the IFIs holding the key of access to vital international credit, LDCs come to the "negotiating table" with little or no bargaining chips. Is IMF conditionality therefore an affront to the principle of the sovereign independence of states? Bank and Fund officials usually insist that it is not, pointing out that LDCs enter into such agreements in full exercise of their sovereign prerogatives. One of the few scholars to have thought deeply about this question is the French political economist, Marie-France L'Hériteau. Her work on the relations between the Fund and the LDCs leads to the conclusion that conditionality does in fact imply an erosion of state sovereignty.[51]

Adjustment programmes have led to the involvement of external donors in virtually all areas of economic policy. Countries are no longer able to set long-term objectives of national development. The growth of aid-related countervalue funds has become the pretext for imposition of external directives on the setting up of national priorities in the annual budgets. In Zaire, Liberia and Zambia, for example, foreign experts have either taken over control of vital ministries or have become their *eminences grises*. In the case of Ghana, E. Hutchful observes that

> the erosion of national sovereignty and the autonomy and popular direction of the regime . . . is more readily perceived. What has emerged in Accra is a parallel government controlled (if not created) by the international lender agencies.[52]

There have been instances when the IFIs have had to approve appointments of key officials such as ministers of finance and governors of central banks. In what could be regarded as perhaps a Freudian error, World Bank Vice-President for Africa, Edward Jaycox, seemed to be confirming this view when he declared in an interview that, "for African authorities, the rhetoric of independence now rings hollow and breeds cynicism instead of energizing people".[53]

AFRICAN ATTITUDES TO IMF/WORLD BANK PROGRAMMES

As a consequence of their experience with Bank and Fund reform programmes, African leaders and articulate publics have altered their perceptions of those institutions. In the 1960s and 1970s the role of the IFIs was seen as essentially technical and politically innocuous, merely complementing efforts of UN agencies such as FAO, UNDP and UNCTAD in the sure-footed path of economic development and modernization. This image was largely a product of history. The Bank had arrived on the African scene much earlier than the Fund. In the late 1950s the first World Bank missions were already in several SSA countries helping to map out their ambitious post-independence economic plans. Since the 1960s, the Bank has been a prominent donor to SSA countries, beginning with infrastructural projects in the 1960s to agriculture and the "Green Revolution" in the 1970s.[54]

The IMF, for its part, was largely preoccupied with the needs of the developed market economies in the 1960s. It was not until the 1970s that African countries began to borrow heavily from the Fund in response to their protracted balance of payments crises. By the 1980s, with the establishment of the Fund's Structural Adjustment Facility (SAF) and the Extended Structural Adjustment Facility (ESAF) the IMF had become a dominant actor in policy-based lending. Between 1986 and 1991, some SDR1,881 billion was approved for thirty-five LDCs under the SAF, of which twenty-six were SSA countries.[55] Under the ESAF, SDR1,907 billion was approved for nineteen LDCs, of which fifteen were SSA countries.[56] During the clamour for the NIEO, African states had joined their Southern counterparts in demanding reforms in the decision-making system in the key international economic institutions.[57] Even then they did not attach as much salience to the IFIs as they were to do in subsequent years.

As a result of the adjustment experience, African attitudes towards the Bretton Woods institutions have been tempered with a sense of critical realism. One of the severest critics of the Bank and Fund is former Tanzanian President Julius Nyerere. He has criticized their coercive approach to conditionality, describing it as an attempt to use their structural power in a subterranean effort at re-colonization of Africa.[58] Having retired from government in 1985, at a critical time in Tanzania's relations with the IFIs, Mwalimu Nyerere became Chairman of the South Commission, from where he has sought to foster Southern collective solidarity against what is perceived as a new international social Darwinism.[59]

Radical African scholars have been at the forefront of the critique of the IFIs, whose role they view as fostering even deeper asymmetries in North–South relations. The Nigerian economist Bade Onimode describes Structural Adjustment Programmes as:

> a strategy for ensuring that African countries pay their debts, and a means of gaining effective leverage over the industrial policy of the poor countries. Trade liberalisation, tariff restructuring, and related policies are seen as being designed to dump manufactured imports and wreck the industrialisation of these countries.[60]

The argument about industrial strangulation is probably borne out by the de-industrializing effects which analysts have observed in Africa in recent times.[61] Onimode censures IMF and World Bank policies for "trying to impose a capitalist model of development on the poor countries", an accusation which is true, even if banal. Anyone who is acquainted with the articles of agreement or the historical background and operational principles of the Bank and Fund should not have expected them to support, or even encourage, non-market principles. That the IFIs espouse free enterprise is therefore hardly a new discovery. In their organizational set-up and decision-making procedures, they have incarnated the structural power of the United States and the dominant capitalist economies who, by definition, have a vested interest in shaping a global market for the free flow of capital, investments and goods. Indeed, one writer has argued that the IMF is, in the strict sense, "not an autonomous, self-styled entity but an *agent*".[62] The Malawian economist and Executive Director of CODESRIA,[63] lamented that, under the cloak of monitoring economic reform programmes, an "incredible number of peripatetic *experts*" were invading Africa, jetting "from one part . . . to another, prescribing one standard drug against all ills, leaving behind them enormous suffering with absolutely no accountability to anyone".[64]

The ECA and the politics of adjustment

To appreciate fully the role of the ECA in the debate on Africa's adjustment, it is perhaps useful to give a brief historical background to its emergence. The Economic Commission for Africa (ECA), a UN regional agency based in Addis Ababa, Ethiopia, was established in 1958 to promote economic cooperation in Africa and to offer research and technical support for African development efforts.[65] Just as its Latin American counterpart did under the leadership of the Argentinian economist Raul Prebisch earlier in the 1950s and 1960s, the ECA has come to play an activist role in the diplomacy and politics of structural adjustment in the 1980s. In the 1960s its Executive Secretary had been the Oxford and Cambridge-educated Ghanaian economist, Robert Kweku Gardiner. Well schooled in the best traditions of the British civil service culture, he was a rather self-effacing technocrat, whose style was that of quiet but meticulous effort in the public interest. During his time the role of the ECA was central in the establishment of the several regional trade groupings and in the creation of the African Development Bank in 1964.

In the 1970s Dr Adebayo Adedeji of Nigeria took over as Executive Secretary. A graduate of London and Leicester Universities, he did postgraduate work in finance and public administration at Harvard. After the Nigerian civil war, he was drawn from his Deanship at the Faculty of Public Administration at the University of Ife to become Minister for Finance and Economic Planning. He was widely respected as a competent public servant and technocrat. Far from being self-effacing, his experience in government had given Adedeji some fondness for the political arena. He came to the ECA at a time of profound change and crisis in Africa, and up to his retirement in 1990, he never fought shy of taking the path of active debate, some would say even open confrontation, with the international institutions.[66]

In June 1987, the ECA organized an international conference at Nigeria's new federal capital, Abuja. Although the main object of the conference was to assess the extent of the progress made so far in implementing the programmes resulting from the 1986 UN Special Session on Africa, the discussions extended to issues of structural adjustment and economic reforms, and became the first open political position taken by the ECA on this question.[67] The conference assembled more than 200 delegates from Africa, some donor countries and from twenty-four international agencies. The conference noted the very modest achievements that had been made and stressed the need to direct efforts at sustaining domestic policy reforms; improving macroeconomic management; increasing debt-relief and development assistance; and ensuring that Structual Adjustment Programmes harmonize with long-term goals of recovery and growth.

The conference seemed to have been reconciled to the fundamental requirements of adjustment. What apparently was at issue was how to reorientate the reform programmes to bring them in line with African priorities and long-term goals. Interestingly enough, the conference called for an African development strategy based on a programme of "structural transformation". While the content of such a strategy was not clearly spelt out, the ECA underlined the political requisites for its success:

> The democratization of the African society and increased accountability of those entrusted with power are vital for the mobilisation of greater popular participation. . . . African political perspectives *vis-à-vis* external political interests will also have to be sharpened to become more decisive and enlightened so that the destiny of Africa is assured to be in the hands of the African people.[68]

In March 1988, following the Abuja conference, the ECA sponsored yet another conference, this time in the Sudanese capital of Khartoum. Unlike the former, this conference's purpose was to examine the impact of adjustment on African development. It was to be of crucial importance because it led to the "Khartoum Declaration on Structural Adjustment in Africa". The declaration largely echoed the views of UNICEF in decrying the adverse effects of adjustment on vulnerable groups, and calling for a more humanized version of economic reform based on a human-centred approach to development:

> We the delegates will not tolerate economic formulas, will not apply economic indices . . . which fail to assert the primacy of the human condition. Nutritional imbalances are as crucial as trade imbalances, and high infant mortality rates require as much immediate action as high rates of inflation.[69]

Although the conference did not deny the rationale behind adjustment programmes, it reaffirmed the need for "home-grown" varieties to reflect African interests and priorities more accurately. Interestingly enough, the conference emphasized its difference from the humanitarian version of "adjustment with a human face": it stressed the direct relationship between malnourishment, disease and economic production. This was perhaps an emphasis that did not quite feature in the UNICEF study, which rather emphasized the humanitarian dimension. Dr Adedeji was quoted as saying: "We squander the most precious resource we have for effecting economic and social growth when we neglect the welfare of the majority in our search for production gains which have often remained illusory."[70]

In terms of diplomacy, the conference was well timed in anticipation of the mid-term review of the programme (a programme launched following the United Nations Special Session two years earlier). It was a collective statement of principle which could not be ignored by donor countries, nor by the international agencies, although the extent to which it did influence subsequent policy responses is uncertain. Perhaps the subsequent adoption of the Programme of Action to Mitigate the Social Costs of Adjustment (PAMSCAD), a US$70 million programme of social investment on public works employment, provision of drugs and educational rehabilitation, could be seen as a possible outcome of the ECA's critique.

In 1989 the World Bank published a report on Africa in which they maintained that structural adjustment was proving to be a success in the region.[71] Their optimism was based on what was regarded as "encouraging signs" in such areas as agriculture and exports. They estimated that the GDP of SSA had grown by more than 2.3 per cent in the three years 1985–87. Agriculture was singled out for praise as a particularly remarkable sector of increased output, thanks to structural adjustment. The report maintained that, as a result of increased agricultural output, Africa's combined share of world exports of ten major non-oil primary commodity exports had grown by 30 per cent during 1984–86, for the first time reversing the declining trends of the 1970s.

The Bank's report was to lead to one of the most embarrassing political and intellectual responses, this time from the UN Economic Commission for Africa. The ECA came out with an official rejoinder which questioned the statistical as well as factual basis of the report's conclusions.[72] The ECA stopped short of calling the Bank's integrity into question, accusing it of inconsistency in the use of statistics and even of departing from its normal way of using data in analysing the impact of its programmes.

Was the Bank engaging in the politics of statistical manipulation? Were the Washington technocrats anxious to manufacture evidence of success in their reform programmes? Why did the ECA choose the path of open confrontation instead of the discreet style characteristic of international technocrats? The answers to the first two questions may never be satisfactorily resolved. From a technical point of view, economists will always differ on the best way to measure success of adjustment programmes and on what the criteria of success ought to be. There is always the problem of the "counterfactual", i.e., of determining results from probabilistic permutations of what might have been if there had been no adjustment in the first place. Owing to changing world conditions, it is difficult to compare results during an adjustment period with economic performance in the years preceding adjustment. It is equally difficult to disentangle the real effects of an adjustment programme from those which derive merely from additional financial resource inflows which are triggered off by Bank/Fund "seals of approval".

The "African Alternative" to adjustment

The most wide-ranging African collective response to the new politics of structural adjustment has been the ECA Alternative Framework, which was officially released in the spring of 1989.[73] But it would be a mistake to describe it simply as an ECA document. After all, it did emerge as the final outcome of a series of extensive consultations with African governments, OAU finance and planning ministers and African scholars and researchers.[74] It was a response to what were perceived as the general failings and inherent defects of orthodox adjustment programmes, with their monetarist approaches, short-term horizons and neglect of the social, political and capacity-building aspects of development.

What seems clear from the start is that the "African Alternative" does not question the need for structural adjustment. Where it parts company with the IFIs is with regard to what and how to adjust. The document calls not for structural adjustment but for what it terms "adjustment with transformation". What is offered is a supposedly more comprehensive "political economy" framework going beyond the narrow economic and monetarist assumptions of the Bank and Fund:

> to situate the process of adjustment in the objective realities and conditions of African societies – the reality of the multiplicity of political, social and economic forces that in the end determine the success or failure of policy reforms.[75]

A strategy of structural transformation is expected to be implemented through the following key policies:

- allocation of at least 20 to 25 per cent of total public investment to agriculture;
- agrarian reforms and facilitating better access to land;
- creation and strengthening of rural financial institutions;
- reduction of defence budgets;

- improvement of tax systems;
- selective use of trade policy;
- strengthening African regional cooperation;
- reduction of debt-service ratios;
- greater mass participation in decision-making and in implementation of programmes.

There are aspects of the document which are confused, confusing, populist and clearly only of rhetorical interest. Is popular participation the same as democratization? What does "mass participation" in policy formulation and implementation mean in practical terms? But the problem is not only in relation to some of its rhetorical licence. There are technical issues that are inadequately treated, for example, the question of exchange rates; the role of foreign investment, and the rationalization of policy systems. However, to its credit it does question the size of African military budgets in a context where children cannot be properly fed and the threat of hunger is always on the horizon. Until very recently, the IFIs have always been reticent even to discuss the question of defence budgets, arguing that it is very sensitive and might be considered to be political interference in internal affairs. The African Alternative's central orientation remains its emphasis on the social and human dimensions of adjustment, especially in the key areas of provision of social services and basic needs, shielding the most vulnerable groups from adversity of harsh policies, and improving human and institutional capacity. The ECA clearly felt the need for African countries to reassert their initiative in matters of economic policy instead of depending on external actors for ideas which might not be in their own best interest.

Responses to the African Alternative have been varied. Former World Bank President Robert McNamara hailed it as a "remarkable document . . . a set of extraordinarily wise and advanced principles", which are crucial to Africa's long-term development.[76] Similarly, the French government gave its approval because, according to them, it took account of the social and political realities of the region.[77] The then Secretary-General of the United Nations, Javier Perez de Cuellar, officially welcomed the report as a recognition of the need for structural transformation in Africa and to protect the weakest segments of society from the negative effects of orthodox reform programmes.[78]

During the debate at the UN General Assembly over the resolution to adopt AAF-SAP as a reference document for "constructive dialogue and fruitful consultation" between Africa and the international community (read donors and the finance institutions), France's Paul Lemerle, spokesman for the European Community group at the UN, accepted the main arguments of the report, pointing out that orthodox programmes did not always take into account the specificities of African political economies.

The resolution was successfully passed on 17 November 1989, with a 137 vote in favour, no abstentions, but with the United States casting the sole dissenting vote. The United States Ambassador, James Wilkinson, insisted that the American government could not accept that structural adjustment was not working. He reaffirmed support for the IMF and the Bank and criticized the African states for overlooking what he believed to be "the progress which has occurred over the past several years, largely as a result of internationally supported adjustment programmes".[79]

Power imbalance

Although positive acceptance of the African document was near-universal, opposition from the United States has probably proved to be a decisive stumbling block. In expressing staunch opposition, the United States was not only defending its dominant position within the international finance institutions, it was also expressing its unwillingness to give up the prerogative in setting agendas and determining the character of international aid regimes. The strong support expressed by France and the European Community illustrates an instance of lack of cohesion between the two Atlantic communities with regard to international development questions. France's response could be said to derive from its traditional posture in international fora as "the friend of Africa" as well as its Gaullist antipathy to the alleged Anglo-Saxon domination of international economic decision-making.

From adjustment to political conditionality

Political conditionality refers to the tying of aid to fulfilment of stated political reforms. A major change in Western development policy after 1989 was the increasing use of political conditionality as a complement to macroeconomic conditionality. Owing in large part to the collapse of the Soviet bloc and the ending of the Cold War, Western donors no longer found it politically expedient to prop up despotic allies with aid money. The World Bank report on Africa which was published in November 1989 set the tone when it underlined "governance" and "institutional capacity" as essential complements to sustainable growth in sub-Saharan Africa.[80]

In June 1990 the British Foreign Secretary, Douglas Hurd, gave a policy statement at a press conference in which he declared that "good government" is a necessary condition for success in economic development. He warned that LDCs "which tend towards pluralism, public accountability, respect for the rule of law, human rights and market principles", would be encouraged, while those who "persist with repressive policies, corrupt management, wasteful and discredited economic systems should not expect us to support their folly with scarce aid resources which could be used better elsewhere".[81] A year later, the Minister for Overseas Development, Baroness Chalker, was to outline the conditions of "good government" as being: sound social and economic policies; free markets and enhanced role for the private sector; provision of essential services and reduction in the military budget; competence in government and administrative capacity; pluralism; public accountability; and political openness. She announced that British aid policy would give positive support to good government and capacity-building in sectors such as electoral and legal reforms, public administration, public expenditure management, and improvement of financial institutions.

Political conditionality has often entailed giving direct support to pro-democracy movements and to encouraging multi-partyism. One of the most notable examples of political conditionality has been in Kenya, where aid consortia led by the United States and Britain were active in pushing through political reforms.[82] In February 1991, the Director of the United States Agency for International Development (USAID) announced that the agency would "direct an increasing amount of funds to those countries that are moving towards economic and political liberalization".[83] Under the influence of Senator Edward Kennedy, 1990 aid appropriations for Kenya were explicitly tied to human rights improvement. Both the USAID representative and the American Ambassador became directly involved in Kenya's domestic politics, giving open support to the main opposition group, the Forum for the Restoration of Democracy (FORD). The British approach to political conditionality has been contrasted with the "punitive approach", of American aid policy in Kenya. Whereas the British approach in Kenya was to seek positive signs of improvement in the government's determination to enhance improved governance, the United States was demanding immediate action in specific human rights areas, especially in the release of political prisoners, putting an end to the physical maltreatment of prisoners, restoration of judicial independence and freedom of speech. In November 1991, the multi-donor Kenyan Consultative Group, in its meeting in Paris, resolved to suspend all aid to Kenya for at least six months, pending improvements in terms of economic and political reforms. These actions succeeded in forcing the government of President Daniel Arap Moi to agree to the demands for multi-party elections in 1992.[84]

Most African countries have at least acknowledged the inevitability of democratization and political reforms. In July 1990, the OAU Summit of Heads of State and Government affirmed their commitment to democracy and popular participation in governance, human rights, the rule of law and public accountability.[85] By 1990, no less than twenty-eight African countries were explicitly committed to a programme of political reforms.[86]

What factors account for this change in political orientation by international donors? The first and most obvious is the fall of the Soviet empire, which Lord Dahrendorf has appropriately termed "the Revolution of 1989". African publics and governments alike could not have remained immune to these changes.[87] The European Bank for Reconstruction and Development, which was soon to be established by the European

Community to assist the transition to market economies in Eastern Europe, established political criteria for the use of its funds. Its mandate was clearly stated as to give loans only to those countries in Eastern and Central Europe that commit themselves to the principles of multi-party democracy, pluralism and the market system.[88]

Another contributory factor was the increasing frustration with the lack of effectiveness of economic reform programmes. The 1989 World Bank Report, with its theme of "adjustment with growth", "capacity building" and "good governance", was widely hailed as signalling a progressive "learning curve" by the IFIs, an awareness of the inherent limitations of neo-liberal reform strategies.[89] There was now acceptance of the need to go beyond stabilization, to achieve "a genuine transformation of productive structures". The Bank explicitly drew a causal relationship between democracy and economic performance, citing the examples of Mauritius and Botswana, where openness and democracy have been correlates of economic growth. This report has virtually set the agenda for recent international development efforts which have all tended to chorus the tune of "good governance" and its accompanying elements of institutional development and capacity building.

The third factor to account for the change in the international donors' political stance was that now popular groups were vociferously demanding civic participation. Even as the African state had crushed most forms of dissent, there were groups who had never relented in the struggles for democratization.[90] What was new about the current libertarian spirit, according to Ambassador Olara Otunu, President of the International Peace Academy, was "the sense of confidence and legitimacy with which democratic demand is being made".[91]

Criticism of political conditionality has often centred on the question of whether there is a direct correlation between economic performance and democracy. The well-known argument of Lee Kuan Yew, former Prime Minister of Singapore, is that democracy could actually prove harmful to rapid economic growth. The Swedish scholar Björn Beckman has addressed the political implications of the new World Bank perspective from the viewpoint of legitimation.[92] He discerns in it a legitimation project which is "managerial and populist rather than democratic". He disclaims the view that democratization can be derived from adjustment, when in fact it is resistance to such programmes that offer the source of democratization. Using class analysis, he maintains that adjustment has empowered the domestic bourgeoisie, and being a foreign imposition, directly negates nationalism and "popular struggles".[93] Beckman perhaps fails to see the wider global context in which new democratic struggles have emerged, as well as the undeniable fact that political conditionality has opened up new possibilities of free expression in many countries.

Indeed, it has been suggested that one of the major political consequences of structural adjustment is increased repression.[94] The introduction of "austerity measures", removal of subsidies, massive retrenchment of workers, drastic increases in prices of essential consumer items, in the context of a non-existent social safety net, inevitably bred political resistance by urban workers, students, university teachers and other articulate sections of society.[95] In Zambia, Nigeria, Côte d'Ivoire, Sudan and a host of other countries, the so-called "SAP riots" were suppressed only through quasi-military means. In Sudan the bread price riots of 1985 led to the downfall of President el Numairy, and the 1989 food riots greatly weakened the civilian government of el Mahdi, paving the way for a military coup d'état.

Finally, there has been the question of the legitimacy of externally imposed political liberalization and its inherent conflict with the principle of national sovereignty. Within the OAU, for example, African leaders, while reaffirming the need for democratization, have expressed concern about "the increasing tendency to impose" political solutions as a condition for aid.[96] One African observer has dismissed the entire "governance" project as an attempt to uproot the last remaining tendencies of socialism in Africa while constructing a framework of legitimation for Western hegemony and political control.[97] It is perhaps inevitable that support for democratization will stop where vital Western economic and political interests are at stake.[98] Whatever the political motivations, the strengthening of public-policy institutions, the encouragement of democratic accountability, and the promotion of the rule of law, remain issues of crucial importance for economic and political change in contemporary Africa.

CONCLUSION

In this chapter we have discussed the international responses to Africa's economic decline, from the World Bank's Berg Report to the current preoccupation with adjustment and political conditionality. Structural Adjustment Programmes have had at best an ambiguous effect on African development. Particularly for the poorest sections of the African people, life-chances have worsened dramatically, and life has become, as Thomas Hobbes depicted the "state of nature": nasty, brutish and short. Conditionality may be a "bargaining process", but it is a bargain between unequals, in which the stakes are overwhelmingly tilted against poor and weak states.

Adjustment, then, is only marginally about "development"; its *raison d'être* appears to be to ensure that (a) debts to western creditors are collected and (b) that the dominant economic powers, led by the United States, are able to utilize their structural power in constructing a global economic and political environment which is conducive to international finance capital. African states have sought to enhance their political autonomy through collective counter-hegemonic programmes, from the LPA to the AAF-SAP.

These have largely failed owing to their inability to sustain a common programme of action and resistance from dominant forces in the North who are opposed to all such initiatives. The introduction of political conditionality into the development lexicon is an important development in the international aid regime. Support for human rights and democracy has had a modest impact on political change in contemporary Africa, compelling African leaders to institute varying programmes of political reform. Political conditionality serves to ration increasingly limited aid funds while increasing the political leverage of donors in recipient countries.

3

THE ORIGINS OF EC–AFRICAN DIPLOMACY, 1957–71

In the *Periplus*, an ancient Roman inscription of the fifth century BC, dedicated to Hanno the Carthaginian, we read of a trade and navigational route which begins in the Mediterranenan, traversing the heart of Africa and ending somewhere in what is today the modern republic of Cameroon. From this inscription we know that trade relations between the two continents have existed for at least 2,500 years.[1] Although Africa's encounter with Europe dates back to classical antiquity, it was the history of slave trade in the sixteenth century and of colonialism in the nineteenth that was to shape the modern structure of Euro-African relations.

Contrary to the generally accepted wisdom, the Euro-African association regime which emerged in 1957 under the Treaty of Rome was not accomplished in a feat of absent-mindedness. Although taken up with reluctance by the majority of the negotiators, it was an inevitable stepchild of history, a product of the "Dual Mandate" which underlined European colonial ideology in Africa.[2] The core of the argument in this chapter is that between 1957 and 1971 Euro-African relations metamorphosed from colonialism to neo-imperial paternalism. To grasp fully the historical background to this relationship we have to go back to the era of colonization in the late nineteenth century, when European powers were mobilizing various ideological arguments in support of colonial adventures in Africa.[3] A new kind of discourse was emerging, one that was based, to borrow the terminologies of French philosopher Michel Foucault, on hierarchy, difference and exclusion.[4] Although diplomatic exchanges were known to have been established as early as the fourteenth century between, for example, Portugal and the Bini and Itsekiri kingdoms in what was to become south-Western Nigeria, it was the nineteenth century which marked Africa's entry into international society.[5] This initial phase was marked by the primacy of the imperial idea, when African communities and kingdoms became appendages of the great powers in the European-dominated society of states.

The second phase came soon after the Second World War. This period coincided with the rise of anti-colonial nationalism in Africa and Asia. The dominant international temper was also decidedly in favour of national self-determination for all colonized peoples. Anti-colonial nationalism was encouraged in particular by the new superpowers, the United States and the Soviet Union, who had risen triumphant from the ashes of the war. Both countries shared a common interest in the dissolution of old imperial systems. For its part, the United States hoped to gain access to new markets by dismantling colonial preference systems, while the Soviet Union had as its global ambition the recruiting of new allies in the global ideological contest which was then emerging.

In this postwar international environment, if a framework of Euro-African association did not exist, it would have had to be invented. *Realpolitik* as well as economic considerations would have dictated that, in the period of decolonization, the ex-colonial powers would want to ensure alternative forms of control in Africa in line with their perceived long-term strategic interests. "Association" thus came to replace "Eurafrica" as the dominant idiom of Euro-African diplomacy. "Association" conformed to the concept of "informal empire", by which formal colonial structures were to be replaced by diplomatic and trade arrangements which would ensure continuation of European influence in Africa.[6]

EURAFRICA AND THE GEOPOLITICS OF EMPIRE

The idea of "Eurafrica" dates back to nineteenth-century German grand strategists who believed that the structure of the continental land masses demarcated the natural "spheres of influence" for the great powers. Writing in 1897, for example, Friedrich Ratzel, author of *Politische Geographie*, developed concepts about *Raum* or space, which came to be seen as one of the main arguments in favour of colonial incursions into Africa.[7] Just as North America was seen as having South America as its natural sphere of influence, Africa came to be regarded as Europe's strategic entitlement. As an ideological construct, "Eurafrica" derives from the belief in certain European circles that the continents of Africa and Europe have a natural affinity towards each other, an affinity derived from their supposed complementarity and interdependence. According to Guy Martin, it is "a body of thought, originating in the colonial period, according to which the fate of Europe and Africa is seen as being naturally and inextricably linked at the political, economic, social and cultural levels".[8]

During the advent of the Age of Empire, Eurafrica aimed at promoting European international cooperation while minimizing conflicts over the colonial question. The Berlin Conference of 1884–85 which came to be known as the "Scramble for Africa", was remarkable as an exercise in peaceful diplomacy amongst the European powers in carving out their African "possessions". Although Germany, France and Britain had their own separate and conflicting ambitions, the conference was, according to

John Chipman, the "first true act of European cooperation in Africa".[9] Eurafrica, however, was not only an instrument of external policy; it was also seen as a vehicle by which European states could cooperate in promoting peace and amity within the continent itself. The British pacifist, E. D. Morel, for example, was writing in support of a common European African policy as a means of reducing international conflicts to prevent Africa from becoming a battleground of rival European ambitions. He argued that "the very fact of international action being designed to this end will . . . assist Europe in ridding herself of one of the most dangerous incentives to international tension".[10]

It was in France, however, that the myth of Eurafrica acquired an enduring resonance as an ideology of empire as well as of post-colonial influence. In its peculiar version as "*France Afrique*", it became a rallying political maxim for winning domestic support for colonial adventures as well as for legitimizing imperialism in the eyes of the colonized Africans. Why it was in France rather than elsewhere that this idea became such a potent political force is in itself an interesting question for historians of ideas. Since the eighteenth century, France, perhaps alone amongst the great powers, had reinvented her national vocation in terms of certain immanent universal principles of civilization. Whether in terms of the beauty of its language, the nobility of its culture or its political ideals, France saw herself as Europe's leading light in extending the benefits of civilization to the non-European world.[11] Writing in 1862, the influential French statesman Jules Ferry declared that France should not be content to pursue the ideals of a free republic like Switzerland or Belgium. Rather, it should seek national greatness and *rayonnement:* "exercising on the destinies of Europe all the influence . . . [France] should spread this influence over the world, and carry everywhere its language, its customs, its flag, its arms, its genius".[12]

Apart from "*la mission civilisatrice*", in the era of classical balance of power politics, France often turned to Africa in the hours of its defeat, as it did after the Franco-Prussian war of 1870–71, in order to reassure herself that she was still a power of the first rank.[13] Inspired by statesmen such as Jules Ferry and his like-minded compatriots, France took up the banner of colonization, spurred on, according to Immanuel Wallerstein, by a combination of "Jacobin egalitarianism" and "aristocratic romance".[14] Prominent amongst the early French apologists of empire were writers such as Eugène Guénier, Joseph Caillaux and Anton Zischka. They were arguing essentially along the following lines:

> The African soil is too poor for Africa to be able to do without Europe. The African sub-soil is too rich for Europe to be able to do without Africa. Thus, it must be admitted that Africa is an indispensable complement to Europe.[15]

In his book, *L'Afrique Champ d'Europe*, written in 1933, Eugène Guénier called for the incorporation of Africa into Europe, since Africa was allegedly a natural extension of the Old Continent. Africa would supply Europe's needs in raw materials while Europe would provide Africa with the benefits of industry and civilization.[16]

John Chipman has argued that "Eurafrica" was not an idea shared exclusively by Europeans, since in 1953, at the height of the discussions on European unification, a "leading African statesman and intellectual", Leopold Sedar Senghor, was advocating the same idea. Senghor, who was later to become President of Senegal, was calling for the establishment of a Eurafrican community, which would be led by France, since according to him, "the vocation of France is an African one".[17] While its foundations would be economic, Senghor envisioned such a community as a "third force" in the bipolar international system:

> What is interesting is that the two continents . . . are also complementary, while the two antagonistic blocs think only of victory and prepare themselves to achieve it. . . . [Europe and Africa] can constitute a larger force of culture proceeding from peace.[18]

"Eurafrica" may be properly understood as one of the dominant myths of the Age of Empire. In the era of decolonization, it was proffered as a counterforce to the rival ideological pulls in the Cold War. In the era of independence it was to be advanced as a basis for the "special relationship" between Europe and Africa. In particular, it was to form the moral bedrock of the Franco-African alliance which enabled France to exercise political influence in its erstwhile dependencies. Together with the monetary arrangements under the Franc Zone and a web of military alliances, France had effectively institutionalized her "informal" imperial hegemony in post-colonial Africa.[19] In the wider context of the postwar era, the Euro-African relationship could be interpreted as another version of the American "Monroe Doctrine", as Europe and in particular France, sought to establish a sphere of exclusive influence as guardian of Western interests in Africa.[20]

THE ROME TREATY AND THE EMERGENCE OF ASSOCIATION

In the conduct of international relations, associations between states or international organizations serve to broaden the arena of participation without leading to all-out inclusion in a given system. According to Carol Twitchett, associations are:

> political devices enabling states to participate in international organisations, without either the full benefits or obligations of membership . . . [it is] an institutional link between an organ, composed of full members,

> and other states who may participate in some, but not all, activities of the organisation.[21]

It is important to distinguish between associations of a voluntary nature and those that are essentially coercive. For the nature of an association may depend ultimately on the political framework in which it was constructed. We may therefore use the term "coercive association" to refer to situations where states have no choice or say in whether or not to associate, and "association" proper, as applying to arrangements freely agreed upon between sovereign and legally equal political entities. This distinction is crucial because the 1957 Rome Treaty made provision for two fundamentally different forms of association. Part IV, Articles 131–6 of the Treaty provides for an association status for overseas dependencies and territories. The aim of association, according to Article 131, is "to promote the economic and social development of the countries and territories and to establish close economic relations between them and the Community as a whole".[22] The ultimate goal is to foster "the interests and prosperity of the inhabitants of those countries and territories, in such a manner as to lead them to the economic, social and cultural development to which they aspire". Article 238, on the other hand, provides for an entirely different type of association, "with a third country, a union of states or an international organization agreements . . . embodying reciprocal rights and obligations, joint actions and appropriate forms of procedure".[23] The first relates to association between unequals. What is on the agenda here is neither rapid industrialization nor economic restructuring, but a commitment to a vague form of social and economic development "to which they aspire". The second resonates with the language of reciprocity and mutually defined rights and obligations. It clearly supposes a more voluntaristic agreement between equal sovereign states and was obviously aimed at countries on a similar level of development with Europe.

The history of "coercive association" between Europe and Africa predates the Rome Treaty negotiations. During the Hague Congress in May 1948, which was to lead to the formation of the Council of Europe, some reference was made to the need to adjust "the economic ties which at present link the countries of Europe to the Dominions and associated states or dependent overseas territories".[24] The Westminster Conference in London the following year emphasized the need to include the colonies in the European integrative process and to extend colonial trade preferences to all the other European states. Although this principle was rejected by the final Statute of May 1949, the Consultative Assembly of the Council, which included representatives from the colonies such as Leopold Sedar Senghor, did not give up on the idea. Their deliberations were to lead to the Strasbourg Plan, which proposed increased investments in the colonies, the establishment of a European Bank for overseas development, the formalization of long-term contracts to ensure stabilization of commodity prices, and ultimately, an economic grouping embracing Europe and all overseas dominions and territories.[25] This Plan was vetoed mainly by France on the grounds that it was too pro-Commonwealth in its orientation. Most of the other colonial powers also opposed it because it implied a multilateralization of colonial privilege.

According to former Commission President and one of the early architects of European integration, Professor Walter Hallstein, "association was an inheritance left by history, which was taken on with reluctance rather than enthusiasm".[26] During the initial stages in the negotiations between the original Six (France, Belgium, the Netherlands, Luxembourg, Italy and West Germany), there was virtually no discussion about the status of colonial territories in relation to the nascent EEC. Neither the inter-governmental meeting at Messina, Italy, in June 1955, nor the subsequent committee under the Belgian statesman Paul-Henri Spaak, made any reference to the issue of overseas territories.

French colonial interests and association

It was not until a year later, at the 1956 Venice Conference, that France brought up the issue of association for the colonies and even declared it a non-negotiable condition for her signing the Treaty. The inclusion of *France d'outre-mer* in an association status was seen by France as a means of assisting its colonies to gain access to the large market of the EEC. The government of the socialist Mollet also nurtured the sentiments that a prosperous Europe had a duty to assist in the development of the Third World. The reasons why France left this vital issue until almost the very end of the negotiations will continue to be a matter of speculation. The most plausible explanation is that France wished to avoid any embarrassing debates on the status of its colonies in general, whilst putting the other negotiators in a position where they had no choice than to accept the French proposition.

Behind these noble sentiments, however, there was an underlying calculation of national self-interest.[27] France wanted the other EEC members to share the financial burdens of its *Sûrprix* system of subsidizing raw materials export earnings from its colonies and the assistance provided by the *Fonds d'Investissement pour le Développement Économique et Social* (*FIDES*). Indeed, France went to the extent of making an association provision for overseas territories a precondition for its own membership of the EEC.

In order to grasp fully the import of France's position on this question, it would be necessary to consider, albeit briefly, the economic and financial structure underlying France's colonial policy in Africa. In the 1930s the Franc Zone was established as a trade and monetary system to protect France's economic and colonial interests and to counteract the international commercial and financial instability of the interwar years.[28] After the Second World War, this structure became institutionalized with the establishment of the dual franc. There was the metropolitan franc, which was used in France, and the colonial franc, which was the legal tender in the colonies. Both were mutually convertible and had a mutually fixed parity. The Caisse Centrale, which was founded in April 1946, was launched as a development bank to promote investment in the colonies and to finance development projects.[29]

Table 3.1 Volume of French investments in the African colonies, 1900–40 (000s 1940 francs)

Sector	*Companies*	*Private individuals*	*Total*	*% by sector*
Business	8,761,962	1,752,392	10,514,354	39.0
Construction	814,953	81,495	896,448	3.5
Banking	1,556,732	—	1,556,732	6.0
Industries	2,176,801	435,460	2,612,261	9.6
Mines	1,860,304	186,030	2,046,334	7.5
Transport	879,150	87,915	967,065	3.6
Plantations	2,451,848	2,451,848	4,903,696	18.0
Livestock	71,450	14,290	85,740	0.3
Forestry	1,933,236	1,449,927	3,383,163	12.5
Total private investments	20,506,436	6,459,357	26,965,793	12.5
Public investments (loans)	7,033,014	—	7,033,014	
GLOBAL TOTAL	27,539,450	6,459,357	33,998,807	

Source: Jean Surêt-Canale, *Afrique noire occidentale et centrale,* Paris: Presses Universitaires 1964[30]

To aid the economic recovery process in the 1950s France took a number of measures to centralize its economic control of the colonies. This included centralization of monetary and fiscal policy, greater emphasis on extractive industries and supporting infrastructural development. The FIDES had been set up in 1946 with the aim of increasing French investment in extractive raw materials which were vital to the postwar economic reconstruction. Between 1946 and 1955 France invested an estimated US$ 1 billion in its colonies.[31] A monopoly was established on transportation between the metropole and the colonies, with exclusive rights guaranteed to French commercial firms.

Crucial to this overall strategy was the system of reciprocal subsidies between France and its colonial dependencies. It was estimated that in 1957 the prices of raw material imports from the colonies were between 15 and 65 per cent above world market prices in France, while French exports to the colonies carried prices of between 8 and 85 per cent above world prices.[32] This served to cement the economic and political relationship between France and its colonies, securing France's influence and interests, while guaranteeing market outlets for her uncompetitive manufactures. Sectors such as textiles which were labour-intensive and had not benefited from rationalization were exporting up to 90 per cent of their products to the colonies. About a third of all of France's exports went to her colonies, with about 300,000 of the 5 million workforce engaged in production for colonial markets. Table 3.1 shows the estimated volume of investments by sector in the French African colonies between 1900 and 1940. During this period French investments amounted to about 34 billion francs, of which the dominant shares were in the distributive or business sector (39%), plantations (18%) and forestry (12.5%). After the Second World War official France favoured increased investments in the colonies as a means of supporting the economic recovery process. Investments were increased in sectors such as textiles so as to overcome the hard-currency constraint for imports which would have required massive availability of dollars. Between 1940 and 1958 an estimated 10.5 billion (1914) francs of public investments were made in tropical Africa as against 2 billion by private French investors.[33] Such economic measures led to increased volume of trade between France and its African territories. Between 1949 and 1955 imports from the colonies increased by an estimated 115 per cent while France's exports to the African dependencies increased by 100 per cent.[34] The total value of exports from French West Africa and Equatorial Africa amounted to more than 75 billion CFA (Table 3.2) by 1957.

Given these intensified commercial links with the colonies, the debate on France's policy in the Community was bound to evoke strong reactions. There was a division between industrial groups who favoured continuation of colonial economic arrangements and those who wanted a change. The most modernized sectors, the so-called "competitive productive capital", favoured the latter scenario, which provided the prospect of an enlarged European market, while the less efficient sectors tended to favour the colonial preference regime, which guaranteed them the security of protected traditional markets.[35] Powerful interests in the textile industry, led by industrialists such as Marcel Boussac, founder of the Comptoir de l'Industrie Cotonnière, were opposed to decolonization.[36] Other interests which favoured intensification of colonial links included those in sectors such as sugar, groundnut refining, clothing manufacturing, engineering and chemical goods. France's position in the final stages of the Rome Treaty negotiations could thus be seen as a compromise between these two conflicting interests.

But it was not just a case of conflict between two rival fractions of the industrial bourgeoisie. French policy was also dictated by the political logic of decolonization. The French state had to contend with violent revolu-

Table 3.2 Total exports of French West Africa and Equatorial Africa in 1959 (French and EEC tariffs)

Product	*Value (CFA mn)*	*French tariff* %	*EEC tariff* %
Unroasted coffee	16,139	20.0	9.6
Shelled peanuts	14,918	10.0	—
Cocoa beans	6,579	25.0	5.4
Cattle	271	—	—
Crude oil	480	—	—
Unprocessed wood	7,064	10.0	—
Processed wood	1,475	15.0	10.0
Cotton	4,398	—	—
Diamonds	424	—	—
Fresh bananas	1,839	20.0	20.0
Palm nuts	1,839	10.0	—
Crude peanut oil	7,315	18.0	10.0
Refined peanut oil	1,196	18.0	15.0
Oil cake	1,759	10.0	—
Other	9,479	4.4	2.7
TOTAL	75,175		
Weighted average (all items)		8.1	4.8
Weighted average (preference items)		8.7	5.1

Source: Marjorie Lister, *The European Community and the Third World*, Aldershot: Avebury, 1988, p. 23

tionary upheavals in Indochina and Algeria during this period. These colonial wars imposed severe budgetary constraints on the state, leading to high inflation, economic difficulties and political crises towards the end of the 1950s. Association status for its colonies therefore offered a politically prudent way by which to get other EEC members to share the burdens of Empire. There was the inescapable question of the political future of the colonies. The earlier French Union had been superseded by the *Loi Cadre*, which was passed by the French parliament in June 1956. It consisted essentially of broad principles for political and administrative reforms aimed at increasing local autonomy and decentralization in the colonies. Whilst the basic anti-federalist constitutional principle of a "One and Indivisible Republic" was to remain unchanged, reforms were effected in the following areas: extension of universal suffrage and of the single electoral college system to enable colonial peoples to express their views; administrative decentralization; and Africanization of the *cadres administratifs* at all levels of the administrative machinery to absorb the growing number of educated elites.[37]

While these reforms were expected to stem the tide of demands for political independence, the emergent African elites saw things in a different light. For them the *Loi Cadre* represented the hope of eventual political emancipation.[38] Paradoxically, the reforms tended to create even more grievances against French colonialism. Influential figures such as Leopold Senghor opposed the reforms from the pan-Africanist viewpoint, because they encouraged the dissolution of the Federations of French West Africa and of Equatorial Africa.

With the exception of Belgium, most of the European states were opposed to the idea of association.[39] Italy and Germany, both of whom had lost their colonies after two world wars, were quite unwilling to subsidize what they considered to be France's colonial liabilities. The Netherlands was also opposed to association because she had just emerged from her colonial entanglements in Indonesia and was politically ill-disposed to new colonial engagements. Indeed, the Dutch government did not support association status for her two remaining dependencies in the Netherlands Antilles and Surinam.[40] According to one of the architects of the Rome Treaty, Spaak of Belgium:

> the political and psychological aspects were even more vital. The Italians and the Germans, who after two world wars had been stripped of their colonies, some of which now belonged to their new partners, were to be asked to contribute to development schemes drawn up by the new owners of these territories. This was not an easy concession for the Germans and the Italians to make.[41]

A compromise was finally reached whereby Germany agreed to contribute to the proposed European Development Fund (EDF), in exchange for which there would be a special trading regime for the imports of Latin American bananas into Germany as well as non-discriminatory right of establishment for companies originating from all the other members of the EEC. A compromise was also struck on the duration of the EDF, which was now to last for five years instead of being of unlimited duration as had been originally planned.

Internationally, both the Soviet Union and China raised political objections on the grounds that association between Europe and the Africa would ensure perpetuation of colonialism, which was in direct opposition to their own international objectives as "natural" partners of colonized peoples struggling to throw off the colonial yoke. According to Walter Hallstein, Soviet attitudes towards the Community were rather ambiguous.[42] On the one hand, the Soviets were against European integration because they saw in it the emergence of an independent power-base against *Pax Sovietica* in Europe; on the other hand, they were said to have encouraged Euro-Communist parties and movements to take an active interest in European affairs so as to influence its future course. At the early stage the Soviet Union seemed to have underestimated the political significance of the Community because of what they regarded as the inherent impossibility of any sustained international capitalist cooperation. Indeed, they sometimes saw the emergence of the Community as heightening the potential of the "inter-imperialist struggle" between Western Europe and the United States and Japan.[43]

Opposition also came from the United States and some Latin American countries, this time with economic rather than political arguments. The Latin Americans took exception to the discriminatory aspects of the trade arrangements under association with their potentially negative effects on their exports, particularly coffee, cocoa, bananas and vegetable fats. United States opposition was based on the argument that a preference zone of this kind was a dangerous protectionist precedent which in the long term might undermine the spirit of GATT.[44] The Community response to this attribution was that association was a matter of practical necessity, as they could not simply abandon old colonial economic arrangements without creating economic and political chaos in the African countries. They also held that association was a way of initiating the African Associates into the world economic system based on the principles of GATT. They pointed out that even the GATT Council and its Director-General, Olivier Long, had given a dynamic interpretation to EC–African association as a most favoured nation arrangement "with a provisional superstructure of non-discriminatory preferences granted by the developed to the developing countries, and by the latter to each other".[45]

The objectives of association

Three main objectives were specified under the association clause of the Rome Treaty. The first was to expand trade between the Community and the Eighteen, based on the principle of reciprocity. A transitional period of 12–15 years was set when the AASM were expected to abolish tariff barriers on Community exports while the latter would undertake to increase the imports quota and reduce its Common External Tariff (CET) for tropical products originating from the AASM. The second objective relates to the creation of an investment regime based on reciprocal "right of establishment" for the Community as well as the Eighteen. The third aim pertains to the provisions of financial aid, for which two institutions were to be established, namely, the European Development Fund (EDF) and the European Investment Bank (EIB).

The main source of EDF finance was to be through direct contributions from the Six. The first five years had an EDF allocation of US$581.25 million, of which the major contributors were France and West Germany (Table 3.3); the subsequent five years had another US$730 million, while the third five-year period had an allocation of US$918 million. A sum of 65 mua (million units of account) was set aside to finance emergencies such as famine, natural disasters or drastic falls in world prices of commodities.[46] Most of the funding was by way of grants, with only a minimum of loans

Table 3.3 Contributions and allocations of EDF funds, 1958, from member states to dependencies

Member state	*mua**	*%*	*mua*	*%*
Belgium	70.00	12.04	30.00	5.16
Germany	200.00	34.40	—	—
France	200.00	34.40	511.25	87.80
Italy	40.00	6.90	5.00	1.02
Luxembourg	1.2	0.22	—	—
Netherlands	70.00	12.04	35.00	6.02
TOTAL	581.25	100.00	581.00	100.00

Note: * mua refers to million units of account; 1 ua = 1 US$ (1973)
Source: P. N. C. Okigbo, *Africa and the Common Market,* London: Longman, 1967, p. 38

given by the EIB. The key sectors for funding were infrastructure (especially road construction), modernization of agriculture and, to a lesser extent, manpower training and health services. Financing was also directed at investments and diversification of production. By January 1963, some 438.9 mua had been committed to 316 projects in the dependent territories, and by August 1965, a total amount of 581.25 mua had been fully committed. In terms of sectoral distribution, infrastructures took the overwhelming share of EDF financing commitments, having an allocation of slightly over a half of the total (54.4 per cent).[47] Transport and communications alone took 44.5 per cent of all disbursements. The next sector is social services (education and health) with a total of 26 per cent. Industrial production was accorded the least allocation, with only 0.7 per cent of the total. The very low priority given to the productive and particularly the industrial sector reflected the pattern of economic development which had been prevalent during much of the colonial epoch in general.[48]

THE YAOUNDÉ CONVENTIONS

The Implementation Convention under the Rome Treaty was to last from 1958 to 1962. It had been an agreement imposed "from above", as the colonial territories had no say on how they were to be associated with the EEC. By 1960, however, "the wind of change", about which Prime Minister Harold Macmillan had warned the world, was blowing all over Africa. All the French colonies and Somalia became independent nations. Clearly, some modification of the association arrangement was necessary to reflect the changing international order. Whereas the initial phase of association was undisguised paternalism, the Yaoundé negotiations were novel in being a series of elaborate negotiations between formally equal sovereign states.

The EEC opened the negotiations by putting forward a Commission

Table 3.4 Common external tariff rates applied to non-associated third countries by the EEC

Products	*Rome Treaty*	*Yaoundé I*	*Yaoundé II*
Coffee	16	9.6	7
Cocoa	9	5.4	4
Bananas	20	20.0	20
Palm oil	9	9.0	6
Fresh pineapples	12	9.0	0
Vanilla	15	11.9	—
Tea	18	10.8	—

Source: Agence Européenne d'Informations, Brussels, 1978

report to the Council of Ministers in July 1971. The report suggested the elimination of tariff, quota and consumption taxes for tropical exports of the African associates and the acceleration of the process leading to the establishment of a CET. By the time of Yaoundé II, most of the tariff advantages which the Eighteen had enjoyed were being eroded (Table 3.4). In return for a lowering of the CET on competing products from other LDCs, the EEC offered to compensate the African associates by way of direct aid to production. The Six also offered to enlarge the financial resources of the EDF while demanding the continuation of the right of establishment on a reciprocal basis. The EEC expressed their wish for the

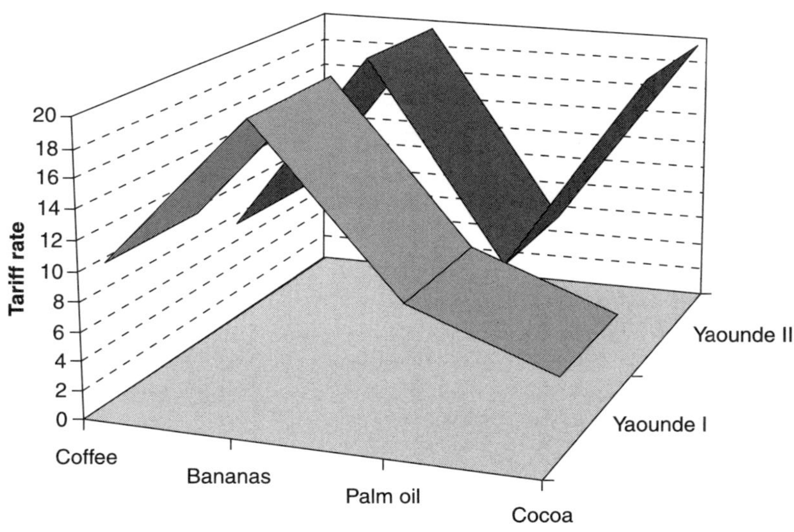

Figure 3.1 EEC tariffs on selected products

establishment of an investment guarantee scheme to secure their investments in Africa. Their other proposals were for the setting up of institutions such as a council, a committee, a secretariat and a joint assembly. The CET reductions for non-associated LDCs were occurring against a backdrop of decline in AASM commodity exports.

For example, AASM coffee exports had declined from 160 million tonnes in 1958 to an estimated 141 million tonnes in 1967, while Latin American exports of the same commodity had improved by more than 30 per cent over the same period.[49]

The African states on the other hand wanted a stabilization fund for their exports and price, marketing and anti-dumping provisions for fats and oils. The Yaoundé Group were anxious to maintain their preferential access to the EEC market against competing LDC exports. They demanded also joint management of the key institutions of cooperation and a voice in major EEC decisions which are likely to affect them as a group. At the insistence of the Dutch, the EEC committed itself to extending associate status to the other African states if they so desired. After nearly two years of negotiations, the first Yaoundé Convention was signed in Yaoundé, Cameroon, in June 1963.

Youndé I and post-colonial development policy

The agreement conceded tariff preferences to the Yaoundé Group without, however, the system of export subsidies and the stabilization scheme which they were demanding. The EDF resources were increased, but not to the amount that was asked for. Four main areas were covered by the new Convention:

1 The trade provisions of the Rome Treaty were expanded. The French *Sûrprix* system of subsidies was phased out while import liberalization was to be mutually reciprocal;
2 continuation of the reciprocal right of establishment, with provision for more liberalized movement of capital, services and payments with respect to investment in the African states;
3 EDF finances were increased to the tune of 730 mua for the five-year period from 1964 to 1969;
4 new institutions were to be established to implement the new Convention. These were: a Council of Association, a Parliamentary Council of Association and a Court of Arbitration.

From every indication the first Yaoundé agreement fell short of the expectations of the African associates. According to Joanna Moss:

> While the trade flows had increased between the two regions, the exports of some non-associated developing nations increased in per-

centage terms more rapidly than those of the Yaoundé Group. Nevertheless, the trade preferences offered under the EEC arrangement were, it was felt, better than no preferences at all.[50]

In evaluating the impact of association during the ten-year period from 1958 until the end for the first Yaoundé Convention, Johann Galtung, concluded that its benefits were at best very modest:

1 The associated countries remained cash crop exporters.
2 Average imports from non-associated countries had grown at 8% p.a. while those from associates grew at 5% p.a. The value of exports grew from US$86 to US$89 per capita.
3 EEC exports to the associates grew much faster than imports during the period.[51]

At the commencement of the Yaoundé II negotiations, President Hamani Diori, Niger's Head of State and President of the African and Madagascar Common Organization (OCAM), toured the capitals of the Six on behalf of the AASM, armed with a report which detailed the main criticisms of the Eighteen with regard to the impact of the Yaoundé aid regime. The report noted that while exports from Latin America to the Community had increased by 6 per cent between 1964 and 1966, exports from the AASM to the EEC had increased by less than 1 per cent during the same period. Presumably, this was an indication that even without the benefit of a Yaoundé-type agreement, Latin American trade with the Community was at a more advantageous position than that of the AASM. On the other hand, between 1966 and 1967, Community exports to the Eighteen had risen in value from US$847 million to US$926 million, an improvement of 10 per cent.[52] The report was critical of the system of "reciprocal" preferences which enabled the Six to export their products to the AASM at price levels higher than those of the world market, whilst the terms of trade between raw materials and manufactures continued to deteriorate to the detriment of the former.[53]

Criticism of the EDF centred on approaches, procedures and content. The Eighteen pointed out the following defects in the aid system:

1 Only 4 per cent of EDF investments had been devoted to the industrial sector.
2 Aid for agricultural development and diversification had not been effectively channelled into import-substitution.
3 The ratio of "genuine aid" to loans had become quite high, together with higher interest rates.
4 Aid for training and manpower development had fallen from 22.5 per cent of the EDF Social Fund (before 1964) to 14.5 per cent.
5 European aid did not take account of recurrent costs for upkeep of hospitals and other social services.

6 The time lag between EDF approval of projects and implementation often caused increased costs of between 10 and 20 per cent.[54]

Continuity and change under Yaoundé II

Yaoundé I expired at the end of 1969 while Yaoundé II was signed on 29 July 1969, to be effective from January 1970. In the course of the second round of multilateral negotiations, the Yaoundé Group put the emphasis of their demands on a price guarantee scheme for their exports and for the increase of the EDF to the tune of US$1,500 million. Yaoundé II negotiations proved to have been rather acrimonious and difficult. The Eighteen wanted the Community to grant them comprehensive most-favoured nation treatment, essentially implying the same level of tariff preferences offered to Greece and Turkey. However, this was rejected by the Six.

There was a division within the Community itself, between the "regionalists" and the "universalists". The latter were represented by the Dutch and the Germans, who were yet again expressing their opposition to the Yaoundé trade regime and their unwillingness to commit more funding to the EDF. They felt that an exclusive association was too constricting and narrow in scope and they would have much preferred a more inclusive and universal arrangement within the framework of UNCTAD. The "regionalists", France and Belgium, on the other hand, wanted a continuation of the trade preferences, while the Italians took a neutral position.[55] Disagreement centred also on the future shape of Euro-African association. France and the Commission seemed to favour a permanent and quasi-political arrangement, whereas the Germans and the Dutch perceived association as essentially temporary and primarily as a vehicle of economic and commercial cooperation.

Yaoundé II was essentially a continuation of the previous agreement. The principles of the first convention were preserved with only minor modifications. The clauses regarding the right of ownership and the institutions and procedures were left intact. In the trade sector, however, some changes were noteworthy. The free trade zone was maintained while the common external tariff for three African exports (coffee, cocoa and palm oil) was slightly lowered. Rice and cassava were two products on which the community could not offer more favourable treatment. France, herself a rice grower, was reluctant to grant further preferences whilst Germany, with surplus animal feeds, did not wish to encourage further importation of manioc. A special protocol also made provision for African states to participate in a possible generalized system of preferences. Unlike the previous Convention, Yaoundé II did not provide for automatic price support for primary exports. In its place an Emergency Fund with a maximum funding of 80 mua was allocated to give price support in the event of "exceptional" falls in world prices or occurrence of natural disasters such as famine and floods.[56] The Eighteen were quite divided on this question. Countries such as Chad and Senegal, with heavy dependence on a single commodity (cotton for Chad and groundnuts for Senegal), wanted most of the funds to go for their export commodities. Many of the others, however, were opposed to the idea of an Emergency Fund which would take resources away from the EDF allocation.

Perhaps the most important political and diplomatic significance of the negotiations, according to the spokesman of the Eighteen, Konan Bedié of Côte d'Ivoire, was that they provided valuable experience for the newly emerging states in the intricate art of multilateral economic diplomacy, whereby the Eighteen negotiated with a powerful European trade bloc "as equals and on the basis of a true dialogue".[57]

Funding for the EDF was raised to 918 mua, a slight increase from the previous amount of 800 mua which was allocated under Yaoundé I. Of the 918 mua allocated under Yaoundé II, some 748 mua were in grants, while 80 mua was to be in special loans and 90 mua as European Investment Bank (EIB) loans.[58] In terms of aid programming, emphasis was put on regional economic integration efforts amongst African states, the development of public enterprises, and on industrial projects. A minor but significant concession was made to the AASM by way of a 15 per cent preference for African companies bidding for supply contracts for EDF-financed projects and a general preference for local firms in the awards of contracts of less than US$500,000.[59]

THE ANGLO-AFRICAN COMMONWEALTH AND ASSOCIATION

During the 1962 Commonwealth Prime Ministers' Conference, the United Kingdom, having applied for membership of the Community under the conservative government of Harold Macmillan, was eager to get the Commonwealth countries into considering association. All the African leaders, with the exception of Sir Milton Margai of Sierra Leone, rejected the offer of association. It certainly did not help matters that Britain had taken it upon herself to negotiate on their behalf without consulting them. What came close to a consultation was the tour in June 1961, by the British Labour Minister, Mr Hare, to West and Central Africa. His brief, so it appears, was limited to "explaining" the meaning of "association".[60]

Politically, the offer of association could not have come at a less auspicious moment. The bitterly fought Algerian war was still raging, while French atomic test explosions in the Sahara also served to alienate several African countries, leading countries such as Nigeria to break off diplomatic relations with Paris. Perhaps the most important factor was the fact that association, in the words of Professor Dennis Austin, "still bore the stamp of inferiority which it acquired at birth. . . . Not only had it been devised for dependent territories; it seemed . . . to perpetuate the colonial relationship in a new guise."[61]

Between scepticism and ambition

Within the rest of Africa, three different responses were discernible. The first was the attitude of outright rejection, championed by radical Pan-African nationalists such as Kwame Nkrumah of Ghana and Sékou Touré of Guinea. Nkrumah was against association because he saw it as condemning the whole of Africa to remaining producers of cheap agricultural exports and that Africa could not develop on that basis, and much less by keeping its population "solely as workers in rural areas".[62] He saw association as a form of collective neo-colonialism which would entail "continuation of the same old imperialist relationship of the European rider on the African horse".[63] He was also quoted as saying:

> Nobody is against the European countries coming together but why do they want to draw us into their association? With my little knowledge of world economic problems, it is because they want to enslave us economically. They want to make us hewers of wood and drawers of water.[64]

President Ahmed Sékou Touré of Guinea argued essentially in the same vein to the effect that association would reduce Africa to being the proletarian continent of the world.[65] The radical nationalist position thus tended to view association as being diametrically opposed to the dream of Pan-African unity, a continuation of the age-old European project of dominance and exploitation of the African continent. Nkrumah, who had emerged as symbol and champion of Pan-African unity and liberation, had inspired the formation of the Ghana–Guinea–Mali Union, and therefore saw association with Europe as being in fundamental opposition to his own vision of *Pax Africana*.[66] A second attitude was that of relative indifference so long as Africa was not dragged into European affairs. The ECA was concerned not so much about the inherent effects of association as about its impact on African integration:

> If the associated territories were to diversify their economies, by increasing the protection of their local industry against the competition of the EEC, it is doubtful if the EEC countries will continue to offer the same advantages to the export of primary products by the associated countries. . . . Association with the EEC can easily . . . turn out to be a long-term disadvantage to the country concerned.[67]

The third and perhaps the most dominant attitude was the one which conceded that while association might be beneficial, it was necessary to bargain for more reasonable terms from the Community. This seemed to have been the perception shared by the Nigerian government and its chief negotiators when they negotiated a trade agreement with the Community.[68]

In 1962 the Commonwealth African Group turned down an offer of association from the Six. While the Yaoundé Group were themselves anxious to exclude other African and Third World states from their privileged association, at the insistence of the Netherlands the EEC had to make a Statement of Intention in April 1963, by which other African states were given options of negotiating association status with the Community should they so desire. In spite of their initial misgivings, however, Nigeria and the East African Commonwealth states of Tanzania, Uganda and Kenya were later to request negotiations for association with the EEC. They were driven largely by the need to secure a guaranteed market for their export products within the EEC.

The Nigeria–EEC agreement was signed in Lagos in July 1965. The agreement established a modified trade area between Nigeria and the Common Market.[69] This granted Nigerian products free entry into the EEC at EEC internal tariff rates, with the exception of groundnut oil, palm oil, cocoa beans and plywood, which had specific quotas. In return, Nigeria granted marginal tariff preferences of between 2 per cent and 10 per cent to twenty-six EEC products, amounting to £8.7 million, which was about 4 per cent of the total value of Nigeria's imports.[70] The Lagos Agreement, however, was never ratified due to the outbreak of the Nigerian civil war in July 1967. France in any case had refused to ratify the agreement. This was most probably due to her own diplomatic problems with Nigeria which followed from her recognition of secessionist Biafra. In September 1968, during a debate in the European Parliament, a Belgian deputy had advocated suspension of the Lagos Agreement in protest against Nigeria's conduct in the Biafran war. The Development Commissioner, Henri Rochereau, had promised to refer the matter to the EEC Council, in view of the "highly political" nature of the question.[71] Nigeria responded with a strongly worded renunciation of the idea of association between Europe and Africa. Lagos declared that failure to ratify the trade agreement meant that there had been in actual fact no legally binding treaty between her and the Community. They added that in any case Nigeria could not derive any benefit from such "neo-colonialist" arrangements, as the civil war had already demonstrated the resilience and independence of the Nigerian economy.[72]

On balance, the prospective of the trade agreement could only have been of marginal importance to the Nigerian economy at this time. Especially for cocoa, the country's most significant export item to the Community, rising prices in the late 1960s meant that the EEC probably needed the agreement more than Nigeria did, at least in the short term.[73] But Nigeria's new-found confidence was also a product of her gradual emergence as a potentially rich, major oil-exporting nation. In 1965, oil had been only 26 per cent of her total exports; by 1968, it had risen to the position of 78 per cent. Projections under the Second National Development Plan had estimated even more spectacular earnings from petroleum exports.[74]

The East African Commonwealth states, following the Nigerian example, reached their own agreement with the Six at Arusha, Tanzania, on 24 September 1969. The Arusha Convention was to run concurrently with Yaoundé II from 1970 to 1975. It provided for tariff preferences within the Common Market to be extended to most exports from the three East African states. The EEC, however, imposed quota restrictions on coffee, cloves and tinned pineapples, which were in competition with the exports of the Yaoundé Group. The Arusha Group, for their part, removed all customs duties and quantitative restrictions on some imports from the EEC, covering sixty products, ranging from 2 to 9 per cent.[75]

The Nigeria and Arusha Agreements were politically significant to the extent that they reflected the ability of some of the newly independent members of Commonwealth Africa to launch their own diplomatic initiatives without British support or involvement.[76] This was partly made possible by the fact that their economic and commercial ties were much more diversified than those of French-speaking Africa in relation to France.[77]

The performance of the association regime

In her interesting statistical evaluation of the impact of these trade agreements, Joanna Moss has shown that although African exports to the world and the EEC expanded in dollar value, the relative importance of the EEC as a purchaser of African exports had continually declined. While African exports expanded at an average annual rate of 13 per cent between 1964 and 1975, its percentage share of exports to the Common Market dropped by 10 per cent.[78] Table 3.5 shows the annual rates of change for imports and exports between the Eighteen and the Six, while Table 3.6 illustrates the annual rate of AASM exports to the Community in comparison with other LDC regions. Although the annual increase for the SSA region was

Table 3.5 EEC–AASM trade, annual rates of change, 1958–71

	France	*Belgium and Luxembourg*	*Netherlands*	*W. Germany*	*Italy*	*EEC*
AASM exports to EEC	+3.1	+6.8	+10.7	+11.2	+12.6	+6.2
EEC Exports to AASM	+5.1	+4.6	+11.2	+11.9	+14.7	+6.5

Source: Agence Européenne d'Informations, Brussels, 1978

Table 3.6 AASM exports to the EEC, annual rates of change, 1958–71

	AASM	*Total LDCs*	*Latin America*	*Far East*	*Middle East*	*North Africa*	*SSA*
All products	+6.2	+7.7	+6.4	+6.1	+8.2	+11.1	+8
Excluding petroleum	+6.2	+5.5	+6.9	+6.5	+9.6	−2.9	+5

Source: Agence Européenne d'Informations, Brussels, 1978

marginally above the LDC average, it was well below that of non-associated countries of North Africa and the Middle East.

As far as trade is concerned, therefore, it is clear that association did not improve the export performance of the African states. Under the first Yaoundé Convention the fourteen former French African dependencies had to abandon the system of guaranteed prices and outlets for their products. They had to align themselves to lower world price levels in exchange for the markets of the Community of Six. Whatever preferences they still enjoyed were immediately eroded, first, by the Community"s external tariff reductions in 1964, just before the conclusion of Yaoundé I, and again in 1971, during the conclusion of the second Yaoundé agreement.

Germany continued to insist on its special protocol which allowed it to import bananas from Latin America, while the pledge by the Community to "take account of the interests of their African associates when formulating their . . . Common Agricultural Policy (especially in the case of sugar and vegetable oils) was virtually ignored in practice".[79] In July 1971 the Community had also introduced a system of generalized tariff preferences which the associates justifiably saw as a further reduction of their trading privileges. Even though their exports of manufactures and semi-manufactures were comparatively modest, they saw generalized preferences as a further limiting factor in their future prospects for industrialization. With regard to financial assistance, the first three EDFs (580 mua under the Implementation Convention; 730 mua and 900 mua for Yaoundé I and II respectively), amounted to a total of 2.21 billion units of account (about US$1.93 billion)[80] between 1958 and 1975. With an average disbursement of more than UK$150 million per annum to the AASM, the EDF was clearly an important source of development finance capital for these newly emerging nations (Table 3.8). Table 3.9 shows the volume of financial aid under the first three EDFs. EDF financing procedures required that project proposals had to emanate from recipient countries themselves, with financing approval resting with the EDF Committee. The Community could also initiate projects proposals, which had to receive approval of recipient governments.

Table 3.7 EEC exports to the AASM and other LDCs (FOB basis) – annual rates of change, 1958–71

AASM	*Total LDCs*	*Latin America*	*Far East*	*Middle East*	*North Africa*	*SSA and other LDCs*
+6.5	+5.7	+5.4	+6.1	+9.4	+0.9	+78

Source: Agence Européenne d'Informations, Brussels, 1978

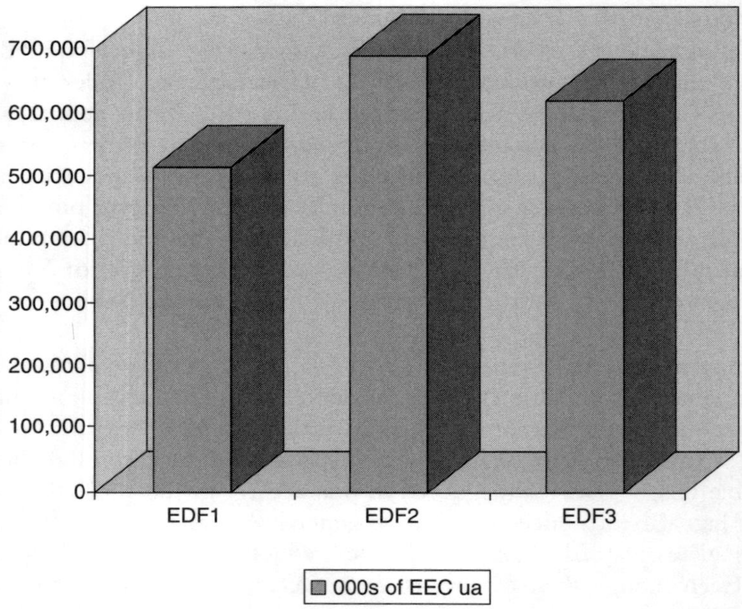

Figure 3.2 Volume of the first three EDFs (in mua)
Source: European Development Fund, 1973

There were no clear-cut principles of financial allocations for each country, although the EDF did indicate that considerations would be given to population, level of economic development, absorptive capacity, and availability of other sources of external finance.[81] Projects had to be seen not to be competing with private enterprise and nor could EDF funds be used as public subsidy. Once approval was formalized, tenders would then be invited, followed by evaluation and signing of implementation contracts. A fundamental principle of EDF development contracts was that all funds had to be spent within the Community.

Table 3.8 Bilateral and multilateral aid to the AASM, 1962–73 (US$ million)

	1962	*1968*	*1969*	*1970*	*1971*	*1972*	*1973*
1 Bilateral aid	485.5	412.1	461.2	455.3	524.5	587.1	737.6
of which:							
– W. Germany	6.5	17.6	32.9	34.0	40.7	28.9	74.7
– Belgium	53.4	60.6	65.8	72.8	81.3	102.5	122.3
– France	288.1	269.0	288.8	269.7	294.6	351.8	269.5
– Italy	10.8	11.0	12.6	8.6	16.8	9.6	128.7
– Netherlands	—	—	—	2.9	4.7	4.6	7.0
– EEC TOTAL	358.8	358.2	400.1	388.0	438.1	497.4	602.1
USA	94.0	43.0	44.0	37.0	48.0	39.0	74.0
2 Multilateral aid	96.4	135.6	175.7	200.6	235.8	226.9	341.7
of which:							
– EEC	50.7	101.3	112.5	137.1	155.7	148.0	208.5
– UNO	15.3	25.3	41.9	38.0	56.1	56.1	68.3
– Others	30.4	9.0	21.3	25.5	24.0	28.7	65.5
3 Total aid (1+2)	581.9	547.7	636.9	655.9	760.3	814.0	1,079.3
of which:							
– EEC	409.5	459.5	512.6	525.1	593.8	645.4	810.7

Source: Agence Européenne d'Informations, 1978

Table 3.9 Breakdown of EDF Aid by Country, December 1973 (in 000s of EEC ua)

Country	*EDF1*	*EDF2*	*EDF3*
Burundi	5,058	18,921	26,966
Cameroon	52,515	51,597	50,574
Central African Republic	17,806	51,597	50,574
Chad	28,422	32,759	26,739
Congo	24,498	19,308	19,287
Côte d'Ivoire	39,769	55,901	39,242
Dahomey	20,674	21,874	22,095
Gabon	17,501	20,230	18,042
Madagascar	57,097	69,235	50,390
Mali	42,340	32,479	41,021
Mauritania	42,867	59,692	46,162
Niger	15,432	18,000	15,157
Rwanda	31,115	30,578	40,477
Senegal	42,867	59,692	46,162
Somalia	9,733	25,344	22,588
Togo	15,815	18,793	24,526
Upper Volta	29,521	29,118	30,327
Mauritius	—	—	1,569
Zaire	18,021	72,055	44,849
TOTAL	511,051	687,173	616,747

Source: European Development Fund, *Annual Report*, 1973

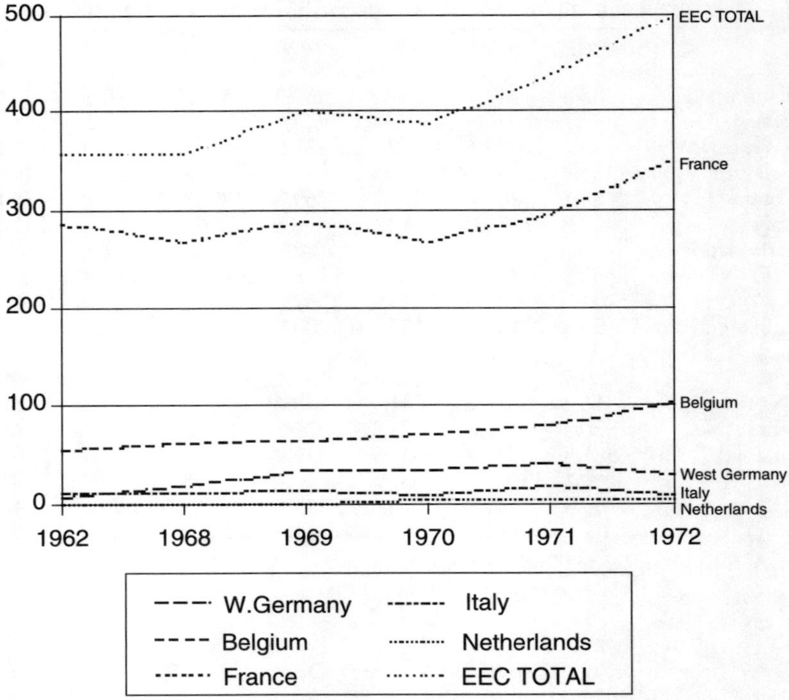

Figure 3.3 Volume of first three EDFs by country (in US$ million)
Source: European Development Fund, 1973

EDF procedures under the Yaoundé regime followed the so-called "World Bank rule", whereby project proposals were submitted randomly from the AASM, with financing decisions based on the determination of technical viability. This means that there were no objective criteria for the equitable distribution of the funds between countries, leaving thereby a wide opportunity for subtle political manipulation in ways that would have been difficult to detect. Such procedures underlined the deeply asymmetrical relations between the Community and the associated countries. Financing decisions appeared to have been little short of capricious. As Ravenhill explains:

> Community procedures for distributing aid between recipients are quite extraordinary: for none of the EDFs has the Commission made public on an *ex ante* basis its country allocations. Nor has it been willing to provide a detailed explanation of the criteria used in the decision-making process.[82]

But there were a number of shortcomings, both regarding EDF financing procedures as well as implementation of projects. The AASM had complained about the delays with respect to financing decisions and disbursements which compounded the problems of project implementation.

What was the guiding philosophy of EDF financing during this period? After the conclusion of the Yaoundé II negotiations, the Commission submitted a report to the EEC Council of Ministers, in which it outlined the principles of Community aid policy. The report stressed that effort should be concentrated on granting aid for "limited projects" while larger enterprises should follow joint co-financing actions with the World Bank. In fact, the paper emphasized the need to adopt the Bank's philosophy with regard to the strategy of investment combined with technical assistance.[83] It is therefore evident that the "triangle of development diplomacy" was operative even at this early stage, as Community development policy aspired to closer links with the World Bank.

Another major criticism of the EEC's development philosophy relates to its apparent bias against the industrial sector. This reflected an explicit policy on the part of the Commission, which insisted that "as a general rule it is not in the nature of the EDF to act as an industrialist".[84] The Commission's argument was that only the private sector was well placed to operate in the industrial sector. Whatever financing that was undertaken in this sector was channelled through the EIB, and was limited to no more than 25 per cent of the total capital cost of a project.[85]

There is also some evidence to suggest that the EDF financing system was both inefficient and open to political manipulation. What came to be known as "the Mannesmann Affair" was perhaps the most well known of such cases of financial misjudgement. In 1964 representatives of a German steel company, Mannesmann Limited, had approached the Government of Senegal with a proposal to undertake a water piping project estimated at the cost of US$24 million (6 billion CFA). The company was said to have been facing a massive pile-up of steel piping after a previous Russian steel contract fell through.[86] The project idea was to convey water through steel pipes from a lake on the Senegal river to the capital, Dakar. The Senegalese government was persuaded to pay an advance of 5 per cent of the total costs on the understanding that it would be provided with a loan and EDF financing to cover 60 per cent of the entire cost. Under normal EDF procedures, projects which had already been partly financed were not eligible for funding, but a special case was made for the Mannesmann project.

The Commission proceeded to appraise the project and came out with the expert conclusion that it was not viable. The irregular water levels of the lake were said to have high risk of salinity, and it was pointed out that cheaper and closer artesian sources of water were available and could be more easily tapped. The Commission then recommended an alternative scheme using available artesian resources. The Mannesmann scheme was shelved but was resubmitted in 1965. Both the Senegalese and West

German governments, however, were insistent that the project should proceed irrespective of the opinions of the technical experts. During an official visit to Paris the Senegalese President had reportedly received a pledge from de Gaulle that France would not oppose the German proposal whenever it came up before the EDF Committee. Pressure was eventually put on the Commission to accept the project.[87] Given that France and Germany controlled between them the majority of votes on the funding Committee, it was clear that the other four did not stand much of a chance in opposing the scheme. Even on such a relatively modest issue, the so-called "Franco-German axis" in the Community was crucial in pushing through an important financing decision. This decision, however, turned out to be a costly mistake, as the project proved to be technically unviable and had to be abandoned eventually. Underlying this disastrous experience was an attempt not only to dump steel products in a poor African country but an unabashed effort by the West German government to increase its share of what was popularly known as the "boomerang effect" of EDF funding, whereby financial aid gets recycled back to the donors through lucrative contracts.

CONCLUSION

This chapter has examined the origins of EC–African diplomacy and the evolving pattern of development cooperation between 1957 and 1971. We argued that EC–African relations have metamorphosed from the era of classical imperial control, to the post-colonial phase of "association". As we have seen, association was initially conceded to placate French political interests; however, once taken up, it was enthusiastically pursued as the mainspring of European policy in Africa. France's external policy, and in particular her neo-imperial interests, were the major driving force behind the association idea. The Yaoundé Conventions, as we saw, offered a minimum of aid and trade concessions in exchange for continuation of European influence in the former colonies. EEC aid was oriented towards financing of infrastructures and was markedly biased against industrialization. It is therefore safe to conclude that association did not mark a major departure from the historical pattern of colonial development. Whilst it offered the AASM an invaluable experience in economic diplomacy, the balance of power was clearly tilted in favour of the Six. Their political influence over the allocation of funds and the procedures of EDF financing were clearly reflective of the asymmetrical relations between Europe and Africa which had been firmly established since the previous century.

4

THE EMERGENCE OF LOMÉ AND ITS INSTITUTIONS, 1973–78

In the previous chapter we examined the origins of EC–African diplomacy. We argued that the association regime was characterized by neo-imperial paternalism. In this chapter we shall consider the emergence of Lomé in the 1970s and its key institutional features. The core of our argument in this chapter is that Lomé marked a qualitative change in the dominant idiom of EC–African diplomacy, although in real terms, it has not effected any structural changes in the economic condition of African states.

Three factors were crucial in the emergence of the Lomé agreement in 1975. The first was the imminent ending of Yaoundé II by 1975. During the negotiations of the first Yaoundé Conventions the "universalists" within the Six had expressed reservations about the narrow scope of association membership. They had therefore hoped that Britain's accession would lead to a broadening of association. However, this hope was not fulfilled owing to President de Gaulle's veto of the British application in 1963. A compromise was reached in the 1963 "Declaration of Intent", by which the EEC had undertaken in principle to extend the Yaoundé association or other similar instrument to other developing countries having an "economic structure and production" comparable to the eighteen associates.[1]

The second factor is related to Britain's renewed application to join the Common Market.[2] The second Yaoundé Convention had not yet been ratified when the Six gave approval at the December 1969 summit meeting for resumption of negotiations on Britain's accession. Britain's second application had been submitted as early as May 1967. The French government, however, insisted that Britain's membership should not be considered before its economy had sufficiently recovered, especially following the November 1967 devaluation of sterling.[3] The election of Georges Pompidou as President and the formation of a new government under M. Chaban-Delmas in June 1969 led to a more favourable attitude from France regarding the enlargement of the Community to include Britain and the other three applicants: Norway, Denmark and Ireland.

It is instructive that the government White Paper which gave an "Economic Assessment" of the implications of Britain's membership in the Community accorded only scant attention to the Commonwealth Preference Area.[4] During the opening session of the negotiations in Luxembourg in June 1970, the Commission and Council set out what they regarded as the main principles for the enlargement of the Community. On the question of association, Pierre Harmel, the Belgian Foreign Minister, said that Britain's Commonwealth African states were in principle eligible to become associates if they so desired, providing this did not weaken the already existing regime with the AASM.[5] In his official presentation to Parliament in July 1971, the Prime Minister, Harold Wilson, explained the official position of the government regarding association for Commonwealth and Dependent Territories:

> We made it clear in the negotiations that we needed to ensure that trade relations between these countries and the enlarged Community should be safeguarded either by the establishment of association arrangements, comparable with those already accorded to developing countries . . . or, where this is not appropriate, by alternative solutions.[6]

The British Treaty of Accession to the EEC was signed on 22 January 1972. Britain of course had its own Commonwealth commercial and political interests which it could not jettison without damage to its long-term economic and geo-strategic interests.[7] There was the Commonwealth Sugar Agreement which was due to expire in 1974, and the financial and trading arrangements which were vital to British trade. It was therefore inevitable that Britain would seek association status for its Commonwealth partners just as France had done for its former colonial dependencies.

The third factor was the changed international economic environment of the 1970s. The postwar Bretton Woods regime of fixed exchange rates was unilaterally repudiated by President Nixon in the summer of 1971. African states were not represented in the negotiations leading to the establishment of the postwar regime, nor could they insulate themselves from the negative effects of its demise.[8] African states, like most other developing countries, were, according to Ravenhill:

> simultaneously the principal beneficiaries and principal victims of the new international economic disorder: beneficiaries in that the weakening of prevailing rules and norms of international economic relations enabled them to challenge the existing distribution of gains from international economic [relations]; . . . victims in that the selective exceptions to the liberal trade order imposed by industrialized countries occurred primarily at their expense.[9]

The breakdown of the Bretton Woods regime contributed to the "politicization" of trade and North–South relations in general. Linked to this was the sudden emergence of OPEC as an international cartel following the

Middle Eastern conflict in October 1973. The ensuing oil crisis fuelled the sense of Western insecurity regarding raw materials, compelling the advanced industrial economies to acquiesce to Southern demands for dialogue on a new world economic order.

The emergence of Lomé was partly an outcome of this "politicized" international economic environment, an environment in which the South found itself for the first time in an advantageous bargaining position. Indeed, the speeches on the signing of the Convention echoed the ideas of the NIEO and of the need for North and South to reach a deeper understanding of their common interests and mutual goals.

Opposition to the continuation of the Yaoundé-type association regime came from both outside and within the Community. The United States, supported by Japan and the Scandinavians, expressed strong views against the system of reverse preferences which they saw as discriminatory. The United States had gone to the extent of threatening that it would not extend the benefit of the OECD system of preferences to developing countries that discriminated against American goods.[10] These attitudes were reflective of the worsening US balance of payments crisis, which was later to lead to President Nixon's unilateral repudiation of the system of fixed exchange rates and in effect, the end of the Bretton Woods international economic architecture.[11]

Within Europe itself, opposition was still being expressed by Germany and the Netherlands. Again, France stood out as the strongest defender of Euro-African association, because she stood to benefit from it much more than any other Community member state. With the discussions of Britain's accession, France was insisting that Yaoundé should not be diluted by the entry of the Commonwealth countries, and that instead of a separate series of negotiations, Yaoundé III should be negotiated with the Eighteen and presented as a *fait accompli* to the Commonwealth countries on a "take-it-or-leave-it" basis.[12]

The initial attitudes of the Anglo-African Commonwealth to the prospects of a Yaoundé-type association could not be deemed enthusiastic. Countries such as Zambia and Sierra Leone showed little interest because their chief exports, copper and iron ore respectively, were in any case not subject to custom duties within the Community. Ghana expressed interest due to her position as a dominant cocoa exporter. In 1970 a ministerial committee in Accra was said to have been set up to prepare a study on Ghana's future relations with the Community.[13] Similarly, the East African states were known to have been positively disposed to association with Europe. They obviously sought more benefits in financial terms than was possible under the Arusha trade agreement which had yet to come into effect owing to lack of parliamentary ratification.

Nigeria's reticence stood out rather conspicuously in this context. The country's envoy in Paris, Ambassador Leslie Harriman, had stated that his country was interested in a strictly commercial agreement which did not include financial aid. Some officials were reported to have expressed the view that Lagos was suspicious of any comprehensive, institutionalized link with Europe which would jeopardize self-reliance and inter-African cooperation. Although the Lagos Treaty between Nigeria and the Community never became operational owing to the interruption of the Biafran war, Nigeria saw its long-term interest in Europe largely in terms of trade access for its exports. After her civil war, she had emerged as an important subregional power with her own geo-strategic ambitions in the continent generally and in the West African subregion in particular.[14] Association with Europe was therefore seen as a potentially limiting vertical alliance.

In April 1972, four months after the British Treaty of Accession, the Franco-African associates held a meeting in Nouakchott, Mauritania, where they agreed to join with the Commonwealth *associables* in the negotiations to enlarge the Euro-African Association.[15] At the African trade ministers' conference in Abidjan in May 1973, agreement was reached among the African group to engage in a "bloc-to-bloc" negotiation with the Community, a decision which was to be confirmed two weeks later at the OAU summit in Addis Ababa.

Many of the Commonwealth *associables* were hesitant about joining the negotiations because of the issue of trade reciprocity which the Community had come to regard as indispensable under the GATT. The English-speaking Africans argued that the UNCTAD principle of generalized preferences did indeed justify non-reciprocity. The Six themselves were divided on the issue, and this probably delayed the preparation of the Community's framework for the negotiations. It was not until April 1973 that the Commission came up with a draft Association Agreement. The basis of the Community's negotiating position was contained in the Déniau Memorandum which was released following the first enlargement of the Community. The Memorandum was based on a creative interpretation of Protocol 22 of the Rome Treaty on Association, and was seen as reconciling the principles of the Community's development policy with an awareness and sensitivity to the interests of the *associables.*[16] It contained elements of the Yaoundé formula as well as provisions on financial aid, access to European markets, non-reciprocity, and stabilization of export earnings for specified products.[17]

The Brussels Conference in July 1975 was the high point of the multilateral negotiations. The forty-six ACP countries presented their positions through three spokesmen chosen from the three regions. The ACP position was essentially based on the principle of non-reciprocity in respect of access to the European market, improved terms of trade and systems of payments for basic products, industrial cooperation and financial assistance. A subsequent conference was held in Brussels in October 1973, while the

OAU trade ministers held another summit meeting in Addis Ababa to consolidate their bargaining position.

FORGING A COMMON AFRICAN FRONT

There had been fears that African states would not be able to negotiate as a group, and that the older associates would view the new *associables* as rivals. Instead of negotiating separately, the OAU had pressed for a common front in bargaining with Europe. During its tenth Summit, it urged for "a platform or negotiations . . . which would embody a number of principles agreed by common accord by the African countries as a whole".[18]

The achievement of a common African position was all the more remarkable, having been attained only after considerable tensions and difficulties. There were disagreements between the French-speaking African states and the English-speaking *associables.* At the Lagos meeting of African trade ministers, the OAU Secretary-General was openly accused by the Senegalese Trade Minister, Babacar Ba, of exceeding his constitutional powers in trying to push through a common set of negotiating principles.[19] One of the issues was the question of reciprocity, which the French-speaking countries, led by President Leopold Sedar Senghor of Senegal, had insisted should not be part of the agenda.[20]

The OAU came out with eight negotiating principles:

1 non-reciprocity in the trade and tariff concessions which was being offered by Europe;
2 ensuring possibility of extension to third parties, on a non-discriminatory basis, the trade concessions which the EEC would grant the associates;
3 the need to revise the Community's "Rules of Origin";
4 the reform of the arrangements for movements of capital and finance to safeguard the interests of African "monetary independence" and intra-African monetary cooperation;
5 removal of any forms of linkage between aid and political relationships with the EEC;
6 stabilization of exports prices to ensure that the associates could improve their export earnings;
7 free and guaranteed access for all African exports into the Community, regardless of whether or not they were processed, semi-processed or fell within the CAP;
8 guarantees that association with Europe would not stand in the way of intra-African cooperation.[21]

Two issues lingered on until towards the very end of the negotiations. The first was the question of agricultural produce. The ACP were anxious to avoid repetition of the Community's 1972 refusal to grant concessions to the associates' early fruit and vegetables exports. They therefore began by demanding total and unrestricted access to the EEC market for their agricultural produce. Although the Community did agree to relax its agricultural protection by granting reductions in customs tariffs and agricultural levies, it nevertheless was insistent that Community agricultural policy was not a subject of negotiation.[22]

The ACP were also concerned about non-tariff barriers such as health regulations, technical standards and non-tariff customs duties affecting tropical produce. The Community argued that such regulations arose out of national regulations and therefore could not be subject to multilateral negotiation. In frustration, the ACP pointed out the contradiction in the Community's responses to both demands. In the case of the first, the Community claimed it could not take any substantive action because it was an internal Community policy, and in the second, because it was a bilateral issue for the member states of the Community. Another major issue during the negotiations was the question of sugar. Although the Community had offered to buy 1.4 million tonnes from the ACP and to pay a price equivalent to the price guaranteed to beet producers in Europe, they said they could not offer more without incurring major political risks with Community producers.

These differences of opinion were significant enough to cast an atmosphere of gloom within the negotiations. The political initiative came from the ACP who invited the Nine to a meeting in Kingston, Jamaica, in July 1974. This gave a new impetus to the negotiations, resulting in a meeting of minds on some of the burning issues. The EEC finally abandoned its insistence on reciprocity in trade relations. The Community also made a definite commitment on the system of export earnings stabilization as proposed by the Commission; they also agreed to place higher priority on industrialization.

The issue of the size of the EDF remained unresolved until the very end of the negotiations. The Chairman of the Community ministerial Council, Jean Sauvanargues of France, had revealed that the Community was willing to make a financial commitment to the amount of 3,000 mua (Table 4.1 and Figure 4.1). This figure was considered inadequate by the ACP, with its spokesman, Babacar Ba of Senegal putting the alternative figure of 8,000 mua as a more acceptable sum to the associates. Two other conferences were to be held on 13 and 30 January 1975, to deal with outstanding issues. At midnight on 31 January, amid immense fanfare and pageantry in the Togolese capital, the Lomé Convention was finally signed by the Nine and by the forty-six ACP states.[23]

Lomé was widely regarded as a major turning point in the history of North–South relations. In terms of the issues covered, it was a comprehensive agreement embracing trade, commodities, financial aid and joint institutions for continual consultation. The ACP partners comprised nearly half of the member states of the United Nations with a population of about 510

Table 4.1 Comparison of financial aid under Lomé I and II (in mua)

	Lomé I	*Lomé II*
EDF TOTAL	3,150	4,542
of which:		
Grants	2,165	2,928
Special loans	470	504
Risk capital	100	504
Stabex	395 (+20) (a)	550
Sysmin	—	280
EIB TOTAL	400	685 (+200) (b)
Administrative costs	—	180 (c)
GRAND TOTAL	3,550	5,607

Notes:
(a) Reserve
(b) EIB funds for investments in the minerals sector
(c) Allocation to ACP administrative costs

Source: EC Commission, 1979

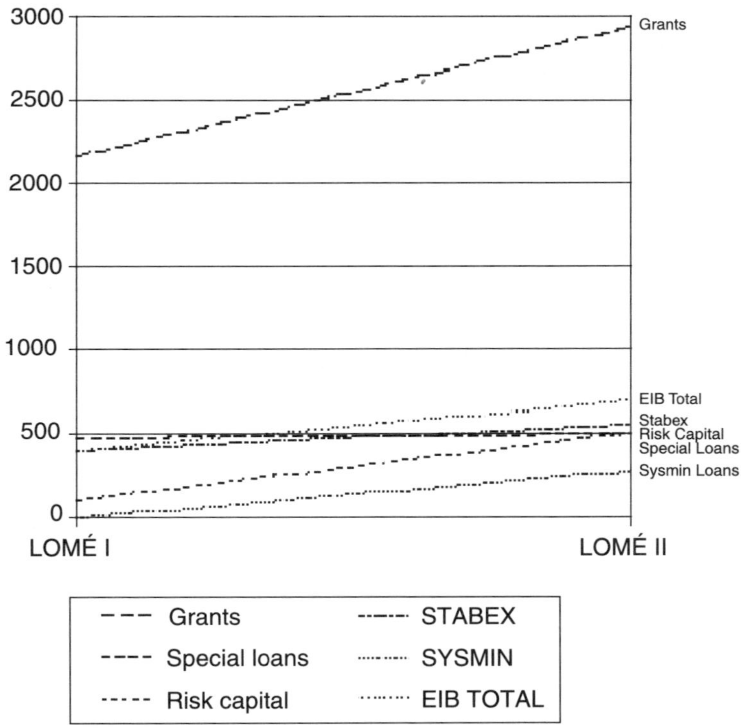

Figure 4.1 EDF aid under Lomé I and II (in mua)
Source: European Commission, 1979

million. Its contractual character offered a source of guaranteed aid and trade concessions at a time of uncertainty and turbulence in international economic relations.

THE MAIN PROVISIONS OF LOMÉ

The main provisions of the Lomé agreement covered six major issues:

1 free market access for ACP exports into the European market without reciprocity;
2 commodity stabilization fund (Stabex) to compensate ACP countries for losses resulting from falls in export earnings from their principal export commodities;
3 financial and technical cooperation with an allocation of 3,000 mua from the EDF and 390 mua from the EIB;
4 industrial cooperation, with a centre (CDI)[24] to assist in the promotion of industrial and technological development of ACP states;
5 a Sugar Protocol to enable ACP countries to export up to 1.4 million tonnes of sugar into the Community;
6 establishment of joint institutions to promote EC–ACP dialogue and to oversee observance and implementation of the Convention.[25]

Compared to the preceding association regime, there were a number of important innovations both in terms of general principles and in specific details. In the area of trade and commercial cooperation, the abandonment of reciprocity was certainly one of the most important innovations. It had been one of the contentious issues in the negotiations, as the Europeans themselves became divided in their opinions. The central issue was whether international obligations under the GATT did not conflict with non-reciprocity. The ACP argument was that the inequality between North and South and the imbalances in the international system did justify non-reciprocity in trade relations. Its final resolution in favour of the latter argument was seen as a major victory for the ACP Group. The abandonment of reciprocity, however, was an economic victory with a political cost: in political terms it meant an erosion of the principle of formal equality between the Community and the ACP Group.

Access for ACP products into the Community market was guaranteed to be free of customs duties and taxes of equivalent effect, and also without quotas and other quantitative restrictions. An exception, however, was made with regard to goods falling within the Community's Common Agricultural Policy (CAP). ACP exports to the Community in 1973 were valued at US$7,600 million, of which $1,000 million or 13.4 per cent of the total consisted of products (including sugar) falling within the CAP regime.[26] The Community went a step further in guaranteeing free access to the EC market for 71.9 per cent of those ACP agricultural products that fall within the CAP.

Sugar, which alone made up 2.3 per cent of this group of commodities, was subject to a special arrangement under the Sugar Protocol. In the case of the remaining 5.8 per cent, the Community offered a more favourable margin of preferential treatment than had been granted to any outside countries. In general terms, therefore, the new trade regime amounted to 99.2 per cent of free access for ACP exports, with the remainder subject to admission on preferential terms. The only corresponding undertaking which was required of the ACP Group was that they would give a most-favoured nation treatment to EC member states with regard to all their external trade relations with third parties.

An important qualification to the principle of free access is the Rules of Origin clause, which sought to define which goods could be regarded as having originated from the ACP. This Rule had been the subject of intense negotiation, as the Community were anxious to maintain a uniform definition of the Rules of Origin to all goods coming into its market. The ACP, on the other hand, wanted as generous a definition of the rules as possible, with allowance being made for special situations. Two concessions were in the end agreed to by the Community. The first was that they had accepted to consider the ACP states as a single customs area, allowing for successive processings and partial manufactures in several ACP countries. The second concession was acceptance by the EC to consider applications by ACP states for temporary derogations for industrial development purposes. In return the ACP agreed to a list of exceptions which the Community had put forward.[27]

Another important innovation in the trade provision was the establishment of an export stabilization scheme, Stabex. A Commission study had underlined the critical issue of commodity price instability. The study had concluded that the problem was best tackled through a mechanism that avoided creating new obstacles to free market operations and to international trade in general. An export receipts stabilization policy was finally adopted in the expectation that it would not only affect the general economic structure of the exporting country but also "mitigate the difficulties of producers".[28] Unlike the Emergency Fund under Yaoundé II, Stabex was to be operated separately from the EDF, with an allocation of 375 mua, to be disbursed at an annual rate of 75 mua (Table 4.2). Any unused surplus which remains in any particular year is automatically carried over to the next.

Lomé and aid programming

The main approach to development policy was based on "project aid" and on "integrated rural development". The rising tide of population and rapid

Table 4.2 Summary of principal exports covered by Stabex in 1975

Country	*Product as % of total exports*
Botswana	leather and hides (9%)
Burundi	coffee (86%), cotton (3%), leather and hides (2%)
Cameroon	cocoa (23%), coffee (26%), timber (12%)
C.A.R.	coffee (23%), timber (21%), cotton (18%)
Chad	cotton (69%)
Congo (Braz.)	timber (42%)
Côte d'Ivoire	cocoa (15%), coffee (23%), timber (29%)
Dahomey	palm products (34%)
Ethiopia	coffee (38%), leather and hides (13%)
Fiji*	coconut oil (5%)
Gabon	timber (32%)
Gambia	groundnuts, oil and cattle cake (94%)
Ghana	cocoa (61%), timber (19%)
Jamaica*	bananas (4%)
Kenya	coffee (22%), tea (11%)
Liberia	iron ore (71%)
Madagascar	coffee (30%), sisal (3%)
Malawi	tea (17%), groundnuts (7%)
Mali	cotton (39%), groundnuts (7%)
Mauritania	iron ore (93%)
Niger	groundnuts (61%), groundnut oil (4%)
Rwanda	coffee (61%), raw hides (4%)
Senegal	groundnuts (9%), groundnut oil (9%)
Sierra Leone	iron ore (10%), palm kernel (5%)
Somalia	bananas (26%), copra (25%)
Sudan	cotton (56%)
Swaziland	cotton (3%)
Tanzania	coffee (19%), cotton (13%)
Togo	cocoa (26%), coffee (13%)
Tonga*	copra (50%)
Uganda	coffee (66%), cotton (15%), tea (5%)
Upper Volta	groundnuts (8%), cotton (22%)
Western Samoa	cocoa (28%)

Note: *Non-African members of the ACP Group
Source: *The Courier*, March 1975, p. 28

urbanization with its attendant problems of food shortages and urban social crisis was cited as the background against which EC development policy under Lomé I was devised. Through the project approach, the Community hoped that more food could be produced to feed the teeming urban populations and to reduce the unmanageable rate of urbanization. According to a Community policy review paper, during the 1970s:

> The rural urban exodus had swollen and was still swelling the towns . . . urban expansion increased by an average of 6%. To feed these populations, often living in slums around the big metropolises on the coast, the leaders sometimes opted to import cereals, particularly rice and wheat. . . . At the same time, the city dwellers started to prefer white bread and long grain rice to local cereals, a change in habits which . . . increased food dependency and the deficit in these States' trade balance by the same amount.[29]

Aid financing focused on both "project aid" as well as "integrated rural development". Large-scale rice projects were set up in Senegal, Cameroon, Surinam, Ethiopia, Niger and Madagascar.

The idea of integrated rural development was centred on the need to put "economic considerations in a wider social and cultural context". This meant integrating the various components of rural development, from provision of credit and irrigation to rural extension and construction of rural tracks and stores. Even in this approach, the Community was not offering a unique or original approach to "development". In fact, the World Bank was already promoting this form of approach, and the EEC could be said to have been only following the Bank's lead. Prominent among such EC-funded projects were the Iringa (Tanzania) and Djebel Mara (Sudan) and the Benué (Cameroon) integrated rural development projects.[30]

THE INSTITUTIONAL FRAMEWORK OF LOMÉ

The institutional framework of Lomé consists of three types of institutions: the "joint institutions", the EC institutions, and the ACP institutions (see Figure 4.2).

The joint institutions

The joint institutions consist of the Joint EC–ACP Council, the EC–ACP Committee of Ambassadors and the Joint Consultative Assembly.

The **EC–ACP Joint Council** is the supreme arm of the Convention, consisting of members of the EC Council of Ministers, Commission, and representatives of each of the member governments of the ACP states. There are normally joint chairmen, one from both sides. Under Lomé I, the Presidency was on annual rotational basis by the two sides. The Council

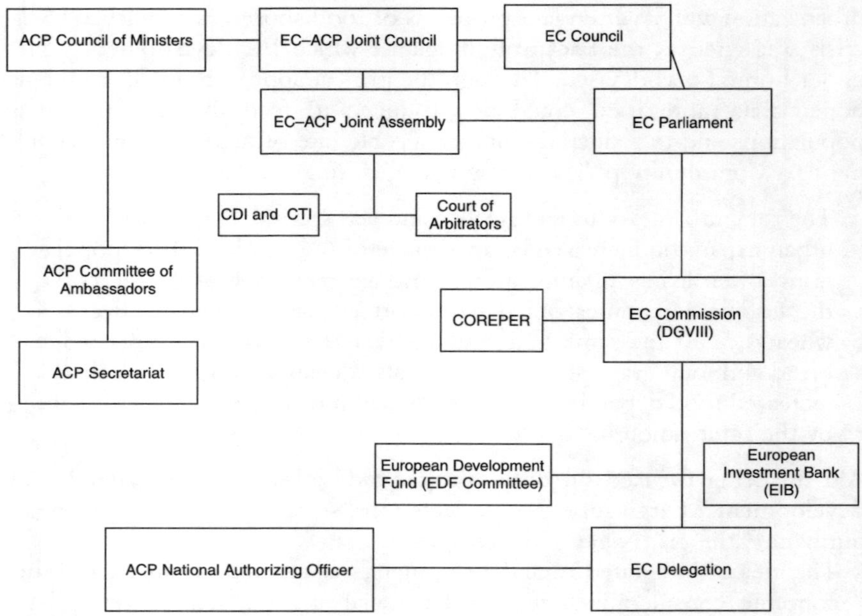

Figure 4.2 The institutional framework of Lomé

meets once a year at the initiative of the President. Under its Rules of Procedure, it may meet at any other time if the circumstances warrant it. The Council lays down the general guidelines for the implementation of the Convention. Its decisions are legally binding on the contracting parties. The main responsibility of the Joint Council is to administer the Convention, for which it enjoys the powers of decision and consultation. In principle, any matter that is deemed to impact on the Convention can be brought before the Council. It may also undertake consultations at the highest levels in Europe as well as in the ACP states.[31]

The EC–ACP **Committee of Ambassadors** assists the Council in the performance of their role, carrying out all such tasks as the Council may direct. It also has supervisory powers over functional organs of the Convention, whether these are ad hoc or permanent.

Third, there is the **Joint Consultative Assembly**, consisting of members of the European Parliament and representatives from ACP countries, with the two sides appointing the same number of delegates. The Joint Assembly comprises an equal number of parliamentarians or designated representatives from ACP countries and from the EC Parliament. The work of the Assembly since 1980 has involved examining the operations of financial and technical cooperation, with the Resolution of 26 September 1980, which followed upon an earlier report by Mrs Katerina Focke, MEP

(Germany). The Assembly has addressed questions ranging from financial disbursements of EDF resources and famine to indebtedness and human rights. The Assembly may discuss any matters which it regards as important in relation to EC–ACP relations. It may then pass resolutions on these matters. In recent times their meetings have become increasingly frank, with resolutions on questions of human rights, freedom of the press, and democracy receiving considerable attention. Procedures have also been established for dealing with disagreements or conflicts which may arise between or amongst the partners. Difficulties which are not settled within the joint institutions may be raised through the "procedure of good offices" or through the services of an "ad hoc arbitration committee".

EC institutions for Lomé cooperation

The EC institutions consist of the EC Council of Ministers, the EC Parliament, the Committee of Ambassadors, the Commission and the EDF Committee.

The Committee of Ambassadors (COREPER)[32] assists the Council, doing most of the groundwork for the former as well as participating in the Lomé negotiations with its ACP counterparts. It acts as an intermediary body between the Commission and the Council. According to a former EC Commissioner:

> *Coreper* constitutes a sort of legislative chamber for the member countries and examines, amends and approves (or disapproves with relegation to the files) a large part of the proposals for rules or directives made by the Commission. It is an accepted constitutional custom that when an agreement is reached in *Coreper*, the Council ratifies it without further discussion. *Coreper*, for its part, passes to the Council only those points on which the Permanent Representatives have not [reached] . . . agreement.[33]

The EC Council of Ministers may be said to be the executive arm of European government. It is the highest decision-making body. Its decisions are legally binding and take precedence over national rules and regulations. It is composed of ministers representing each of the EC Twelve. In the case of Lomé and EC development cooperation in general, the Council is represented by Development Ministers from each of the member states. As Juliet Lodge has pointed out, the EC Council is hardly a collegiate body: "It has several, and often twelve, competing opinions as to what constitutes an acceptable compromise on a draft Commission proposal."[34] Contributions to the EDF derive from the member states, which means that the Council jealously guards its right to determine how aid money is spent and on the broad outlines of policy underlying Lomé aid.

The EC Parliament, perhaps among all EC institutions, has seen its powers gradually increased in recent times, with the first direct elections in 1979, and subsequently with the passing of the Single Market Act in 1985. An inherent conflict seems to exist between the Parliament and the Council, owing to what has been termed the EC's "democratic deficit". As a result, the Parliament often adopts a confrontational attitude in relation to both the Council and the Commission. It currently enjoys powers of control over the budget, and the right to be consulted on most important policy matters. It has a Committee on development which has often held debates and sponsored major resolutions on development issues such as famine, food aid and human rights

The EC Commission has sometimes been disparagingly termed a "Eurocracy". Often seen as the "motor of European integration", its role is quite unique in international organization. It enjoys enormous powers in proposing decisions, regulations and directives for consideration and adoption by the Council. It comprises seventeen Commissioners, each in charge of a division, which is akin to a governmental ministry. Directorate-General VIII is the development division of the Commission, with the fisheries portfolio recently added to the incumbent Commissioner, Manuel Marin (Spain). Although all divisions are legally equal, it is known that a hierarchy of prestige does exist. Two of the most "powerful" departments are said to be DGI (External Relations) and DGVI (Agriculture). Observers have noted the relative decline of DGVIII, with the addition of the fisheries portfolio, and the general impression in EC circles that it operates at the margins of Community affairs.[35] The various divisions, like all bureaucratic entities, are very protective of their domains, leading to the anomalous situation whereby EC food aid, which is a vital development operation, is handled almost exclusively by the agriculture division.[36]

The EC Delegation comprises a Delegate and other officials who play the role of diplomatic representation as well as helping to coordinate and implement EC development policy in the ACP states. He generally liaises with the National Authorizing Officer, normally the Permanent Secretary in the Finance or Planning Ministry, who has responsibility for implementing Lomé aid projects. The status of the Delegate has been a matter of some controversy. Although some host states have accorded him an ambassadorial status, other states have been hesitant to accord the full rights and privileges of legation under international law. Although the Delegate enjoys a high profile within the aid and economic policy circles of ACP states, he has very little autonomy in practical terms, as most decisions have to be referred back to Brussels for final approval.

The European Development Fund (EDF) is a financing agency under the development division. It does not have an independent existence outside EC development financing. While it finances the national indicative programmes allocated to each ACP state, which are almost all by way of grants, its counterpart, the European Investment Bank (EIB), has only marginal responsibility for development. Its principal role is to promote European investment. It also provides risk capital and soft loans for investment in ACP states.

The EDF Committee was originally established in 1963 as a result of an internal agreement by EEC governments on the management and financing of Yaoundé aid programmes. It was renewed in 1969 to cover Yaoundé II and subsequently in 1975 to manage the Lomé Convention.[37] The Committee consists of representatives of all the member states, with a non-voting Chairman who is normally a representative of the Commission. It also has representatives from the European Investment Bank, and from the General Secretariat of the EC Council (the latter having observer status). It is the organ responsible for approving project proposals submitted by ACP states after their National Indicative Programmes have been agreed with the Commission. Its decisions are taken on the basis of qualified majority of 69 per cent of the votes, providing that the combined votes of Germany, France and the United Kingdom do not constitute this majority.[38]

The EDF Committee is the main avenue through which EC member governments exert influence on Lomé aid decisions. ACP states have been unsuccessful in their bid to be involved in the work of the Committee and the EC has rejected even their request to be granted observer status. The Committee has also been the focal point of an evolving EC development philosophy. It provides member governments with an opportunity to compare notes on their aid experience and to coordinate joint efforts in the development field.[39]

Although the duty of the Committee is to approve projects, the Commission is responsible for technical preparations and financing decisions. The Committee itself was established in 1963 during Yaoundé I, as an internal arrangement among EEC countries on the management of Community's aid. If a proposed project is rejected by the Committee, it may be withdrawn or an appeal could be made to the EC Council. Delays have often resulted from the need to translate all proposals into the six EC official languages, with an interval of six weeks before projects would be considered.

The EDF Committee provides the actual forum for member states to influence decisions on projects. They normally compare notes on their bilateral aid experiences and seek to evolve a common philosophy on development policy.[40] Outside the EDF framework, there is a provision for ad hoc consultations between the Commission and the European Investment Bank and member states. ACP countries are also allowed to take their cases directly to EC governments if their projects were turned down by the Committee.

The Commission has diplomatic delegations in forty-six ACP countries, comprising more than 300 professional staff, mainly economists, agriculturalists, engineers and technicians.[41] The responsibilities of the Commission Delegate consist of five functions:

1 providing technical assistance in project preparation and appraisal and helping to prepare financing proposals;
2 providing a link between Brussels and ACP host governments as well as information gathering;
3 liaising with the host authorities in the monitoring and supervision of projects and ensuring that projects are being implemented according to acceptable financial and technical conditions;
4 preparation of annual reports on the operations of all EDF aid programmes in the host country; and
5 the function of representation, i.e., serving as the "eyes and ears" of the Commission and of the European Community with regard to aid and development in the ACP country.

Although their powers are quite limited, EC Delegates are now empowered to take certain key decisions on the spot on behalf of the Commission, such as award or approval of certain contracts and authorizing payments to contractors.

The Joint Council meets once a year and their meetings are prepared by the Committee of Ambassadors. Under Lomé I the Council passed the Suva Resolution of 14 April 1977 and the Nairobi Resolution of 9 May 1980, both of which relate to improving the policy framework for implementing Lomé aid programmes. Central to the work of the Council is the role of the Article 108 Committee, consisting of ministers drawn from both sides, who are mandated to examine means of strengthening financial and technical cooperation. This Committee is endowed with the political authority to review progress in the implementation of the Convention. Under Lomé III it was renamed Article 193. Article 193 (6) of Lomé III authorizes the Committee to hear cases of complaints on any aspects of EDF aid programmes: "any specific problem arising in the implementation of financial and technical cooperation may be submitted to the Committee which shall examine it within 60 days with a view to providing appropriate solutions". This Committee has seen its role considerably strengthened in recent times. It now prepares annual reports on the progress and problems in the implementation of the Lomé agreement.

ACP institutions

The ACP Group currently consists of sixty-nine African, Caribbean and Pacific states. The main legal instrument which established the legal basis of the Group was the Georgetown Agreement of 1975. The Group grew out of the concertation of the African, Caribbean and Pacific states during the Lomé I negotiations. The objectives of the Group are to promote their "solidarity" as a group, promote trade and economic relations among the ACP states, promote "effective regional and inter-regional cooperation" by the ACP states, and "to ensure that the Convention of Lomé contributes fully to the realization of the common aspirations of countries of the developing world".

Although its founding Instrument defines its objectives as being to promote South–South integration and to monitor implementation of the Convention, it is difficult to imagine its existence outside of the Lomé Convention.[42] An amorphous group, with diverse cultural, regional and historical identities, it is very much an artificial creation. There have been conflicts between the Caribbean and Pacific on the one hand, and the African states, on the other.[43] Added to this is the traditional divide between English-speaking and French-speaking Africa.

The ACP Council, like its EC counterpart, is the highest decision-making body within the ACP Group. It oversees the implementation of the Lomé Convention and the conduct of intra-ACP relations.

The ACP Committee of Ambassadors assists the Council in its work, and undertakes all such other tasks as the Council may assign it. Its duties extends to monitoring the implementation of Lomé and overseeing the activities of the ACP Secretariat-General. The Ambassadors meet routinely each week at ACP House, the headquarters of the Secretariat in Brussels.

The ACP Secretariat-General is the administrative and servicing organ of the ACP Group. The Georgetown Agreement of 1975 had provided for a Secretariat to help administer ACP–EC relations, assist with technical work, and provide administrative service to the Council and Committee of Ambassadors. The history of the Secretariat, however, goes back to the Yaoundé I period. It was established in 1964, to service the African associates. During the Lomé negotiations an African Secretariat was set up to coordinate African negotiations, and was later merged to form the ACP Secretariat.[44] Under the Georgetown Agreement, the task of the Secretariat is to monitor the implementation of the Lomé Convention, to service the various organs of the ACP Group, to perform any task required by the ACP Council. The Secretariat has a staff of seventy-three, representing all sections of the ACP Group. Article 3 of the Georgetown Agreement set out the following roles for the organization: monitoring and implementation of the Lomé Convention; providing services to the principal organs of the ACP Group and the joint EC–ACP institutions; and undertaking any other tasks as may be determined by the Council of Ministers and the Committee of Ambassadors.

The Secretary-General is the chief administrative officer of the organization.[45] He is appointed by the Council of Ministers, and his functions are to administer the Secretariat and to ensure effective financial management of the Secretariat's budget. As in other similar Third World organizations, his role is very limited. It is not part of his duties, for example, to coordinate the

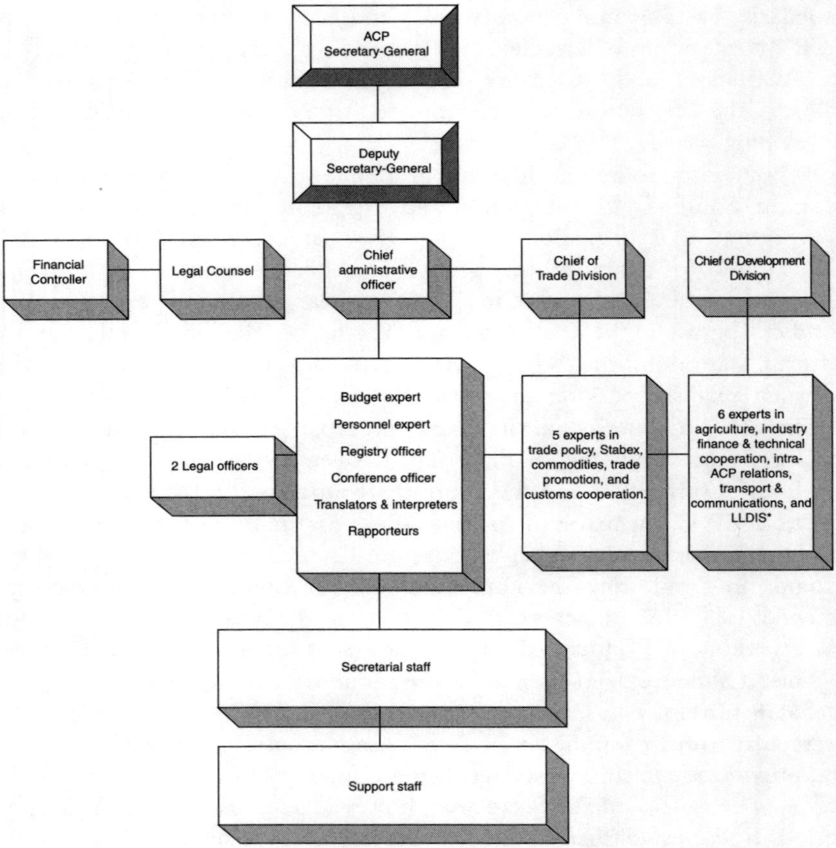

Figure 4.3 Organizational structure of the ACP Secretariat. *Land-locked Least Developed Island States

activities of the ACP Group or to act at the highest political levels within the Group to ensure that the goals and ideals of the association are promoted.

In October 1985 the Harare Declaration was adopted, as follow-up to the earlier Montego Bay Plan of Action, to improve intra-ACP cooperation.[46] As part of this project a Committee was set up to advise on the reorganization of the Secretariat. As early as 1960 the EC Parliament had opined that "the European Communities by virtue of their international legal personality enjoy the active and passive right of legation".[47]

At the head of the Secretariat (Figure 4.3) is the Secretary-General, whose task it is to ensure the smooth running of the administration and to promote the interests of the ACP Group. In the performance of this task he is assisted by officials from five principal divisions, namely, the Chief Administrative Officer, the Financial Controller, the Legal Counsel, the

Chief of Trade Division and the Chief of the Development Division. In November 1981 the ACP Ambassadors set up an eight-member "Committee of Wise Men" to look into the problems of the Secretariat. This Committee was chaired by Ambassador Séydina Oumar Sy (Senegal). Their report revealed a state of low morale and widespread irregularities within the organization.[48] While staff complained of poor working conditions and lack of regular consultations with the Chiefs of Division, the Secretary-General himself decried the problem of excessive intervention by Ambassadors even in routine personnel matters, which he said was fostering an environment of indiscipline within the organization. The report concluded that the "Secretariat has not yet managed to institute an effective system which is properly organized and coordinated and through which it can deploy all its staff to their utmost".[49]

During the negotiations for the Fourth Convention, the problems of the Secretariat were once more brought into the forefront of attention. The Secretariat itself identified some of its own shortcomings as those of chronic deficiency in the requisite technical personnel. Consequently, it was having to seek assistance from other international organizations, notably the Commonwealth Secretariat, UNCTAD, the Caribbean Commission (CARICOM) and the ECA.[50] The Committee of Ambassadors underlined the abolition of the post of Deputy Secretary-General, who hitherto had done most of the technical work, as a major factor in the problems of the Secretariat, including lack of expertise in certain sectors, notably minerals, fisheries, structural adjustment, debt, population and research/scientific cooperation.[51]

The Secretariat is so deficient in terms of personnel and expertise that it has to depend on other agencies such as the ECA and the Commonwealth Secretariat for technical studies.[52] Morale of staff has been noticeably low, due to the Secretariat's uncertain financial position. Some staff have also complained of undue interference from some members of the Committee of Ambassadors in even very routine matters.[53] Although there have been some improvements under the incumbent Secretary-General Dr Berhane Gebray of Ethiopia, who is a competent international lawyer and diplomat, the Secretariat's manifold problems seem unlikely to disappear in the near future. Indeed, its failings may reflect even deeper problems relating to the intrinsic artificiality of the ACP's collective identity.

At the ACP Council of Ministers' Conference in April 1986, the financial problems of the Secretariat once again were brought up by Secretary-General Edwin Carrington. The EDF had offered to make financial contributions, but this was rejected by the Council, even though countries were left with the discretion of where to find the money for their contributions.[54] Under Lomé IV, the EC has undertaken to pay emoluments of staff. Whilst this had done much for staff morale, the obvious implication is that they may come to see themselves as EC staff, and the senior officials in particular may find it increasingly difficult to take publicly strong positions against the Commission.

LOMÉ AND DEVELOPMENT POLICY

The formal provisions of the Lomé trade regime are quite generous, offering free access to 95 per cent of ACP products. In practice, however, there have been protectionist pressures, especially in sectors such as textiles and clothing, which are declining industries in the European Community. In the area of manufacturing exports, which in the ACP are admittedly marginal, there is evidence, according to Stevens, that "in cases where an ACP is able to take advantage of its theoretical rights, it runs the risk of administrative action to discourage it".[55]

During 1975–79 the ACP share of EC imports fell by 1 per cent from 8 per cent in 1970–74 to 7 per cent during 1975–79, while other LDCs increased their share from 39 per cent to 43 per cent during the same period.[56] Table 4.3 shows the trade balance between 1975 and 1979. Although the trade balance was heavily in deficit by 1976, it registered significant improvement in 1978, only to record a massive deficit of ECU3019 billion (the equivalent of Lomé I EDF funding by 1979).

In terms of product composition of exports, there was no change in the eleven manufactured products which constituted a paltry 0.05 per cent of total ACP exports.[57] However, some countries, notably Mauritius, Kenya, Côte d'Ivoire and Cameroon, recorded significant diversification into non-traditional exports. In the case of Mauritius, for example, Lomé did make an important difference to its textiles exports. In 1970, two years after its independence from Britain, Mauritius set up an Export Processing Zone (EPZ) to boost its export sector. By 1980, textiles and clothing accounted for 45 per cent of all enterprises and 76 per cent of employment. Although the Community was not the only outlet for Mauritian exports, it was by far the predominant one, with the UK and France absorbing between 57 and 70 per cent of the island's products.[58]

Lomé was expected to contribute to ACP trade in four ways:

Table 4.3 EEC–ACP trade balance, 1975–79 (mua)

1975	−593
1976	−588
1977	+43
1978	+800
1979	−3,019

Source: EC Parliament, *The Katerina Focke Report*, 1981

1 tariff-free restrictions, preferential access with regard to processed exports and manufactures;
2 through stabilization of export earnings or Stabex;
3 through aid to boost agricultural exports and trade promotion;
4 through the special protocols on products such as sugar, banana and rum.

The record of these provisions have been modest, for reasons ranging from the Rules of Origin to EC protectionism and the "safeguard clause".[59] The Rules of Origin require that the value-added of goods originating from ACP countries must be no less than 50 per cent in ACP and/or EC inputs. The safeguard clause permits the Community to make derogations to the general rule of free access for ACP products.

Another demonstration of the structural weakness of the EC is in investment promotion. In the case of Mauritius, for example, the CDI was able to attract only one EC company to invest in the island while the French-funded trade agency (which was later to receive EDF funding) was able to attract fifty-five investors to the EPZ.[60]

There were also the crucial shortfalls in the Stabex funds. Stabex shortfalls rose further to ECU31 million, and to ECU375 million in 1987. By 1987 payments to legitimate claimants had to be reduced by 58 per cent for most ACP states and by 53 per cent for the poorest states.[61] Dissatisfaction

Table 4.4 Stabex transfers by product, 1975–89

Product/group of products	*Period*			
	Lomé III (1985–89)		*Lomé I–III (1975–89)*	
	Allocation (ECU)	*% of total*	*Allocation (ECU)*	*% of total*
1 Coffee	589,494,410	40.40	850,571,356	33.78
2 Groundnuts	168,023,123	11.52	440,641,445	17.50
3 Cocoa/cocoa products	203,098,818	13.92	353,456,761	14.04
4 Cotton	846,119,740	5.80	164,505,748	6.53
5 Timber	107,111,119	7.34	147,493,817	5.86
6 Coco/copra products	101,336,328	6.95	143,532,914	5.70
7 Palm oil products	77,727,124	5.33	92,239,282	3.66
8 Tea	45,905,104	3.15	56,531,537	2.24
9 Iron ore			61,789,536	2.45
10 Oil cakes	20,848,292	1.43	52,434,242	2.08
11 Others	60,894,295	4.16	155,027,537	6.16
TOTAL	1,459,050,587	100.00	2,518,224,175	100.00

Source: *The Courier*, 132, March–April 1992, p. 7

with the general record of Lomé trade was perhaps a contributory factor in leading some in the EC to seek a reorientation of Lomé from trade to a greater emphasis on aid and macroeconomic reform. Table 4.4 shows the value of Stabex transfers by product from 1975 to 1989. In 1980, the shortfall in Stabex amounted to ECU123 million, compelling the Community to reduce payments by 53 per cent (reduced to 40 per cent for the least developed, landlocked and island states).

In the area of aid projects, Lomé performance seemed similarly weak. Figure 4.4 shows the eight-level programme cycle of the Lomé aid process. The ACP–EEC Joint Council report of 1980 noted that the Community programming missions in ACP states were characterized by three failings:

1 There was a feeling by recipients that EEC points of view were being imposed on the recipients.
2 Several recipient countries said it was a major hurdle getting the Commission to accept additional information or other important facts regarding projects.
3 On several occasions the Commission tended to reject important technical amendments to projects which had already been submitted.[62]

The European Court of Auditors had listed the following types of shortcomings in Community-funded projects:[63]

1 totally unjustified projects;
2 inadequate preliminary studies;
3 failure to adapt designs and techniques to local conditions;
4 narrow technical approach to projects;
5 faulty maintenance;
6 faulty execution;
7 no coordination of physical and human resources;
8 lack of coordination in financing;
9 unsatisfactory comparison of tenders;
10 objectives not fulfilled;
11 failure to consider running costs;
12 little lasting impact on national/regional welfare and productivity.

If the records of aid and trade performance were not impressive, at least it could be said that the institutional framework of Lomé was an encouraging sign of institutionalized dialogue, based on a sense of mutual respect and solidarity. The unique framework provided by the joint institutions cannot be denied. Certainly no other Northern institution has offered such a forum, least of all the World Bank and the Fund. On the surface, the joint institutions seem to reflect an outlook of genuine equality and "mutual interests". However, as Isebill Gruhn explains, they have never transcended

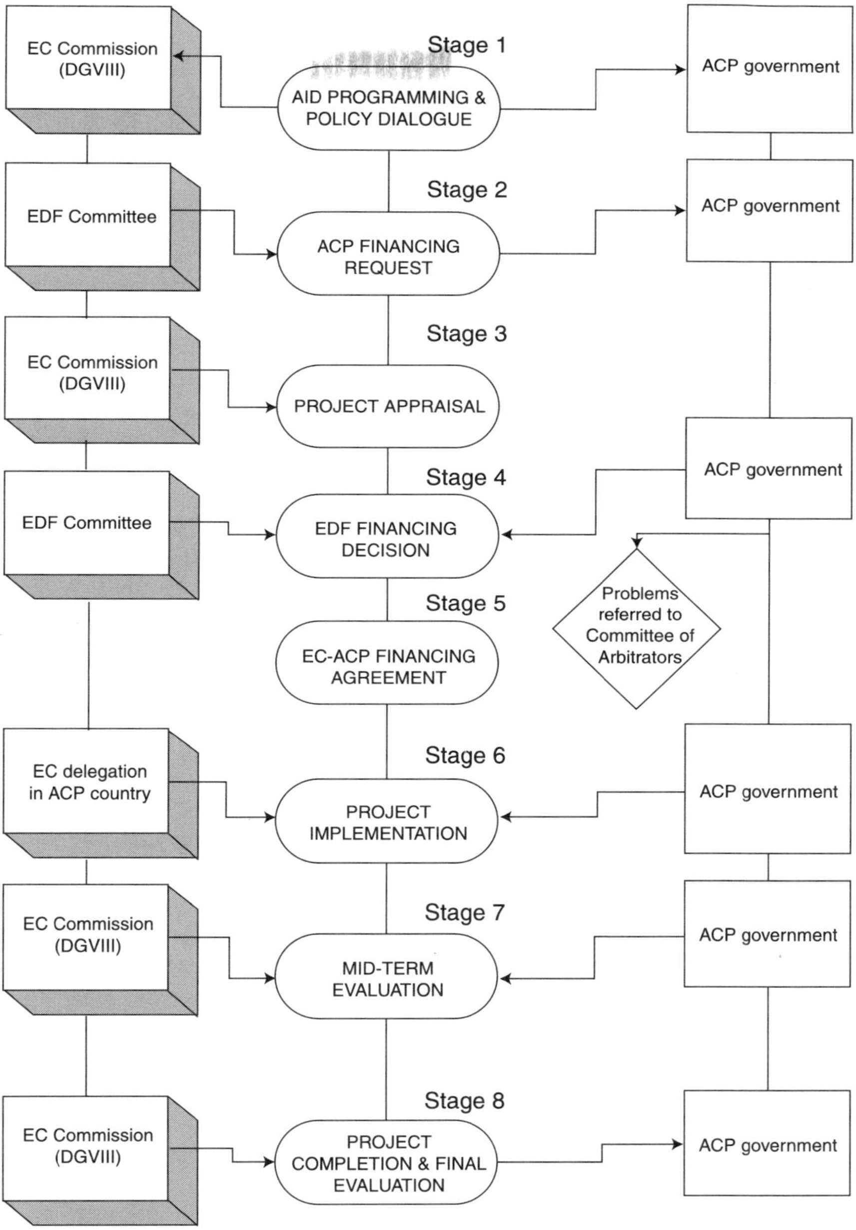

Figure 4.4 The Lomé aid programming and implementation cycle

the basic asymmetry in the relationship. According to her, when the Community speaks of:

> "policy dialogue", "joint decision making", or even an ACP country's right to determine which projects it wants financed, it is the EEC and EDF, more frequently than not, which determine which projects it wants financed . . . which determine which projects are in fact funded.[64]

Decisions on projects and NIP allocations are entirely a matter for the Committee, the Commission and the Council, with no ACP representatives involved. Inequality is reflected as well in the way funds are spent. During the Lomé II negotiations the ACP called for a separate industrial fund to be jointly managed by both parties, but this was rejected by the Community. According to one observer, while frank dialogue does take place in Lomé diplomacy, "there ought to be no pretence that the ACP states are really equal partners when it comes to utilizing aid monies. The paymaster calls the tune, lays down the rules and supervises their implementation."[65]

CONCLUSION

What emerged in 1975 was an aid and trade regime which offered the ACP some modest assistance in exchange for clientelist loyalty and influence. It also offered long-term guarantees of raw material sources for the Community at a time when the North was made uneasy by the semblance of Southern power. The rhetoric and elaborate institutions which accompanied Lomé enhanced the world status of the European Community, enabling it to buy, in the words of John Ravenhill, "substantial international prestige – at relatively little cost".[66] The actual record of Lomé aid and trade policy, as we have seen, was far from being impressive, even if such innovations as Stabex and Sysmin could be regarded as a gesture of positive commitment to LDCs commodity stabilization. The declared principles of Lomé resonate with the ideas of interdependence, "partnership" and equality, which marks a significant departure from the more obvious paternalism of the association regime. This was to some extent an important departure from the unabashedly neo-imperial assumptions which underpinned the association regime. In real terms, however, such protestations of equality have been clearly tenuous, as the decision-making structures and procedures clearly reflect the dominant position of the Community. Decisions on aid and financing have remained firmly in the hands of the EC. Lomé may have been a novel experiment in development diplomacy, but it soon proved to be a far cry from the project for "international social justice" that it was made out to be.

EC dom.

5

LOMÉ, POLICY DIALOGUE AND STRUCTURAL ADJUSTMENT

In the last chapter we analysed the emergence of Lomé and we underlined the idiom of interdependence and "mutual interests" which defined the political basis of EC–African relations. In this chapter we consider the changes in EC development policy since the beginning of the 1980s. We shall examine in particular the emergence of "policy dialogue" under Lomé III and its culmination in the new politics of structural adjustment under Lomé IV. Our central argument in this chapter is that the emergence of adjustment and "policy dialogue" marks a qualitative shift from the norms of interdependence and formal equality which had underpinned the Lomé aid regime in the previous decade.

In September 1979, following the first direct European parliamentary elections, the new Parliament undertook a major reassessment of the Community's development policy. Under the chairmanship of an Italian socialist, Mr Ferrero, the work of the Parliamentary Committee on Development Cooperation eventually led to the final resolution at Strasbourg in September 1980.[1] The "Ferrero Resolution", as it was later to be known, was essentially a broad reassessment of the key issues of development, particularly agriculture and food aid, the impact of the CAP on LDCs, the effectiveness of commodity stabilization, and the possibilities of a Common Fund for Commodities.[2] The aim was to draw up a coherent set of responses within the framework of the North–South negotiations and the third UN Development Decade. The second objective of the resolution was to coordinate joint efforts with EC member states and international organizations for a policy that would ensure food availability to the LDCs.

Whilst calling for increased food aid and financial assistance, the resolution urged specific actions on the establishment of a mechanism for the recycling of petro-dollars, extension of World Bank financing to embrace structural adjustment reforms in the South, and substantial increases in IMF and IDA resources in support of economic reform programmes.[3] It showed a significant difference in thinking that the EC Parliament was calling for increased contributions to the IFIs at a time when some of the major share-holders – notably Reagan's United States, Thatcher's Britain and Kohl's Germany – were advocating the reverse.[4]

Perhaps the central issue which dominated the attention of the parliamentarians was how to boost agricultural production and ensure food security. It was recommended that EC development intervention ought to give particular attention to "all sectors of development policy, including the commercial aspects".[5] In other words, aid was expected to shift from the traditional approach of project financing as had been the case under Lomé I and II, and to focus instead on key macroeconomic sectors.[6] With specific regard to food strategies, the resolution urged the EC to support local, national and regional food initiatives with technical assistance in the planning of such strategies and through provision of requisite financial backing on a multi-donor basis. It underlined the vital requirements for a viable food strategy as being:

1 adoption of national farm prices to stimulate production;
2 organization of a system of agricultural credit adapted to the special situation of small farmers;
3 improvement of production-consumption structures, and in particular, the establishment of marketing networks to boost national and regional markets.

Many aspects of these recommendations were indeed novel from the viewpoint of EC aid. Given that infrastructural development had been the dominant sector of EC project financing, the focus on a sectoral approach and on food in particular was a significant change in policy. However, it was a strange omission that the report did not highlight the role of the World Bank which was already becoming influential in SSA.[7]

In March 1981 the Commission had submitted proposals to the European Council on the Community's strategy for the Western economic summit which was due to be held in Ottawa in July of the same year. The Commission's position was that the economic problems of the industrial nations could only be effectively solved in the context of a North–South strategy.[8] Stressing the "geopolitical dimension" of the LDCs' economic problems, the Commission called for action in three related areas:

1 easing the scarcity constraint in food and energy;
2 improving the framework of development financing which would lead to improved economic performance in both North and South;
3 effective industrial restructuring in the EC as well as more access for LDC exports.[9]

In October 1981, seven months after its communication to the Council, the Commission drew up a "Plan of Action" to implement its new food strategy approach.[10] To give concrete backing to this plan, the EC Parliament voted ECU50 million in the 1983 budget to be devoted to food sector strategies. This met with considerable opposition from some member states, notably Britain, who argued that the plan should be targeted at the poorest countries and not necessarily restricted to the Lomé associates. This disagreement delayed implementation of the programme by a year.

The impasse was resolved by the inclusion of Bangladesh within the programme. The EC food strategy finally took off, consisting of thematic activities directed at nine countries, four of which were from SSA: Zambia, Kenya, Mali and Rwanda.[11] EC support was to take the form of financial assistance to each country programme as well as aid coordination with member states to ensure policy consistency. The initial condition which was attached to the food strategy was that the EC had to be convinced of the genuineness of the country's commitment to the implementation of a viable food strategy.[12]

This was a major departure from the Lomé financing approach, which normally allowed the ACP state to come out with its own portfolio of projects. Given that the food strategy funds were coming from the EC budget rather than the EDF, the legal hurdle of existing contractual obligations and financial procedures could easily be overcome.

THE PISANI MEMORANDUM ON DEVELOPMENT POLICY

In the spring of 1981 Claude Cheysson resigned his post as Development Commissioner having been appointed Foreign Minister by President François Mitterrand. His successor was another Frenchman, Edgard Pisani. A former Agriculture Minister, he was a socialist by conviction and an idealist by temperament. Pisani came to DGVIII with an eagerness to put his stamp of authority on the direction towards which he felt the Community's development policy should be heading. The "Pisani Memorandum", like the "Ferrero Resolution" before it, emerged out of a profound dissatisfaction with the performance of the EC aid regime and what was seen as its lack of responsiveness to the development climacteric of the late 1970s and early 1980s.

The memorandum was critical of the prevailing orthodoxy in EC development policy which had resulted not in balanced and self-reliant development, but in the construction of "cathedrals in the desert".[13] According to Bernard Lecomte, a member of Pisani's *cabinet* at DGVIII, such dissatisfaction derived from poor conceptualization of the development process and failure to reconcile aid practices to the culture of the recipient countries.[14] Coming at a time when the Community was going through "Eurosclerosis", a search for a coherent external development policy could be seen as partly a reaffirmation of a European identity in international affairs, a search for a fulcrum of collective energies which would give character and specificity to the European integrative experience.[15] Indeed,

Pisani himself stressed development policy as a major pillar of EC integration, "an expression, not multinational but collective, of a Community which has neither the attributes nor the ambitions of a state but which nevertheless has great capabilities".[16]

The memorandum stressed a greater role for the EC in determining how its aid resources were to be used. The necessary effect of this increased power to the Community would be reduced autonomy for the ACP states. On the question of conditionality, the EC was anxious to score the moral high-ground of moderation. The memorandum orchestrated a "middle way" which accepted neither of the two extremes of rigid conditionality or the "irresponsibility" of non-conditionality. What it hoped to achieve was a more effective approach to development intervention, based on "policy dialogue between external providers of funds and local decision-makers".[17]

In support of this new initiative, the Commission urged the Ten to increase the percentage of their total aid being channelled through Lomé from 0.05 per cent to 0.1 per cent over the next decade. The memorandum also urged the EC to transfer aid under the EDF to the common budget and to expand EIB operations to non-associated developing countries. Whilst reaffirming the contractual nature of the Lomé relationship, it urged extension of its five-year duration to become of unlimited duration, so that only specific issues could be renegotiated over the short term. The Caribbean and Pacific states were particularly opposed to this aspect of the memorandum because they saw it as a form of "divide and rule" tactic, with bias towards sub-Saharan Africa. It probably also implied increased use of conditionality, although this was strenuously denied by the Commission. However, the tendency towards increased conditionality was to be seen in the new guidelines on greater flexibility in the use of EC aid, with a de-emphasis on project financing and more on "maintenance aid" or balance of payments support as well as sectoral aid.[18]

The attempt by the EC to implement a food strategy approach was hardly original.[19] As Michael Lipton has reminded us, it was reminiscent of the World Bank's earlier move from agricultural projects to sectoral strategies based on policy dialogue.[20] Apart from the lack of an adequate research and information base, which is a requisite for formulating effective rural-agrarian strategies, particularly in Africa, there were also the institutional constraints within the Commission and DGVIII. There was the additional fact that EC food aid policies were yet to become more than just an appendage of the Common Agricultural Policy.[21]

POLICY DIALOGUE AND LOMÉ III

The 1980s began with the most severe economic downturn in Africa's development experience since the last quarter century. At a time when the

Ethiopian famine was making headlines, the parched regions of the Sahel and southern Africa were undergoing their worst drought in decades. Even hitherto prosperous countries such as Nigeria, Kenya and Côte d'Ivoire were undergoing severe economic problems. Commodity prices had deteriorated drastically between 1980 and 1983, as illustrated by Table 5.1. Out of ten selected ACP commodities, all but one had registered negative change in price. Commodities such as groundnuts and sisal had registered a price deterioration of −36 and −24 per cent respectively.[22] Compounding this bleak scenario was the emerging debt crisis, as the loans which were incurred after the last two oil shocks had matured, while interest rates rose and new credits had dried up. Politically, the neo-conservatives were anxious to distance themselves from the liberalism of the Carter–McNamara era. They therefore tended to cut back on aid or to direct it more strictly as an instrument of foreign policy rather than for "development".[23] Thanks to the changed political climate and to diplomatic disarray amongst the LDCs, the North–South dialogue gave way to a new unilateralism in international economic relations. As Tony Hill has observed: "the international recession and the realignment of Northern politics to the right after 1979 . . . effectively ended – or at least postponed for the foreseeable future – the South's challenge to North".[24]

The EC negotiating position

The Lomé III negotiations could be said to have commenced as early as September 1981, with the Pisani Memorandum. It anticipated what were to be the key issues in the new round of negotiations. The guidelines submitted by the Commission to the Council called for a complete reorientation of EC development policy:

Table 5.1 Price changes for ten selected ACP commodities between 1980 and August 1983 (based on IMF financial statistics)

Commodity	*% Change*
Cocoa	−11.3
Coffee	+44.9
Copra	—
Cotton	+10.5
Groundnuts	−31.5
Palm oil	−4.1
Rubber	−19.3
Sawn wood	−18.8
Sisal	−23.5
Tea	+6.3

Sources: IMF, IFS, October 1983, and Adrian Hewitt, 1984, p. 15

> The alternatives can be starkly expressed: either we launch a new cooperation policy with self-sufficiency as its goal or most African and some Caribbean and Pacific countries will sink back into the paralysis of increasing dependency, malnutrition, under-investment and uncontrolled urbanization. The Community could [not escape] . . . the consequences of that situation.[25]

In spite of this broad consensus, there were a number of conflicts over certain vital policy issues within the EC. There was a division within the Community itself, between the "liberals" and the "conservatives". The former, comprising France, Italy, Luxembourg, Italy and Belgium, favoured an increased role of EC-wide development policy, while the conservatives, namely, Britain, West Germany, Denmark and the Netherlands, were against increased EC aid role.

Another source of division within the EC was with regard to its external trade regime. One level of conflict was within the Commission bureaucracy itself, between DGVI and DGVIII. With a prime responsibility for agriculture and the management of the CAP, DGVI resisted proposals by DGVIII to grant free and automatic access to all ACP agricultural products. In the end a compromise was reached to improve transparency of the trade provisions by giving access to all ACP exports, including agricultural goods, with the exception of products that were specifically restricted under the CAP list.[26]

The trade issue was also a source of friction between countries, led by the United Kingdom, who favoured more trade access and less aid, as against France and the Mediterranean countries who favoured the reverse. Clearly, the latter were anxious to safeguard their vital agricultural sectors from competition from ACP countries. Trade and aid became counterposed as mutually exclusive issues, leading to a situation where there was universal support for neither.

The ACP negotiating position

During its Thirtieth Session in Brussels in December 1982, the ACP Council of Ministers mandated the Committee of Ambassadors, with assistance from the ACP Secretariat, under Resolution 6 of 1982, to prepare a draft memorandum on ACP negotiating position and strategies for Lomé III. This memorandum was expected to be submitted to ACP capitals by 30 June 1983, with the comments from the latter to be submitted to the ACP Secretariat by 30 August of the same year. The memorandum that emerged took as its point of departure the global economic environment of recession, inflation and unemployment in the industrialized countries, and the general trends towards reduced enthusiasm for aid in the OECD states.[27] The Mediterranean enlargement of the Community was also seen as a negative development from the ACP viewpoint, since Portugal and Spain had agricultural products which would compete with ACP exports. All the three new members were also potentially net receivers of EC financial aid, a situation which could lead to aid diversion from the EDF. The ACP position also inevitably sought to respond to the challenges of the Pisani Memorandum in forging the framework for a new EC – Lomé development aid approach.

The report identified the main economic problems facing the ACP states as massive food imports and energy import bills, and debt servicing difficulties resulting from sharp increases in interest rates in international capital markets. The causes were linked to "over-dependence on the world economy, weak internal structures, lack of regional complementarity, shortage of technical know-how and management skills".[28] Quoting the *Lagos Plan of Action*,[29] the report blamed "global development strategies" for ACP states' economic stagnation. The ultimate solution was seen in terms of "collective self-reliance".

The ACP Committee of Ambassadors put forward ten principles which they saw as the bedrock of the Lomé regime:

1 Development of ACP economies was to be seen as primarily a responsibility of the ACP states themselves, and Lomé could only be a form of assistance to the domestic efforts self-reliant development.
2 The Lomé Convention should be seen to support ACP economic strategies, cultural values and development priorities. The activities to be supported by Lomé aid had to conform to ACP development plans and priorities and remain the ultimate choice of the ACP states themselves.
3 Those "acquired rights" which had accrued to the ACP states, and all other such privileges which emerged in the future, had to be protected against "all forms of non-compensated dilution", whether as a result of Community policy or any related international effect.
4 Reaffirmation of the principle of interdependence and "mutuality of benefits" as the *raison d'être* of the Lomé partnership. Moreover, to enhance equality in the partnership, it was mandatory to have joint management and consultation with regard to key decision-making in the Lomé partnership as well as in the interpretation of the provisions.
5 To achieve its stated objectives, Lomé should be backed with the requisite financial resources; the enlargement of Community membership should also mean an enlargement of the financial resources available to the Convention.
6 As an instrument of the development of ACP states, Lomé should aim to promote social and economic advancement not only in the ACP states, but also in their cooperation within a regional framework and in their relations with other LDCs.

Table 5.2 Lomé III funds as compared to Lomé I and II (in ECU million)

	Lomé I	*Lomé II*	*Lomé III*
Total Convention	3,483	5,428	8,855
EDF	3,093	4,743	7,755
Grants	2,174	2,977	4,920
Special loans	446	525	600
Risk capital	96	274	600
Sysmin	—	282	415
EIB loans	390	685	425

Note: *Under Lomé III, part of the amount provided for risk capital has been included in the national indicative allocation for least-developed ACP states

Source: EC Commission, 1989

7 The scope of the Convention should not be restricted by a legalistic interpretation; rather, any issue which militates against the achievement of the aims of the Convention should in principle be open dialogue within the institutions of the Convention.

8 With regard to the rights and obligations of the partnership, due account should be taken of the differences in levels of development between the Community and the ACP countries; the needs of the least developed, island and land-locked countries also require special consideration.

9 The Lomé Convention should be dynamic in its responses to the changing needs of ACP states, in particular the projected long-term needs of the coming decade.

10 Protectionism should not be used against the ACP states' products.[30]

Table 5.2 shows the breakdown of Lomé III funding in comparison to the prevous two EDFs. Although total financial resources had been substantially increased (by 61 per cent), they were far below the figure which the ACP were demanding. Perhaps as a reflection of the bleak investment climate in Africa and the ACP in the early 1980s, EIB loans were reduced from ECU685 million in Lomé II to ECU425 million under Lomé III, with marginal increases being registered in the sector special loans and risk capital.

Under Lomé III, aid was oriented to what was termed the "principle of concentration". This meant prioritizing one or two sectors for at least 80 per cent of the NIP funding exercise, with agriculture and rural development as the principal areas of concentration. The aim was to ensure that aid programmes were implemented through a "package of actions" which would be "internally consistent" and harmonize with the wider macroeconomic framework.

To accomplish this, "policy dialogue" or the "exchange of views" had to

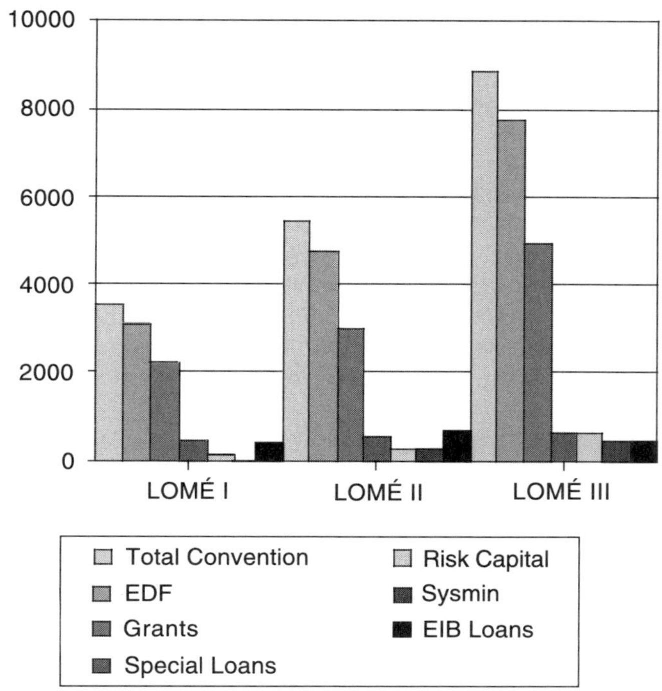

Figure 5.1 EC financial aid resources, Lomé I–III (in ECU million)
Source: EC Commission, 1989

be institutionalized as part of the aid programming process. Within the framework of such dialogue, the merit of projects would be judged not only by their internal rate of return (IRR), but also by how they related to macroeconomic performance in general. In agriculture, for example, this implied raising questions about pricing policy, incentives, and restructuring of production and marketing.

Many ACP states were opposed to this new orientation, as they considered it as giving a *carte blanche* to the EC to "interfere" with virtually all aspects of their economic and public policies.[31] The idea of sectoral concentration, however, had its own inherent shortcomings within the Lomé aid framework. As Christopher Stevens has observed, the principle was generally ill defined. "Rural development" seemed to cover everything "from projects and technical assistance aimed at increasing food security . . . to activities that would have been described in previous Conventions as infrastructure".[32]

THE EC COUNCIL RESOLUTION ON STRUCTURAL ADJUSTMENT IN AFRICA

In May 1988 the EC Council of Ministers finally adopted a resolution on structural adjustment in the SSA region.[33] This emerged in response to an earlier Commission submission which had outlined proposed Community responses to the challenge of the adjustment process in Africa. The Commission had called for a "more realistic, pragmatic, more differentiated approach" that would avoid "the stereotyped, often dogmatic and too exclusively economic and financial approach of the Washington institutions".[34] The Commission's view was that reform policies needed to take into consideration the human dimensions of adjustment and the goals of long-term development. A sense of realism, combining considerations of economic and financial efficiency with an appreciation of economic and social constraints, was seen as the best way of ensuring the viability of adjustment programmes.

The Council enunciated seven principles of an EC approach to adjustment in Africa. First, the Council accepted the Commission's diagnosis which saw the economic problems of Africa as deriving from both internal and external factors. Not only were internal structural rigidities a major constraint to African development, there were also external factors such as the debt-servicing burden, the collapse in commodity prices, and inadequate financial inflows. Given the problems and constraints which have dogged most reform programmes, the Council proposed a new strategy which would ensure their viability. It called for a "pragmatic and differentiated" approach to the implementation of reforms, taking into account the specific situation of each country, and especially in getting recipient countries involved "to the greatest extent in analysing the difficulties to be resolved and in preparing reform programmes".

The EC ministers stressed the role of the Community's own sectoral strategy and support for food security as an integral part of an effective reform programme. Apart from consideration of such issues as the environment and cultural factors, which were recommended to be integrated into the adjustment process, the greatest emphasis was laid on the question of equity and justice:

> it is important, from the stage of planning any adjustment measure, to take into account its social dimension, particularly in order to reduce any negative effects it may have on the most vulnerable sections of the population and to promote simultaneously the objectives of economic growth and social justice.[35]

The preconditions for the sustainability of reform programmes were said to lie in the pacing of the reform process and in effective financial backing through quick-disbursing import schemes such as those launched under the

Special Programme of Assistance. In support of this process, the Community declared its commitment to increased action through quick-disbursing sectoral import programmes in aid of adjusting countries. The Council urged the Commission and the member states to ensure that aid instruments such as Stabex, sectoral import programmes, and food aid were more effectively and efficiently coordinated so that adjustment support for each receiving country would be based on a coherent approach.

Although the EC underlined a coordinated strategy involving all its member states as an essential element to the success of adjustment, the United Kingdom insisted that the minutes of the Council meeting include a qualification that such coordination should be undertaken only "as far as possible".[36] This proviso could be interpreted as a political limitation in the Community's attempt to evolve a common framework on adjustment, as some member states were determined to preserve their autonomy and independence of action in that area.

In 1988 Dieter Frisch, Director-General of DGVIII, published a statement in *The Courier* which gave additional insight into the Commission's thinking on adjustment.[37] Writing with specific reference to the African experience, Frisch declared that whilst there could be no question of the EC having its own doctrine of adjustment, he maintained that orthodox models were failing due to their lack of pragmatism and failure to adopt a case-by-case approach. He argued that a viable adjustment model had to fulfil certain fundamental conditions. First, it had to evolve from the country itself, both in terms of the diagnosis of the problems and in the choice of strategies for implementation. The role of external donors would then be to support and not supplant local initiatives.

The second condition, according to Frisch, is to adapt reform strategies to the situation of each country:

> The case-by-case approach recommended in other fields takes on its full meaning in the adjustment sector if the aim is to respond to Africa's diversity of practical situations and this should lead to a relativisation of the theoretical concepts which are usually there when adjustment programmes are drawn up.[38]

Whilst concepts such as comparative advantage, protection, market allocation, flexibility of exchange rates are useful theoretical guides, he argued that the orthodox adjustment model needed to be applied with greater circumspection in the African environment. Experience with past adjustment programmes, he pointed out, had shown that estimates of key parameters such as statistical data, market imperfections, commodity price forecasts, and the extent of real imbalances were often far off the mark.

The third condition for a successful adjustment was said to be the linkage of economic reforms to long-term development needs. In other words, adjustment should be based on a convergence between the triad processes of stabilization, growth and development. Stabilization should not lead to too restrictive a monetary policy, which discourages investment, or to repeated devaluations, which can lead to inflationary spirals and impede growth. The short-term horizons of the IMF often not only negate growth, they hardly relate to the needs of long-term development. Not only should adjustment focus on development, but the goals of development should not be defined in narrow economic terms:

> all states need economic growth for their development, but at the same time they have other, vital targets of their own and they are not purely economic ones either. They want a national identity, regional cooperation, proper income distribution, food security, environmental protection and more – all of them aims which do not add up to a real GDP growth rate but which in fact define a certain kind of growth.[39]

Frisch argued for integration of the social dimension into the adjustment process. Alluding to Bank and Fund poverty-alleviation schemes such as those in Ghana, Guinea Bissau and Madagascar, he called for their integration as an inseparable component of adjustment and, indeed, as a measure of the efficiency and sustainability of all economic reform programmes.

LOMÉ IV AND STRUCTURAL ADJUSTMENT

If the Lomé III negotiations were overshadowed by pessimism, those of Lomé IV were even more bleak.[40] There was the mounting debt which, for all ACP states, was estimated at US$130 billion, of which US$102 billion was owed by SSA alone; the estimated overall ACP debt-service ratio stood at 34 per cent. As a consequence, more than half of the ACP Group were undergoing IMF and World Bank-supported economic reform programmes. Second, there was the virtual collapse of commodity prices, which, excluding oil, accounted for nearly 90 per cent of total ACP export earnings. Of particular concern for ACP countries was the pressure of competition from other LDCs, which was eroding their share of EC imports. In addition, there were the Uruguay Round of GATT negotiations and the EC Single Market Act, both of which seemed to portend negative trends for ACP trade.[41] For the EC Twelve, the renegotiation of the Lomé Convention was no longer an issue of political significance. According to Myriam Vander Stichele:

> the EC member states' own economic restructuring and changes in world markets had significantly reduced their dependence on ACP raw materials. They were far more intent on overcoming internal difficulties in completing the Single Market by 1992 and defending [their] interests at the GATT talks. Towards the end of the . . . negotiations, all eyes were on Eastern Europe. The Community was also coming under

internal and external pressure to give more assistance to other developing countries . . . [such as] Latin America.[42]

The multilateral negotiating framework

On the eve of the negotiations, therefore, the ACP states were in a far weaker bargaining position than they had ever been before, in contrast to a Community which, according to John Ravenhill, was "more self-confident than in any previous negotiations, buoyed by the prospects of the Single Market in 1992, and of other European countries lining up to seek admission thereafter".[43] Given this situation, the EC wanted as little change as possible in the text of the Convention.

As in the three preceding rounds, the Lomé IV negotiations were a series of "multi-level games".[44] Within the Commission, there were the negotiations between DGVIII on the one hand and DGI (Directorate for External Relations) and DGVI (Directorate for Agriculture) on the other. Within the EC itself, the Commission had to negotiate with member states and the EC Parliament. During Lomé IV negotiations the Parliament was enjoying an enhanced role, with additional powers under the Single Act of 1985 which gave it a right to be consulted and to veto the final agreement if it did not approve of it.[45] Multi-layered games also took place within the ACP Group, although at a less complex level than within the EC.

Within the EC, in July 1987, the Commission had set up a "think-tank" of half a dozen officials from DGVIII to determine the broad outlines of the Commission's negotiating mandate. In March 1988, the proposed guidelines were submitted to the EC Parliament and Council of Ministers, and were to be the subject of arduous negotiations amounting to about 150 man-hours of negotiations.[46] A clear North–South schism seemed to have emerged between the Twelve. Whilst the "Northern" countries, among them Britain, Germany and the Netherlands, were in favour of more trade liberalization instead of increased aid, the "Southern" Mediterranenan countries, Portugal, Greece and Spain, were opposed to increased trade concessions, preferring instead greater aid. Among the newer Mediterranenan members of the Community, Greece was particularly opposed to expansion of the Sysmin because of the fear that it would adversely affect its own bauxite mining industry. Whatever changes they envisaged were those in response to the agendas set by the IFIs and the requirements of the GATT.

The debate on adjustment was also a major source of division within the EC. The initial Commission guidelines had indicated its intention to reorient its aid policy towards adjustment, given the gravity of the problems facing the ACP countries, and the negative effects reform policies were having on number of EC projects. The Commission was especially dissatisfied with a situation whereby the EC was being reduced to playing the role of a "social fire brigade", being called upon to support social victims of adjustment programmes designed by the IFIs and over which it had no initial say. The Commission therefore proposed a new framework for EC development aid which "would enable the Community and its member states to play a more active part in consultations and dialogue with – other donors as well as the ACP countries themselves – on general macroeconomic reforms".[47] Germany, the Netherlands and Britain were firmly in favour of a new EC structural adjustment initiative, which they insisted should be clearly linked to IMF and World Bank conditionalities. However, they were against the idea of establishing a separate fund for structural adjustment support. On the opposite side were France, Italy, Ireland and Belgium, who preferred the status quo of traditional EC project aid, while insisting that the Community should distance itself from the conditionality of the IFIs.

Two former Development Commissioners, Claude Cheysson and Edgard Pisani, who had been invited to make their views known, pitched themselves firmly in the anti-conditionality camp. Pisani warned that "using the Convention as an instrument for adjustment policies" was a fundamental error in judgement, because, according to him: "Lomé would not be Lomé if it concerns itself with adjustment. Lomé is for development."[48] Perhaps this attitude reflected, in part, the feelings in some European circles, especially in France and the Latin countries, that the IFIs are dominated by the "Anglo-Saxons", and that the EC Commission should therefore evolve its own independent line to serve as a counterweight to the alleged domination.

On the ACP side, the opening position centred on their dissatisfaction with the incremental changes within Lomé. They underlined three pillars as the foundation of their future relations with the Community: First, the need to reaffirm the contractual character of the relationship; second, the validity of the special and differentiated treatment of countries according to their level of development; and third, the need to maintain and improve upon their acquired rights or *acquis*. These *acquis* were listed as:

1 a status of equality between all the partners to the Convention;
2 full recognition of, and mutual respect for the sovereignty and the political, social and cultural identity of all the contracting parties;
3 the notion of interdependence and "mutual interests" as the underlying fundamental character of their relations;
4 the security and continuity of the relationship based on a system of law and joint institutions;
5 a comprehensive or "global approach" to the partnership, incorporating a variety of instruments, a differentiated approach to the developmental needs of a variety of ACP states, based on their own priorities as sovereign states;

6 the right to innovation and improvement in the quality of the relationship without compromising the ACPs' acquired rights as partners.[49]

In the course of the negotiations the ACP expressed considerable fears about the likely consequences of the EC Single Market and the changes in Eastern Europe. These changes were leading some to question not only whether the Community might become a "fortress", but also whether resources might not be diverted to the East. Speaking for the Caribbean, Erskine Sandiford observed:

> There is the talk of a Marshall Plan for Eastern Europe . . . a frantic search for means to deal with Polish debt and assistance to the Hungarian economy. . . . In some areas, the Mediterranean countries [of North Africa] have been given more preferential terms of trade than ACP countries.[50]

The ACP position on structural adjustment

The ACP demands with regard to adjustment consisted of six principles:[51]

1 The ACP states were calling for more support for balance of payments aid as a means of cushioning some of the constraints posed by adjustment.
2 There was a need to adopt a Lomé approach to adjustment, as opposed to simply following the neo-liberal orthodoxy.
3 In evolving a Lomé approach, a realistic account should be taken of the domestic needs of ACP states and the constraints of the international environment.
4 The resources of a future adjustment fund should derive from supplementary EC financial resources and not from normal EDF resources.
5 Financial commitment to structural adjustment should not lead to a diversion of resources away from long-term development, and should safeguard their "acquired rights", while respecting the sovereignty and independence of ACP states.[52]
6 Whilst pointing out that coordination between the EC and the Bretton Woods institutions was unavoidable, such coordination should not involve "undue conditionalities" and should give attention to the "human and social dimensions of adjustment".[53]

The ACP Group were critical of the EC's proposed criteria of eligibility, especially terms such as "significant adjustment measures", "sustainability" and "transparency", which could politicize adjustment support and discriminate against countries that were implementing their own independent programmes. In addition, they were anxious about its implications for their autonomy. They pointed out that such preconditions could lead to "interference in decision-making," with the real possibility that they could be used to exert pressure on ACP countries to fall in line with World Bank/ IMF conditionalities.[54]

An alternative set of criteria was proposed by the ACP to guide adjustment support under Lomé:

- Adjustment programmes should be launched at the express request of the ACP states.
- Adjustment support should take into account the "socio-political dimension of development".
- External support should be determined by the "magnitude of the socio-economic problems of the ACP state assessed on the basis of macro-economic performance indicators".[55]

The ACP argued that their own experience with reform programmes had led them to the conclusion that financial resources, rather than conditionalities, were the determining factor in the success or otherwise of adjustment. Echoing the OAU Alternative to Adjustment (AAF–SAP), they observed that adjustment should go beyond short- or medium-term policies, and should focus on "structural transformation", with its objectives of "diversification, reduction of unemployment, increasing per capita income, and attaining greater self-reliance".[56] Underlying the ACP position could be said to be the desire to secure financial support while protecting their autonomy in domestic decision-making.

Continuity and change in the Lomé IV provisions

The question of the volume of financial assistance was not raised until towards the end of the negotiations. Whilst the ACP states were asking for ECU15.5 billion, the Commission recommended the sum of ECU12.8 billion. By the 26 November, when up to a third of EC Development Ministers met in Brussels to discuss the concluding phase of the negotiations, they finally agreed on the sum of ECU10.8 billion (Table 5:3).[57] Although the broad framework of Lomé remained unchanged, a number of modifications were made to the trade and financial aspects. With regard to trade, access to EC markets in products such as strawberries and dried fruits have been increased, while Stabex has been extended to cover commodity earnings of countries that trade heavily with non-Community countries. Lomé IV is characterized by elements of both continuity and innovation. The broad framework of cooperation and the fundamental objectives of EC–ACP relations have remained unchanged. The new Convention reaffirms the principles of mutual interests, non-interference, reciprocal respect for sovereignty of all partners, and dialogue, security, predictability of aid and trade advantages. Indeed, the ten-year duration of the new Convention, albeit with a five-year renewable financial protocol,

Table 5.3 Financial resources under Lomé IV

Sector	*(Million ECU)*	%
Grant	6,845*	63.38
Risk capital	825	7.64
Stabex	1,500	13.89
Sysmin	480	4.89
Structural adjustment	1,150	10.65
Soft loans	—	—
TOTAL EDF	10,800	100
EIB	1,200	
TOTAL RESOURCES	12,000	

Note: * Part of it can be used for structural adjustment support
Source: EC Commission, January 1990

is a guarantee that Lomé will endure, in form if not in spirit, until the end of the millennium.

Membership of the ACP Group has expanded from 66 to 69, with the accession of Haiti, the Dominican Republic and the newly independent Republic of Namibia. Financial allocation to the new Convention for the first five years is to stand at ECU12 billion, of which ECU10.8 billion will consist of EDF resources (a nominal increase of 46 per cent and in real terms, 25 per cent), while ECU1.2 billion will consist of EIB resources.[58] Whilst this financial commitment is inadequate in comparison to the needs of ACP states, its increase in percentage terms cannot be said to be negligible. The most important innovations include chapters on the environment, regional food security and the role of women in rural development, the development of services, industrial development (broadening the role of the CDI), nutrition, population and demography. Although the EC has resisted any major action on EC debt, Lomé IV has included a section on debt (Articles 240-242), which essentially relates to assistance for debt management and debt negotiation in "appropriate" multilateral fora.[59] The most crucially important innovation is on structural adjustment support. Under Lomé IV, some ECU1,115 million has been set aside for structural adjustment support. ACP countries can also request that some of their NIP funds be transferred adjustment support, a process which is expected to raise the total of funds for adjustment to ECU1,500 million.

Adjustment and EU Aid Management

After the ratification of the Fourth Lomé Convention, Community action in the area of structural adjustment began with a series of internal reorganizations and actions within DGVIII itself. The first task was centred on information-gathering and consciousness-raising. A series of workshops and intensive seminars was held in Brussels to familiarize DGVIII and

EC Delegation officials with structural adjustment policies. This training scheme aimed at getting all relevant officials within the Commission bureaucracy to understand and follow the new economic and political objectives set by the EC. The focus was on the following areas:

- general guidelines;
- procedures for implementation of import programmes;
- arrangements for the constitution and utilization of counterpart funds;
- model for financing proposals;
- early-warning system for monitoring reform programmes in each country.[60]

The administrative reorganization of DGVIII has taken the form of the creation of a new Unit for Structural Adjustment Support. Under the direct responsibility of the Director-General for Development, the Unit has as its main functions the programming and coordination of Structual Adjustment Programmes both within the EC Commission and in monitoring these programmes and liaising with other international aid agencies.

Following the experience of the multi-donor SPA, the EC approach to adjustment support consists largely of sectoral import and general import programmes. For countries that have embarked upon a macroeconomic adjustment programme, the EC uses General Import Programmes (GIPs) as the main form of support; whereas for countries where reform measures are deemed not to have progressed to the stage where price, exchange rate and credit allocation mechanisms are properly adjusted, Sectoral Import Programmes (SIPs) are the preferred alternative. In the first quarter of 1991, Commissioner Marin of DGVIII prepared a communication to both the Commission and Council on EC official guidelines on structural adjustment.[61] The report sought to address the root causes of the economic difficulties facing ACP states in the 1980s. It underlined both external causes – such as commodity prices – and internal domestic structures as the principal factors responsible for the development crisis. Unlike the traditional position of the IFIs, which view the economic difficulties of the 1980s as predominantly determined by domestic policy failures, the EC seemed to adopt a more balanced view in locating the problems in terms of both domestic and international conditions.

However, the Commission shared the view of the IFIs that adjustment programmes are an "absolute necessity" to overhaul the structural disequilibria in LDC economies: "The choice for them is no longer between adjustment and the status quo but between a managed, orderly adjustment and forced adjustment."[62] The EC has outlined six principles which will guide its structural adjustment operations:[63]

1 consistency of the measures with long-term development;
2 the social dimensions of adjustment;

3 a realistic pace of implementation;
4 tailored to the needs of individual countries;
5 adjustment programmes should be internally generated;
6 the regional dimension.

The first concern about the integration of adjustment with "development" derives from the consideration that "the baby should not be thrown away with the bathwater". IMF and World Bank reform programmes have often been criticized for their failure to take into account the needs of long-term development. According to the EC perspective, long-term development puts a major premium, first and foremost, on food security, followed closely by development of human resources, regional integration and environmental development. Stabilization and adjustment measures must be seen to advance these long-term objectives, and not to negate them. The "social dimension of adjustment" is aimed at filling the hiatus between adjustment on the one hand, and growth and equity on the other.

The regional aspect derives from the perceived historical vocation of the EC itself. More than perhaps any other aid-giving agency, it has often awarded special importance to regional cooperation. The Commission seeks to have a regional dimension to adjustment so that a reform programme in one country, such as in relation to domestic prices and exchange rates, does not result in disruption to regional economies. The unilateral liberalization of imports, for example, might have quite a different impact from the liberalization of trade on a regional and reciprocal basis. Similarly, sharp changes in domestic prices and exchange rates may have negative repercussions on regional economies.[64] This is clearly an important difference from orthodox strategies which give very little attention to regional aspects of economic reform programmes.[65]

The question of countervalue funds

Another important element in the EC adjustment policy is the large amounts of counterpart or countervalue funds (CVFs) which will inevitably accompany import programmes. In line with its normal practice under Lomé III, the Commission has decided that such funds would be included in the ACP countries' budget planning. Under this arrangement the Commission will participate in the planning and regular reviews of public expenditure in recipient countries.[66] Counterpart funds will therefore no longer be a one-off operation but will constitute part of the regular aid intervention to improve recipients' monetary and financial balances. The EC has earmarked the social sector, especially health and education, for the use of counterpart funds in support of the social dimensions of adjustment. Other related areas which may benefit from counterpart funds include the environment, redundancy payments, project financing, and repayment of domestic debts to commercial banks.

Emphasis on the use of CVFs entails considerable influence by the Commission over public expenditure and the budgetary process in the ACP states. The Commission declares that: "In the years ahead, control of the budgetary process will be central to the Community's approach and the Commission's involvement in the adjustment process."[67] The EC seeks to take charge of the budgeting process because it believes that it is in public expenditure and public investment that development policy choices will have to be made. The Commission presumably wishes to influence public spending in order to ensure effectiveness as well as, in its words, "integrity, efficacy and equity". The Commission acknowledges that this kind of involvement may be politically sensitive, but is nevertheless regarded as unavoidable in ensuring effectiveness of its aid programmes. Particular importance is attached to coordination with other donors in review of public expenditures, in light of past apparently successful joint World Bank–EC reviews of public spending in Mauritania, Mali, Burkina Faso, Papua New Guinea and Madagascar.[68]

Eligibility for adjustment financing

According to Article 244 of Lomé IV, any country that is undertaking a Fund or Bank-supported adjustment programme shall be deemed as "automatically" qualifying for EC adjustment support. The first criterion of eligibility is therefore a situation whereby a country is already receiving financial or other form of support from the main multilateral donors. The second criterion is less clear-cut. It refers to the eligibility of countries that are carrying out "autonomous" adjustment programmes, subject to the proviso that the EC and the country in question have reached a common understanding based on a "joint assessment". Inevitably, the determination of the viability of a "home-grown" programme would lie largely with the Community, not the receiving country.

Under the first criterion, the EC extended adjustment funding to thirty-one countries which were already implementing orthodox reform programmes. So far, no country that is implementing an autonomous reform programme has been a beneficiary of the Lomé Structural Adjustment Facility. The reasons for this may be either because the Commission lacks the technical personnel to evaluate such programmes in order to determine their level of support, or because it inherently shies away from countries that have decided on independent programmes of their own. Even though the Commission insists that nothing prevents it from carrying out initial assessment of reform programmes in such countries or in helping others to introduce their own programmes, it seems evident that the bulk of the funds will go mainly to countries who are implementing orthodox reforms.[69]

Coordinating with the Washington institutions

The 1988 EC Council resolution had stressed the need for coordination between the EC and the Bretton Woods institutions both at the operational level as well as "upstream" in order to ensure political convergence on questions of fundamental strategy as well as conceptualization of reform programmes. Coordination between agencies is acknowledged to be essential for the success of policy-based lending. As Stevens and Killick have explained:

> With traditional project aid a lack of co-ordination may be wasteful but it need not vitiate the efforts of donors; with policy-based lending this degree of tolerance disappears. A recipient government can only follow one set of recommendations for a given policy variable; if those providing advice do not proffer the same prescriptions, it will be forced to reject some of them.[70]

The Commission describes its relations with the World Bank as "exemplary". When Commissioner Marin visited Washington in 1990 he agreed on a "code of conduct" between the Community and the IFIs, setting out the EC approach and working out a framework for avoiding any conflict or resolving it whenever it was surfacing. They also agreed on future joint missions, regular contacts between key officials, and exchanges of relevant information on preparation and implementation of adjustment programmes.[71]

The Commission obviously considers coordination to be vital to the success of reform efforts. However, it intends to do so without losing its own independence of judgement. The Commission has maintained that it would not "subordinate its . . . financing operations to decisions in which it has not played an active part".[72] This is perhaps one of the major contradictions in the EC approach to structural adjustment. On the one hand, the EC position does not pretend to represent an alternative to Bank and Fund strategies, since, according to the Commission, "there can be only one reform per country"; on the other hand, the Commission insists its approach is "different" or "unique".

In February 1990, barely two months after the signing of Lomé IV, Commissioner Marin made an official visit to Washington, where he met with Michel Camdessus, Managing Director of the Fund, Mohammed Qureishi, a Vice-President of the World Bank, and with Edward Jaycox, the Bank's Vice-President for Africa.[73] This visit was intended as a first operational contact with the Bretton Woods institutions to acquaint them with the Community's new orientation towards structural adjustment and to discuss possibilities of joint efforts and coordination with regard to adjustment support.

The ACP have tended to view EC coordination with the IFIs as leading to subservience to those institutions by the Community. On this question, Marin's response was to reaffirm that the Community's approach is "to stand alongside you [the ACP states] and make sure that this programme – the contents of which you will have negotiated with the World Bank and the IMF – really does include the essential things laid down in the Convention".[74] He maintained that coordination was necessary to ensure coherence of reform programmes. He was at pains to distance the Commission from the IFIs: "We want neither to align ourselves with these institutions nor to subject our financing to decisions in which we have not been involved."[75]

It seems evident that whilst the EC seeks to express its own distinctive accent on adjustment, it does not seek to present an alternative to the orthodox IMF/World Bank approach. If anything, it seeks to act as intermediary in helping adjusting countries faithfully to implement orthodox reform programmes. The EC thus defines its role in terms of helping countries "that so wish to implement a programme that in time will receive backing from all donors, while at the same time ensuring that the essential aspects of the Lomé approach are retained. The Commission's role would thus be one of facilitator or intermediary".[76]

Table 5.4 shows the structure of World Bank conditionality which accompanies structural adjustment and sectoral loans in LDCs.[77] While agricultural, public enterprise, exchange rate, public expenditure and industrial policies have had a higher level of conditionality requirements than in other LDCs, the latter have had higher conditional levels in areas such as financial and fiscal reforms, trade and energy policies.

Table 5.4 The structure of World Bank conditionality

	% of conditions	
Item	*Africa*	*All LDCs*
1 Exchange rate	4.2	1.9
2 Trade policies	25.0	28.1
3 Fiscal policy	8.3	11.4
4 Budget/public expenditures	11.8	9.9
5 Public enterprises	19.4	15.5
6 Financial sector	3.5	10.9
7 Industrial policy	6.9	3.3
8 Energy policy	1.4	6.0
9 Agricultural policy	17.4	11.3
10 Other	—	—
TOTAL	100.0	100.0

Source: The World Bank, 1988

In practical terms, there is no evidence to sustain the view that the EC pursues a clear alternative to the orthodox adjustment model. The ambivalence and contradiction in the EC perspective is a factor of the Community's internal incoherence, with conflicts between Commission, Parliament and Council on the one hand, and between various member states on the other. Conflicts are also known to occur even within the various divisions of the Commission itself. Within the EDF Committee, for example, Germany, the Netherlands and Britain are known to favour a closer alignment of EC adjustment support with the programmes of the Bretton Woods institutions, whereas the Southern countries generally do not.

Macroeconomic reform and aid programming

Adjustment has led to changes in the aid programming process and in the "development" role which the Commission has traditionally pursued. EC development policy has gone beyond the judicious, technocratic negotiations which have characterized Lomé national indicative programming in the past. DGVIII officials have played activist roles on key adjustment issues in a number of countries. Examples include public expenditure review in Mauritania, a reform programme for the cereals sector in Kenya, and in negotiations with striking public sector workers in Togo.[78] In both Burkina Faso and Zambia, the EC has been a central actor in implementing social programmes, while in Benin it has been a key player in creating a link between democratization and budgetary support.

The programming process under Lomé III, with its focus on sectoral aid, has formed the basis for EC intervention under Lomé IV. The new Convention builds on this previous model to include macroeconomic aspects, particularly debts, public expenditure and financial management, and the social dimensions of adjustment. According to Michael Laidler, a senior DGVIII official, the Commission's approach to adjustment programming is to ensure that reform programmes are part of an "integrated" approach, which relates short-term requirements to long-term needs. According to him, adjustment programming is based on the following assumptions. Structural reform is viewed not as "an add-on, or a separate development tool"; rather, it is to be seen as an "essential part of the development process, designed to remove short- and medium-term barriers to growth".[79] A major difficulty from the Commission's viewpoint is its limited manpower resources.[80] The administrative reorganization of DGVIII led to the establishment of a Structural Adjustment Unit and a small pool of structural adjustment specialists. However, the additional workload seems overwhelmingly greater than the available expertise within the Commission is able to cope with.

In June 1990, in accordance with Article 281 of the Fourth Convention, the EC Commission gave notice to thirty-five ACP states, most of them

Table 5.5 Adjustment resources under Lomé IV, 1991–93 (ECU million)

Resource	*Amount*
Specific resources under the Convention	1,150
Share earmarked in indicative programmes (estimate)	850
TOTAL (estimate)	2,000
Amount of 1st allocation (from specific resources)	415
Balance specific resources	735

Source: Commission of the European Communities, 1991

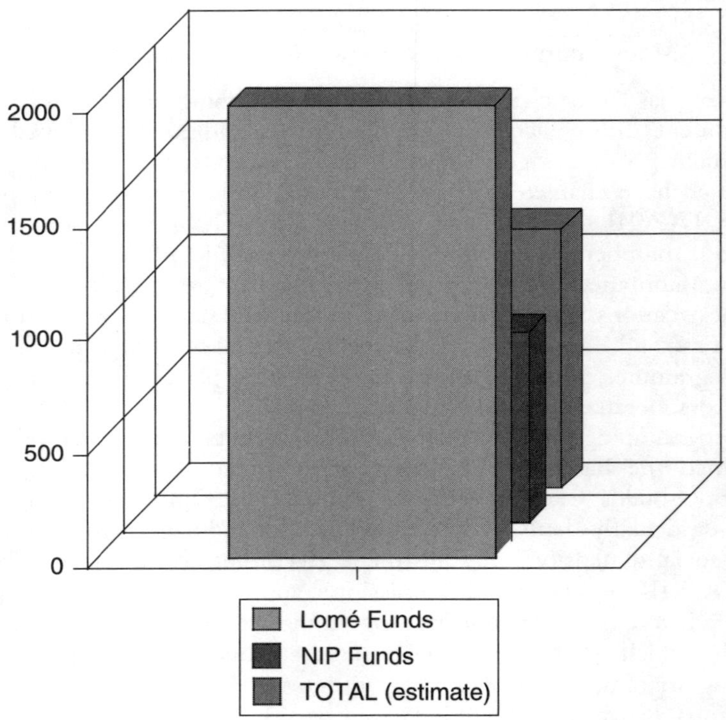

Figure 5.2 Structural Adjustment Funds under Lomé IV (in ECU million)
Source: EC Commission, 1991

from SSA, which were deemed eligible to receive structural adjustment support. Although financial allocation for adjustment support under Lomé IV amounts to ECU1.150 billion, additional resources from indicative programmes are expected to raise this figure to ECU2 billion, of which 415 million is to be committed to adjustment support during 1991–93 (see Table 5.5). By the end of 1991, eight countries (Benin, Burkina Faso,

Gambia, Ghana, Guyana, Mali, Papua New Guinea and Uganda), six of them from SSA, received a total of ECU150 million in support of economic reform programmes.

During the Sixteenth meeting of the EC–ACP Council of Ministers, the Lomé approach to adjustment and the Lomé IV programming process were the main focus of attention. Commissioner Marin sought to clarify what he regarded as a "misunderstanding" about structural adjustment, especially on the questions of eligibility, the Community's relations with the Washington institutions, and the Twelve's contribution to the SPA for Africa.[81] Mr Marin defended the EC's support for the thirty-five ACP countries considered eligible for structural adjustment financing. He argued that the consideration of eligibility for other countries pursuing "autonomous" reform programmes would depend on joint assessment to ensure that the criteria for support, as laid down in the Convention, were being followed. What clearly worried the ACP Ministers was the fact that thirty-five beneficiaries of the EC adjustment support scheme were made up only of countries who were implementing orthodox IMF and World Bank reform programmes. The solemn declaration that the EC would exercise its independence of judgement with regard to countries that were implementing their own programmes was clearly not being followed in practice.

The EC approach to macroeconomic conditionality

In September 1988 Germany, Britain and the Netherlands blocked an ECU24.5 million Sectoral Import Programme (SIP) for Tanzania on the grounds that the country had failed to reach an agreement with the IMF on the devaluation of its currency. As it turned out, the disagreement was supposedly derived from a misunderstanding over technical issues, which was in the process of being resolved. The EC Commission was later to approach the Fund to confirm that this was indeed the case. Upon confirming the situation, Germany withdrew its opposition to the SIP, thereby forcing both Britain and the Netherlands to give up their opposition, as they no longer had sufficient votes successfully to oppose the programme.[82] In November 1988 the funds for Tanzania were unblocked. The significance of this case shows the possibilities of implicit conditionality which underlies Lomé aid in general, even before Lomé IV was agreed upon. According to Parfitt and Bullock:

> EC member states' blocking power is not restricted to the funding designated to SAPs. On the programming Committee, while having no formal power of veto, member states are able to influence the design of national indicative programmes . . . on the EDF Committee, an alliance of as few as three member states can be sufficient to block the financing of a project. This could well prove to be a mechanism for covertly introducing conditionality for all Lomé aid through the backdoor.[83]

Two factors which the EC sees as predefining its approach to conditionality is that (a) a reform programme being implemented in a given country *must be that country's own*; and (b) the Commission has to operate within a framework of contractual obligations which *assumes an independence of judgement on the progress of adjustment.* Explicit conditionality under Lomé IV is understood to be applicable only to the fund for adjustment support. Even then the word "conditionality" has been avoided in preference to "joint assessment" between the Community and the ACP states.[84] Such joint assessment is expected to apply to EC import programmes to ensure that they directly support the economic reform process.

As far as the Commission is concerned, its approach to conditionality has to reconcile these two aspects whilst avoiding what it terms the "stop/go syndrome" of the Bretton Woods institutions, in which "a country becomes ineligible when it runs into problems with them, then re-eligible when an agreement is reached, then ineligible again when new problems arise, and so on".[85] The EC is committed to three levels of conditions which will guide it in assessing the progress towards the implementation of adjustment programmes:

1 an assessment of "general, qualitative conditions", including measurement of economic indices such as exchange rates and interest rates, budgetary equilibrium, the balance of payments, and public expenditure to ensure that they are at a "satisfactory" level;
2 assessment of specific conditions, particularly sectoral conditions linked to utilization of counterpart funds;
3 transparency in the administrative and financial procedures, especially those relating to the constitution and use of counterpart funds, and acceptable standards of documenting import invoices, bank statements and public expenditure accounts.[86]

Another distinguishing feature in the EC approach is the inclusion of NGOs and socioeconomic organizations from the wider civil society in the debate on adjustment. A certain populist element has always informed the rhetoric of aid and cooperation within Lomé. Lomé IV states that social, economic and cultural organizations would be encouraged to put forward and implement initiatives that would advance the development of ACP states. The concept of "decentralized cooperation" is often used in this context as a means of democratising decision-making and mobilizing all the relevant segments of civil society for development.[87]

From adjustment to "Governance" and political conditionality

As we have previously indicated, the 1989 World Bank report, with its theme of "adjustment with growth" and "good governance", was widely hailed as signalling a progressive "learning curve" by the IFIs.[88] For the first time the Washington institutions were openly acknowledging the need to go beyond stabilization in order to achieve "a genuine transformation of productive structures".[89] This report has virtually set the agenda for international donors who have all tended to chorus the tune of "good governance" and its accompanying elements of institutional development and capacity building.[90] Internal pressures by popular groups demanding civic participation could no longer be ignored.[91]

The new discourse on "democratic adjustment" has not escaped the EC's Lomé diplomacy. The notion of "decentralized development" (under Articles 20–22 of Lomé IV) allows private groups such as NGOs, trade unions and cooperatives to approach EC Delegations in ACP states for direct support for their development efforts. The programming process for Lomé IV has evidently placed human rights and democratization at the forefront of the agenda. According to a senior DGVIII official, "Lomé is the expression of a political attitude, and we cannot pretend that politics do not have a role to play in its implementation".[92] In March 1991 the EC Commission submitted a communication to the Council and the European Parliament on the question of human rights in the context of development cooperation.[93] During the Lomé II negotiations the EC's proposal to include a human rights clause in the new Convention was met with decisive opposition from the ACP Group, which felt it would give the EC undue right to interfere in matters which they regarded as being strictly within their own domestic jurisdiction. They were eventually to adopt a linkage approach to the question, bringing up the issue of the Republic of South Africa, and the EC's failure to condemn human rights abuses there.[94]

The fourth Convention has included a clause on "human dignity", which asserts that development shall be centred on man and on the promotion of human rights:

> Hence the parties reiterate their deep attachment to human dignity and human rights, which are legitimate aspirations of individuals and peoples . . . non-discriminatory treatment; fundamental human rights; civil and political rights; economic, social and cultural rights.[95]

This provides as broad a definition of human rights as it is possible to have in the framework of a multilateral cooperation regime such as Lomé.[96] The Commission defines its own approach as "positive" in terms of assisting countries to evolve institutions and practices that lead to pluralism, democracy and "good governance", as opposed to the approach that attempts to "impose democracy" from outside. In other words, the EC does not intend to impose political conditionalities in its aid programme; rather, it would give support to groups or institutions that promote those political ideals.

The Commission's official policy, which was submitted as part of its political union recommendations, proposes two aims for development cooperation. First, cooperation is to promote economic and social development and the fulfilment of basic human needs; second, it should aim to "ensure development and consolidation of democracy and human rights and the rule of law, and respect for human rights".[97] Marin goes on to explain that this grows out of the Commission's belief in the inseparability of "democracy and human rights on the one hand, and the right to development, on the other".

Within the framework of the EC–ACP Joint Assembly, resolutions have been sponsored condemning human rights violations in ACP countries, notably in Malawi, Sudan, Zaire and Chad.[98] According to Giovanni Bersani, human rights have now become "one of the most meaningful subjects dealt with in the recent history of the Assembly".[99]

CONCLUSION

The transformation of EC–African economic diplomacy in the 1980s was largely in response to the economic and social predicaments which Africa has undergone since the last decade. The nature of the response has been determined both by the extent of the difficulties and Europe's own changing economic and political interests and priorities. With the new agenda of conditionality and adjustment, the relations of formal equality have been replaced by a more paternalist form of relations. Africa and the ACP Group have sought to safeguard their political autonomy while securing financial and aid resources which will assist them in rebuilding their economies. Their inability to do so reflects the limits of their collective power. The ACP were successful in blocking the inclusion of the phrase "policy dialogue" in the Lomé III document; but it was an unreal victory, as the actual conduct of EC development policy and its sectoral strategy was already shifting in subtle but effective ways, to the policy dialogue approach.

The advent of Lomé IV marks the EC's explicit commitment to the goal of adjustment, with a set of conditions which have to be fulfilled by implementing countries. The guidelines set out are sufficiently broad to give the EC a wide margin of interpretation. The EC approach is indistinguishable from that of the IFIs in stressing macroeconomic changes in such areas as exchange rates, trade liberalization and public subsidies. The main differences are in the rhetoric on the "human dimensions" of adjustment, consideration of equity issues, and popular participation in the development process. The emphasis on import support and the accompanying build-up of countervalue funds gives the EC increased influence on the budgetary process in ACP countries. The recent emergence of political conditionality derives from the growing realization that political reform is a necessary corollary to economic reform. The EC, as we have seen, was historically in advance of the IFIs in its concern with human rights in the context of economic development.

6

EUROPE AND THE AFRICAN EXTERNAL DEBT BURDEN

In the last chapter we considered the evolution of European development policy in the 1980s. We saw how the questions of policy dialogue and adjustment emerged as the new dominant issues in Lomé aid diplomacy. This chapter extends the discussion to the problem of Africa's external indebtedness. Indeed, it can be argued that the changed international aid regime was in direct response to the global debt crisis of the 1980s. We shall examine, first, the international context of the African debt problem, its origins and structure, and the political responses by international creditors; second, we shall consider the responses by the European Community in the context of Lomé diplomacy.

THE AFRICAN DEBT IN INTERNATIONAL PERSPECTIVE

The global "debt crisis" no longer excites the imagination of economists and development experts. Whilst it has by no means disappeared, it is no longer considered the threat it once was to the stability of the global financial system.[1] The total volume of LDC debt currently exceeds US$1,000 billion, the greater part of which is owed by the countries of Latin America and some of the Asian NICs.[2] The debt crisis, however, did not emerge until the summer of 1982, when Mexico announced that it was no longer in a position to service its debts. What was at stake in this threat of default was not only the future of some large Western commercial banks but indeed the stability of the international financial system itself. The IMF and the American Federal Reserve had to mobilize hastily a financial aid package in support of Mexico as well as rescheduling the country's debts in order to stem the tide of imminent disaster. In the years following the Mexican crisis, the global debt problem gained considerable salience as a major issue in North–South diplomacy.

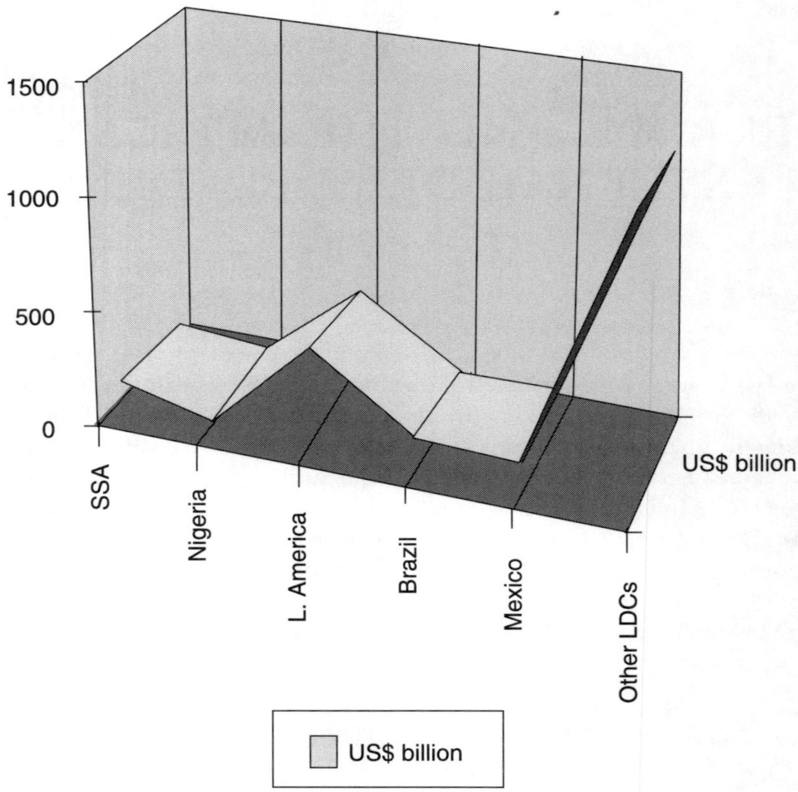

Figure 6.1 SSA external debt in comparison with other LDCs, 1988 (in US$ billion)
Source: The World Bank, Washington, DC,1989

It was the Cambridge economist Joan Robinson who once declared – perhaps echoing Marx – that the problems of underdeveloped countries do not derive from the misfortunes of capitalist exploitation but from the fact that they were not exploited enough. Such an ironical statement may be a fitting way of describing the problem of African indebtedness. The low salience given to it in North–South debt negotiations is primarily due to its comparatively small size.[3] The World Bank estimates that Africa's external debts at the end of 1989 were about US$147 billion, which amounted to only 12 per cent of total developing countries' debts.[4] This contrasts with the figure of US$422 billion for Latin America and US$288 billion for Asia during the same period. The total debts of SSA countries hardly surpass those of the largest Latin American debtors such as Brazil, Mexico and Venezuela. In contrast with the bigger debtors, the size of the African debt reduces the leverage which African states could wield *vis-à-vis* external

Table 6.1 External debts of sub-Saharan Africa, 1970–87 (in US$ billion)

	1970	*1975*	*1980*	*1985*	*1986*	*1987*
Total external debt (+ IMF)	6.0	15.8	97.2	97.2	112.7	126.5
Excluding IMF	5.8	14.7	45.1	80.8	98.9	113.3
Publicly guaranteed	5.4	13.8	41.8	74.7	92.3	106.4
To private creditors	1.6	4.4	15.0	20.8	23.2	25.1
IMF	—	0.5	2.8	6.9	6.4	5.9

Source: IMF, *World Economic Outlook*, 1988

creditors. Volume alone, however, does not tell us the whole story about Africa's "debt burden". Account has to be taken of the nature of the debt itself and of the country's debt-servicing capacity, which can be measured against the volume of exports.

According to Table 6.1 and Figure 6.2, African external debts grew from

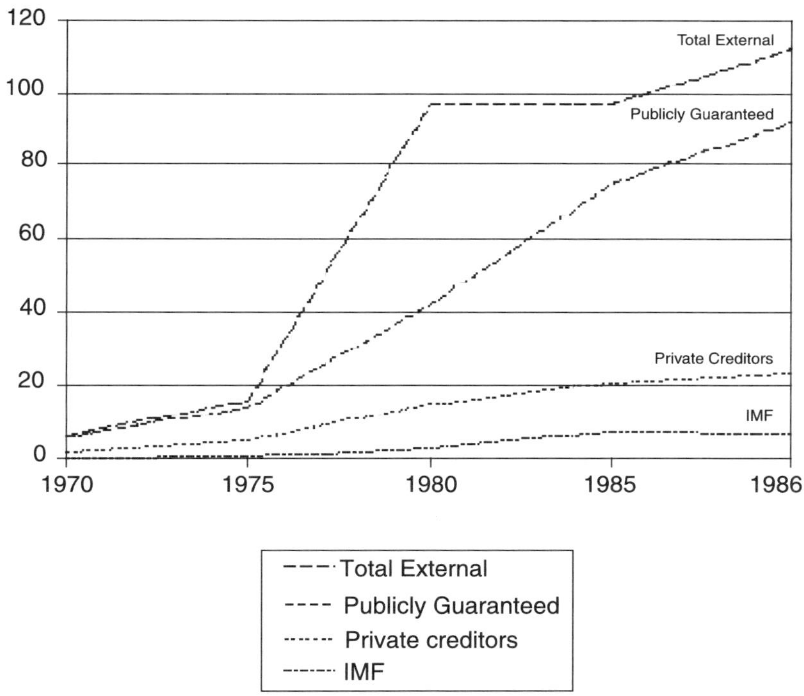

Figure 6.2a External debts of sub-Saharan Africa, 1970–87 (in US$ billion)
Source: International Monetary Fund, 1988

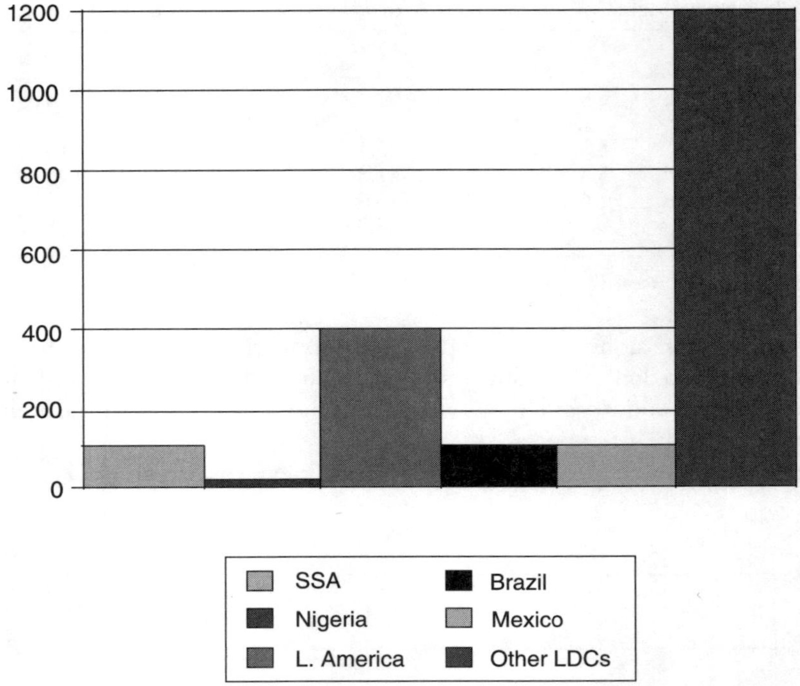

Figure 6.2b SSA debts in relation to total LDC debts (in US$ billion)
Source: World Bank, 1988

US$6 billion in 1970 to US$126.5 billion in 1987, an increase of more than 650 per cent. SSA debts are overwhelmingly long term, public or public guaranteed. In 1987, commercial or private debts were only about US$25 billion dollars or 15 per cent of total debts. Loans from the IMF were not recorded in 1970. By 1980, however, they rose steadily from US$2.8 billion to US$5.9 billion in 1987.

Table 6.2 provides a comparative overview of SSA debt in relation to total developing countries' debt at the end of 1986. The figures show that SSA debts[5] were only 8.6 per cent of the LDC total of US$1,192 billion. Within this period the debts of Brazil and Mexico were 9.3 and 8.5 per cent of the world total respectively. Total SSA debts virtually equalled its gross national product while for Latin America, they amounted to only 59 per cent.

World Bank estimates put the total debt of the subregion at US$147 billion in 1989, of which US$125 billion (90 per cent) was incurred from official

Table 6.2 Sub-Saharan Africa's external debt as a share of total developing country debt at the end of 1986 (in US$ billion)

Region	*Amount*	*% share*
Sub-Saharan Africa	102	8.6
of which:		
IDA-eligible countries	57	4.8
Other countries	45	3.8
of which:		
Nigeria	22	1.8
Latin America	399	33.5
of which:		
Brazil	111	9.3
Mexico	102	8.5
Other LDCs	838	91.4

Source: World Bank, *World Bank World Debt Tables*, 1987–88

creditors.[6] The most heavily indebted countries were Nigeria (US$32.8 billion), Côte d'Ivoire (US$15.4 billion), and Sudan (US$12.9 billion).

The ratio of export earnings to debt repayment obligations has been particularly high in the case of countries such as Mozambique and Madagascar, which stood at 246 per cent and 118 per cent respectively.[7] The average for the entire subregion is slightly over 40 per cent, which is still a heavy burden compared to the Latin American countries which have a significant manufacturing exports sector.

Table 6.3 and Figure 6.3 show trends in the SSA debt between 1982 and 1990, including accumulation in interest arrears, which were US$830

Table 6.3 Growth of the sub-Saharan African debt burden, 1982–90 (in US$ billion)

	1982	*1986*	*1990(E)*
Total debt disbursed and outstanding (DOD)	71.69	116.72	159.69
of which: Official bilateral	20.35	41.40	64.59
Official multilateral	15.46	28.51	42.88
Private long-term guaranteed (LTG)	22.26	27.51	29.61
Private LT unguaranteed (LTU)	3.89	5.36	7.31
Private short-term (STD)	9.73	13.94	15.30
Total private DOD	36.72	45.50	54.83
Interest arrears due	0.83	2.76	72.48

Source: Percy S. Mistry, *African Debt Revisited*, Amsterdam: *AWEPAA*, 1991, p. 18
Note: (E) = estimated figures

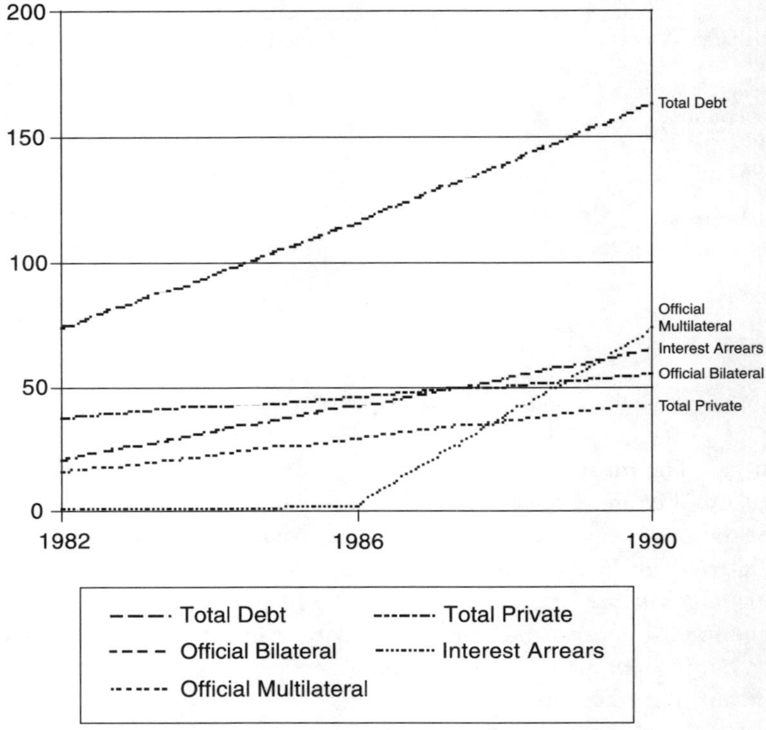

Figure 6.3 Growth of SSA debt burden, 1982–90 (in US$ billion)
Source: Percy S. Mistry, *African Debt Revisited*, The Hague: AWEPAA, 1991

million in 1982, rising to US$2.76 billion in 1986 and US$7.99 billion in 1990. Table 6.4 illustrates the extent of debt-servicing problems of SSA countries in 1989. Whilst 86 per cent of multilateral debts were paid up, including nearly a half of all official obligations, most countries were in arrears with respect to private and bilateral debts, in which only 29 and 21 per cent respectively were paid up. The debt burden in Africa is even more onerous given the prevailing situation of general economic stagnation, deteriorating terms of trade, famine, and the virtual collapse of public institutions in many countries of the subregion. The complexity of the debt problem is best seen against the background of falling exports and dwindling GNP (Table 6.5). In 1982 the SSA debt was only 38.63 per cent of GNP. By 1990, however, it had exceeded GNP, to reach a figure of

Table 6.4 Scheduled and actual debt service payments of sub-Saharan Africa, 1989 (in US$ million)

Payment	*Amount due*	*Actual paid*	*Paid as % of amount due*
1 Official	10,203	4,869	48
of which:			
Multilateral	4,206	3,604	86
Bilateral	5,997	1,265	21
2 Private	7,994	2,405	29
TOTAL (1 + 2)	18,197	7,174	39

Source: *World Bank, World Debt Tables*, 1990-91

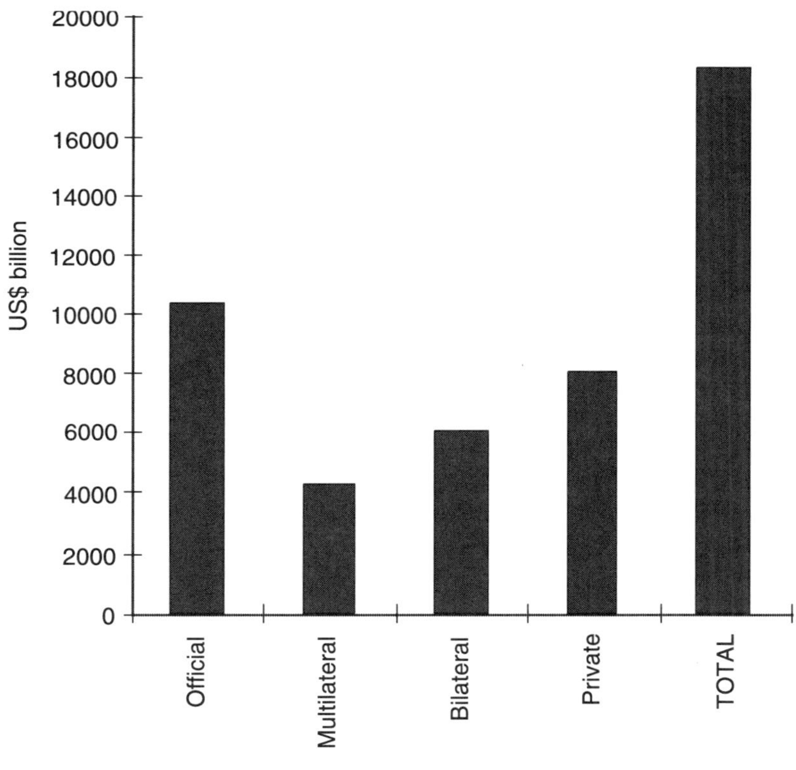

Figure 6.4 SSA debt service payments in 1989 (in US$ billion)
Source: *World Debt Tables, 1990–91*, Washington, DC: World Bank, 1991

Table 6.5 SSA debt burden relative to GNP and export capacity, 1991 (in US$ billion)

	1982	*1986*	*1990*
Total outstanding debt	72.48	115.40	162.87
Total GNP	187.94	154.25	147.65
Total exports	38.63	35.13	47.20
Debt/GNP ratio	38.57%	74.81%	110.31%
Debt/exports ratio	187.62%	328.49%	345.06%

Source: Mistry, *African Debt Revisited*, 1991, p. 21

110.31 per cent. The debt-exports ratio, at 187.62 per cent in 1982, had almost doubled to 345.06 per cent in 1990.

Another important characteristic of SSA debt is that, unlike Latin America and the Asian NICs, much of it is public rather than commercial, deriving mostly from bilateral loans, export credits and multilateral loans. In 1987, for example, claims by American commercial banks against the SSA region amounted to no more than US$1.53 billion (Table 6.6). A crucial implication is that African debts are largely viewed as a concern for multilateral agencies and creditor governments and therefore not a direct threat to the international financial system. This further reduces the political influence which African governments can have on their creditors. Consequently, African debts have not acquired the prominence of those highly publicized international meetings between debtors and lenders.

Table 6.6 United States bank claims and exposure to sub-Saharan Africa, 1987 (in US$ million)

	Claims	*Less amounts guaranteed by external entity*	*Plus amts externally guaranteed by borrower*	*Equals US bank exposure*
Non-oil Africa	2,734	806	46	1,974
Less:				
Egypt	546	337	31	240
Morocco	845	99	8	754
Tunisia	134	42	0	92
Plus:				
Nigeria	864	274	28	618
Gabon	41	9	0	32
Equals: SSA	2,114	611	35	1,538
SSA less:				
Nigeria and Côte d'Ivoire	883	330	1	554

Source: United States Federal Financial Institutions Examinations Council Country Exposure Lending Survey, March 1987

Given also that African governments have not sought a coordinated action on debt in the way some Latin American states attempted in the early 1980s under the so-called Cartagena Group, they were bound not to be seen as a major political threat to Western financial interests.[8]

Having examined the nature of the African debt, I shall discuss its origins. The debate on the origins of the African debt has been part of the wider debate about the global "development crisis" of the 1980s.[9] At one extreme, there are those who blame the wrong-headed policy choices made by LDCs and their failure to adapt to changing international conditions. This has been largely the underlying assumption of the IFIs in their responses to the crisis. At the other extreme is the view, shared by certain radical circles in the South, that the crisis largely derived from external sources.[10]

Perhaps a more balanced explanation must lie somewhere in between these two extremes. Korner *et al.* have moved the debate forward by focusing instead on the factors that limit the returns on external loans in poor countries.[11] These are, according to them:

1 the historical legacy of colonialism and the inherited economic, social and political structures which lead to "indebted development";
2 the types of financial, economic and development policies pursued by LDC governments and their state-classes;
3 external shocks, global market developments and other international changes.[12]

Seen from this perspective, Africa's debts can be said to derive from a combination of unfavourable international developments and inappropriate domestic policy choices. Amongst the unfavourable external factors were the oil price shocks of the early and late 1970s; the collapse of commodity prices; and the rise in interest rates.[13] Sharp oil price increases led to the growth of deficits for oil-importing developing countries, from US$11.3 billion in 1973 to 37 billion in 1974; expanding further from 42 billion in 1978 to 88 billion in 1980.[14] These deficits had to be financed either through the expansion of export drives or through foreign borrowing. Given the massive earnings by OPEC and the ensuing increased liquidity, the commercial banks were more than willing to give out loans to the developing countries. Much of the surplus could not be absorbed in the industrialized countries which were still enjoying a period of steady growth. In the words of Bertrand Schneider:

> The Eurodollar market became an important source of financing African countries, for whom financing had never been previously available. This increased access to capital markets was encouraged by financial agents who travelled from one African country to another looking for potential financial investments.[15]

The commercial banks sometimes appeared over-zealous in persuading some LDCs to take out loans which they did not really need. An example of this is the US$1 billion which the military government of Nigeria took in 1979. In a year when the country recorded its highest earnings ever from petroleum exports, the Nigerian military government under General Olusegun Obasanjo was persuaded to accept a jumbo loan of US$1 billion from the commercial banks. Such a loan was incurred at a time when the country did not need it and was in fact in a position to give out such a loan itself. The Nigerian public were never given a credible explanation about the purpose for which the loan was incurred. According to Susan George, many of such loans were state-guaranteed and went into public projects which, in some instances, were neither properly designed nor effectively implemented.[16]

Another external factor which contributed to the rise in Africa's debt

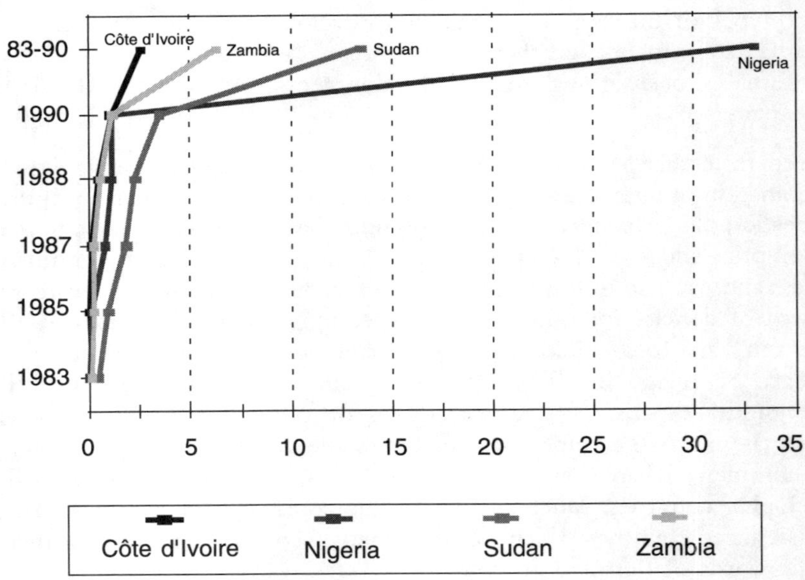

Figure 6.5 Africa's major debtors, 1983–90 (in US$ billion)
Source: International Financial Statistics, 1991

burden was the collapse in commodity prices after the late 1970s. Whilst the first oil shock coincided with the period of general increases in commodity prices, the second one occurred at a time of massive decline in commodity prices. The tendency towards the deterioration in the terms of trade became quite acute in the late 1970s. The World Bank estimated that between 1980 and 1982 the prices of non-oil primary commodities fell by 27 per cent, leading to a 2.4 per cent decline in the earnings of low-income SSA countries.[17] To finance these shortfalls, African states had little or no option other than to acquire external loans.

A third external factor was the rise in interest rates in the 1980s. At the beginning of the decade Keynesianism as an economic philosophy was largely in retreat in the countries of advanced industrial capitalism. The new orthodoxy was monetarism, with its essentially deflationary approach to economic policy. The Reagan administration, for example, believed that to keep down inflation it was necessary to raise interest rates. High interest rates, coupled with the rise in the value of the dollar, entailed an increase in the volume of indebtedness for many LDCs whose debts were denominated in dollars. High interest rates had a more severe effect on the Latin American debtors and were of comparatively lesser impact on SSA countries because most of their debts are official rather than commercial. However, the effect is still significant. Schneider estimates that the total SSA debt subject to floating interest rates rose from 9.3 per cent in 1973–74 to 20.6 per cent in 1981–82.[18]

However, these external factors by themselves cannot provide a sufficient explanation for the African debt. There were other factors deriving from the nature of the African political economy. Given their monocultural export-dependence, SSA economies were hardly in a position to absorb the cyclical shocks which are endemic in the world capitalist economy. Given also the phenomenon of excessive *étatisme* in their economies and the tendency to maintain high exchange rates, SSA countries were oriented towards the massive importation of artificially cheap goods from abroad. Whilst monetarist policies in the OECD countries reduced the money supply from an 11 per cent rate of increase in 1978 to a 6.5 per cent rate of increase in 1984, SSA countries were pursuing expansionist monetary and fiscal policies which saw the growth in the money supply rate rising from 15.1 per cent to 18.4 per cent over the same period.[19] Central government deficits were estimated to have increased from 5.5 per cent of GDP in 1978 to 7.3 per cent by 1983. To finance such deficits, recourse to external borrowing, at a time when western commercial banks were awash with liquidity, became a particularly attractive option.

The debt problem is therefore traceable to the interaction between wider macro-factors and domestic micro-factors and the resultant weakening of productive investment.[20] In particular, the forms of clientelist politics in countries such as Zaire, Nigeria, Côte d'Ivoire and Kenya underpinned the failures of public management and economic policy.[21] Structural distortions, coupled with governmental incapacity and rent-seeking, were the fertile ground on which a culture of external borrowing and conspicuous consumption became a substitute for discipline and productive effort.

INTERNATIONAL RESPONSES

Comparatively small as the SSA debt has been in global terms, the growing arrears in repayments and the worsening development predicament in the region were compelling donors and creditors to give some attention to the problem. Severe repayment difficulties with regard to World Bank and IMF loans in particular, had become an increasingly worrisome question. Total annual interest arrears for the region rose from US$0.95 billion in 1983 to 7.99 billion in 1990, with total arrears over the seven-year period estimated at US$33.66 billion (Table 6.7).

International responses to the African debt have ranged from bilateral initiatives by some creditor-nations to rescheduling arrangements by the Paris and London Clubs of official and private creditors. Multilateral policy actions by the Bank and the Fund, however, have been the broader framework within which the international debt strategy was launched. We shall briefly review these responses after which we shall consider in some greater detail the responses by the Community and assess the role of the EC in North–South debt diplomacy.

It is necessary to commence by briefly reviewing the responses by the African countries themselves. In June 1984, at a meeting in Addis Ababa, African leaders adopted a draft memorandum on the debt problem.[22] They identified the debt burden as a major impediment to their developmental aspirations and called for urgent measures to redress the situation. They suggested, among other things:

Table 6.7 SSA interest arrears in selected years, 1983–90 (in US$ billion)

	1983	*1985*	*1987*	*1988*	*1990*	*1983–90 (E)*
Total debt service	8.56	11.75	8.87	10.06	11.75	81.21
Total interest arrears	0.95	1.98	4.70	6.52	7.99	33.66
of which: Côte d'Ivoire	0.05	0.01	0.11	0.45	1.05	2.53
Nigeria	0.01	0.08	0.76	1.05	1.10	3.65
Sudan	0.38	0.90	1.79	2.25	3.43	13.47
Zambia	0.08	0.17	0.16	0.52	1.12	3.31

Source: Mistry, *African Debt Revisited*, 1991, p. 26
Note: (E) = Estimated figures

- strengthening of administrative structures to deal with the problem;
- increased national savings to enhance domestic investment and reduce dependence on external loans;
- exchange of vital information on debt management;
- the need for the donor community to take measures towards cancellation of debts for the most impoverished states;
- conversion of public and private debts into long-term obligations;
- imposition of a ceiling on debt repayment as a percentage of GNP;
- the extension of grace and rescheduling periods;
- the holding of a special conference under United Nations auspices to discuss the reorganization of the international monetary and financial system.

This memorandum was the expression of an emerging African consensus on the debt problem. But in practical terms it had little to it beyond its declaratory significance. It did not result in the mobilization of African collective will, nor was its orchestration of across-the-board cancellation of external debts likely to impress the international creditors. The call for a UN conference to "reorganize" the global monetary and financial system was little more than wishful thinking. Coming as it did in the heyday of Reaganism and Thatcherism, it betrayed a limitation of judgement regarding the climate of the times. Beyond this broad perspective, African countries have not articulated a clear position in the search for an effective international debt strategy.[23]

At the December 1987 OAU Special Summit on debts, African leaders once more drew the world's attention to the debt repayment problems of the region. They underlined the combined effects of low commodity prices and net resource outflows as the main causes of Africa's inability to service its debts.[24] They urged international creditors to accept multi-year debt reschedulings, including a ten-year moratorium on debt service payments, and with repayment spread over fifty years at zero per cent interest rates. Among the main recommendations were the following:

- conversion of all bilateral loans into grants;
- the Fund should consider rescheduling of its loans to Africa and extension of the repurchasing period;
- establishment of a special compensatory fund to offset the effect of increasing interest rates of the currencies in which debts are denominated;
- an additional SDR allocation of 15 billion units to improve the financial liquidity of LDCs;
- conversion of commercial credits into transferable securities, with lower interest rates and maturities of at least twenty-five years;
- easing of conditionality clauses on debt rescheduling and abolition of cross-conditionality;

- doubling of the World Bank's capital base and increase in the eligibility ceiling for IDA financing.[25]

Soon after the OAU summit, a multi-donor meeting under the auspices of the World Bank in Paris (3–4 December 1987) pledged about US$2.9 billion in new disbursements for twenty low-income, debt-distressed African countries.[26] These funds, which were targeted at countries implementing reform programmes, were to cover the period 1988–90 and were additional to finances already earmarked for these countries under the Bank's "soft window". By the end of December the IMF also announced the establishment of its Extended Structural Adjustment Facility (ESAF), with an additional infusion of US$8.4 billion to the 3 billion which was still to be spent under the original facility.[27]

Debt rescheduling, mainly under the auspices of the Paris Club, has been one of the ways of providing debt relief for debt-burdened SSA countries. Rescheduling, however, is at best a temporary palliative, providing some "breathing space" for the debtors rather than offering a permanent solution to the problem. What it does is to restructure the timing and sometimes the terms of repayment.

Table 6.8 and Figure 6.6 provide some data on the number of multilateral reschedulings which have taken place in SSA between 1980 and 1990. On the whole, 134 rescheduling arrangements were effected. Countries such as Benin and Burkina Faso registered no rescheduling agreements, whilst a country such as Zaire had as many as thirteen.[28] The general criticism against rescheduling arrangements is that they often do not take account of long-term needs which require longer grace and maturity periods as well as lower interest rates. The first part of the criticism has been assuaged by the introduction of the Multi-Year Rescheduling Agreement (MYRA) which some countries have enjoyed.

Table 6.8 SSA debt restructuring, 1985–89 (in US$ million)

	1985	*1986*	*1987*	*1988*	*1989*
Principal rescheduled	1,558	3,210	4,166	1,567	4,387
Interest rescheduled	440	1,202	1,408	792	2,052
Principal forgiven	6	30	0	9	101
Interest forgiven	1	4	0	9	82
Disbursements from rescheduled	4,408	9,059	10,867	4,385	12,128
Debt stock reductions	0	0	0	47	257

Source: Economic Commission for Africa, *Annual Report*, 1992

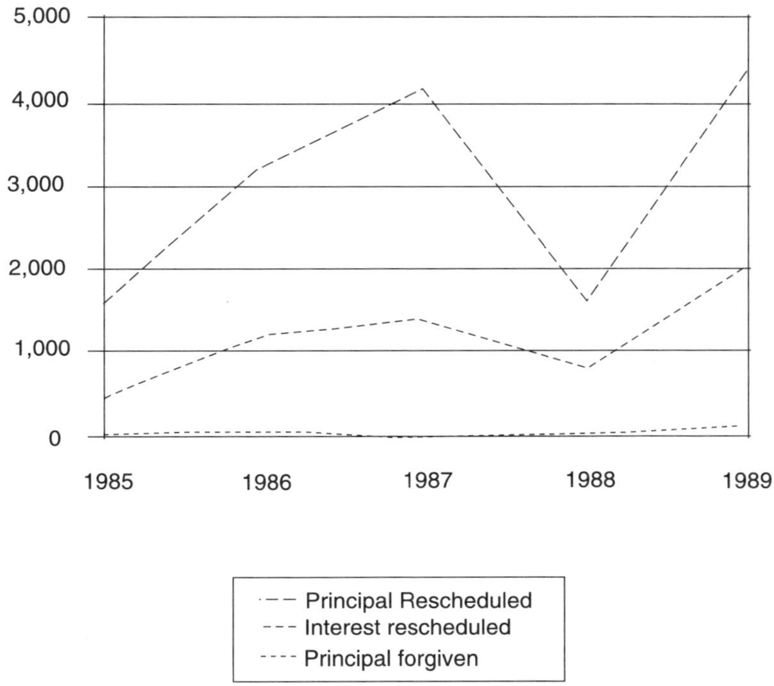

Figure 6.6 SSA debt restructuring, 1985–89 (US$ billion)
Source: Economic Commission for Africa, 1992

The Toronto principles on international debt

One of the most important multilateral debt initiatives was the Toronto Agreement by the Group of Ten of the OECD. In the meeting of September 1988 they agreed on a plan to soften the terms of debt rescheduling for non-concessional loans which are mostly owed to export credit agencies. The plan consisted of a menu of three options which Paris Club creditor governments could choose from, either singly or in combination with other options, depending on the circumstances. These options were:

1 cancellation of 33 per cent of debt service covered by the agreement;
2 reduction of interest rates by 3.5 percentage points or 50 per cent, whichever of the two is less; or

3 extension of grace periods to 14 years and maturity to 25 years (8 and 14 years in the case of the other two options).

The Toronto principles have been seen as an important improvement in the search for solutions to the problems of LDC debts, especially the allowance for below-market terms for non-concessional debts. However, the ODI has estimated that the benefits from the Toronto Agreement are not likely to exceed US$700 million during 1989–2000, a figure which is less than 1 per cent of the 1989 debt of the most debt-distressed SSA countries.[29]

From the Baker Plan to the Brady Initiative

At the multilateral level, it is the IFIs which have played the dominant role in managing the debt crisis. Their responses have ranged from provision of additional financial resources for structural adjustment to technical assistance on the management of external debts.[30] Indeed, it would not be incorrect to say that the debt problem has been one of the main underlying factors in the emergence of structural adjustment as the new ideology of development.

The first major policy initiative emerged with the Baker Plan in October 1985. At the Seoul meeting of the Bank and Fund, James Baker, who was then US Treasury Secretary, put forward a plan which came to be known by his name. The so-called Baker Plan consisted of three main elements. First, private commercial banks were to provide additional loans to the tune of US$20 billion to the fifteen largest debtors.[31] Second, these new loans were to be supplemented by additional inflows of US$9 billion over a three-year period by the World Bank and the Inter-American Development Bank. The third element was the new accent on a "growth-oriented adjustment strategy" as the preferred policy option to overcome the debt problem and to put the economies of the affected countries on a more even keel. Perhaps for the first time the United States was conceding the fact that a strict austerity or shock treatment was not necessarily the best way of dealing with the problems of the most heavily indebted developing countries.

The main criticism against the Plan is the fact that the commercial banks did not respond positively to the needs of the indebted countries for additional capital inflows. It was only the Bretton Woods institutions which increased their financial commitments to the amount advised by the Baker Plan. The banks were predictably not enthusiastic about "throwing good money after bad". According to Rainer Erbe, they were instead hoping for "direct or indirect government guarantees and/or massive government lendings to debtor countries in order to resolve the precarious situation for which these banks themselves were partly to blame".[32] There were also conflicting perspectives among the industrialized countries about how to share the burdens likely to arise from implementing the Baker Plan. Differences emerged between the Japanese, European and US banks concerning how to share the costs of the US$20 billion net loan figure proposed by Baker. Another major defect was that the Baker Plan gave more priority to the Latin American countries. Only two SSA countries, Nigeria and Côte d'Ivoire, were affected by the terms of the Plan. It virtually overlooked the least-developed and debt-distressed countries, whose debts, though small in comparison with those of Latin America, were an enormous burden on those countries.

The Brady Plan was launched in March 1989 by US Treasury Secretary Nicholas Brady. It emerged as an attempt by the new administration of President George Bush to come to terms with the debt problem. The plan is made of three elements:

1 the declared commitment to examine the legal implications of voluntary debt reduction by commercial banks on a case-by-case basis;
2 governments of respective creditor countries were to undertake certain measures to reduce the administrative and fiscal obstacles impeding debt reduction;
3 support of the Bank and Fund in the debt reduction process.

Under the Plan, countries undergoing economic reform programmes are eligible for US$30–35 billions within the period 1989–92. The Plan was adopted at the IMF/Bank meeting in April 1989. Among the new aspects were the involvement of Fund and Bank resources in voluntary debt-service reduction schemes, reimbursing debtors for the costs of buying back their loans and providing financial guarantees in respect of the debts to be repaid.[33] As a precondition, debtor countries were expected to be implementing viable reform programmes and to have firm measures to attract capital which had left the country.

Criticisms of the Plan have ranged from political problems of debt-equity conversion schemes, to reluctance of commercial banks to engage in debt cancellation.[34] It is clear that the Brady Plan has not resulted in any dramatic improvements in the debt situation of the poorest countries. Indeed, from the very beginning, commercial creditors and some creditor governments expressed reservations about the possibility of debt forgiveness, which they contended would only further destroy the creditworthiness of the debtor countries while also devaluing the reform efforts of countries which had managed to keep up with their debt repayment obligations. Moreover, it was vigorously argued in certain quarters that the most important issue was the need to overcome the temporary liquidity gaps rather than to engage in debt cancellation.[35]

From the Lawson Initiative to the Trinidad Terms

During the IMF/Bank annual meeting in Washington in April 1987, the British Chancellor of the Exchequer, Nigel Lawson, made proposals on debt alleviation with special focus on the poorest countries.[36] The Lawson Plan entailed more widespread conversion of aid loans to grants; rescheduling of other public debt, especially export credits with repayments increased to between 15 and 20 years and with grace periods of up to 10 years. The Lawson Plan also called for a reduction of interest rates to below market levels. The main conditions to be attached were that beneficiaries had to be heavily indebted with a high debt-service ratio and should be implementing appropriate economic policies. At the G7 Economic Summit in Toronto in June 1988 the main ideas of the Lawson Plan had been accepted and were to be implemented under what became known as the "Toronto Terms".

In June 1990, at the Commonwealth Finance Ministers' meeting in Trinidad, the then British Chancellor, John Major, made another proposal on the debt question. This initiative called for more debt cancellations by creditors and more rescheduling for the poorest LDCs. The "Trinidad Terms" called for immediate write-offs of a third of a country's debt and rescheduling of the remaining debts. It called for a grace period of five years and for subsequent agreements on repayments to be worked out on the basis of countries' ability to pay.[37] At the bilateral level some creditor nations have undertaken measures such as debt rescheduling and debt cancellation. Countries such as France, Canada and Sweden have written off the debts of some of the least developed and debt-distressed countries. The former Soviet Union has either written off or granted 100-year moratoria on its aid debt. For most OECD countries, debt cancellations are often conditional on countries pursuing an appropriate adjustment programme. Between 1986 and 1989 over US$3.5 billion of LDC debts were written off, with a further US$3.5 billion cancellation pledged for countries that agreed to undertake Structural Adjustment Programmes. However, the net value of these debt cancellations for SSA have been quite modest. It has been estimated that during 1986–89 low-income SSA saved only US$250 million in debt service from debt cancellation.[38]

EUROPEAN COMMUNITY RESPONSES

Before discussing the EC's responses to the African debt, it is pertinent to begin by considering its status as a creditor to the SSA region and to the ACP group. A distinction should be made between the debt owed to the EC member states and those owed to the Community as a legal person. Whereas the one is quite substantial, the other is comparatively small. We have not come across any data on the details of the debts owed to

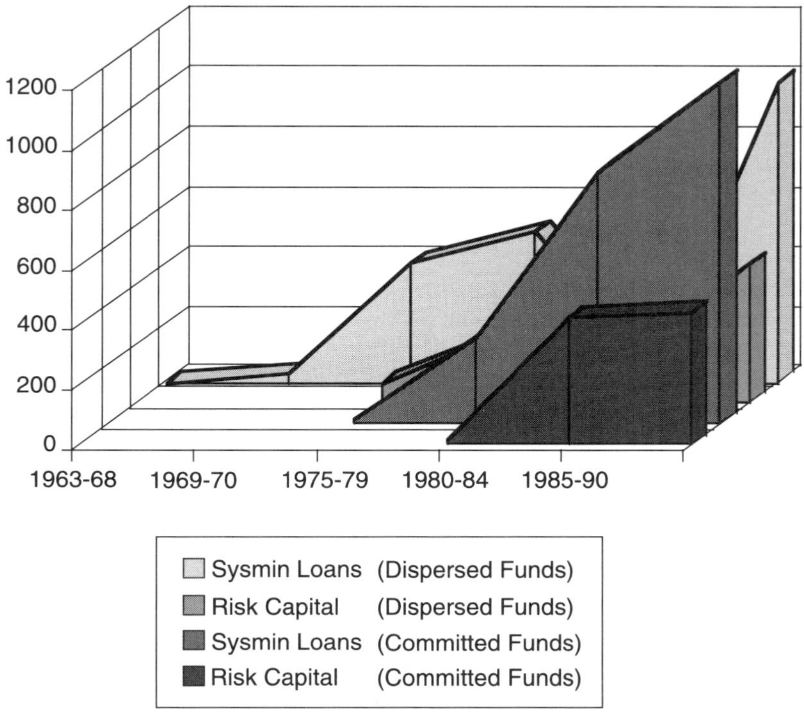

Figure 6.7 ACP debt to the European Community, 1963–90 (in ECU million)
Source: *The Courier*, 1991

individual EC member states by the African states. From available statistics, however, Vincent Cable, an official at the Commonwealth Secretariat, estimates that the EC Twelve account for 55 per cent of ACP long-term debt owed to bilateral DAC creditors, who in turn account for 62 per cent of total long-term debt.[39] Most of the remaining debt is owed to the multilateral institutions, of which the Twelve, as major contributors to the Bank and the Fund, can be regarded as an important part of the international community of creditors.

In terms of ODA debt, the governments of the EC states account for over 60 per cent of ACP debt, and in the case of Francophone Africa, their share is in the region of 100 per cent. On the other hand, there is the debt which is owed to the Community as an international organization. This is mostly by way of loans within the framework of the Lomé regime. Such credits derive from EDF special loans, EDF risk capital, EIB resources, and

Table 6.9 ACP debt to the European Community as at 30 September 1990 (in ECU million)

	Yaoundé I	*Yaoundé II*	*Lomé I*	*Lomé II*	*Lomé III*	*Total*
	1963–68	1969–70	1975–79	1980–84	1985–90	
Disbursed funds						
Sysmin loans	4.7	31.5	404	510	59.5	1,010.2
Risk capital	—	—	70.5	236.5	167.9	474.9
Committed funds						
Sysmin loans	—	—	15.5	290.1	845.9	1,151.5
Risk capital	—	—	—	18.5	432.1	450.6

Source: *The Courier*, 125, January–February 1991, p. 9

Table 6.10 Estimated global debt service due to the EC (in ECU million, approx.)

	Year	*ECU (million)*
TOTAL DUE	[1990–1995]	675
	[1990–2000]	1,135
of which: EIB's own resources	[1990–1995]	425
	[1990–2000]	600
EDF Risk Capital	[1990–1995]	125
administered by EIB	[1990–2000]	250
EDF Special Loans	[1990–1995]	120
	[1990–2000]	285

Source: Commonwealth Secretariat, London, 1990

Stabex and Sysmin transfers. Table 6.9 presents some figures on ACP debt to the EC in September 1990. Amounts already disbursed totalled ECU1.01 billion in special loans and ECU450.6 million in risk capital. Loans which were yet to be disbursed were ECU1.15 billion in special loans and ECU450.6 million in risk capital.

Table 6.10 provides some estimates of ACP debt service obligations to the European Community. The accumulated debt of over ECU1.7 billion would have been payable at an annual average of ECU130 million. Both the debt and debt service obligations in 1989 were hardly more than 1 per cent of ACP total debt obligations. Between 1990 and 1995 the amount of ECU675 million would have had to be paid, while the sum of ECU1.3 billion would have had to be paid over the ten year period 1990–2000.

In what follows we shall examine the politics of the African debt as it has featured within the framework of Lomé. In doing this we shall assess the adequacy and effectiveness of the EC responses to the problem and its relevance to the search for a viable international debt strategy. We shall also see to what extent the EC approach to the debt question compares with the approach taken by the IFIs.

During the Lomé III negotiations the debt issue was a subject which was quite peripheral to the discussions. The dominant issues were those relating to food security, rural development and policy dialogue. In October 1983, when the negotiations commenced in Luxembourg, the African states and their Caribbean and Pacific partners saw their priorities in terms of improving their agricultural productivity, ensuring food self-sufficiency, and increasing their export earnings. The debt problem was largely consigned to the sidelines. However, some reference was made to the issue in the Lomé III document. Article 198 states that:

> At the request of the ACP states, the Community shall lend technical assistance in studying and finding practical solutions to their indebtedness, debt-servicing and balance of payments problems.[40]

The emphasis seemed to have been on technical assistance in the management of debts rather than a commitment on the part of the Community to finding long-term solutions. The EC certainly was not to blame for this rather non-committal attitude, as the ACP themselves did not voice any really strong demands on the debt issue. It is clear that the Mexican debt crisis in the year preceding had not sufficiently impressed itself upon the minds of both parties to the Lomé III negotiations. The relatively small size of the ACP debt and the more pressing concerns about food, agriculture, drought and desertification ensured that the debt issue was kept on the backburner.

By the second half the 1980s, as the African "crisis" worsened and the debt burden was gaining salience as one of the major factors in Africa's economic predicament, the EC official attitude was far from being committal. The main argument was that the debt issue was outside the competence of the Lomé Convention as such and was best handled within a wider multilateral framework such as was then beginning to emerge within the OECD and the Group of Ten. In any case, they pointed out that EC debts were a mere 1 per cent of total ACP debt and that the Lomé regime already contained elements which could be supportive in overcoming the debt problem. Those elements were identified as:

- concessional EDF assistance which helps in filling the "financing gap" of indebted ACP countries;
- existing trade provisions which could assist the process of export growth and trade diversification, thereby helping to alleviate the debt burden;
- compensatory finance by way of Sysmin and Stabex which would contribute to debt service even under circumstances of dwindling export earnings;
- the existence of provisions for industrial cooperation which would facilitate direct investment.[41]

These initial attitudes betrayed the fact that the North was unwilling to weaken its common front on the debt issue by adopting divergent policy initiatives, while at the same time insisting that the LDC debt issue had to be approached on a case-by-case basis. The fundamental principles of Lomé espouse an EC–ACP partnership based on equality and solidarity. In principle, no issue which affects the long-term development of the ACP partners can be excluded from Lomé discussions. Finally, the argument about the adequacy of existing provisions was both ironical and factually doubtful. Ironical, because these same provisions accounted for a sizeable part of ACP debt in the first place. And factually doubtful, because in some cases such as investment and trade diversification, there have not been any significant improvements in the economies of the ACPs which could be seen as a contribution to debt alleviation. In the words of Vincent Cable, an official of the Commonwealth Secretariat:

> the overhang of debt and widespread debt servicing difficulties simply prevent these traditional instruments working effectively. Highly debt-distressed countries have to give priority to maintaining existing services and projects rather than launching new ones, for which local and recruitment costs financing may in any event be an impossible burden.[42]

Following the EC–ACP Joint Assembly resolution of February 1987, a committee was set up under the chairmanship of Ambassador Joseph Iroha of Nigeria to examine the nature of the African debt problem and the policy options that could be adopted within the framework of Lomé. The Iroha Report perhaps influenced the launching in 1988 of the Special Community Programme for highly indebted low-income African countries. Under this arrangement, unspent EDF allocations, reflows and additional EC funds were to be pooled into a quick-disbursing fund to be used by countries undergoing Structural Adjustment Programmes. The fund amounted to some ECU500 million. Of this amount, 100 million were new financial resources from the EC; 40 million were from the outstanding balance of unallocated funds from previous Lomé EDF finances; 60 million came from partial reflows of special loans and EIB risk capital provided under previous Lomé Conventions; while the remaining 300 million was derived from a reallocation of Lomé III funds.[43]

The criteria of eligibility were not explicitly stated.[44] One of the criteria was that beneficiaries would have had to introduce reform policies that could be considered adequate in dealing with domestic economic imbalances. This implied an understanding with the Bretton Woods institutions. Funds could be used to supplement Structural Adjustment Loans (SALs) or Sectoral Adjustment Loans (SECALs) as the case may be. However, in the absence of such adjustment funds, the EC could form its own independent judgement on the adequacy and effectiveness of reform programmes. When such judgement was positive, then funds could be disbursed to the country in question.

The EC special debt programme for Africa

At the Venice Summit in December 1987, the EC Council adopted a decision to launch a special programme of import support for debt-distressed SSA countries. Under Article of 188 of Lomé III, provision had been made for quick-disbursing import support to relieve the import constraints faced by highly indebted countries. The import programme was organized in two different forms. First, there was the Sectoral Import Programme (SIP), which itself was in the form of either (a) supplies of inputs and other goods, or (b) by way of direct provision of foreign exchange for financing imports in specified sectors. There was also the General Import Programme (GIP) which entailed provision of hard currency for all kinds of imports except those explicitly disallowed under the "negative list".

The choice of which kind of support to be given was to be determined by the Commission according to the extent to which a country was judged to be implementing a Structural Adjustment Programme and the appropriateness of its exchange rate regime.[45] The rationale for the SAP is the alleviation of the external financial constraints faced by indebted countries by providing the entire economy (GIP) or specific sectors (SIP) with foreign exchange to finance a range of imports in exchange for which the recipient would undertake to implement a programme of sectoral or macroeconomic reforms.

The EC programme was part of a bigger programme, the Special Programme of Assistance (SPA 1), a multi-donor programme, comprising around twenty bilateral and multilateral donors and coordinated by the World Bank. Some US$16 billion was mobilized for fifty countries, and was estimated to have filled up to 95 per cent of those countries' current account deficits. The volume of the total EC contribution was second only to that of Japan. The EC objectives in the first phase of the SPA were:

- to mobilize enough resources to reduce the external constraint of highly indebted SSA countries;
- to provide financial support for the economic reform programmes;
- to enhance policy coordination between donors in supporting structural adjustment efforts.

The overall objective was to support macroeconomic stabilization so that "adjustment with growth" could be pursued.

The total financial commitments by the EC amounted to ECU572 million, of which ECU331 million were in addition to amounts already available under Lomé. The SPA was to have a three-year life-span (1988–90). It could be said to have marked the entrance of the EC decisively into the politics of adjustment. The Commission came out with a set of eligibility criteria for recipients of the programme:

1 They had to be low-income countries entitled to IDA funding.
2 There had to be evidence that the country's debt burden was such that its debt service ratio was at least 30 per cent of export earnings.
3 Evidence also had to be provided that the countries were making a "significant effort to carry out economic adjustment".[46]

Although these criteria were the same as those of the World Bank, the EC Council was "anxious to give a special Community slant to the assessment of adjustment efforts". The Commission thus launched its own policy dialogue with SSA countries and made its own assessments of macroeconomic reform efforts in the prospective recipient states. On this basis, for example, Benin was considered by the EC to be eligible in December 1988, even though she had no reform programme with the IFIs. The Bank did not reach an agreement on its own SPA contribution to the country until six months later. This is evidence that though their understanding of the requirements of adjustment was essentially the same as the IFIs, the EC did depart from the IFIs occasionally in making their own independent judgements.[47] Of the original twenty-seven countries which were to benefit from the programme, three were later disqualified for having failed to meet the third criterion of having in place a viable economic reform programme: Sierra Leone, Comoros and Sudan.[48]

Four General Import Programmes (GIPs) were undertaken for Burundi, Guinea, Guinea-Bissau and Mauritania, all four accounting for 11.5 per cent of the total SPA. Sectoral Import Programmes (SIPs) accounted for 88.5 per cent of the total funds (see Table 6.11) and were concentrated in five main sectors: agriculture, industry, transport, energy and education. The country allocations varied from the highest amount of ECU70 million for Mozambique to ECU60 million for Zambia, to ECU1.15 million for São Tomé & Principe. It is not clear what criteria the EC used in determining the specific needs of each country. It can only be surmised that political considerations as much as the requirement of macroeconomic adjustment would have been taken into consideration.

The Commission explained its preference for SIPs because of the difficulties of monitoring GIPs. It therefore preferred to focus on sectors where it already had some experience under Lomé III. In Kenya, for example, the SIP focused on restructuring of the production and marketing of cereals, which was undertaken jointly with the World Bank and other donors.[49] In the Franc Zone, however, the SPA did not really take off because monetary arrangements with the French franc meant that the acquisition of foreign exchange was not a constraint as such.

The operations of the programmes were monitored by EC Delegations with support from technical assistance teams. The final report, which derives from a Commission internal evaluation, predictably scores it as an important success. Given the traditional snail pace of Lomé funding, the SPA's quick-disbursing and targeted financing procedures were seen by ACP states as a positive development.[50] Whilst it was difficult to assess the extent to which the programme directly influenced the course of macro-economic reforms, the assessments for nineteen countries showed that SPA funds covered in most cases a significant percentage of the total volume of imports. These were estimated to have ranged from as much as 23% in Malawi and 20% in Togo to as low as 3% in Kenya and 1.3% in Senegal. In at least six countries (Guinea-Bissau, Togo, Madagascar, Burundi, Malawi and Somalia), it accounted for more than 10% of the total volume of imports.[51] Table 6.11 shows the financial allocations and their classifications, while Table 6.12 shows the breakdown of country allocations under the EC–SPA programme.

With regard to filling the gap in the current account deficit, the benefits were estimated as ranging from 26% in Mali, 13% in Madagascar, to 5% in Mauritania and 8% in Kenya. The Commission estimates that on average, the SPA filled up to 12% of the current account deficit for beneficiary countries. They also constituted a significant source of public revenue by way of customs duties and taxes, which in the case of Uganda were estimated as high as 28 per cent of direct additional revenue to the government. In Benin the counterparts generated were used in making redundancy payments to civil servants who had been retrenched as a result of the adjustment programme in the country.[52]

The SPA experience has influenced the EC approach to adjustment under Lomé IV, both in emphasizing the "human dimensions of adjustment" and in coordinating with other donors, especially the IFIs. According to a Commission report, the SPA provided "a fillip to relations between the World Bank and the Commission, which now works closely with the Bank on structural adjustment policy and action".[53]

The EC Special Programme was far from being a comprehensive and original approach to the African debt problem. It was essentially a form of financial support for IFI-approved reform programmes. It aimed to offset the import gaps of countries undergoing structural adjustment rather than addressing the debt issue as such.[54] Another major problem was the coverage of the programme. Beneficiaries were restricted to only a few countries while many other deserving cases could not benefit. There was also the issue of the adequacy of the funds. The volume of new funding under the programme was only ECU100 million, a figure which pales into insignificance in comparison with the actual extent of the African debt situation. In political terms it may be said that the programme, while being a welcome initiative to the debt-distressed African countries, actually served to buttress further the legitimacy and power of the Bretton Woods institutions with respect to reform policies and adjustment programmes in Africa.

During the Lomé IV negotiations the debt problem emerged as one of the most prominent issues on the agenda. Even before the formal negotia-

Table 6.11 Classification of EC import programmes, 1987–90

*Country**	*Programme*	*Year*	*ECU millions*
Benin (1)	SIP *K*	1988	11.00
Benin (2)	SIP *K* + *C*	1989	20.00
Burundi	GIP	1988	12.00
Chad	SIP *K*	1989	9.50
Gambia	SIP *K*	1988	5.00
Ghana	SIP *K*	1988	20.50
Guinea-Bissau (1)	GIP	1988	6.00
Guinea-Bissau (2)	SIP *K*	1988	3.40
Guinea-Conakry	GIP	1988	12.50
Guinea-Equatorial	SIP *K*	1990	1.50
Kenya (1)	SIP *C*	1988	35.00
Kenya (2)	SIP *C*	1990	7.00
Madagascar (1)	SIP *K*	1988	17.25
Madagascar (2)	SIP *K*	1988	2.50
Malawi (1)	SIP *K*	1987	42.10
Malawi (2)	SIP *C*	1990	12.50
Mali	SIP *K*	1988	25.00
Mauritania	GIP	1989	7.00
Mozambique (1)	SIP *K*	1987	40.00
Mozambique (2)	SIP *K* + *C*	1989	30.00
Niger	SIP *K*	1988	14.00
RCA (C.A.R)	SIP *K*	1989	1.15
São Tomé and Principe	SIP *K*	1988	11.50
Senegal	SIP *K*	1988	0.00
Somalia (1)	SIP *C*	1988	15.00
Somalia (2)	SIP *C*	1989	16.00
Sudan (1)	SIP *K*	1988	7.00
Sudan (2)	SIP *K*	1989	7.00
Tanzania	SIP *C*	1988	24.50
Togo	SIP *K*	1989	10.00
Uganda (1)	SIP *C*	1987	17.25
Uganda (2)	SIP *C*	1988	15.00
Zaire	SIP *C*	1989	30.00
Zambia (1)	SIP *C*+ *K*	1987	40.00
Zambia (2)	SIP *C*	1990	20.00
TOTAL			548.15

Source: EC Commission, 1991
Notes:
* (1) or (2) after the name of a country indicates that this is the first or second of two financing programmes
K = in kind
C = in currency

tions started, the government of Senegal proposed a seminar on debt, structural adjustment and commodities. The aim was to forge a framework of intellectual understanding on these key issues in preparation for the imminent negotiations. An underlying motive was perhaps the fact that the

Table 6.12 Financial disbursements under the EC Special Programme of Assistance as at 31 December 1990 (in ECU million)

Country	*Amount*	*Commitments*	*Payments*
Benin	31.00	30.90	28.70
Burundi	12.00	11.90	7.02
Gambia	5.00	5.00	4.90
Ghana	20.50	17.10	12.20
Guinea-Bissau	9.40	9.40	7.00
Guinea-Conakry	12.50	12.50	9.10
Guinea-Equatorial	1.50	1.50	1.40
Kenya	42.00	42.00	42.00
Madagascar	19.75	17.25	17.02
Malawi	54.60	40.30	36.60
Mali	25.00	25.00	23.20
Mauritania	7.00	7.00	7.00
Mozambique	70.00	55.60	40.50
Niger	14.00	13.50	10.30
RCA (C.A.R.)	7.00	6.90	6.20
Senegal	11.50	11.50	11.50
São Tomé & Principe	1.15	1.14	0.83
Somalia	31.00	29.30	22.50
Tanzania	24.50	24.30	20.00
Tchad	9.50	9.50	9.50
Togo	10.00	9.90	9.20
Uganda	32.25	32.25	32.25
Zaire	30.00	30.00	29.40
Sudan	15.00	10.30	6.30
Zambia	60.00	45.60	35.90
TOTAL	556.15	499.64	430.50

Source: EC Commission, 1992

African countries were anxious to get a feel of what the current thinking was in the EC and in European development circles generally. This would have served to prepare them for what to expect during the multilateral negotiations and perhaps to come to terms with the kinds of bargaining posture that would yield the most effective results.

The seminar took place in Dakar from 11–12 July 1988. It brought together a cross-section of parliamentarians, ambassadors, ministers and high officials from both the Community and the ACP region. The ACP Secretariat took charge of the groundwork in terms of practical organization and monitoring of the proceedings. The discussions were quite open and frank, although both sides avoided anything that could be interpreted as their definitive negotiating position. However, the feelings in African circles were well represented in the address by President Abdou Diouf, when he remarked that the ACP debt was now so large that it threatened the long-term development of the countries as well as the stability of the international financial system. He then called for an immediate and constructive response from the international community.[55] At the end of the seminar ACP ministers held a meeting to review the outcome of the session and to consider the implications for their bargaining approach in the forthcoming negotiations.

The success of the Dakar seminar, from the African viewpoint, could be measured by the fact that it underlined the key issues of debt, adjustment and commodities as the core of the agenda for the Lomé IV negotiations. The particular issue of debt was no longer one that could be shelved for deliberation in other multilateral fora, which was the position that the EC seemed to have been maintaining up until then. It also provided a non-political platform for intellectual interchange which might have served to prepare a common ground of understanding between the EC and the ACP Group on the debt problem and the other related issues.

During the course of the substantive negotiations the ACP Group came out with a common position on the debt question. In the official memorandum which embodied this common position,[56] they stressed what they regarded as the main factors responsible for the emergence of the debt problem. It was a repetition of the familiar litany of external woes: the collapse of commodity prices; deterioration in the terms of trade; effect of past borrowing and the hardening in the terms of credit; effects of past rescheduling which had worsened the debt burden; rise in interest rates and interest rate fluctuations; and decline in capital inflows and increase in non-concessional as opposed to concessional credit.

In making only perfunctory reference to the failures of domestic policy in the rise of their external debts, were the ACP states manifesting the all-too-familiar penchant in African circles to blame outside forces for most of the continent's misfortunes? The diagnosis in the memorandum certainly lacked the moral courage to acknowledge the wrong policy choices and in some cases gross economic mismanagement, which have interacted with unfavourable factors in the international environment to create what has become a continental nightmare.

In proposing a Lomé approach to their debt problems, the ACP countries called for a comprehensive approach both within the framework of the EC–ACP partnership and in other international fora. With regard to the latter, they invoked the spirit of Article 1 which has remained one of the fundamental principles of the Lomé regime, which states that the partners resolve "to work together to affirm in the international context the principles underlying their cooperation". In other words, the ACP were trying to prevail upon the Twelve to defend their interests in international fora such as in the policies of the Bank and Fund and in their negotiations with the Paris Club of creditors. While such an expectation cannot be dismissed, the ACP Group perhaps did not realize that international treaties are replete with pious intentions which have largely remained dead letters. They also blamed the EC for being "insensitive" to the need for it to play a "special" role in the search for a constructive international debt strategy.

Within the framework of Lomé IV, the ACP position on the debt included the following:

1 need for a separate chapter on the debt issue;
2 need for dialogue between debtors and creditors and a "special" role for the EC in this regard;
3 debt relief through cancellation of all EC debt and of all least-developed ACP countries' debts owed to EC member countries, debt-conversion schemes, technical assistance in debt management by way of training and improvement of expertise in external debt management;
4 provision of financial resources for debt relief in addition to other resources provided under Lomé;
5 use of foreign exchange available under the National Indicative Programmes for debt servicing of EC loans and an Action Programme to enable utilization of EC aid already available for debt servicing;
6 review and improvement of debt-increasing instruments such as the Stabex, EIB risk capital and special loans;
7 improved terms of trade and enhancement of foreign direct investment.

For its own part, while the EC conceded that the debt issue was a major constraint on ACP development, they were unwilling to accept the invitation to play a "special" role in the international discussions on the LDC debt. The EC Council in particular did not regard the subject of ACP debt to member states as falling within the competence of the Lomé negotiations. In a separate declaration annexed to the Lomé IV Convention the EC expressed its willingness to engage in exchange of views with their ACP partners on the debt problem "in the context of international talks without prejudice to specific talks within relevant forums".[57]

Nevertheless some compromises were reached. Lomé IV contains a new chapter on debts (Articles 239–242). The main innovations are in two main areas. One approach is to assist the process of debt relief through improvement of the terms of trade. The new Convention has removed the issuance of special loans and the requirement to replenish the Stabex funds, both of which have been seen as major debt-creating schemes. The Sysmin has also been reviewed. Under the new arrangement, Sysmin operations will be undertaken in a two-stage process of grants to countries who would then on-lend to final borrowers. In order to avoid future increases in debts, Lomé IV financing, with the exception of Bank loans and risk capital, will now be in the form of grants.

The second aspect of the debt provisions commits the EC in assisting ACP countries to improve their technical capacity in managing their debts. Such capacity-building measures are to be undertaken through training programmes in external debt management and international financial negotiations, including workshops, seminars and courses in this area. It also spells out the need for structural adjustment measures as the long-term solution to the problem of indebtedness. Article 241 lists the main areas in which the Community will assist the ACP Group. These are:

- in undertaking reforms aimed at improving the performance of their economy;
- in strengthening debt management mechanisms and improving control over public sector borrowing;
- in reversing the outflow of capital;
- in enhancing the quality of investment;
- in providing incentives to projects that generate or save foreign exchange;
- in the development of subregional capital markets to tap ACP funds invested abroad;
- in adopting measures to improve intra-ACP trade through development of regional payments mechanisms, clearing arrangements and credit insurance.

Another important innovation relates to future arrangements for the repayment of EIB credits, special loans and risk capital. Under Article 242, ACP countries may, after a case-by-case understanding with the Commission, effect such repayments in their local currencies. Such arrangements are to be enhanced through the operation of domiciliary accounts denominated in ECUs or in the currencies of one of the EC member states. Such accounts will be operated in the name of the Commission and will be overseen by a national public or semi-public financial institution of the ACP state under mutual agreement between the Commission and the country concerned. This is a particularly interesting innovation from the viewpoint of ACP debtor countries and could be regarded as a unique innovation under the Lomé regime.

Whereas the ACP states were pressing for EC action on the debt problem, they did not succeed in getting any new innovations included in the Fourth Convention. The EC position has always been that (a) Lomé is not the appropriate framework for discussing the debt problem and (b) the EC on its own is not competent to discuss issues of sovereign or multinational debt. Again, this illustrates a major limitation of Lomé: the Community tends to be selective in its definition of what it considers to be the really pressing problems besetting its ACP partners.

Whilst acknowledging that massive debt-servicing obligations are a constraint on development and growth, EC responses will be limited to the following measures (Articles 239–242):

- provision of technical assistance for ACP debt management;
- encouraging more financial inflows for debt-distressed countries and to reverse the capital flight;

- Stabex and Sysmin funds to be converted to grants to reduce debt-inducing financing;
- use, on a case-by-case basis, of the resources of past indicative programmes for attenuation of debts;
- assistance of training in international financial and debt negotiations.

Although most of the demands by the ACP Group could be said to have been met, at least in the legal text of Lomé IV, it is clear that not all of them have been addressed. The document is silent on the demand for more financial resources for debt relief in addition to normal Lomé funds. What was conceded was the allowance for greater fungibility of resources from past indicative programmes not already committed through the quick-disbursing instruments to be used for the purpose of debt relief. The Twelve were both unwilling to engage in a wholesale cancellation of ACP debt or to commit themselves to the pursuit of debt strategies which might be prejudicial to the prevailing norms in the international management of ACP and other LDC external debt. Their interests as creditors took precedence over any commitment to the development of their Lomé partners.

The issue of debt cancellation was particularly a source of division within the Community itself, between the EC Council of Ministers on the one hand, and the Parliament and Commission on the other. Until the end of the negotiations in November 1989, no firm agreement had been reached on the subject. In his speech at the signing ceremonies in the Togolese capital in the following month of December, Manuel Marin, Vice-President and EC Commissioner for Development and Fisheries, promised that the Commission, "within the limits of its competence, will be studying in a constructive spirit the situation in respect of ACP debt to the Community", adding that it was an open question for the future for which constructive answers had to be found.[58]

The solution finally came a year later in December 1990, when the EC announced the cancellation of over ECU2.6 billion worth of ACP debts owed to the Community.[59] Señor Marin stated that the decision had been taken after careful consultation between the Commission, Parliament and EC–ACP Joint Assembly. The debt written off was the one deriving from the application of the financial instruments of the Lomé regime, namely, special EDF loans, Sysmin funds, Stabex transfers and EDF risk capital. Excluded from this were loans from the European Investment Bank (EIB).[60]

To what factors could one attribute this apparent change of heart on the part of the European Community? The first answer is purely speculative. It could be that it was realized in the inner chambers of the Community that the disillusionment amongst the ACP Group which greeted Lomé IV could be partly assuaged by the decision to annul their multilateral debt to the Community. The ACP fears attendant upon the establishment of the

European Bank for Reconstruction and Development (EBRD),[61] and the greater attention being focused upon Eastern Europe, perhaps required some dramatic gesture of reassurance to the ACP partners that the "spirit of Lomé" was not dead. The second explanation could be attributed to the pressures exerted on the EC Council by the Commission and Parliament on the one hand, and the personal commitment of Manuel Marin himself, on the other. Both the Parliament and Commission did argue vigorously in favour of a more liberal approach to the debt issue. In the case of Development Commissioner Marin, being relatively new to the job, he was perhaps labouring under the shadows of his distinguished predecessors, notably Edgard Pisani and the late Lorenzo Natali. He might have been quite anxious to establish his credentials as a statesman who is assiduously committed to the ideals of multilateral cooperation and international development. There is some evidence to show that, for whatever reason, Señor Marin seemed to have been personally committed to finding a solution to the ACP debt problem.[62]

It now remains to say a word about the consequences of the EC decision to cancel most of the debts owed by the ACP countries. It must be stated that, welcome as this move was to the ACP countries, the amount involved related to only 2 per cent of the estimated total ACP debt of over ECU130 billion. The debt forgiveness of ECU2.6 billion was thus a mere drop in the ocean. However, the political significance of the decision cannot be overlooked. According to Marin, it was a positive signal to EC member states and other creditors to do likewise:

> This expression of solidarity goes hand in hand with, and indeed complements, the bilateral actions of the member states. Emanating from the Community in its own right, the initiative gives a political signal which is all the more worthy because it is directed towards countries which are among the poorest in the world and because it will encourage them to continue reforms, and to give new impetus to their economic and social development.[63]

CONCLUSION

We have argued in this chapter that the origins of the SSA debt were traceable to a combination of misguided internal policies and negative developments in the international environment. We considered the paradox of the African debt, whereby its relatively small size and its structural composition have reduced its importance in the politics of international debt. In considering the political responses to the African debt, we wanted to evaluate the extent to which the EC could be said to offer a different and perhaps more effective solution. There is little doubt that Lomé does offer its own peculiar accent to the debt issue. That it allows the discussion of debts within a North–South multilateral group system is an important achievement that may not be easily appreciated. Its significance becomes clear when it is realized that the vast majority of Northern OECD creditors have rejected any discussions of the debt problem from a multilateral approach, the preferred approach being the case-by-case, individual consideration of debtors under the tutelage of the London and Paris Clubs. Lomé can be said to offer a framework that is unique in this respect.

Lomé clearly has not offered an approach to the debt problem which could be said to be substantially different from orthodox approaches. Whilst EC member countries may accept collective actions on debts owed to the EC as an international organization, they have been opposed to any suggestion that the debts owed them as individual countries could be a subject of multilateral negotiations within Lomé. They have vigorously argued that such debts are outside the legal competence of the Lomé regime.[64] Individual EC governments have undertaken some bilateral initiatives, such as the Mitterrand and Lawson initiatives, which have been an improvement on prevailing multilateral strategies. However, most such actions have been largely conditional upon SSA countries reaching agreements with the Bank and the Fund on structural adjustment and reform programmes. In the final analysis, it can thus be seen that Lomé does not offer a fundamentally unique approach on the debt question.

7

ECONOMIC DECLINE AND POLICY CHOICE IN ZAMBIA

In the last chapter we examined the question of external debts as a major factor in the international politics of adjustment and conditionality-based aid. In this chapter we shall focus on the particular experience of Zambia. We shall consider some of the key issues in the politics and economics of Zambia's development, in particular the nature and origins of its economic decline, and the role of the Bretton Woods institutions in the country's quest for macroeconomic reform. This will clear the ground for our subsequent analysis of EC intervention in Zambia's reform process, which is the subject of the last two chapters of this study.

COLONIAL POLICY AND UNDERDEVELOPMENT

The area which today comprises Zambia became integrated into the international economic and political system by the late nineteenth century, following the earlier activities of European explorers and missionaries.[1] After the treaty which Charles Rudd signed with King Lobengula of the Ndebele on behalf of Cecil Rhodes, the British South Africa Company (BSAC) took control of all mining rights "north of the Transvaal and west of the Portuguese possessions".[2] Northern Rhodesia was under BSAC rule from 1899 to 1924. Apart from its role as supplier of cheap labour, the territory suffered "relative neglect" during this period. Cecil Rhodes' real interests were in the mining fields of Katanga in the north-west and Mashonaland in the south. With the beginning of mining in the Copperbelt in 1902, the BSAC strengthened its political and administrative presence in the territory. European and white immigrant farmers from the south were encouraged to settle on the fertile lands along the railway line.

The 1922 plebiscite which voted in support of "responsible [self] government" in Southern Rhodesia was to pave the way for transfer of power from the BSAC to the British Colonial Office. In 1924 the territory of Northern Rhodesia formally came under British rule. The consolidation of British imperial administration coincided with the intensification of mining activities in the area. British, American and South African mining interests increased their investments and reaped considerable profits.[3] Far from creating an integrated or balanced industrial base, colonial economic policy sowed the seeds of uneven development, mass rural migration, and the dislocation of traditional socioeconomic structures:

> the peoples and minerals of the north were exploited for the advantage of the settlers in the south, the shareholders in South Africa, Europe, and North America and the British government. The railroad . . . was meant simply to serve the mines of the Copperbelt and Katanga and did not reach out into the rural areas to help the African peasant. . . . Consequently, Northern Rhodesia's inhabitants existed in an unequal society with a regionally unbalanced economy.[4]

The colonial experience was to inspire the emerging educated urban elite to begin to question the rationale and justice of foreign rule. However, it was not until the amalgamation of Northern Rhodesia with Southern Rhodesia and Nyasaland in 1953, that there was a quickening of nationalist elan amongst the African population.[5] Most Africans opposed the Central African Federation because they saw in it the widening of the circle of colonial exploitation and settler domination. Opposition to Federation became the rallying focus of the anti-colonial struggle in general.[6] Nationalist agitations culminated in the granting of political independence by the British on 24 October 1964, under the leadership of Kenneth Kaunda and the United National Independence Party (UNIP).

Zambia's post-independence orientation in the international system can thus be said to have been shaped largely by its historical experience of colonial rule and by the challenge posed by colonial and racialist regimes within the subregion. Underlying this orientation has been, of course, its inherited imbalances in regional development, over-dependence on copper for government revenues and export earnings, a political economy characterized by the dominance of the urban sector *vis-à-vis* the rural countryside, with the obvious implications in terms of class formation and intra-elite conflicts in the ensuing decades.[7]

THE RISE OF THE SINGLE-PARTY STATE

Although Zambia was constitutionally a multi-party state at the time of independence, regional and intra-elite conflicts became a major threat to the stability of the political order. There was the question of the Lozis of Western Province, who wanted to maintain their regional autonomy in an independent Zambia.[8] President Kaunda came to rely increasingly on patronage and personal influence in attempting to resolve these conflicts. In 1971, the schism within the ruling party broke into the open, when a prominent Kaunda associate and Vice-President of UNIP, Simon

Kapwepwe, led his largely Bemba-speaking followers to form the United People's Party (UPP), while Harry Nkumbula's African National Congress enjoyed a largely Tonga following. There was also the defection from UNIP by the Lozi of Western Province. Regional as well as ethnic loyalties were invoked by the politicians in what was largely an intra-elite struggle for power.[9] In 1973, all political parties other than the ruling UNIP were outlawed and Zambia became a de facto single-party state, officially committed to the concept of "participatory democracy". Electoral and administrative reforms were put in place to strengthen the position of UNIP and to ensure its organizational supremacy over state and civil society.

Ideology and political mobilization

Kaunda stumbled upon the philosophy of humanism, which both party and state came to embrace as the national ideology.[10] An amalgam of Fabianism and Christian ethical socialism, Zambian humanism aimed to integrate African communal values with a socialist strategy of development in an attempt to create a classless society.[11] In concrete terms, however, Kaunda's humanism never really transcended the level of rhetorical and emotional appeal. It placed naïve hope in the belief that it is possible to change society simply by appealing to man's superior moral nature.[12]

Although largely ineffective as an ideology of societal mobilization, Kaunda's humanism is central in explaining certain aspects of Zambia's international behaviour, notably its emphasis on morality and ethical principles with regard to racism and imperialism; in the quest for peace and global solidarity; and in the search for international social justice.[13] Its "socialist" dimension has shaped its disposition towards economic nationalism and the bias in favour of a welfare/statist economic strategy.

Regional insecurity and foreign policy

At the regional level, Zambia occupies a strategic location in Southern Africa, a fact which imposes certain inescapable imperatives in terms of its regional policy and security calculations. The country attained independent statehood at a time when eight of its neighbours were either under colonial or minority regime rule. Geographical contiguity alone would have rendered it impossible for Zambia to remain aloof from the political ferments which were sweeping through the region. Given also its avowed anti-colonial stance and sense of moral outrage against all forms of racial oppression, the country gave support to various liberation movements as well as to refugees fleeing from areas of violent conflict.

Such a position inevitably put the country on a collision course with the colonialist and minority regimes further south. Economic and political destabilization inevitably became a constant threat. Apart from the sabotaging of vital transport and supply routes, there have been numerous military raids into Zambia's southern provinces.[14] The country also incurred heavy economic and financial losses in trying to uphold international sanctions against, first, Southern Rhodesia and later, the Republic of South Africa.[15] By the late 1980s it was estimated that the country was losing as much as US$500 million per annum due to destabilization as well as increased transport costs and trade losses.[16]

The central dilemma therefore has been how to reduce the level of dependence and vulnerability on the south. In 1968 an oil pipeline was completed, from Zambia to Dar es Salaam in Tanzania. Perhaps the attempt to disengage from the south is best symbolized by the construction of the Tanzania–Zambia Railway (TAZARA).[17] In the search for a *modus vivendi* with the south, President Kaunda personally drafted the Lusaka Manifesto which was adopted by the East and Central African states in April 1969, and subsequently by the OAU and the United Nations General Assembly. The Manifesto espoused a nonviolent approach to liberation in Southern Africa. In light of the futility of this stance in the circumstances of Southern Africa, the Lusaka Manifesto was replaced in 1970 by the Mogadishu Accord, which accepted violence as a legitimate instrument in the struggle for liberation. Zambia played a major role in setting up the Southern African Development and Co-ordination Committee (SADCC),[18] and also joined the East and Central African Preferential Trading Area (PTA), in the continuing search for "collective self-reliance" and less dependence on the south.

Within the wider African circle, Zambia has been active in OAU affairs and has embraced its ideals of "non-interference in the internal affairs of member states" and respect for their territorial integrity.[19] Perhaps a major anomaly in this regard was Zambia's recognition (with Tanzania) of Biafra in May 1968. Support for the secessionist group in the Nigerian civil war was certainly in conflict with the avowed principle of respect for existing African boundaries. Neither could acceptance of the "Balkanization" of African States be justified from the viewpoint of Pan-African unity.[20] At the international level, Zambia has continued to affirm its faith in the ideals of the United Nations. Indeed, its choice of 24 October as its independence day, which is also United Nations Day, could not have been a mere coincidence. It did reflect the country's identification with the principles and aspirations of the universal international organization. Twice Zambia was elected as a non-permanent member of the Security Council.[21] Kenneth Kaunda became one of the elder statesmen in the Commonwealth of Nations and in the non-aligned movement, in both of which bodies he orchestrated his country's concerns against colonialism and injustice, and against what he saw as the inequities of the international system.[22]

Although Zambia has been avowedly a non-aligned country, it is clear that its historical, cultural and structural orientations put it squarely in the orbit of the Western system.[23] Trade, investment and aid figures clearly show the dominance of Western countries and Western mining companies. In 1982, Zambia's most important trading partner was Japan, followed by the United Kingdom, West Germany and China. Aid and credit from the OECD by far outstripped that from China, the Soviet bloc and OPEC. The dominant actors in the aid business have been the Netherlands, Sweden, West Germany, the United Kingdom and the European Community. Western donors increased their aid to Zambia from US$360 million in 1984 to US$400 million in 1985, an amount which covered the external payments gap of the period in question.[24]

MINERAL DEPENDENCE AND DEVELOPMENT POLICY

During the first decade of independence Zambia enjoyed a period of economic prosperity owing to high copper prices and a conducive international environment. Living standards were amongst the highest in sub-Saharan Africa. The state used surplus earnings from the mining sector to subsidize the rapidly increasing population of urban dwellers in an effort to create the so-called "humanist" welfare society. In line with its commitment to economic independence and self-reliance, the government gave increasing attention to nationalization of the copper industry.

At independence, international mining concerns, notably the Anglo-American Corporation of South Africa, AMAX and Selection Trust, controlled the production, sale and marketing of Zambia's copper. The initial measures centred on increasing tax revenues from the mining companies to put more Zambians at decision-making levels which were then almost exclusively occupied by expatriates.[25] Following the 1968 Mulungushi reforms, the government asked twenty-six foreign-owned companies, most of them in retailing, construction, road transport and brewing, to sell a majority (51 per cent) of their equity shares to the state.[26] A new parastatal organization, INDECO, was created to oversee the new enterprises (see Figure 7.1).[27]

In August 1969, at a UNIP national council meeting in Matero, in the outskirts of Lusaka, President Kaunda made an official demand for a 51 per cent equity share in the mining assets of RST and Anglo, a move which shocked the companies and concerned business interests in Britain, the United States and South Africa.[28] Much of the political rhetoric of the nationalizations echoed the notion of capturing "the commanding heights of the economy" as a means of securing the country's "economic independence".[29] In a period of rising copper prices in the world market, it was indeed an attractive option. Control over the country's economic lifeline was seen not only as means of maximizing rent from the mining industry; the political imperatives of the times required that the fruits of political independence be consolidated through the reduction of economic depen-

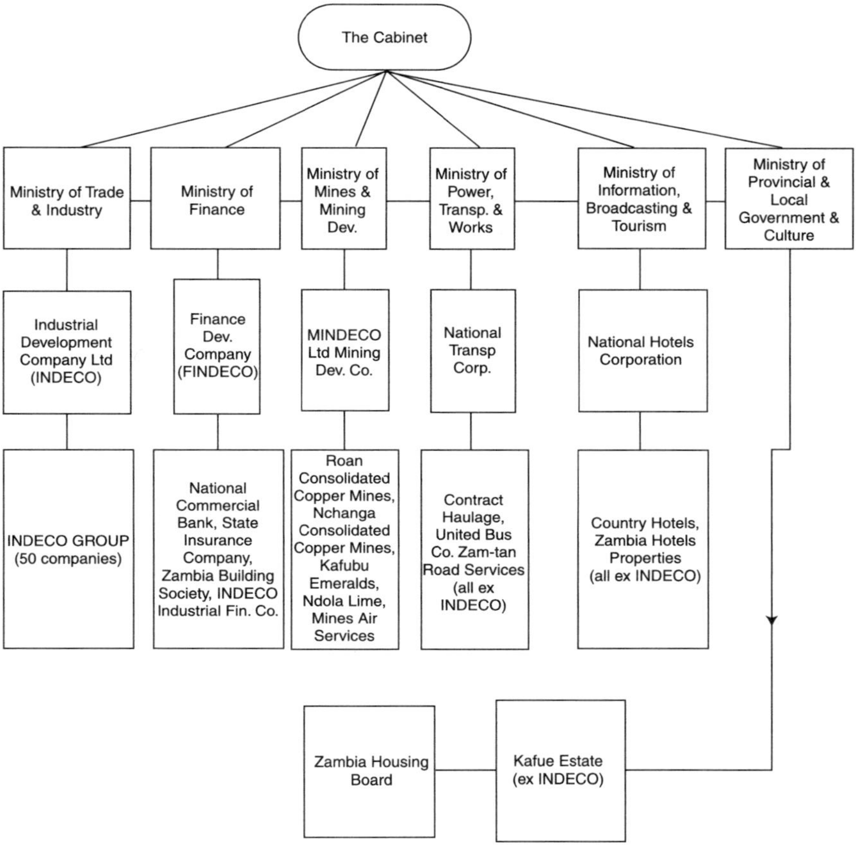

Figure 7.1 Structure of government participation in the Zambian economy, 1971
Source: Jonathan Chileshe, *Third World Countries and Development Options: Zambia*, New Delhi: Vikas Publishing House, 1987, p. 141

dence and vulnerability on transnational companies. In furtherance of this goal, Zambia, together with Chile, spearheaded the establishment of CIPEC,[30] an organization which sought to give LDC producers greater control over the production, pricing and marketing of copper.[31]

By the mid-1970s, as a result of the decline in world copper prices on the one hand, coupled with rising petroleum import bills and the recession which was gripping the developed market economies on the other, Zambia's post-independence success was gradually turning into a nightmare.[32] Copper production fell in volume from 713,000 tonnes in 1976 to 479,000 tonnes in 1985; whilst world prices for the commodity fell from (US) 95 cents a pound in 1975 to (US) 63 cents in 1984/85.[33] Export receipts

Table 7.1 Zambia: Terms of Trade Index, 1970–82 (1970 as base year)

Year	*Export price Index (A)*	*Import price Index (B)*	*(B) − (A)*	*Terms of Trade*
1970	100	100	00	100
1971	78	105	27	74
1972	80	111	31	72
1973	117	126	9	93
1974	134	157	23	85
1975	84	194	110	46
1976	100	217	117	46
1977	97	248	151	34
1978	103	299	196	35
1979	185	374	189	50
1980	201	486	285	41
1981	198	584	386	34
1982	180	695	515	24

Source: John Clarke, *Zambia: Debt and Poverty*, London: Oxfam, 1989, p. 6

deteriorated sharply from US$1.6 billion in 1980 to a mere US$700 million in 1989. Table 7.1 shows figures for the Terms of Trade Index between 1970 and 1982. With 1970 as base year, the terms of trade fell from 100 in 1970 to 24 in 1982, representing an annual loss estimated at K353 million (in 1970 prices). The problem of terms of trade deterioration was further aggravated by rising production costs in the copper industry, which in 1982 actually exceeded the export price.[34]

The inevitable result of these adverse changes was the drastic contraction of imports,[35] leading to low capacity utilization in manufacturing industry, massive shortages, high inflation, negative real per capita income growth, and a burgeoning parallel market. Tables 7.2 and 7.3 show trends in population and GDP respectively. Real per capita GDP fell by an annual average of 2.7 per cent in the 1970s and over 3 per cent a year by the 1980s. Real per capita GDP fell by an estimated 26 per cent in the decade between 1977 and 1987 while the rate of fixed investment fell from 18.2 per cent in 1980 to 10.7 per cent in 1987.[36] Inflation rose from 15 per cent in late 1970s to about 50 per cent by 1986.[37]

Rising food price subsidies, especially on the staple product, maize meal, were exerting additional pressures on dwindling budgetary resources, in addition to their effects on the money supply and inflation.

External borrowing and the debt build-up

Believing that the first shock in copper prices was a temporary aberration, international creditors agreed to extend massive loans to Zambia. Most of this borrowing was in commercial terms. Since 1972 Zambia had also been

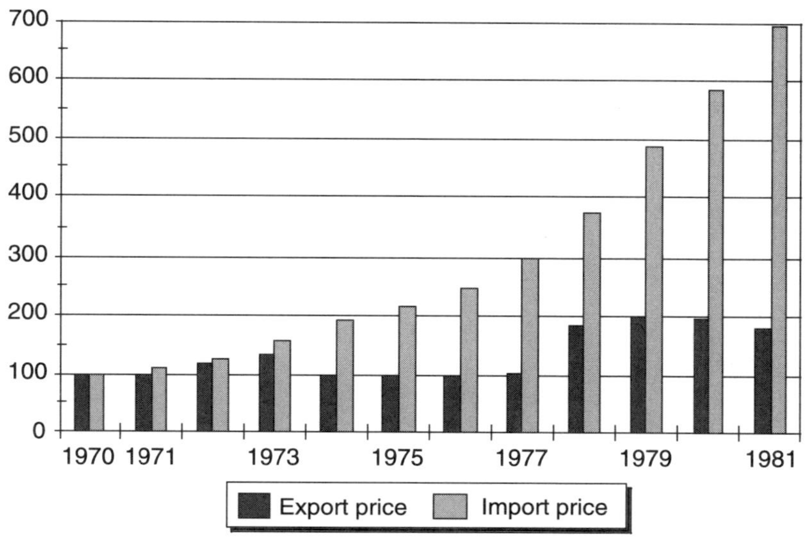

Figure 7.2 Evolution of Zambia's Terms of Trade, 1970–82
Source: John Clarke, *Zambia: Debt and Poverty*, London: Oxfam, 1989, p. 6

borrowing considerably from the IMF on relatively hard and non-reschedulable terms. By 1987 the country's external debt reached the level of US$6.51 billion, about US$1,957 million of which was owed to the IMF. Zambia's total external debt was equivalent to more than nine times its total export earnings, a situation which put it amongst the five countries with the worst debt/exports ratio in sub-Saharan Africa.[38] By the second half of the 1980s external capital inflows were drying up as Zambia began to acquire low credit rating due to its accumulation of large payments arrears. Loan disbursements fell from US$284 million in 1980 to a low US$31 million in 1986.[39]

THE PATH TO ECONOMIC DECLINE

In seeking to explain the root causes of Zambia's economic difficulties in the 1980s it is necessary to consider the nature of the country's political

Table 7.2 Zambia population and labour force, 1980–90

	1980	*1985*	*1987*	*1988*	*1989*	*1990*
Total population (million)	5.68	6.72	7.15	7.35	7.57	7.79
Growth rate %		3.30	2.8	2.9	2.9	102.90
Urban population (million)	2.26	3.00	3.4	3.6	3.8	4.00
Labour force (million)	1.65	1.99	3.74	3.78	3.82	3.86
Formal sector employment	0.38	0.36	0.36	0.36	0.37	0.38
Urban population as % of total population	40.00	45.00	48.00	49.00	50.00	51.00
Formal sector employment as % of labour force	23.00	18.00	90.00	10.00	10.00	10.00

Table 7.3 Long-term trends in Zambia's GDP in selected years, 1970–90

	1970	*1975*	*1980*	*1985*	*1987*	*1990*
1 GDP at constant (1977) prices						
(A) kwacha million	1,775.0	2,013.0	1,996.0	2,245.0	2,114.0	2,187.0
(B) 1975 = 100	88.2	100.0	99.2	111.5	105.0	108.6
(C) Previous year = 100	—	97.5	103.0	111.6	102.7	98.3
2 GDP at current market prices (kwacha million)	1,279.0	1,583.0	3,064.0	7,072.0	19,779.0	107,602.0
3 GDP per capita						
(A) at constant (1977) prices	427.0	412.0	351.0	334.0	290.0	270.0
(B) 1975 = 100	103.6	100.0	87.6	81.1	70.4	65.6
(C) Previous year = 100		93.8	94.1	106.7	98.6	94.7

Source: National Commission for Development Planning, Lusaka, November 1990

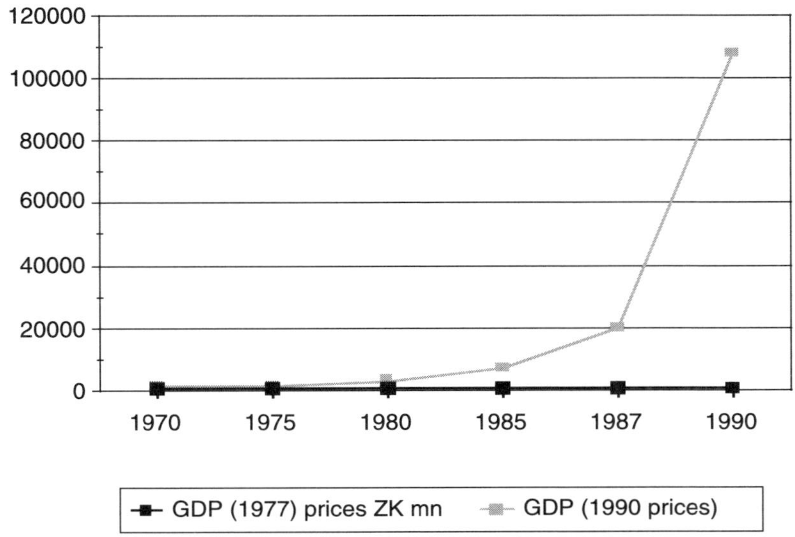

Figure 7.3 Trends in Zambia's GDP, 1970–90 (in kwacha million)
Source: National Commission for Development Planning, Lusaka, 1992

economy and its fragile position in the international system. The most salient factor is the problem of mineral export dependence. President Kenneth Kaunda used to remark that Zambians were "born with a copper spoon", an expression which properly conveys the extent of the country's dependence on a single commodity. By the late 1980s the entire mining sector accounted for about 95 per cent of all export earnings (copper for 83 per cent, cobalt for 8–9 per cent, zinc and lead for 3–4 per cent).

Although, as we have seen, the state had made some efforts to assume full control over the mining sector largely through nationalization, it is clear that transnational mining interests are still dominant in the control of the technology of production and marketing of the country's copper. The Zambian state also has no control over pricing, which is determined by the international capitalist market, notably in the London Metal Exchange (LME). We have already referred to Zambia's futile attempt to organize a Third World copper cartel in the form of the CIPEC which has not been effective. Fluctuations in copper prices are thus bound to impose a deleterious effect on the Zambian economy.[40]

The Zambian mining sector has been a large consumer of investment capital and has historically attracted a considerable percentage of the skilled labour force. Rural–urban migration was increasing rapidly, with the urban population growing at the rate of 7 per cent annually. With the urban population around 51 per cent (1991 estimates), Zambia has become the most urbanized country in sub-Saharan Africa. This trend has been accompanied by a terms of trade loss in the rural sector. Whilst the manufacturing sector was growing at an annual rate of 10 per cent, agriculture grew at the rate of only 2 per cent between 1964 and 1974.[41] The political regime thus has to contend with a growing urban population with an ever-expanding demand for food and social services, a sector, which, unlike the agrarian, is politically articulate and has a relatively well-unionized working class.

A third factor in the Zambian development crisis has to do with the prevalence of policy-related distortions in the country's economic management. Ravi Gulhati has shown "policy failures in managing aggregate demand and in securing a sensible allocation of resources compounded the devastating impact of exogenous shocks".[42] The state preferred to maintain the level of aggregate demand by external and domestic borrowing rather than directly cutting down on demand. Related to this were the distortions in prices as the government resorted to price controls instead of the market mechanism. A passive exchange rate policy was maintained, with the kwacha pegged initially to British sterling and subsequently in 1971 to the US dollar. Although in 1976 the kwacha underwent a 20 per cent devaluation and became linked to the SDR, with a further 10 per cent devaluation in 1978, the exchange rate misalignment was evident in the import bans, quantitative restrictions and administrative controls in the foreign trade sector.

Policy bias against agriculture

During the first decade of independence, policy bias was markedly oriented against agriculture in favour of manufacturing.[43] With the establishment of Namboard in 1969, the state assumed a virtual monopoly over maize marketing and over the sale of vital agricultural inputs. There were also the Provincial Cooperative Unions (PCUs), which, together with Namboard, served to keep down the maize price, an issue which was becoming of vital political importance to the Zambian government. Government subsidies on maize grew from K1 million in 1965 to K205 million (38 per cent of the government budget) in 1980.[44] The underlying logic of this policy bias against agriculture is quite clear. Given the fact that the articulate and relatively well-organized urban wage sector is potentially capable of undermining the regime, government policies, as elsewhere in Africa, were often geared towards protecting or placating this sector at the expense of the rural-agrarian sector.[45]

Public management and the princely state

Another level of explanation of the Zambian crisis relates to the pattern of its national politics and governmental machinery. Given the inherited imbalances in the country's political economy, the post-colonial state resorted to centralization under the leadership of Kaunda and the UNIP. Riding on the wave of his popularity as "Founder of the Nation", Kaunda took personal control of key policy-making organs, surrounding himself with trusted advisers and party loyalists and often by-passing the established channels of decision-making.[46] Public appointments and key policy decisions reflected a patron–client system of politics which characterizes the phenomenon of personal rule, a syndrome which the sociologist Max Weber described as "Sultanism".[47] State and parastatal positions were seen as part of a collective patrimony to be given out to party faithfuls and to be used to balance competing ethnic and class interests.[48] To bolster his control over the state, Kaunda adopted the technique of rotating public functionaries at short, irregular intervals.

> This raised the President's autonomy and reduced threats to him, but demoralized administrators, impaired efficiency and frustrated efforts to improve state capacity and insulate its institutions from outside pressures.[49]

The market and private enterprise were virtually squeezed to the margins of productive economic activities, the most resilient private companies surviving only as part of the existing framework of political patronage.

Economic policy thus took the form of a bargaining process between various elites – national as well as international – rather than being an outcome of rational decision-making.[50] The result was that technical rationality was undermined while bloated bureaucracies became an obstacle to efficiency.[51] In the words of Patrick Ollawa, motivation seemed to have "outrun understanding", as the "primacy of politics" became the sole consideration in the allocation of scarce resources.[52] It was in this kind of environment that the "crisis" of the 1980s emerged and is to be properly understood. Alex Chikwanda, a former Finance Minister and Chairman of the Zambia Confederation of Industries and Chambers of Commerce has described the Zambian mind-set thus:

> The absence of accountability and transparency have led to crippling inefficiency and costly corruption. . . . When the corrupt, indolent and irresponsible elements are rewarded lavishly, the incentive for diligence and civic duty is discouraged. When privileged groups in any commu-

nity prosper not through hard work and honest accumulation but through graft . . . the general public will develop a tendency to frown at hard work and honesty.[53]

The road to the IMF

Zambia, like most other African countries, joined the IMF shortly after her independence.[54] However, she did not avail herself of the Fund's resources until the beginning of the 1970s, when she resorted to the Compensatory Financing Facility to the value of SDR19 million to rehabilitate the country's biggest copper mine at Mufulira which had collapsed. In March 1972 Zambia also bought the equivalent of another SDR19 million under the Gold Tranche. These funds were aimed at improving the country's balance of payments position and to ease budgetary constraints rather than to undertake wider macroeconomic reforms. With the persistence of the deteriorating economic situation, especially with regard to export earnings, Zambia approached the Fund again for another SDR19 million to cover the period from May 1973 to April 1974. This standby facility was aimed at relieving the situation of dwindling foreign reserves and to improve the budgetary position of the country. These measures were essentially aimed at improving the domestic economic performance rather than to effect diversification and external balance of the Zambian economy.

These measures proved rather ineffective in improving the country's economic prospects. Towards the end of 1975 there was a severe shortage of foreign exchange, due mainly to the fall by about 40 per cent in copper prices, from K1,327 per tonne in 1974 down to K794 per tonne in 1975. Total copper production also dropped from 709,000 tonnes to 648,000 during the same period.[55] The financial crisis was aggravated both by soaring oil import bills after the OPEC price rise in 1973 and the concomitant rise in prices of manufacturing imports from the industrialized countries which ensued. Zambia resorted to yet another IMF standby in August 1976, but this time with the explicit objective of economic diversification so as to make the economy less vulnerable to the endemic fluctuations in world copper prices. The aim was to redress external and domestic disequilibria by reducing aggregate demand and enhancing domestic production. Measures included a three-year wage freeze, a 60 per cent reduction in consumer subsidies, reduction of the budget deficit through a cut on capital expenditures, while raising interest rates so as to enhance savings and curb excess credit demand.

These policy measures, however, could not stem the drift towards a further economic downturn. The balance of payments crisis was worsening with the growth of payments arrears which rose from SDR88 million in 1976 to SDR393 million in 1977.[56] Dwindling foreign reserves led to intensification of foreign exchange controls, which in turn precipitated massive shortages of essential consumer items, inflation, and a general decline in the level of economic activities.

A more comprehensive IMF programme was agreed upon for the period 1978–80, with a financial value of SDR250 million. The programme sought to use the economic instrument of demand management to effect a healthier balance of payments position and to set the country back on the path towards sustained growth. The programme also sought to revamp the mining sector so as to enhance its viability and economic performance. This was to be done through rationalization of production processes, massive retrenchment of staff and cutbacks in certain employee social services. The agricultural sector, hitherto neglected in most public policies, received some attention under the new programme. Emphasis was placed on the need to reduce the unfavourable terms of trade of rural farmers through higher producer prices. Food production was also to be enhanced through improved extension services. Industrial performance was to be improved through development of local sourcing for industrial raw materials, and the creation of a more attractive environment for foreign private investment. Emphasis was equally placed on monetary and fiscal discipline. Domestic credit expansion was slowed down while the kwacha was devalued by 10 per cent in March 1978. In the same year the government met with a consultative group in Paris under the auspices of the World Bank, a forum which proved quite effective in mobilizing much-needed funds and improving the international credibility of the reform programme.[57]

The 1978–80 programme was only partially successful in attaining its stated objectives. The mining sector's financial viability had positively improved whilst better monetary and fiscal discipline brought down the level of inflation. External balance also improved as the balance of payments became positive in 1979, after having been negative in the previous year.[58] On the deficit side, however, GDP fell in real terms due to reduction in volume of copper production. Agricultural production also fell due to unpropitious weather conditions during 1978–79. The government had to import food at massive cost in terms of scarce foreign exchange. The second oil shock in 1979 also contributed to the worsening economic situation, as did rising transport costs in connection with the Zimbabwean war of independence.

THE IMF EXTENDED PROGRAMME, 1981–83

Table 7.4 shows Zambia's transactions with the IMF from 1971 to 1983. Given the persistent nature of the Zambian crisis, and the awareness of the need for more profound structural and macroeconomic reorientation in policy and management, the Zambian government negotiated a major extended facility to cover the three-year period from 1981 to 1983.

The IMF approved the amount of SDR800 million for the programme

Table 7.4 Zambia's transactions with the IMF, 1971–83 (SDR millions)

Year	*Drawing*	*Repurchases**	*Net IMF credit*	*Use of Fund credit*	*Charges*
1971	19.0	—	19.0	19.0	—
1972	38.0	—	38.0	38.0**	—
1973	19.0	—	19.0	57.0	0.6
1974	—	—	—	57.0	1.6
1975	56.9	38.0	18.9	75.9	1.3
1976	38.5	19.0	19.3	95.2	4.1
1977	19.0	19.0	—	95.2	5.3
1978	148.8	—	148.8	245.1	7.9
1979	100.0	26.3	73.7	320.0	13.3
1980	50.0	44.0	6.0	308.3	20.0
1981	359.3	47.3	312.0	627.8	25.3
1982	41.5	86.2	44.7	575.6	48.6
1983	173.7	114.0	59.7	635.3	49.6

Notes:
* Repurchases refer to repayment to IMF in foreign exchange equal to the SDR
** Reserve position in Fund (SDR19.0 million) was used to reduce net use of Fund credited to SDR38.0 million
Source: Marcia Burdette, *Zambia between Two Worlds*, Boulder, Col.: Westview Press, 1988, p. 123

on 8 May 1981. This new agreement was in essence a medium-term Structual Adjustment Programme whose aims were:

1 to move resources to more productive investment through the instrumentality of demand management;
2 to rehabilitate the rural/agricultural sector as well as existing investments, while investing in fast-yielding projects;
3 to maintain the volume of copper production at the minimum level of 600,000 tonnes during the programme period.

The key sectors for the reform programme were thus mining, agriculture and manufacturing.

Agriculture was to be rehabilitated through development of supportive infrastructures such as transport, storage and extension facilities. Particular emphasis was to be placed on production of maize, the country's staple product. There was also the objective of improving prices to ensure that a hiatus no longer existed between domestic and international agricultural prices. With regard to the mining sector, the aim was to rationalize production techniques through recruitment of additional technical staff and through the use of electricity rather than relying on more costly forms of energy such as petroleum. Manufacturing was to be improved through the creation of a more vibrant private sector and a more attractive climate for external investors, enhancing the efficiency of private companies, the development of local sourcing of industrial raw materials, and the elimination of price distortions.

Like its predecessors, the 1981–83 reform programme foundered, largely because of the continuing decline in the mining sector. The price of copper had plummeted from K1,719 per tonne in 1980 to K1,374 per tonne in 1982, while production volume fell from 609,000 tonnes in 1980 to 560,000 tonnes in 1981.[59] The ensuing financial crisis meant that performance criteria could hardly be met. The total domestic credit ceiling, which had been put at K1,999 million, exceeded this limit and rose to the level of K2,013 million in 1981; external payments arrears which were to be reduced by a minimum of SDR21 million from SDR500 million, actually went up by SDR29 million.[60] By 1982, real GDP stagnated, failing to reach the targeted growth rate of 5 per cent, while shortages became widespread.

With these desperate financial and economic circumstances, the Zambian government cancelled the extended arrangement on 3 July 1982, pointing out that the deterioration of international conditions made it impossible for the country to continue with the programme. Backed with an official memorandum explaining his country's financial and economic policies, Zambian Prime Minister and Minister of Finance, Mr Nalumino Mundia, wrote to the Managing Director of the Fund requesting, instead, a one-year standby arrangement for the amount of SDR211.5 million.[61]

The years 1983–86 were to witness an even bolder effort by the Zambian government to come to terms with the country's economic predicament. Past programmes seemed, in retrospect, to be no more than a half-hearted attempt to grapple with the economy's downward spiral. They were based on an over-optimistic estimate of copper prices, an optimism which proved illusory. With the continuing decline in copper and cobalt prices and the failure to restrain government spending, a fiscal and budgetary crisis ensued. The deficit was financed by allowing a build-up of payment arrears and by further borrowing from multilateral and private commercial sources, thereby increasing the already existing debt burden.

It was thus clear that more effective policy changes were required. It was to be spearheaded by technocrats such as Luke Mwananshiku. In 1980, because of his outspoken criticism of government policy, he was summarily dismissed as Governor of the Central Bank by President Kaunda. He was reinstated into government, this time as Finance Minister with enhanced powers over the NCDP and other key policy actors.

Table 7.5 presents the main policy interventions by the IFIs from 1983 to 1991. In April an SDR211.5 million standby was agreed upon to last until March 1984. Its aim was to address the internal and external imbalances, assist in restructuring the payment programme for external debts, and to finance rehabilitation of the mining sector.

The kwacha underwent a 20 per cent devaluation and was delinked from the SDR and pegged to a basket of currencies. There was both a wage and

Table 7.5 Chronology of important policy events, 1983–91

Date	*Policy event*
April 1983	IMF standby agreement (12 months)
May 1983	Paris Club agreement on debt restructuring
March 1984	World Bank export rehabilitation (copper) and diversification loan
July 1984	Paris Club agreement on debt restructuring
July 1984	IMF standby agreement
December 1984	London Club commercial bank debt restructuring
January 1985	IDA/World Bank agricultural rehabilitation project
June 1985	Consultative Group agreement on external aid
October 1985	Import liberalization and Forex auction scheme
October 1985	IDA industrial reorientation credit
December 1985	Consultative Group agreement on external aid
February 1986	IMF standby agreement (24 months)
March 1986	Paris Club agreement on debt restructuring
June 1986	IDA recovery credit
December 1986	Consultative Group agreement on external aid
May 1987	Government revokes IMF programme
August 1987	Government launches the Interim National Development Programme
1989	The Fourth National Development Plan (FNDP), 1989–93
September 1989	Rapprochement with the IFIs (preparation of a joint-policy framework paper)
April 1990	The Social Action Programme (1990-93)
September 1990	Political reforms/programme of transition to multi-party democracy
March 1991	Structural Adjustment Programme relaunched
October 1991	National elections and emergence of a new government

Source: The World Bank and Government of Zambia, 1992

recruitment freeze on the public sector. The programme succeeded in bringing down the budget deficit from 18.9 per cent of GDP in 1982 to 6.9 per cent in 1983.[62] However, performance criteria on debt payment were still unmet by the end of 1983, and the balance of payments problem remained unchanged. The 1984 programme similarly did not record any significant success and, in fact, collapsed. While general living standards were becoming increasingly desperate, socioeconomic inequalities were also widening. Collier and Bates have estimated that by the eve of the auction, the gini coefficient for urban incomes rose from 0.48 to 0.49, while the Consumer Price Index for low-income groups experienced a 16 per cent increase relative to that of high-income groups since 1975.[63]

The 1985 reform programme and the auction

Table 7.6 shows the balance of payments situation between 1982 and 1985. By 1985, it was clear that the external deficit had reached an unsustainable level. The 1985 programme marked an important turning point in Zambian economic policy-making. President Kaunda began to bow to external pressures for more wide-ranging reforms. The strategy of the international finance institutions was to mount a concerted pressure through other external donors and creditors to get Zambia to adopt a structural programme. Within Zambia itself, they targeted their campaigns on the presidency and central bureaucracies, while by-passing the Party. Quite clearly, in the eyes of the Fund and Bank representatives, the Party was not regarded as a legitimate organ of state policy. According to Bates and Collier, "the international agencies revealed that either they did not recognize the significance of the Party or felt it inappropriate to approach its officials".[64]

Indeed, technocrats such as the new Finance Minister Luke Mwananshiku were equally convinced that more drastic changes were needed.[65] This was a view shared by officials such as David Phiri, Governor of the

Table 7.6 Zambia balance of payments, 1982–85 (in US$ million)

	1982	*1983*	*1984*	*1985*
Exports (f.o.b.)	988	988	838	802
Imports (f.o.b.)	−1004	−716	−619	−622
Trade balance	−16	272	219	180
Receipts on invisibles	162	129	104	95
Payments of invisibles	−476	−389	−320	−358
Total invisibles	−314	−260	−216	−263
Current account balance before debt service	−370	12	3	−83
Debt service on existing debt	−433	−365	−329	−769
of which:				
bilateral	(34)	(16)	(30)	(263)
multilateral	(49)	(62)	(61)	(82)
suppliers credit	(25)	(28)	(20)	(69)
private financial institutions	(67)	(17)	(5)	(135)
IMF	(153)	(212)	(137)	(153)
Interest on short term borrowing	(105)	(30)	(76)	(65)
Reduction commercial arrears	—	—	—	(4)
Accumulation of reserves	−91	−25	−5	0
Gross capital requirement	−894	−378	−331	−846
Accumulation of arrears on debt service	0	0	0	586

Source: Bank of Zambia/IMF, December 1985

Central Bank, and Dominic Mulaisho, State House Presidential Adviser. A policy coalition had emerged that was sympathetic to a more technocratic approach to the reform effort. With collaboration of Fund and Bank staff, a series of technical studies was undertaken for a new reform programme. Although there was strong opposition against the programme from the UNIP Central Committee, Kaunda's firm commitment was sufficient to ensure that it was put in place.

A framework was also established for resumption of negotiations with the international finance institutions. Apart from the express commitment to pursue further reform efforts which previous stabilization measures had not effectively undertaken, the new programme was based on three central pillars. These were:

1 liberalization and decontrol of interest rates;
2 abolition of the rent-oriented, import-licensing system and establishment of a foreign exchange auction;
3 a phased removal of subsidies on maize meal and fertilizer.

It was without a doubt the most comprehensive and ambitious reform programme ever to have been launched by the Zambian state, extending from the removal of public subsidies to price decontrol and privatization of certain public enterprises. Other important features of the package included:

> eliminating subsidies on more than fifty commodities by decontrolling prices in the state sector . . . reducing the budgetary deficit by cutting expenditure rather than by domestic and international borrowing or by running down reserves; improving state economic management, especially for budgetary control and debt service; dismantling import restrictions . . . restructuring the parastatal sector to cut costs, improve efficiency, and diminish rent seeking; rehabilitating the copper sector . . . increasing producer prices for maize and other agricultural crops . . . progressively reducing the size of the civil service by 25 percent; increasing export incentives via a foreign exchange retention scheme; compiling a new investment code; and reforming the tax system.[66]

The auction, which was the centrepiece of the adjustment programme, was aimed at liberalizing the exchange rate regime by allowing the kwacha to attain a "realistic" exchange rate *vis-à-vis* foreign currencies. It was based on a set of theoretical assumptions about the positive effects of devaluation on poor, developing, commodity-exporting countries. Exchange rate changes are intended to improve the competitiveness of a country's exports while also encouraging export diversification and eliminating parallel markets. They are also expected to have long-term positive distributional effects, since they tax consumers of imports, mostly relatively high-income urban dwellers, rather than poor rural dwellers, while boosting rural terms of trade.[67]

The auction was organized by the Central Bank which was the official auctioneer.[68] The bidders were the commercial banks who operated on behalf of private companies. A company desiring foreign exchange would normally apply to its bank indicating the amount required and the amount of kwacha it was prepared to pay for it. On a fixed day each week, the banks for their part would lodge their requests with the Central Bank which then would have known precisely how much foreign exchange was being applied for within the week. After receipt of the biddings the Central Bank would then rank all of them, beginning with the highest and working downwards until all the available foreign exchange was exhausted. The exchange rate would then be determined by the marginal bid, i.e., the value of the last successful bid in the rank-order of the biddings.[69]

During the early weeks of the auction the kwacha rose from a pre-auction rate of K2.22 to the US dollar to K6 to the dollar. By April 1986, when President Kaunda decided to replace the "technocrats" Mwananshiku, Phiri and Mulaisho, the value of the kwacha stood at K7 to the US dollar. The auction had come under severe criticism for allegedly being excessive and fuelling inflation and thereby increasing general hardships for the "common man". The "technocrats" were replaced by the "politicians": Leonard Chivuno became Central Bank Governor while Basil Kabwe, a one-time Education Minister and trade unionist was made Finance Minister. Both were known to be protégés of UNIP Secretary-General Grey Zulu, himself a quintessential representative of the old guard.[70] The third man, James Mapoma, was brought to State House as Economics Adviser after years of experience in the mining sector.

The new appointees were widely known to be uncommitted to the auction system, a point which underlined the increasingly widespread lack of confidence in the economy itself, and the speculative effect which this had on prices and economic activities in general. Although it had the salutary effect of removing the bureaucratic delays and rent-seeking which had characterized the old system, the auction favoured the manufacturing sector more than the rural-agricultural sector. In July/August 1986, in spite of dwindling foreign exchange, Chivuno raised the amount of foreign exchange which could be bid for. This created a "pipeline" of successfully auctioned but undisbursed foreign exchange allocations, which by November 1986, had accumulated to the value of US$40 million.[71] Delays on payments were as long as ten weeks for successful bidders.

The problem of foreign exchange scarcity was in large part attributable to the fact that external actors provided only a very limited amount of foreign exchange support to the programme, again because they had reservations about the commitment of Zambian economic managers to pursue the logic of reform. This was especially the case following the introduction of new

Table 7.7 Sources of foreign exchange in Zambia, 1986–89 (in US$ million per month)

	1986	*1987*	*1989*
Copper (gross)	55	89	104
Non-trad. exports	5	9	11
Total exports	60	98	115
Aid & other borrowing	12	5	16
Debt payments*	13	7	4
Net aid	−1	−2	12
Exports + net aid	59	96	127

Note: * Debt payments include payments of arrears, principal and interest but exclude debt payments by ZCCM
Source: Bates and Collier, op. cit., p. 32

controls in July 1986, when the government specified priority sectors and enterprises for foreign exchange allocation.

Donors and the international institutions saw this as an unwarranted interference with the workings of the market. But for Zambian economic managers, it was an attempt to affirm control over the definition of economic priorities in consonance with national developmental aspirations. They did not consider the sudden influx of luxury imports which accompanied the initial phase of the auction as an efficient way to allocate scarce foreign exchange. According to John Clarke, this decision was "greeted angrily by the IMF who saw [it] . . . as unwarranted interference in the market system. This contributed to IMF delaying the disbursement of funds. . . . Bilateral aid pledged to support the auction was also held up as Northern governments meekly followed the IMF's lead".[72]

In Table 7.7 we see the sources of monthly foreign exchange in Zambia during the crucial reform years. Debt payments had become a substantial burden just as external capital inflows were drying up. By 1986 net aid had fallen to nil, and even became negative in the following year. Such a situation obviously aggravated the supply of available foreign exchange which, in turn, brought down the value of the kwacha. Indeed, by the end of 1986, the rate was reduced to K15 to the dollar, a mere 15 per cent of its official value before the auction. By the end of 1987, it was down to K21 to the dollar, which was 11 per cent of its pre-auction value. An additional fault with the auction is the fact that it was not implemented as part of a comprehensive and "integrated" reform package. It was not carefully integrated with the national budget and fiscal policy; nor were supply constraints taken into account; nor was consideration given to the need to avoid imports of unnecessary luxuries.[73]

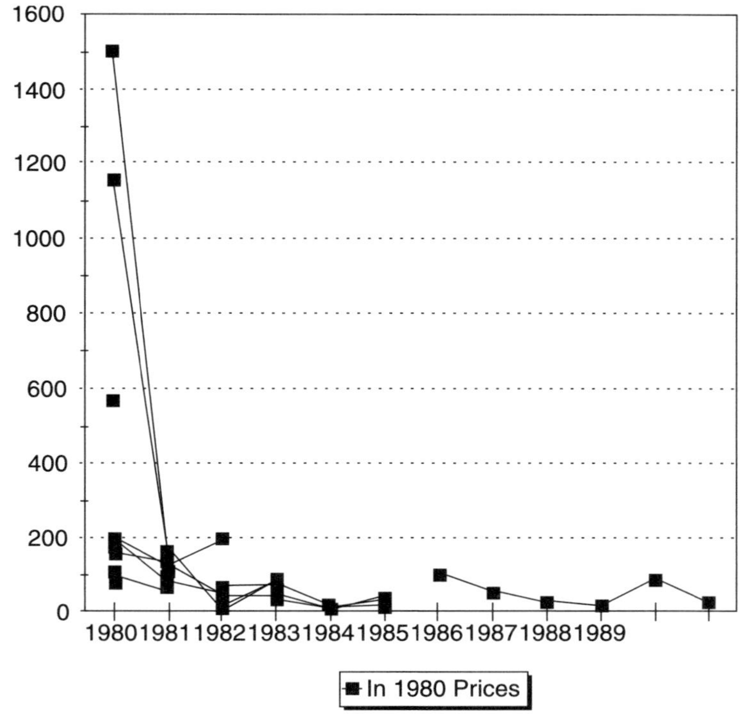

Figure 7.4 Zambia: public expenditure on subsidies, 1980–89 (in kwacha million)
Source: Andersson and Kayizzi-Mugerwa, *Mineral Dependence, Goal Attainment and Equity*, Göteberg: School of Economics and Legal Science, 1989, p. 21

The question of public subsidies

If the auction became a contentious issue in the politics of Zambian economic management, the subsidies issue, particularly on the staple commodity, maize, was to prove the most politically explosive in social terms. Subsidies had been a major bone of contention in the dialogue between the Zambian government and the multilateral institutions.[74]

The Bank and Fund were calling for the massive withdrawal of subsidies which were seen as a major drain on government finances and a cause of the fiscal imbalances which had become endemic in the Zambian political economy. Table 7.8 shows the amount of government expenditure devoted to subsidies between 1980 and 1989. Subsidies rose from K196.8 million in 1980 to K1502.8 million in 1989. In the third column, however, representing amount in terms of 1980 prices, by 1989 they amounted to only K148.8, a drop of 25 per cent from 1980 levels. As a percentage of total government expenditure, subsidies were a massive 27 per cent in 1980,

Table 7.8 Zambian government expenditure on subsidies, 1980–89 (in kwacha millions)

Year	*In 1989 Prices*	*In 1980 Prices*	*% change*	*Index*	*Sub/Rev*	*Sub+net lending/Rev*
1980	196.8	196.8	—	100	27	84
1981	110.2	110.0	−48	52	15	15
1982	156.0	137.6	34	70	15	30
1983	82.2	60.9	−56	31	8	12
1984	91.6	57.2	−6	29	8	13
1985	188.4	83.7	46	43	12	16
1986	569.9	139.0	66	71	18	32
1987	824.0	143.0	3	73	17	24
1988	1156.6	166.4	16	85	20	—
1989	1502.8	148.8	−10	76	19	—

Note: * Sub/Rev is equal to subsidies as a percentage of government revenue
Source: Andersson and Kayizzi-Mugerwa, *Mineral Dependence, Goal Attainment and Equity*, 1989, p. 21

falling to their lowest of 8 per cent during 1983/84, and then rising again to 20 per cent by 1988. It is therefore clear that such high levels of subsidies on consumption could not be sustained under conditions of increasing financial constraints.

In December 1986, the government, following Fund and Bank prescriptions, raised the consumer price on high-grade maize meal by 120 per cent. To cushion the negative effects on the poor, the government pledged to keep subsidies on low-grade maize meal which is normally consumed by low-income groups. The government also declared its intention to compensate private maize millers who were expected to suffer production losses in the process.[75] The result was the shortages of low-grade maize meal whilst the high-grade variety's price had risen astronomically. According to Richard Pearce:

> a substantial proportion of the benefits was received by those who were not the most vulnerable to shortages. Moreover, the high rate of inflation coupled with a shortage of government finance for developmental investment and the slow growth in employment opportunities, meant that the costs of providing the subsidy were borne substantially by the poor.[76]

In an atmosphere of rising tension across the country, riots broke out in Lusaka and in the Copperbelt, in which fifteen people died. Deeply moved by the experience, President Kaunda responded by summarily restoring the maize subsidy. He also proceeded to nationalize the large private maize mills, most of them owned by Greek expatriates, whom he accused of sabotage and "capitalist exploitation".[77]

It was thus becoming evident that the balance of political forces were working against the continuation of the adjustment programme. After months of vacillation, during which pro- and anti-reform advocates argued their case and worked ferociously behind the scenes, it gradually became clear that the anti-reformists were gaining the upper hand. What seemed perhaps to have settled the matter decisively in favour of the anti-reformists was the imminence of the scheduled 1988 national elections. It was widely believed that the elections would be the ultimate litmus test of the legitimacy of the reform programme and indeed of President Kaunda himself and of the one-party state. The leadership feared that people might "vote with their feet" in protest against the hardships of the reforms, with a real possibility that the ensuing embarrassment might foster instability and civil strife.[78] Kaunda ultimately chose the path of capitulation, which he understood as the path of reason; in effect, postponing hard economic choices for the sake of the political "health" of the state.

The break with the IMF

In January 1987, not long after he reneged on the maize subsidy, Kaunda renounced many of the other measures agreed within the reform programme, including the auction. In place of the auction he established a new exchange rate with the kwacha fixed at K8 to the US dollar; the old system of administrative allocation of foreign exchange was also reintroduced. In March, the government brought back the auction, after much pressures from the international institutions, whose high-level officials, according to Thomas Callaghy, "happened" to have been in Lusaka at this time.[79] After the restoration of the auction, the kwacha's value fell once again to K21.01 to the dollar. This was to be followed by intensive discussions with international officials both in Lusaka and Washington. However, these dialogues could not save Zambia's Structural Adjustment Programme. And finally on May Day 1987, President Kaunda officially announced that he could no longer carry on with the IMF programme. It was a move which met with considerable popular support, bordering on euphoria, as shown by the subsequent "sympathy" riots and looting which occurred in Lusaka and in the Copperbelt. President Kaunda declared that the Party and government could no longer accept a situation where the

> social fabric is slowly disintegrating, thereby sowing seeds of unrest and undermining the spirit and unity of the nation. . . . It is patently clear that far from improving our condition, we are not succeeding; hence the need for a fresh look.[80]

It was a major reversal of policy, a classic expression of economic nationalism. In a symbolic and rather baroque gesture, the IMF Resident Representative was locked out of his offices which were located in the Bank of Zambia building.[81] Even before the formal break in relations, conflict was already becoming apparent between the government and the Fund. Just before the rift, deliveries of petroleum to the country's refinery, financed under an oil credit facility by a consortium led by the Bank of America, were suspended after arrears on payments had exceeded US$30 million.[82] In October 1986, it was reported in the Western media that the Fund had made unofficial complaints about arrears of SDR7 million owed by Zambia.[83] Failure to repay these arrears meant that Zambia became automatically ineligible to resume drawings on the SDR286 million IMF standby facility.

Conflicting policy perspectives were also becoming apparent. Prime Minister Kebby Musokotwane had announced that the government was not prepared to accept the IMF position on raising the price of fertilizers by 100 per cent and of fuel by 75 per cent. The Fund for its part took strong exception to the government's failure to meet the agreed targets for controlling monetary growth and reducing the budget deficit.[84] The failure of the auction derived in large part from lack of sufficient foreign exchange. This was decisive in pushing down the value of the kwacha, which in turn lead to an inflationary spiral. Inflation rose from 35 and 39 per cent in 1985 to 52 and 58 per cent in 1986 for high- and low-income groups respectively.[85] Some misallocation of resources and failure to finance priority sectors especially in agriculture and manufacturing was also evident.[86]

A clear balance sheet of the IMF-backed reform programme is yet to emerge. Economists are still debating its impact on the Zambian economy and society. Central to this debate is how to assess the effects of devaluation and the foreign exchange auction, especially on inflation, the CPI (Consumer Price Index) and the general decline in living standards.[87] There is at least some convincing evidence for the argument that devaluation did have an obvious inflationary impact on import prices. The rise in the prices of imports can then be said to have been translated into "accelerated inflation". Devaluation also astronomically raised the kwacha cost of debt servicing, thereby worsening the budget deficit, which in 1986 had reached 30 per cent of GDP. The obvious consequence arising from the ensuing increase in money supply, which rose from 23 per cent in 1985 to 93 per cent in 1986, was an inflationary spiral.[88]

The auction had some positive effects which it would be unfair to ignore:

- It eliminated the corruption and rent-seeking associated with the import-licensing system.
- It removed the bureaucratic delays in foreign exchange allocation.
- Some modest diversifying impact was registered, as profitability of such

non-traditional exports as cotton, textiles, coffee and fresh vegetables was enhanced.
- There was also some import-substituting effect, as the machine tool industry was revived in response to the need to produce more spare parts.
- Finally, capacity utilization improved, given the fact that some manufacturing firms were now able to have access to foreign exchange with which to import their vital inputs.[89]

Social unrest and political resistance

Studies by UNICEF showed an alarming increase in malnutrition, especially amongst children and mothers. By November 1987, 27 per cent of the 433 children admitted to the Lusaka Teaching Hospital in a single week died, and 60 per cent of the deaths were said to be due to protein energy malnutrition (PEM).[90] As a result of inflation and slow wage rises, a manual labourer in 1987 was earning 13 per cent less in real terms than he earnt in 1980.[91] Removal of subsidies as well as rationalization of state enterprises meant a higher cost of living for the average family and a worsening unemployment situation. Social conditions in the Copperbelt, especially among mining workers, had become desperate.[92] It did seem to have aggravated income inequalities while pushing the poor into a condition of greater immiserization. Not only did they face unemployment and massive retrenchments, but also consumer prices soared, food prices doubled, and even the local staple, maize meal, was becoming out of reach in most households. Malnutrition, especially amongst children, was becoming commonplace, while social services, especially health, were in a state of virtual paralysis.[93] Whilst it can be argued that no one can say how much worse the crisis might have become if the Structural Adjustment Programme had not been put in place, it goes without saying that it did not dramatically improve the Zambian economy; indeed, for ordinary Zambians, their life-chances actually deteriorated.

It is hardly surprising, therefore, that strikes and violent unrest became an endemic feature of the social scene between 1985 and 1988. Towards the end of 1985 strikes by hospital staff, students and industrial workers reached a level whereby President Kaunda had to take the extreme measure of invoking constitutional emergency powers.[94] The most serious unrests, however, were the ones following the 11 December 1986 removal of subsidies on the "breakfast" meal, which resulted in a 120 per cent rise in the price of the staple. The government was forced to backtrack on the subsidy and Kaunda proceeded to nationalize the maize milling companies whom he blamed for the rising costs and food shortages.[95] It is thus clear that the lack of a social safety net and of specific programmes of poverty alleviation targeted at vulnerable groups contributed to the eventual collapse of the reform programme.

Kaunda's administration was confronted with what was no less than a crisis of governmental legitimacy. Rumours of a possible military putsch became rife.[96] An alleged coup attempt was uncovered in 1988, involving former army commander and envoy to West Germany, Lt-General Christon Tembo. It was on 30 June 1990 that a coup attempt almost succeeded, when the headquarters of the Zambian broadcasting complex were for a few hours under the control of a mercurial young army lieutenant, Mwamba Luchembe.[97]

How do we explain the failure of Zambia's adjustment effort? A balanced explanation would have to take account of both external and internal impediments as well as the sequencing of the policy reforms.[98] We have already alluded to the lack-lustre support which external actors gave to the Zambian programme. It is obvious that without massive infusions of financial capital, such as was the case in Ghana, structural adjustment packages cannot be expected to achieve their objectives. In the Zambian case, external donors were reluctant to commit more funds because of their lack of confidence in the leadership's commitment to the reform process itself. This lack of confidence can be said to have further fed the Zambian suspicion of Western betrayal and duplicity. "Suspicion fed upon suspicion", thereby setting in motion a vicious circle of mutual disavowal.

The most decisive factor, however, was the political resistance to reform both in political leadership circles and amongst urban groups, especially organized labour. We have already seen how Zambia's development path has historically maintained an urban bias. By comparison with other poorer segments, organized labour in Zambia, particularly in the Copperbelt, had become something of a "proletarian elite" – a well-organized and well-entrenched societal pressure group, able to articulate its demands and able to challenge fundamental government policies which threaten its real or perceived interests.[99] Other important urban elements include students, unemployed youth and lumpen elements, all of whom faced greater hardships as the economic crisis worsened.[100] It is therefore obvious why the numerous "food riots" were a largely urban phenomenon. It also explains why labour leaders such as Frederick Chiluba became the most outspoken critics of the auction and IMF reform programme.

But resistance from workers and urban interest groups alone would not have been enough to bring down the IMF programme. There had to be a contingent coincidence of interests between those disaffected elements and the Party-political class. The latter saw the whittling away of their sources of accumulation, patronage and influence with the dismantling of some of the parastatals, removal of controls and abolition of import licensing. The dominance of the Party within the political structure meant that the apparatchik rather than the technocrats in the ministries and the Bank of

Zambia would have the final say on matters of economic policy. They were therefore reluctant to surrender this privilege and to do what in effect amounted to ministering over the dissolution of a political structure that had served as the pipeline of their material reproduction. With the intervention of the Bank and Fund, who clearly showed their preference for the technocrats, a relentless power struggle ensued between these two factions of the Zambian power elites.

For the party-political faction, therefore, the defence of their interests took the form of opposition to the IMF programme, in the name of humanism, socialism, economic nationalism and national security. The Fund and the Bank, the so-called "terrible twins", were blamed for seeking to undermine the cohesion and stability of the Zambian state. It was ultimately this group that was decisive in bringing down the reform effort. The groups who recorded some gains from the adjustment experiment – farmers, businessmen and industrialists – were, in the words of Bates and Collier, political forces which

> stood at the margins of the polity. They were not lodged in the Party, which constituted the system's core. And they therefore could not provide a political defense for this experiment with the introduction of the market.[101]

THE INTERIM NATIONAL DEVELOPMENT PROGRAMME

After the break with the Fund, President Kaunda launched the Interim National Development Programme (INDP) in August 1987. The main elements of the new policy were: a fixed exchange rate, price control on some twenty-three commodities, fixed interest rates, and a ceiling of 10 per cent on debt service payments. The exchange rate regime was to be administered through a new organization, the Foreign Exchange Management Committee (FEMAC). The programme was presented as a "home-made" package, an attempt to develop from "our own resources". Indeed, it had been designed with the help of academics based at the University of Zambia who were known to be opposed to the IMF programme.[102] In accordance with the nationalist inspiration of the interim programme, the Zambian authorities declared that from now on they would neither accept any foreign assistance nor enter into any aid agreements that contained conditionality clauses. Table 7.9 shows the criteria which the government set out for evaluating all external financial aid.

At the same time, they hoped that external actors would complement their effort with provision of financial assistance, including partial debt cancellation. Prime Minister Kebby Musokotwane made some official visits to Europe in order to sell the new Zambian policy. As was to be expected, he was received with a great deal of scepticism. The programme was seen

Table 7.9 Criteria for selection and prioritization of externally aided projects in Zambia, 1989

General criteria	*Weight (%)*
Projects with high multiplier effect on the rest of the economy	10.0
Manpower development	8.0
Projects with short gestation period	7.8
Projects which substitute imports using local raw materials	7.7
Projects promoting non-traditional exports	7.6
Projects with forward and backward linkages	7.5
Projects using local raw materials	7.3
Government revenue-generating projects	7.1
Employment-generating projects	6.6
Labour-intensive projects	6.3
Projects satisfying basic needs	6.2
Projects with high internal rate of return	5.2
Projects promoting balanced economic development	4.2
Cost effectiveness	3.5
Projects nearing completion	3.0
Loans for maintenance of capital stock	1.5
Externally aided projects with cross conditionalities	0.6
Externally aided projects which impose policy reforms	0.0
TOTAL	100.0

Source: National Commission for Development Planning, Lusaka, 1989

as both misinformed in its economics and patently dubious in terms of its use of statistical data. Even before the announcement of the INDP, the Bank had already stopped further disbursements of funds to Zambia, and in September, the Fund followed suit in declaring the country ineligible to use its resources. The plan consequently did not receive any donor support, with the exception of the Scandinavian countries who continued with their aid programmes and arranged to bail out Zambia from its immediate financial straits by arranging to pay off part of its World Bank arrears.

Heroic as this home-grown strategy might have seemed, it served to bring back some of the ills of the old system: corruption and rent-seeking were back; paralysis encroached upon industry as foreign exchange became scarce; inflation continued to rise as the per capita GDP continued to fall. Table 7.10 presents data for the inflation rate between 1986 and September 1991.

Black marketeering and cross-border smuggling due to currency overvaluation were back. And yet by 1989, on balance, the prospects seemed brighter than they were in preceding years. Real GDP grew by 2.7 per cent while agricultural production increased by an impressive 6.7 per cent.[103] However, these positive improvements are perhaps more attributable to the propitious increase in world copper prices and the fortunate rains during 1987-88. A third factor, the ceiling of 10 per cent on debt payments, did

Table 7.10 Annual rates of inflation in Zambia, 1986–91

Year	*Income group*		*Composite group*
	Low	*High*	
1986	54.0	60.0	54.8
1987	45.6	56.4	47.0
1988	54.7	50.2	54.0
1989	128.7	125.7	128.3
1990	111.0	100.2	109.6
1991 July	100.5	107.1	101.4
August	97.6	106.0	98.7
September	95.6	105.2	96.2

Source: National Commission for Development Planning, Lusaka, *Economic Report 1991*, Lusaka, January 1992, p. 27

reduce the problem of foreign exchange scarcity only through the circuitous path of accumulating arrears of international payment obligations.

THE FOURTH NATIONAL DEVELOPMENT PLAN, 1989–93

In 1989 the Zambian government launched its Fourth National Development Plan to cover the five-year period 1989–93. The plan was essentially a continuation of INDP philosophy, hence it was based on the principle of self-reliance. Over the five-year period, Zambia did not expect much from the outside world in terms of external financial assistance. The plan document assigned a zero weighting to all conditionality-based external aid programmes, while allowance has been made for only K5.7 billion in grants and K1.7 billion in external loans, amounting to about 7 per cent of estimated GDP over the plan period. The plan emphasizes the usual objectives of economic self-reliance, economic diversification, increased agricultural productivity, foreign exchange conservation and reduction of income inequalities. Over the plan period, growth is expected to increase by an annual average of 3 per cent. The fiscal gap is planned to be reduced to 5 per cent of GDP, while inflation is hoped to be reduced to more tolerable level of 20 per cent by end of the plan period.

The Social Action Programme

In April 1990 the Zambian government launched a Social Action Programme as a complement to the INDP and the Fourth Plan. The Programme covers the period 1990–93 and has as its objectives the rehabilitation of social services, alleviation of poverty and the re-establishment of sustainable growth through planned social actions which "contribute a significant increase in investment in the human factor in building a stronger economy and society".[104] The priority groups were identified as the youth, the unemployed, women and children, while the key sectors for action were identified as health, food security, water and sanitation, rural feeder roads and markets, enterprise development, education and training. In order to achieve these objectives the government committed itself to improved capacity-building in policy-making and policy implementation.

Rapprochement with the Washington institutions

Under increasing pressures from donors to resume relations with the international finance institutions, Zambia relaunched discussions with the Fund and the Bank, and by September 1989, they had jointly worked out a policy framework paper.[105] The framework marked an important step in the rapprochement between Zambia and the two international institutions. It was essentially a mutually agreed diagnosis of the policy problems as well as the options in terms of future structural reform programmes. It began with a review of past reform strategies and their attendant problems. It underlined the need to focus on a medium-term strategy with emphasis on parastatal and expenditure reforms, public sector efficiency, creating a favourable environment for foreign investment, strengthening of the financial sector, rationalizing the copper sector and continuing implementation of ongoing institutional reforms in major sectors of the economy.

An assessment of the country's financial requirements were projected to reach an estimated SDR1.501 billion in 1991 and to average SDR490 million a year between 1992 and 1993.[106] Both the Bank and Fund were in principle committed to assisting Zambia acquire additional financial inflows as well as having access to such facilities as the Fund's Extended Structural Adjustment Facility (ESAF) and the Bank's sectoral and project assistance. This was, of course, conditional upon Zambia adopting an acceptable structural adjustment strategy.

RETURN TO MULTI-PARTY DEMOCRACY

These policy initiatives were taking place against a background of simmering political ferment. It may be said that the development crisis of the 1980s seemed to have irreparably eroded the legitimacy of Kenneth Kaunda and the UNIP leadership, leading to pressures for greater political liberalization. Bowing to domestic as well as external remonstrations, President Kaunda, on 24 September 1990, addressing the Twenty-fifth National Council of UNIP, announced that the Party and government had decided that the country should return to multi-party democracy. He found it no longer necessary to have a national referendum for Zambians to determine whether or not they wanted a multi-party system. Soon thereafter, on 8 October, President Kaunda appointed a twenty-one man Constitutional Commission under the Inquiries Act.[107]

The Commission was headed by an academic, Professor Mphanza Patrick Mvunga, and had as its terms of reference to design a new political system in line with the principles of democratic pluralism, a system of government which would ensure the Rule of Law and Separation of Powers, and to determine the status, in relation to the government, of the party that wins an election. The Commission completed its work dutifully and submitted what amounted to a rewritten Zambian Constitution. The government accepted all the most important recommendations, and Zambia became at least by virtue of its new Constitution, a de facto multi-party democracy.[108]

With presidential elections set for October 1991, the Movement for Multi-Party Democracy (MMD) emerged as the main opposition party under the leadership of the trade unionist, Frederick Chiluba. It had amongst its leadership former UNIP "Refuseniks", such as one-time Foreign Minister Vernon Mwaanga, and enjoyed support from such disparate groups as peasants, intellectuals, the elderly and the unemployed.[109] By virtue of its composition and indeed its name, the MMD emerged as an amalgam of disparate socioeconomic groups, interests and tendencies. Without a coherent political philosophy or set of clear-cut ideological principles, it derives its identity and moral force only by virtue of its opposition to the system of one-party rule and especially against Kaunda, UNIP and the old order.

In March 1991, President Kaunda reached yet another reform agreement with donors. However, in the atmosphere of the electioneering campaigns, it seemed obvious that what really counted for him was the need to create enough room for manoeuvre and to brighten his electoral fortunes. In July, Kaunda reneged on an agreement to end the subsidies on maize meal, which prompted the Bank to stay action on the disbursement of a scheduled US$25 million of aid. On 13 September Zambia also defaulted on the repayment of US$10 million to the World Bank, a situation which put back the country automatically on the Bank's blacklist. Figure 7.6 shows the total debt repayment arrears by December 1991. Total debt arrears stood at US$2,112 million, of which US$1,262.9 million was owed to the IMF alone. Vice-President Edward Jaycox was quoted as expressing the Bank's disappointment that the Zambian government had sacrificed economic rationality at the altar of electoral calculations.[110] Kaunda resorted to accusing the West, including the international monitoring team under the chairmanship of former American President, Jimmy Carter, of seeking his overthrow by all means. On 31 October the elections were held and the MMD under Frederick Chiluba won with an overwhelming majority. Clearly, an era had passed in Zambia's chequered post-independence politics. Whether the

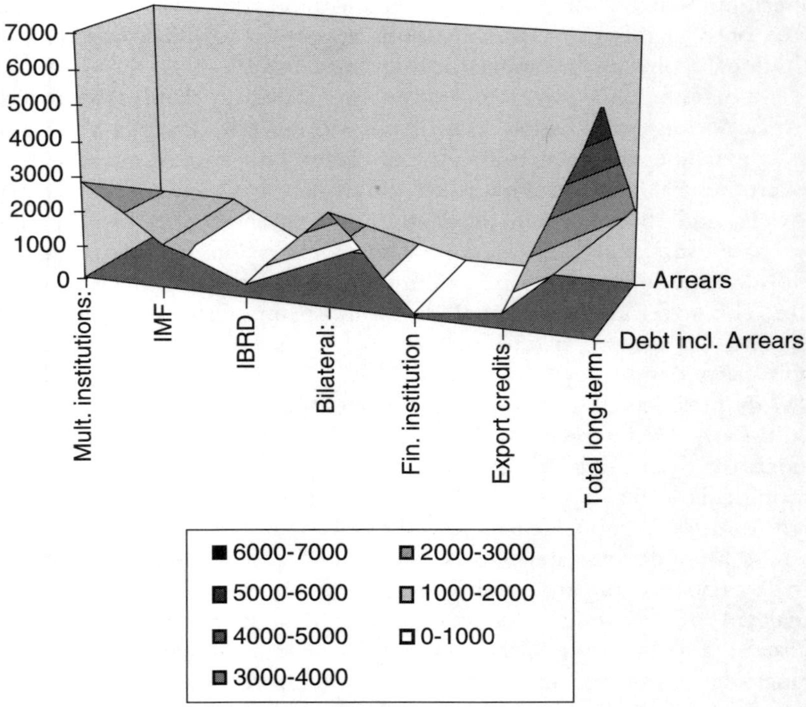

Figure 7.5 Zambia: external debt, December 1991 (in US$ million)
Source: National Planning Commission, Lusaka, 1992

new government will be able to create a new vision for public policy and economic management is a matter which only time will tell.[111]

CONCLUSION

In this chapter we have tried to show that the roots of Zambia's under-development derive from a combination of historical, internal political and external factors. The country inherited a structurally unbalanced model of development from the colonial era. The nationalist bourgeoisie who took over the reins of power in the post-colonial era simply perpetuated the inherited model, with its monocultural dependence on copper exports, neglect of peasant agriculture, and regional imbalance in the development process. The Kaunda regime sought to create a welfarist state without the

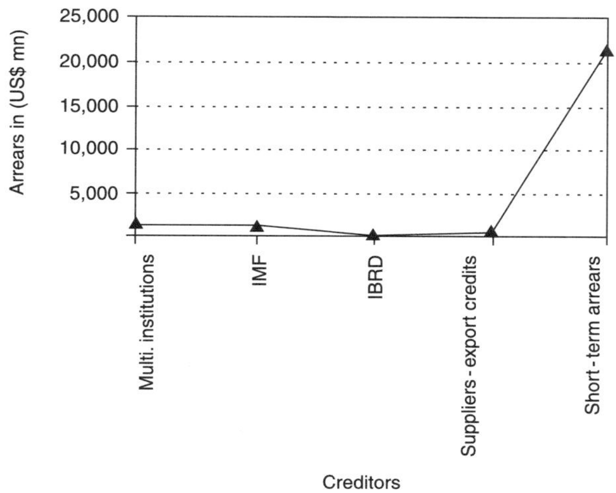

Figure 7.6 Zambia: debt arrears, December 1991 (in US$ million)
Source: National Planning Commission, Lusaka, 1992

productive base necessary to support it. With the collapse of world copper prices, the government resorted to massive external borrowing, with the resultant burden of indebtedness.

The IFIs and external creditors became inevitably involved in the country's structural reform programme. We argued that the foreign exchange auction, while succeeding in liberalizing the foreign exchange market, has contributed to an inflationary spiral and to the deterioration of living standards. We have also seen how it tended to encourage the import of luxury items rather than strategic inputs which are essential to the revitalization of the productive sectors in Zambia. The IMF reform programme has met with a great deal of political resistance not only as a result of the hardships which ordinary people have had to endure, but also because of vested interests in the state and Party, pressure groups such as organized labour and students, and nationalist elements who resent the external control which is entailed by Bank and Fund conditionality.

Structural adjustment in Zambia thus seemed to have been little more than an attempt to ensure that the country was able to service its debt while promoting an economic environment conducive to foreign investment and international capital. Far from being part of a comprehensive strategy for structural transformation, the central economic and political objective of adjustment in Zambia seemed to have been largely informed by the need to balance the accounting books of multilateral creditors while leaving intact the structural coordinates of a dependent, monocultural, mineral-exporting economy.

8

ZAMBIA AND LOMÉ AID DIPLOMACY

At independence Zambia was generally regarded as one of the most promising countries in sub-Saharan Africa. Copper prices were high on the world market and the new government inherited a healthy financial position. With external reserves "almost exceeding the absorptive capacity of the state", finance was not regarded as a major development constraint.[1] Foreign aid was therefore not an issue of high priority for the country's economic managers until the mid-1970s.[2] Between 1971 and 1980 the most important donors were Britain, followed by the United States, Sweden and West Germany (Table 8.1).

Zambia's relations with the EEC date back to 1973, with Britain's accession to the Community. Like many other newly independent African states, she established a diplomatic mission in Brussels, with the Ambassador having multiple accreditation to Belgium as well as the EEC and the Benelux countries. Formal contact with the Community began in early

Table 8.1 Economic aid of the Development Assistance Committee (DAC) countries and international organizations to Zambia, 1971–80

Donor	*Type of assistance*		*Total for years 1971–80*
	Grant	*Loan*	
Britain	175.6	63.2	238.8
USA	14.0	127.0	141.0
Sweden	118.2	13.2	131.4
West Germany	51.5	56.7	108.2
Japan	6.4	81.3	87.7
Canada	27.6	41.2	68.8
Norway	53.9	—	53.9
Bilateral	551.5	403.8	955.3
Multilateral	112.8	314.1	426.9
OPEC	9.5	—	9.5
GRAND TOTAL	673.8	717.9	1,391.7

Source: Financial Flows to Developing Countries, 1978 and 1981, Paris: OECD

1973, when Special Assistant to President Kaunda, Mark Chona, made an official visit to the EEC's Directorate-General for Development to solicit support following the Rhodesian border closure.[3] During the first Lomé negotiations, Zambia played a decidedly low-profile role. Although he was not associated with any major policy position or initiative, Zambia's Ambassador, James Mupoma, was said to have been active in the negotiations.[4]

During this early period Zambia did not accord significant importance to the Lomé partnership. The rather low salience given to the EEC, from the economic viewpoint, was surprising in view of the fact that the Community was Zambia's most important regional trading partner. In 1973 about 52 per cent of the country's exports went to the Community (with the UK alone accounting for 20 per cent) while 38 per cent of its imports were from the EEC (with the UK accounting for 21 per cent).[5] There was a certain degree of wariness, if not antipathy, to the idea of entering into a new relationship with a Community comprising of the erstwhile colonial powers. In 1974 for example, Rajah Kunda, the Minister for Trade and Industry, who was also responsible for EEC cooperation, had described the Community as "new-colonialist" and "exploiter" in the course of a debate in Parliament.[6]

THE FIRST EEC MISSION TO ZAMBIA

During the first ever EEC fact-finding mission to Lusaka in February 1975 in preparation for the first Lomé indicative programme, Dr Corrado Pirzio-Biroli of the DGVIII discovered that there was a great deal of "misunderstanding" on the part of Zambian authorities regarding the workings of the Community. After consulting with EEC Ambassadors in Lusaka, he held a press conference where he sought to counter the negative portrayal of the Community by the Minister for Trade and Industry, arguing that the Lomé partnership was tilted in favour of the less developed ACP countries and was an important vehicle for "international social justice".[7]

The Pirzio-Biroli visit, the first by a senior official from the Commission, underlined the rather low diplomatic status which Zambia attached to the EEC. The responsible government ministry, i.e. the Ministry of Trade and Industry, virtually ignored him, claiming to have lost all the letters of official communication from Brussels. For Pirzio-Biroli himself, it was merely a case of the "hopeless inefficiency" of one particular ministry. Unable to make contacts at the highest levels, he had to content himself with discussions with the Under-Secretary for Budget in the Ministry of Finance.

What factors explain Zambian attitudes towards the EEC during this period? The first answer rests in the confidence deriving from the economic prosperity which the country enjoyed in the first decade after independence. The copper boom ensured availability of foreign exchange reserves and reduced Zambia's dependence on external aid. The second explanation is political. In ideological terms Zambia was close to the Nkrumahist group which dismissed association with the EEC as "neo-colonialism". Although lacking Nkrumah's gift for intellectual analysis, the Kaunda government nevertheless seemed to have reached the same conclusions out of a visceral rather than intellectual or political conviction.[8] Two EEC member states were the main butt of Zambia's anti-Western rhetoric: France, for its arms sales to the Republic of South Africa, and West Germany, for having established a consulate at Windhoek, the capital of the then occupied Namibia, and for its participation in the Cabora Bassa project. Although moderate and pragmatic for the most part, Zambian foreign policy behaviour was also quite adept at using political rhetoric to establish its radical credentials in African international relations.[9]

AID PROGRAMMING FOR LOMÉ I

Following the Pirzio-Biroli visit, the EEC programme mission arrived in Lusaka in early November 1975. The Director-General of DGVIII, Mr Maurice Foley, led the EEC delegation while the Zambian side was headed by the Minister of Finance and Planning, Mr Alex Chikwanda. The discussions were said to have been held in an atmosphere of "cordiality", although the EEC delegation felt disappointed with the administrative arrangements for the mission. Mr Foley had to meet with President Kaunda to ensure that proper arrangements were made and to get firm political commitment to the talks. The ensuing indicative programme for Zambia reflected not only the November discussions, but also the earlier mission by Dr Pirzio-Biroli. The latter's report was influential in shaping the orientation of the new aid programme. The main development constraints which he identified in the country were: the problem of transport; scarcity of trained manpower,[10] lack of infrastructure, and the problem of large subsidies and unproductive investments in certain sectors of the economy.

The Commission's background paper was particularly critical of the policy and planning framework in Zambia. It described the country's public policy as being characterized by a "no-choice" and wavering style, due to the influences of pressure groups such as the highly unionized mining labour, the urban proletariat, commercial farmers, civil servants and the Party. The planning process was also seen as being weak in Zambia, being largely unknown outside the bureaucracy and only referred to during political debates and in discussion with international development agencies. The Commission showed a balanced understanding of the problems of development administration and aid management in Zambia:

> Zambia has inherited from colonialism what perhaps is the weakest administration in English-speaking Africa. Here lies an important reason for Zambia's weak record in project identification and implementa-

> tion, despite a huge army of foreign "experts". The latter were and are at most sufficient to draw up ivory-tower plan documents and to keep the copper mines running.[11]

The EEC noted that in view of a gap of K111 million (US$173 million) in the capital project estimates of 1975 budget, Zambia would need external financial assistance. Since Dr Pirzio-Biroli considered the line Ministries to be inefficient, he advised that the Community should channel most of its EDF aid through parastatals such as INDECO, which had a reputable project management unit. He advised that the EEC should concentrate on boosting agricultural production, especially in wheat, sugar, cotton, maize, seed oil, vegetables and animal feeds, with overall focus on the family farm as the basic agricultural unit. Other areas which could benefit from EDF funds were said to be irrigation; technical assistance and extension services; industrial production of simple agricultural machinery, edible oils and vegetables; regional projects in transport and telecommunications; and technical assistance in terms of research and feasibility studies. Although the two sides concurred on the broad areas of assistance, it appeared that the Zambian authorities favoured a "programme" approach similar to that of the World Bank, although with softer terms for EIB loans. Zambia favoured programme aid because it was thought to give greater scope for flexibility in the use of funds. However, it was clear that the Commission preferred the project approach because it would enable it to keep track of the implementation process and to direct funding to specific projects.[12]

The Lomé I indicative programme

The first indicative programme amounted to ECU 47 million. During this period, i.e. from April 1976 to February 1980, the country also received ECU 15.7 million in emergency aid and ECU 10.5 million in special loans from the EIB, giving a total in financial inflows from the Community to the tune of ECU 73.2 million.[13] About two-thirds of the NIP funds were allocated to agriculture and rural development (ECU 30.3 million). The other major sectors of concern were economic and social infrastructure (ECU 6.6 million) and training and education (ECU 6.2 million). Financial allocation under Lomé I is shown in Table 8.2. Although the Zambian government had expressed preference for a "programme" rather than "project" approach to EEC assistance, particularly since the former was the vogue in World Bank circles, the Community's preference for the "project" approach prevailed. Under agriculture, the most significant projects in financial terms were the Cotton Development Project, Mpongwe Phase I Project and the Kawambwa Tea Scheme.

Education and training were considered to be of crucial importance at this time, given the manpower constraints which confronted Zambia during

Table 8.2 EEC aid programme to Zambia under Lomé I, 1986 (in ECU thousands)

Project/sector	*Allocation*
Kawambwa Tea (loan)	3,100
Cotton Development Project (TA)	1,898
Cotton Development Project (loan)	6,050
Mpongwe Phase I	5,390
Cattle Development Areas	1,937
Batoka Crossbreeding (loan)	1,825
Education and training:	
Multiannual Training Programme	4,550
Economic & social infrastructure:	
Sites and Services (loan)	2,400
Mpika Water Supply (loan)	1,946
Trade promotion:	507
Funds committed to ongoing projects	29,603
Funds committed to completed projects	17,164
TOTAL LOMÉ I	46,767

Source: EC Delegation, Lusaka, 1986

the first decade of its independence. The Multi-annual Training Programme involved scholarships and other forms of manpower development assistance for Zambians in Europe as well as within Zambia. The programming process for Lomé I could be said to have been a one-sided affair, with the Community taking most of the initiatives. This was because, as we have observed, the Zambian Government viewed the new association with some scepticism. Another reason is the fact of the novelty of the Lomé itself, with the new institutions and procedures which were yet to be fully internalized, especially on the Zambian side.

The Kaunda visit to Brussels

During the Lomé I period, 1977 was a particularly significant year from the viewpoint of EC–Zambia diplomacy. In the course of a state visit to Belgium in June, President Kaunda also paid a visit to the Commission where he was received by Commission President Sir Roy (now Lord) Jenkins. In a rather strongly worded speech he called on the EC to increase its aid to Zambia in view of the effects of the Rhodesia border closure. He called on Europe to assist the process of decolonization in Southern Africa and to help prevent further military incursions by Ian Smith's Rhodesian forces into Zambia and other neighbouring countries. Dr Kaunda emphasized the importance which his country attached to the Lomé agreement as demonstrative of the interdependence between North and South:

> We as developing countries possess a huge potential of natural resources. . . . You in the developed world possess a vast reservoir of skills and financial resources, and through cooperation we know you will play your fullest role in forging a new international economic order, an order in which the world at last will recognize poverty and its offshoots of hunger, ignorance, disease . . . for the mortal enemies of humanity that they truly are.[14]

Although no new initiatives emerged from this visit, it could be said to have marked a rapprochement in diplomatic relations between Brussels and Lusaka, a departure away from the latent tensions of the past. Kaunda was conceding the economic and political significance of an emergent Europe, especially at the wake of Zambia's dwindling economic fortunes and increasing international vulnerability.

Towards the end of the year, Zambia also hosted the Fourteenth Session of the ACP Council of Ministers.[15] In his opening address, Dr Kaunda expressed regret that the ideals which had inspired the Lomé partnership were being eroded by the EEC's granting of preferences to third parties, especially under the Generalized System of Preferences (GSP). He advocated South–South cooperation and the strengthening of the ACP Group as the best means of enabling developing countries to survive in "a world characterized by astute manipulations of the weak by the strong to the advantage of the latter".[16]

LOMÉ II PROGRAMMING AND THE FOLEY MISSION

After the signing of the second Lomé Convention, Mr Maurice Foley led another programming mission to Lusaka from 7–11 June 1980, accompanied by some DGVIII officials and representatives of the EIB. The Zambian side of the talks was led by the Minister of State at the Planning Commission, Mr U. G. Mwila. Following the usual "exchange of views", both sides agreed that the priority areas for Lomé funding should be consistent with Zambia's long-term development objectives as spelt out in the Third National Development Plan (1979–83), with its emphasis on rural development, employment creation, food production and import substitution.[17] The programme document therefore specified the areas of intervention as:

- rural development (56 per cent), with the aim of attaining self-sufficiency in food production through promotion of new and ongoing development projects;
- improvement in the quality of life in rural areas by widening opportunities for productive employment and stemming the tide of rural–urban migration;

- helping to boost the production of industrial crops to satisfy the needs of local industrial inputs in manufacturing and processing;
- the establishment of micro-projects to improve the capacity of local communities in order to strengthen grass-roots participation in development.

The second major area of concern in the programme document was economic and social infrastructure, particularly the energy sector. The declared objective was to reduce external dependence on energy requirements through a coherent energy strategy, embracing measures to reduce fuel imports and development of local energy resources. Transportation, water supplies, medical supplies, and sites and services for housing and small-scale industries in rural and urban areas were also highlighted as priority areas. Other sectors included training and technical assistance, support activities such as trade promotion, and EIB credit to small and medium-sized industries.

Financial allocations under Lomé II indicative programme amounted to ECU 58 million, of which 38.2 million were in grants and 19.8 million were in EIB loans.[18] The most important projects in the rural sector from the financial viewpoint were the Maize Development Project in the Central Province, which had an allocation of ECU 5.5 million; Rice Development Project in Northern Province (ECU 4 million); and the Tsetse and Trypanosomiasis Control Project (ECU 5 million). Micro-projects and the Vaccine Production Programme each had an allocation of ECU 2 million. Under the economic and social infrastructure programme, the rural water supply project received ECU 5.2 million for five rural townships while the Health Centres Project received ECU 2 million for construction of five health centres at Northern, North Western, Western and Luapula Provinces. Under the training chapter, which received ECU 3.7 million, the multi-annual programme under Lomé I was continued with provision of scholarships and other forms of manpower development assistance. Outside the NIP funds, a special loan of ECU 55 million under Sysmin I was approved for Zambia in 1982 for the rehabilitation of the copper mining industry. A second Sysmin loan of ECU 28 million was approved in 1986, and was complemented by a grant of ECU 4.5 million from the Italian government.

The Pisani visit to Southern Africa

After the commencement of Lomé II, EC–Zambia relations received a boost with the official visit by the new EC Commissioner for Development Cooperation, Edgard Pisani. Pisani visited Lusaka from 9 to 11 February 1982, after attending an ACP/EEC Joint Committee Meeting in Salisbury (now Harare). The aim of the visit was to familiarize himself with the situation in the Southern African region as a result of the aggressive policies being pursued by the Republic of South Africa.[19] Commissioner Pisani was received by the Minister of State at the Planning Commission, the Prime Minister, Secretary-General of the Party as well as by President Kaunda himself. The discussions centred mainly on the political problems of the region as well as on the implementation of EEC aid in Zambia.

The Zambian authorities expressed concern about the disruption of the country's communication networks as a result of sabotage by the apartheid regime. They were anxious to get Monsieur Pisani to convince EEC member states to impose political and economic pressure on South Africa to stop its aggressive policies and to also grant independence to Namibia in accordance with UN Resolution 435. The Commissioner expressed understanding of Zambia's concerns in this regard and said the EEC would support SADCC as an instrument of "collective self-reliance". He said the Commission would work closely with Zambia as Chairman of SADCC Mining Committee in devising a mining strategy for the regional organization. A special session was devoted to a comprehensive review of EEC projects in the country, chaired by Planning Minister, Dr Henry Meebelo. Both the Ministers of Finance and of Commerce and Industry were expected to attend but were inexplicably absent. The two sides agreed on the imperative of diversifying the economy away from dependence on copper. The agricultural and rural sector was underlined as the area of long-term importance in Zambia's economic development.

Three issues were discussed. The first was the cash-flow problem, in particular, the shortage of funds arising from the unavailability of counterpart funds from the past sales of EEC food aid. It was clear that there was a problem from the Zambian side with respect to proper accounting and utilization of counterpart funds. The second issue was the absence of training for local personnel to take over the administration of projects once EEC technical assistance personnel were withdrawn. The third was the issue of food aid. Both sides were agreed that food aid should only be for a determined period and that the counterpart funds realized from food sales in an open market should be invested in projects that promote food self-sufficiency. It was also during this meeting that Commissioner Pisani announced the approval of the first Sysmin loan of ECU 58 million for the rehabilitation of the copper mining industry. He had met with the Chairman of the ZCCM, Mr Francis Kaunda, when he again reiterated the EEC's desire to devise a Euro-African mining strategy to secure European needs in raw materials as well as assisting in the development of African raw material exports to promote African development. Pisani used the occasion to reassure the Zambian authorities that he had not supported a proposal submitted by the Commissioner for Energy and Industry, Count Davignon of Belgium, whereby the EEC was planning to invest US$ 1.2 billion in Brazil's iron ore and other mineral sectors. He sought to allay the fears of

Zambia and other ACP mineral exporters, pointing out that Europe enjoyed a long "historical association" with Africa and that African countries would therefore have priority in the use of such a fund.[20]

LOMÉ III PROGRAMMING AND THE FOOD QUESTION

The third Lomé Convention programming mission took place in Lusaka from 3–7 December 1985. Mr Dieter Frisch, Director-General of the EC Commission for Development, led the Community's side, while the delegation of the Government of Zambia was led by the Honourable Luke Mwananshiku, who was Minister of Finance and Planning at the time.[21] Even before the mission the Commission had prepared a pre-programming document which presented a diagnosis of the country's economic situation as seen by the EC and the implications for Lomé aid priorities and orientations.[22]

Seven major constraints were identified as the main problems facing Zambia's development:

1 the heavy dependence on copper and cobalt, both declining products in terms of pricing as well as production;
2 the high level of indebtedness (about US$4.5 billion), with a debt-servicing burden absorbing 70 per cent of gross foreign earnings;
3 the severe drought of 1982–84 which severely reduced production of the local staple, maize, and led to deficits in wheat and a general fall in food production levels;
4 constraints in the administrative system, particularly the public service, finance institutions and the parastatals;
5 weaknesses in the financial set-up and in fiscal policy;
6 weakness in the transport system;
7 the demographic explosion and its attendant problems of rapid urbanization and high unemployment.

In terms of the EC's support, the document emphasized agriculture and the food sector as the key area of priority. They felt that emphasis should be on boosting food production with a particular focus on the small farmer. A target was set whereby Community aid policy would seek to increase production of maize from 600,000 million tonnes per annum to 800,000 million tonnes per annum. Alternative staples such as cassava (manioc), sorghum and millet would also be encouraged so as to reduce over-dependence on maize. Non-traditional exports such as coffee, tea and tobacco were to be encouraged. The new thinking in the EC's strategy centred on the idea of geographical concentration, i.e. concentrating on one or two clearly defined geographical areas, instead of having projects scattered all over the country.

In pursuance of these objectives, the EC would put in place the following support activities for agricultural and rural development:

- use of food aid and counterpart funds to improve availability of agricultural credit;
- improvement of systems supplying inputs, particularly to the smallholder;
- a commodity import programme to cover import needs of the agricultural sector in inputs, machinery and spares;
- feeder road and vehicle maintenance programmes;
- development of small-scale agricultural processing and rural artisanal industries;
- manpower, training and technical assistance programmes;
- policies to improve rural housing and water supplies so as to reduce the massive rural–urban drift;
- a "carefully conceived action programme" for controlling population growth;
- research support to improve domestic fuel systems to reduce the problem of deforestation.

In terms of macroeconomic policy, the EC emphasized the importance of the strategy of "restructuring" and "adaptation" as enunciated in the government's June report to the World Bank Consultative Group on Zambia in Paris. The main elements of the policy included:

- the substantial devaluation of the kwacha;
- the adoption of a food pricing structure to reflect relative production and foreign exchange costs, especially with regard to wheat;
- the progressive abolition of agricultural subsidies coupled with a corresponding introduction of incentive prices to farmers;
- the progressive liberalization of agricultural produce marketing.[23]

In many ways Lomé III programming was different from its two predecessors. The two sides undertook a "comprehensive exchange of views" on the country's development objectives and priorities. In contrast to the two previous Conventions, which were only concerned with how Lomé aid could be used to fill important gaps in Zambia's economic development, the EC was now seeking to redirect development policy in line with the imperatives of economic restructuring. Another important departure from previous programming was that a set of conditions was outlined which Zambian authorities were expected to implement, including a detailed timetable specifying the period during which each policy action should be undertaken.

The conditions laid down were expected to provide a consistent framework for the effective implementation of EC development programmes. This included the continuation of pricing policies to provide incentives to agricultural production and to harmonize prices in line with regional comparative advantage. Institutional reforms were also expected in the areas of agricultural credit, research and extension services, and in the provision of economic and social infrastructures in the rural areas. In addition to these, a series of regular quarterly meetings was to be held between the Zambian authorities and the EC Delegation in order to "ensure rapid and effective preparation and implementation of programmes and projects".[24] It was also agreed that implementation of Lomé aid programmes would be undertaken in coordination with other aid agencies within the country so as to avoid duplication of efforts.

Total funding under the Lomé III National Indicative Programme amounted to ECU 85 million, of which ECU 66 million were to be in grants while ECU 15 million were in special loans.[25] This amount did not include other financial contributions from non-programmable EDF funds managed by the Commission, nor amounts from other sources in support of EC development objectives in the country. The agricultural and rural development sector received an allocation of ECU 53.4 million, about 78 per cent of the indicative programme funds. The most important projects from the financial viewpoint were the two Smallholder Development Projects (ECU 23.3 million); the Agricultural Import Support Programmes (ECU 27.2 million). Another sector which received major funding was the Micro-Projects Programme, which was allocated ECU 5.4 million. The education sector received a total funding of ECU 7.9 million, about 11 per cent of all funds, which went to finance the Zambia Maths and Science Teacher Education Project (ECU 3.9 million), the Zambia Centre for Accounting Studies (ECU 4.0 million) and the Copperbelt University Training Programme (ECU 0.2 million).

LOMÉ IV PROGRAMMING AND THE ROAD TO ADJUSTMENT

If Lomé III marked a major departure from its predecessors, Lomé IV could be said to have consolidated this trend towards reorientation in EC–Zambia aid and diplomatic relations. It is markedly different from the others not only in the amount of background analytical work which went into it but also in its clear focus on structural adjustment. Even before the programming process began, the EC Delegation in Lusaka had prepared a detailed policy paper on the economic and social conditions in Zambia. It was perhaps the most comprehensive report ever prepared on Zambia by the Delegation.[26] The paper highlighted the major policy issues surrounding Zambia's Structual Adjustment Programme and tried to indicate the focal areas for EC Lomé support.[27] Discussions on the Lomé IV Indicative Programme took place in Lusaka from 16–20 February 1991. Mr Peter Pooley, Deputy Director-General for Development, led the Community delegation, while the late Mr Gibson Chigaga, then Minister of Finance and Planning, led the Zambian team.[28]

EC FOOD STRATEGY DIALOGUE IN ZAMBIA

The EC food strategy in Zambia can be said to have originated from three parallel factors. The first factor was the 1978 World Food Council meeting in Mexico, when the concept of "food strategy" was initially elaborated as an approach in the fight against hunger and malnutrition in the world. Its particular novelty lay in the fact that it sought to make food availability the focal point of all development efforts and to bring together aid donors as well as the LDC recipients in a process of continual dialogue for the improvement of development policy. This reorientation emerged out of the realization that agricultural and food policies are best seen as an integral part of overall development policy. The notion of food strategy thus began as:

> a comprehensive programme of policies designed to foster the production and availability of food in deficit developing countries. As part of national development plans, food strategies not only define the necessary measures to be pursued by governments of countries in need of food, but they also provide opportunities for aid agencies and donor governments to support these strategies in an active and concrete manner.[29]

The second development in the evolution of the food strategy concept was in September 1980, when the European Parliament passed a Resolution on Hunger in the World. The Resolution was the final outcome of one year's work by the Committee on Cooperation and Development. It expressed the Community's concern with the growing threat of hunger and "its consequences for the lives of hundreds of millions of human beings". It traced the root causes of hunger to underdevelopment and the existing structure of international relations. It therefore called on the EC Council and Commission to launch a renewed effort in the search for a viable food strategy and to link EC food aid to agricultural and rural development.[30] While acknowledging the importance of improved North–South relations, the European Parliament underlined the need for a more effective policy framework for the food and agricultural sector, especially in the areas of farm price policies, greater availability of credits for small farmers, and an improved marketing system for agricultural produce.

The third factor derived from a policy initiative begun by the Kaunda administration itself. In 1980 the government launched the "Operation Food Production" (OFP) Programme in order to reduce the country's dependence on food imports. Before 1978 Zambia had been able to export its surplus maize. By 1981, however, it became a net importer of maize as well as of wheat and rice. According to the EC Commission, during 1981–83 the country was importing an annual average of 143.9 tonnes of maize, 133.1 tonnes of wheat and 7.0 tonnes of rice.[31] Zambia was now having to import about 50 per cent of its domestic maize requirements, a situation which was clearly a strenuous burden on the state budget. It was also a drain on the scarce foreign exchange, which was badly needed for the importation of agricultural inputs such as fertilizers, spare parts and machinery, all of which were needed for the improvement of the agricultural sector.[32] The aim of this programme was therefore to enhance food self-sufficiency as well as agricultural exports so as to diversify the economy away from dependence on dwindling copper export earnings.

The programme's approach was to be based on the revitalization of rural cooperatives, the development of state farms, and support for large commercial farmers as well as small peasant holders. This was essentially a broad statement of policy rather than a concerted strategy plan. In 1981 the Ministry of Agriculture and Water Development (MAWD) initiated a food strategy study with technical assistance from the government of the Netherlands.

The study was supposed to assist the implementation of the OFP.[33] It was in the context of these developments that the EC Commission launched a Food Strategy Programme under what was known as the "Plan Pisani".[34] Food strategy, as it was enunciated in Commissioner Edgard Pisani's "Plan of Action to Combat World Hunger" in October 1981, was aimed at bringing about policy changes as well as integrating food aid into a comprehensive programme to ensure long-term food security. It entailed "policy dialogue" between the EC and recipient countries, with the stated objective of improving the macroeconomic framework and to put in place policies which could enhance long-term agricultural development. Some of the policy changes required would normally entail issues such as price incentives for local farmers through price liberalization, improved marketing and credit and exchange rate adjustments.

In 1982 four countries – namely, Zambia, Rwanda, Kenya and Mali – were selected as the first test cases for the EC's food strategy initiative.[35] In the particular case of Zambia, the EC food strategy was not imposed upon a policy vacuum. The Kaunda government launched the Operation Food Production Programme in 1980. The aim of the programme, as earlier pointed out, was to boost food production and ensure food security as well as to promote agricultural exports to replace the declining mineral exports sector. These objectives were to be pursued through development of rural cooperatives, state farms, commercial farms and small rural peasant farms, in the realization that an "integrated" approach was necessary to sustain food production in the long term.

Perhaps the most controversial aspect of the programme was the issue of large-scale state farms, of which about 20,000 hectares were to be established in each of the nine provinces in the country. However, the emphasis on state farms was to be accompanied by other supportive policies in respect of commercial farmers, especially in terms of tax concessions, allowance for foreign exchange retention, reduction of import duties on agricultural equipment and fertilizers. The government was also committed to the reorganization of the parastatal sector so as to improve its efficiency. Following this broad outline of policy objectives, technical assistance was provided by the Dutch government for a detailed food strategy study. A set of technical reports was then submitted to GRZ between September 1981 and March 1982. When the EC began the process of dialogue with Zambia on food strategy, it was clearly within the framework of an already existing food security policy, albeit one that was in part contradictory; lacking in coherence as well as in clarity regarding priorities and strategy.

The food dialogue process formally began after a meeting between President Kaunda and Commissioner Pisani during his 1982 visit to Zambia. This initial meeting was followed by an exchange of letters over questions of Zambia's agricultural and food policies. According to Jean Gyselinck, a Principal Administrator in the Southern Africa Division of DGVIII, the EC was "both willing to run its scheme as part of the government's Operation Food Production Programme and ready, within this framework, to assist . . . with implementation of this policy".[36]

In May 1982 a high level Joint Committee was formally established to institutionalize the food dialogue process. The Committee comprised high officials of the Zambian government and EC Commission as well as the EC Delegation and representatives of EC member states. It was a particularly novel approach to EC–Zambia development diplomacy in the sense that it elevated the discussions from the technical-bureaucratic level to the political-diplomatic. During the very first meeting in Lusaka, it became quite apparent that each side viewed its *raison d'être* differently.[37] For the Community, it was a forum for "reflection" on matters of economic and food policy in order to reach a consensus regarding the necessary policy changes to be effected. For Zambia, on the other hand, the priority issue was to agree on general guidelines and on a list of projects to be financed by the Community. However, the Community was insistent that its aid programme could not simply be restricted to the implementation of a set of projects. Zambian officials interpreted the EC position as a form of "creeping conditionality".

Following the initial round of discussions, GRZ submitted to the EC a report on its Special Programme of Action against Hunger (SPAH) in October 1982. The report outlined Zambia's objectives as being:

- increased production of maize, sorghum, cassava, millet and rice by small-scale rural farmers;

- development of livestock, fisheries and urban gardening;
- initiation of new pricing policies to provide incentives for small-scale producers as well as to stimulate production of drought-resistant crops.

The report included a list of various project proposals for funding by the Community. Although no explicit reference was made to state farms, it seemed clear that the idea had not been abandoned by the Zambian administration. The SPAH also emphasized the need for commercial farmers to concentrate on import-substituting products such as wheat and on export production. The programme stressed the importance of improved support services (research, extension, input supply and credit) for both "emergent" and subsistence farmers as well as adequate price incentives to encourage agricultural production.

In January 1983 the EC Commission responded to the Zambian report by calling for another round of discussions, especially on the projects and programmes as articulated in the SPAH. Not much seemed to have come out of the subsequent negotiations. A major issue of disagreement concerned the Zambian insistence on state farms and on wheat production. In the words of the Commission, a "real, but containable difference in emphasis . . . was magnified into an ideological dispute".[38] For the Zambians, the need to promote Soviet-style state farms was probably regarded as a cornerstone of their strategy of "humanist" development, and therefore a matter of vital political and ideological principle on which they could not compromise. Although the EC regarded the Zambian programme as a significant step in the direction of a sustainable food strategy, they pointed out the contradictions and stumbling blocks that still had to be resolved. For example, the EC underlined the contradiction inherent in the proposal to eliminate transport subsidies and at the same time maintain uniform producer prices throughout the country. It felt that such prices should have reflected regional disparities and transport costs. The EC also felt that the question of parastatal reform and the exchange rate were not given adequate consideration by the SPAH.

Major differences of policy between the EC and Zambia were becoming apparent. Whereas the Zambians felt it was now time to implement the SPAH, the EC for its part contended that serious policy issues were yet to be satisfactorily resolved. As a symbolic gesture of its new "hard-line" approach, the EC withdrew funding support for a large-scale irrigated wheat scheme, the Mpongwe Development Project. The Zambian authorities however persisted in regarding large-scale agriculture as compatible with a long-term strategy of integrated development focused on the "emergent" as well as subsistence peasant farmers. The EC–Zambia dialogue had entered a stalemate, with both sides realizing that the Joint Committee was no longer a viable framework for "food strategy" diplomacy. According to a Principal Administrator in the DGVIII, relations between the Commission and the Zambian authorities became quite strained as a result of the policy differences, especially over the question of state farms.[39]

During the course of 1983 the World Bank began a series of discussions with GRZ over its food and agricultural policy in preparation for the Consultative Group Meeting which was scheduled for May 1984. The Bank prepared an Agricultural Rehabilitation Project as part of a co-financing arrangement for the revitalization of the Zambian food and agricultural sector.[40] The Bank's analysis confirmed the diagnosis of the earlier Food Strategy Study. The major constraints in the country's agricultural development were identified as:

- inappropriate pricing policies;
- inefficiency of the produce marketing and input distribution system;
- the need for institutional reform of agencies such as the National Agricultural Marketing Board (Namboard) and the Provincial Cooperative Unions (PCUs);
- the need to evolve a more effective research and extension system and to relate technological packages to the requirements of producers, and especially small peasant farmers.
- the need for agricultural credit, which was more acute for the small farmer than for the large-scale commercial or emergent farmer;[41]
- the need to address the manpower shortage in the farm sector through improved technologies and agricultural mechanization;
- the foreign exchange gap, which particularly afflicts the agro-industrial sector in the area of raw materials, spare parts and components.

The multi-donor Monitoring Committee

This was not the first time that the Bank would be involved with Zambian agriculture. Indeed, by 1984, it had financed ten major projects, notably in industrial forestry, livestock/dairy development, tobacco and coffee production. Most of these projects did not achieve any remarkable success.[42] Although the Bank virtually buttressed the EC food strategy approach, it went somewhat farther in stressing the need for macroeconomic adjustment and for enhanced competition between private enterprise and agricultural parastatal agencies in the areas of input and produce marketing. The Bank was equally resolute in its rejection of state farms as an approach to Zambian agricultural development. World Bank intervention was perhaps decisive in inducing the policy changes which the EC and other donors considered vital for Zambian agriculture.

In its official policy paper for the Consultative Group Meeting,[43] GRZ tried to soften its position by incorporating most of the policies that the EC were insisting on during the Joint Committee discussions. They were now committed to an agricultural strategy centred on emergent and subsistence farmers. Although they would still retain the concept of the state farm as joint ventures with private entrepreneurs so as to "utilize" fully the country's agricultural "potential", they would no longer request donor funding for state farms. Following the 1984 Consultative Meeting, the EC–Zambia Joint Committee was dissolved, to be replaced by a broader "Joint Monitoring Committee" (JMC), this time including the Bank, USAID, and several other non-EC bilateral donors.

The JMC was unfortunately doomed to failure, like its predecessor. It proved unable to reach agreement even on the terms of reference for the meetings. Only a few meetings actually took place because there was no standing Secretariat to prepare for the meetings and to follow up on any decisions agreed upon. According to EC Commission sources, the Zambian administration had rejected several offers of technical assistance to set up a Secretariat for the JMC.[44] This was quite clearly an effort by Zambia to reaffirm its autonomy and sovereign prerogative in the face of what was perceived as neo-imperial donor pressure. Zambia's strategy was to shift the locus of monitoring and implementation to the administrative-technical level which was more firmly within its political control. An Investment Task Force had been established in the Ministry of Agriculture to draw up, beginning with the EC Food Strategy, a five-year plan of investment in the agricultural sector. The EC and other donors were welcome to contribute to the efforts of this agency.

Structural adjustment and the food dialogue strategy

Just as the food strategy and economic restructuring dialogue was apparently reaching a deadlock, the IMF was able to reach agreement with Zambia over a structural adjustment package. Central to this agreement was the auctioning of foreign exchange, which led to a substantial devaluation of the kwacha. In agreeing to devalue its currency, Zambia was acceding to one of the demands of the food and economic restructuring dialogue. It changed the terms of trade in favour of rural producers. Imported items became more expensive relative to domestically produced items, a situation which was expected to boost long-term agricultural production.

Other policy measures included increased producer prices and price liberalization for food commodities with the exception of maize. Marketing of crops and agricultural inputs (with the exception of maize and fertilizer) were liberalized. Private enterprise was now allowed to compete with the parastatals. Namboard's monopoly of inter-provincial marketing was curbed and its subsidies substantially reduced. Its staff was reduced from 6,000 to below 2,000. Responsibility for inter-provincial marketing was transferred to the Provincial Cooperative Unions (PCUs). Budgetary allocations to the agricultural sector, and in particular the research and extension services domain, were considerably increased. The Ministry of Agriculture was reorganized so as to increase its operational and technical capacity in the planning and management of agricultural projects.[45]

Although the EC acknowledged that the reforms which Zambia had undertaken were in line with the requirements of its food strategy approach, they were of the view that the reforms were not far-reaching enough. They took exception to the fertilizer subsidy and to the price controls and subsidies on maize, which existed by way of uniform prices for the staple throughout the country.[46]

IMPORT SUPPORT AND THE SPECIAL ACTION PROGRAMME

In support of the Zambia food strategy, the EC increased the monetary allocation to its Lomé II Indicative Programme funds by ECU 5 million, i.e. from 53 million to 58 million. Zambia was also considered eligible to receive the Commission budget funds (under Article 958) for the Special Programme of Action against Hunger (SPAH). In 1983 the first SAP allocation amounted to ECU 4 million. The objective of SAP I was to increase food production through importation of essential farm machinery and inputs such as veterinary drugs, chemicals and vaccines. Another important item to be imported was structural steel, which to be used in the local manufacture of agricultural implements and in the construction of grain stores. There was also the plan to construct grain stores at provincial and district level so as to reduce storage losses. In the following year ECU 2 million was allocated for the SAP II programme. The aim of the second programme was the eradication of tsetse flies from an area of about 4,500 sq km in an important mixed farming area in the southern part of the country. Although its primary focus was on livestock, it was expected that it would be supportive of the crop sector through availability of healthy draught oxen.

SAP I consisted of two phases. The first was the supply of agricultural inputs and steel to various organizations in Zambia which would then sell them to buyers for kwacha. The second phase was to use the local funds generated from the sales for the construction of inputs sheds. According to the EC Delegation, the first programme was successfully completed in 1987.[47] It was the second phase, however, which was admittedly more problematic. The intended construction of grain stores was supposed to have been financed by the countervalue funds generated from the local sales of inputs and the steel. The first problem was that even if all the K14 million of expected counterpart funds were paid up, it would not have covered the cost which in 1987 was estimated at K20 million. However, the EC Delegation was unable to recover much of the funds from the sales.

There was the additional problem of the delay in selecting suitable sites for the grain stores.

According to the Delegation report, the engineering services department of Namboard was originally given the responsibility for the construction of ten to twelve grain sheds in the Eastern Province and Eastern Cooperative Union were to choose the sites.[48] Although the former had completed their part of the job, the latter delayed in finding the suitable sites until February 1988. The situation was rendered more complicated when the assets of Namboard were transferred to the cooperative movement. Responsibility for the sheds therefore reverted to the Zambia Cooperative Federation (ZCF). Although prepared to take up the project, the ZCF was unwilling to accept the financial liabilities of Namboard with respect to the unrecovered counterpart funds. The question of the structural steel was even more confounding. Not only did it remain unused, the EC Delegation actually confessed that it simply could not locate its whereabouts.[49]

It is evident that the first SAP did not benefit from very careful planning. Some consideration should have been given to probable contingencies such as rising costs and institutional changes, which were to affect the programme adversely. The steel issue was even more indicative. Given the "softness" of the Zambian bureaucratic and political environment, the EC should have established a mechanism by which to ensure that some particular agency or legal person would be directly accountable for the whereabouts of the steel. Besides this point, the EC would be hard put to defend the charge that the decision to export steel to Zambia under the SAP I programme was inspired not so much by the need to revitalize a declining European steel industry as by the desire to address the country's long-term food needs. There is in fact no evidence that the programme emerged out of a mutually agreed set of priorities between Zambia and the Community.

A comparative assessment of the Zambian and Mali programmes shows some similarities both in their relative success in the liberalization of the cereals market and in their weaknesses in terms of negligible impact on the small-scale producer sector.[50] On the whole, however, the food strategy appears to have been more successful in Mali. Unlike in Mali, where the strategy was accepted without much difficulty by the government and was even included in the national five-year development plan, Zambia's Kaunda administration was more keen to maintain its autonomy in agricultural and macroeconomic policy. It sought the triumph of ideological politics over the rigours of economic rationality.

The underlying political logic of this stance was informed by the imperatives of regime-survival. The maintenance of large estates (state farms), controlled prices and subsidies were means by which the regime hoped to curb urban unrest while maintaining a basis of legitimation. The fact that the regime backed down on the state farms issue shows that the EC was to some extent successful in its food strategy dialogue. However, the ensuing stalemate in the Joint Committee does show that Zambia was able to hold out on its own "bottom line". What was decisive in tilting matters against the Zambian position was the intervention of the World Bank and the Fund.

If the EC strategy could be said to have ultimately prevailed, it did so riding on the "back" of the international finance institutions, which brought in more resources together with the full weight of their political leverage in terms of conditionality. Indeed, the fact that "economic restructuring" had emerged as the new maxim of public policy confirms that the tactic of gentle persuasion inherent in the EC–Zambia dialogue had given way to the less courtly dictates of the Bank and Fund. Strictly speaking, the EC strategy could be said to have become a mere parenthesis in the new order of economic policy.

SYSMIN AND THE MINING SECTOR

For reasons that are obvious, Zambia has always accorded utmost importance to the mining and "industrial cooperation" aspect of its EC–Lomé diplomacy. Succeeding Zambian Ambassadors in Brussels have always been particularly active on this issue in the various Lomé negotiations. During the early part of the Lomé III negotiations the Zambian representative Ambassador, S. J. Kazunga, chaired the ambassadorial Negotiating Group on Mineral Resources, Energy and Sysmin before leaving to join the Plenary Group which was the coordinating body for the entire negotiations.[51] During the Lomé IV negotiations his successor, Ambassador Kapembe Nsingo, chaired the Negotiating Group on Mining and Industrial Cooperation, winning acclaim from his ACP colleagues as well as from EC Commission officials as a diplomat of rare ability and distinction.[52]

Zambia's strategy has been to maximize the benefits that could be derived from the Sysmin instrument which had emerged as one of the new innovations under the Second Lomé Convention. It is essentially a compensatory finance scheme for an agreed list of minerals, including copper, which would be automatically "triggered" should export receipts fall below a certain determined minimum threshold. Zambian policy aims not only to strengthen the operational effectiveness of Sysmin but also to increase the total volume of finances and to ensure equal participation by the ACP Group and the EC in the decision-making process of the scheme.[53] Under Lomé II and III, Sysmin funds were given on the same terms as special loans, i.e. an amortization period of forty years with a grace period of ten years and a 1 per cent interest rate. Least-developed countries were required to repay the loans at only 0.75 per cent interest.[54]

The background to Zambia's Sysmin application was the persistent decline which had characterized the country's mining industry since the

1970s. In the decade leading up to 1982, total production costs went up by 11 per cent while the real price of copper went down by 60 per cent. The state-controlled copper mining company, ZCCM, recorded decreasing pre-tax profits and subsequently huge losses during 1981–82 and 1982–83 financial years.[55] As a result of rising costs and declining capital investment, productivity in the copper sector had fallen from an annual production average of 12.3 tonnes per employee during 1973–76 to 9.7 tonnes in 1981. There was also the long-term gloomy outlook which forecast a depletion in production to less than 300,000 tonnes per year after the year 2000. Sysmin would therefore not only help the rationalization of production but also the process of diversification away from dependence on copper.

In 1982 the first Sysmin loan of ECU 55 million was approved for Zambia by the Community. In the same year the sum of ECU 50 million was approved for Zaire. In both cases export earnings and production levels had been adversely affected by falling world prices as well as by the wars in Zimbabwe, Angola and the Shaba Province. There was an element of luck involved in Zambia's success in getting its first Sysmin loan. Total annual allocations to the scheme by the EC were about ECU 56 million. The Commission was able to approve the two loans for both countries (a total of ECU 95 million) only because the 1980 and 1981 allocations had remained unutilized. In 1985 a second loan of ECU 28 million was approved, bringing the total of Zambia's Sysmin allocation to ECU 83 million. Consideration of Zambia's eligibility was based on Article 52 of the Second Lomé Convention which states that ACP member states are eligible for Sysmin loans when:

> a substantial fall is recorded or can be expected in the following months in their capacity to produce, or to export, or in their export earnings, to such an extent that it can seriously affect the development policy of the ACP State . . . by seriously compromising the profitability of an otherwise viable and economic line of production, thus preventing it from renewing at a normal or maintaining the production plant or export capacity.[56]

Table 8.3 provides a table of Sysmin allocations under Lomé II. Zambia and Zaire were the most important beneficiaries in terms of the amount of Sysmin loans allocated. The two countries' allocation for the rehabilitation of the copper and cobalt sector totalled ECU 184 million (about 73.6 per cent of all Lomé II Sysmin funding). By September 1990, about ECU 165 million (65.83 per cent) out of the total volume of committed funds had been disbursed.[57] This again illustrates the general slowness which has characterized Lomé aid financing operations.

With respect to the Zambian case, the two Sysmin loans came at a particularly opportune period because the merger of Nchanga Consolidated Copper Mines and Roan Consolidated Copper Mines into ZCCM had only

Table 8.3 Sysmin allocations under Lomé II (in ECU million).

Country	*Amount*	*Product*
Zaire (1)	40.00	Copper-Cobalt
Zaire (2)	41.00	Copper-Cobalt
Zambia (1)	55.00	Copper-Cobalt
Zambia (2)	28.00	Copper-Cobalt
Rwanda	2.84	Tin
Guyana	34.50	Bauxite
Liberia	49.64	Iron Ore
TOTAL*	250.64	

Note: *In 1988 the Commission transferred the sum of ECU 6.36 million to the Stabex fund
Source: ACP Secretariat, Brussels, *Report on Sysmin*, 23 May 1991

recently been completed. The facility was therefore expected to assist the process of reorganization and harmonization.

The main objective of the Sysmin loan was to contribute to the improvement of Zambia's copper and cobalt production capacity and to reduce the problem of rising production costs by replacing obsolete equipment. The first loan went to make up 15 per cent of a US$ 300 million loan package jointly financed by the World Bank, the African Development Bank and the EC for the ZCCM's Export, Rehabilitation and Diversification Programme. The second loan was also added as a supplementary contribution to the programme. Six policy objectives were enunciated as being necessary to the survival of ZCCM as an organization:

1 the restoration of productive capacity;
2 rationalization of production in terms of allocating resources to priority areas and cutting back on others;
3 introduction of policy measures by the government in order to remove certain external constraints;
4 enhancement of employee productivity;
5 development of awareness of the need for cost reduction and income generation;
6 the need to continue the economic diversification process.[58]

An intimate appraisal of the Sysmin programme is somewhat problematic because the loans were utilized for capital expenditure through 265 orders involving some 125 projects. There is the additional fact that the funds did not cover any one project in particular and hence no single project within the programme could be singled out for some kind of detailed economic evaluation.[59] The very first problem that emerged with the scheme was the bureaucratic delay which slowed down the process of implementation. It took about one year from Zambia's formal application in 1981 before the first loan was approved towards the end of 1982 by the EC Commission.

The Commission attributed the cause of the delay to the complex procedures which had to be followed before a final decision could be taken. Even after approval the disbursement of funds was very slow.

By May 1983, only about 4 per cent of the ECU 55 million had been disbursed. It became necessary for Ambassador S. J. Kazunga to seek audience with the Head of the Southern African Division and other key Commission officials. The meeting was held at the DGVIII, during which the Zambian Ambassador was informed that the cause of the delay was due to the slowness with which ZCCM was acting in certain areas, particularly with regard to tenders.[60] It also became apparent that the Commission was not favourably disposed to the decision by ZCCM to take over the purchasing of spare parts which had previously been handled by a British engineering firm, Zambia Engineering Company, based in Kent.

It does appear that both sides share a part of the blame for the delay. On the Zambian side it was clear that ZCCM was unfamiliar with the Sysmin procedures as well as with the purchase of technical equipment. As far as the latter issue was concerned, the financial audit by Coopers & Lybrand identified at least forty-five steps which had to be followed.[61] It has been estimated that it took an average of between 315 and 360 days from the date of tenders publication to the moment of delivery on site. It is therefore safe to conclude that ZCCM was inadequately prepared for the responsibility of purchasing which it had assumed, even though the aim of circumventing huge foreign agency fees which inspired the decision was understandable. Added to this was the delay caused by transport problems in the carriage of the imported machinery from the Tanzanian port of Dar es Salaam to Zambia. By compromising on the most urgent needs, such delays inevitably had an adverse effect on the execution of the programme.

Although the financial audit by Coopers & Lybrand registered no major accounting irregularities or frauds, some major "deviations" were detected. The first anomaly derived directly from the delays in the execution of the project. As a result of the delays, the drawdown procedures of the loan generated an interest amounting to UK£4.3 million. Since this was not anticipated in the loan agreement, no specific clauses were included in respect of the utilization of any interest so generated. The EC Delegate in Lusaka was later to discover that some UK£1.345 million of the interest had been transferred to ZCCM without its knowledge and was used in a manner which could not be properly accounted for.

Another area in which anomalies occurred was in several changes made in the execution of the project, whereby expenditures deviated from the original agreements. Of the 39 projects listed under the first loan, 9 were given up while an additional 49 were included. Under the second loan, 28 were withdrawn from the original 58 projects while another 20 were added. Granted that projects of this nature must take account of contingencies with the requisite changes that these entail, it was not evident that the changes were properly monitored to ensure that they were serving the right purpose. Indeed, the technical evaluation study observed that some of the projects were not properly designed at all:

> it seems that projects have been the name given to boxes in which undefined equipment purchases could take place . . . the general rule consisting in defining Sysmin expenditures is more formal than real and does not allow precise implementation control nor retrospective evaluation.[62]

At the operational level, no single agency or institution was given responsibility for overseeing the implementation of Sysmin and for monitoring the use of funds. Although a team within ZCCM was established to coordinate and monitor the programme, it was largely ineffective because it was technically ill-equipped to follow up such multifarious projects scattered across various departments within the organization. Without effective coordination, it was impossible to keep a close control over cash flows and to check unauthorized transactions.

There were also a number of problems with the equipment purchases that were made. According to the consultancy report, between 1982 and 1989 about ECU 77 million of Sysmin funds were used for the purchase of equipment and spare parts from abroad, representing about 5 per cent of the annual value of US$ 200 million which ZCCM committed to the purchase of technical equipment overseas.[63] Such equipment was spread over a number of capital projects within ZCCM. Here again technical evaluation was reportedly weak, resulting in inefficiency and waste. Equipment that was purchased for the Instrumentation Training School at Kitwe and the intensive care unit at Mufulira Hospital, for example, was said to be considerably under-utilized. Other equipment was purchased for use at Konkola 3 Shaft and at the Chambishi mine, both of which were soon to be closed down in 1987. Although ZCCM pointed out that the equipment had been transferred for use elsewhere within ZCCM, it is indicative of the rather poor planning which was involved.

Part of the problem derived from the tenders restrictions imposed on the loan agreement by the Community. This required that purchases be made only from EC member countries, whereas most of the ZCCM's experience in equipment procurement had been with non-EC suppliers, i.e. American, Japanese, Indian and Scandinavian technology. Some of the sophisticated technology obviously requires long-term commitment and technical partnership in terms of follow-up support services, all of which were negated by the EC insistence on direct purchases exclusively from the Community. Indeed, some ZCCM officials confessed that some of the equipment would never have been purchased but for this insistence on the part of the Community. In what can be regarded as a mild criticism of Sysmin procedures, Dr Edwin Koloko, ZCCM Director of Corporate Planning, stressed that while it is a welcome source of finance for the rehabilitation of the Zambian mining industry, there was nevertheless a need for:

> fair play among manufacturing EEC countries in tendering, giving equal business opportunity to companies in ACP member states . . . the procedures [should] . . . help to ensure . . . choice as far as the price and quality of the materials are concerned.[64]

The training component of the Sysmin programme also left much to be desired. The scheme, which cost about UK£2.1 million, was oriented towards training in Europe. Trainees were apparently selected on the basis of seniority rather than on the long-term operational and training needs of the company.[65] Most of them were sent to the United Kingdom, where they were attached to such companies as the British Coal Board, British Petroleum and Foxboro; many of these companies had not the remotest links to the activities of the ZCCM.

Finally, the use of counterpart funds deriving from Sysmin has raised certain critical questions. According to the first loan agreement, these were to be constituted into a Social Development Fund to be used for social projects. Such projects were to be submitted to the EC Delegation for approval. The second loan agreement extended the scope of the Social Fund to cover projects that contribute to economic diversification. The ZCCM maintains an extensive social and infrastructural overhead for its 60,000 employees. The Social Development Fund was therefore seen as the EC's contribution to the company's rehabilitation of its schools, hospitals, water supply, electricity and other infrastructures. The occasion of the opening of Mufulira mining hospital, financed through the EC Social Fund, was also a public relations opportunity for the EC Delegation, as it publicized their concern with and involvement in, social reconstruction.[66]

It was not possible to get a precise figure of the amount which will be devoted to the Social Fund. ZCCM also turned down several requests by the EC Delegation to discuss the project. It felt, perhaps justifiably, that the EC was seeking a disproportionate influence over its activities even though its Social Fund constituted just a tiny fraction of its annual investment in social and infrastructural development. The Delegation also sought in vain to prevail on ZCCM to avoid its segregationist orientation in the provision of social services. The company maintains separate schools and clubs for management staff and workers, which is a hang-over from colonial days. Non-employees are either barred from access to those facilities or, when allowed access, have to pay exorbitant charges for them. The EC therefore tried, unsuccessfully, to use its funds to enhance socially "progressive" policies in ZCCM. There was also the problem of racial tension between Europeans and Africans in the copper-mining areas which was not touched upon. An official of the EC Delegation confessed that this was a real problem in the Copperbelt.[67]

The consultant's report did raise the issue as to whether the social project which encourages ZCCM to perpetuate its image as a "welfare state" in the Copperbelt is not a negation of the EC's new development orientation in terms of rationalization and economic restructuring.[68] Perhaps a case could be made against supporting a welfarist disposition which fosters an attitude of dependence on ZCCM which itself is dependent on the fortunes of copper. On the whole, this criticism is misplaced. Over the years most of the infrastructures had deteriorated considerably, to the extent that certain basic services could not be met. Social rehabilitation, far from being a luxury, was a matter of practical necessity in order to ensure basic operational activities. Whilst ZCCM would be ill advised to overstretch itself in terms of the provision of social services, such services should be properly seen as positive contribution to a healthy working environment and better community relations, both of which, it can be argued, are conducive to improved productivity.

Towards a general assessment of Sysmin

Between 1988 and early 1989, copper prices at the London Metal Exchange had improved remarkably, attaining a peak of UK£2,008 per tonne in March 1989. Table 8.4 shows trends in copper production within the decade from 1980 to 1990. However, these propitious circumstances did not reflect positively on the levels of copper production in Zambia. Production continued to show a downward trend from 475,000 tonnes during 1987 to 421,590 tonnes during 1990–91.[69] It is therefore safe to assert that although the Sysmin facility was a significant financial input in the Zambian mining sector, it proved largely ineffective to the extent that it could not stop the downward decline in production. It seems obvious that the

Table 8.4 Zambia: copper exports, 1980–90

Year	*'000 Tonne*	*Kwacha (million)*
1980	661.3	870.6
1981	504.4	762.3
1982	606.6	855.4
1983	550.6	930.3
1984	530.8	1,031.2
1985	474.5	1,258.5
1986*	436.3	4,428.6
1987*	475.8	6,845.2
1988*	398.2	8,339.6
1989*	431.5	16,353.1
1990*	441.2	33,733.6

Note: *Preliminary
Source: Central Statistical Office, Lusaka, 1991

problems of the mining industry are highly complex and structural, requiring much more extensive funds and policy actions than had been provided for under the Sysmin facility. The consultancy report by CERNA reached the same negative conclusion in observing that the programme was unable to meet its main objective of stabilizing production and reducing costs.[70]

THE RURAL SMALLHOLDER PROJECT

By the time of the Lomé III Indicative Programme, the food strategy approach had virtually become "internalized" in the EC–Zambia development aid relationship. The change in orientation from large projects to focus on the small rural producer is perhaps best exemplified in the Smallholder Project covering both the Copperbelt and the Central Province.[71] The Copperbelt Project is targeted at a population of about 5,000 smallholder families in an area of 2,500 sq km in the Ndola Rural District. The one in the Central Province is even bigger, involving 30,500 families in an area of 35,000 sq km in the Kabwe Rural and Kabwe Urban Districts. The projects are costed at a total of ECU 12.5 million (a co-financing arrangement of ECU 12 million from the Community and the equivalent of 522,204.03 from GRZ) and are based on an "integrated" approach to agricultural and infrastructural development.

The stated objectives of this strategy are to improve food self-sufficiency, increase farm yields, and raise smallholder incomes.[72] Agricultural production is expected to be boosted through infrastructural development and through increased availability of inputs, credit and marketing facilities. Infrastructures and civil works such as roads, boreholes, pipe-borne water and electrification were to be developed under the scheme. The implementation strategy of the Smallholder Project is to work with existing administrative and institutional services within Zambia. The Ministry of Agriculture was made Executing Authority while the Provincial Agricultural Authorities were given direct responsibility for implementation. A Danish consultancy firm, DANAGRO, was selected to provide technical assistance by sending in a five-man team of technical personnel.

Although it is too early to judge the success or otherwise of the project, the report by the EC Delegation indicates that progress in implementation has been slow. There is also an indication that the farmers' response has not been particularly enthusiastic.[73] During the early stages of implementation, the technical assistance aspect appeared to have been rather problematic. Of the five-man team who were initially deployed by the consultancy firm between August and November 1989, two did not show up. Two other replacements were appointed and reluctantly accepted by the Executing Authority. Another member of the team withdrew from the project after barely spending two months there, and a replacement was not appointed until six months later.

Other problems arose as a result of rising costs due to the changing economic environment. The project quite clearly could have benefited from more careful planning than appeared to have been the case. Too much faith seemed to have been put on the role of foreign technical assistance and consultants, some of whom obviously did not have much experience in working in the African environment. It is curious that ECU 2.946 million, nearly a quarter of the entire funds, were allocated to "Technical Assistance", which obviously contradicts the orchestrated intention of working mainly with existing institutions within the country.

The second programme appears to have been more successful. The project was executed through the Regional Trypanosomiasis and Tsetse Control Programme (RTTCP). The method used was that of "night aerial spraying with ultra-low volume of non-persistent, partly selective insecticide", a method which proved successful in Zimbabwe and Botswana.[74] Aerial spraying was completed in 1987, including the establishment of a 75 km long "holding line" by means of odour baited traps and insecticide-impregnated targets. Implementation was not without problems, however. During the final spraying phase between July and October 1987, the project encountered major technical and organizational problems. The technical aspects of night spraying proved to have been more daunting than originally anticipated. According to the EC Delegation, some of the spraying equipment did not function satisfactorily. The navigational equipment was also poor, a factor which perhaps might have accounted for the tragic plane crash in which the sub-contractor and the EC technical assistance expert lost their lives.[75] There were also negative side-effects such as major fish kills resulting from an overdose of insecticide.[76]

GERMANY AND THE COBALT QUESTION

An important issue which emerged in Zambia–Community diplomacy in the mining area was the decision made by the Federal Republic of Germany to submit an application in August 1989, requesting the Commission to classify cobalt as a category 2 carcinogen under its "Hazardous Substances Directive". Category 2 substances are those which should be regarded as if they were carcinogenic to humans. Such categorization is considered valid if there is sufficient evidence from scientific research to presume that human exposure to such substances can lead to the development of cancer.

Germany's application was based on EC Council Directive 67/548/EEC of 27 June, which aimed to harmonize EC "laws, regulations and administrative procedures relating to the classification, packaging and labelling of dangerous substances". The Zambian Embassy expressed deep concern and reservation about the application and about the Commission's decision to appoint a group of specialized experts to consider the matter. Zambia's national interest was directly involved because cobalt is one of its most important export products.[77] Both countries account for more than 60 per cent of world production of the commodity. Zambia saw this negative classification of cobalt as being detrimental to the long-term interests of cobalt producers.

Ambassador Kapembe Nsingo took up the matter in official communications with the German representative in Brussels and the Commission on the one hand, and with the ACP Group on the other. In its reply to the Zambian request, the German mission to the EC said that, under Community practices, the responsibility for classification of hazardous substances rests with the Commission and neither the German Embassy nor its ministries in Bonn reserved any competence on the matter.[78] It also maintained that under the circumstances bilateral talks between the two countries were therefore unnecessary. The Commission, for its part, said it would welcome a meeting with the Zambian authorities to examine a more detailed submission by Zambia.

At the level of the ACP Group, Zambia sought to convince its colleagues that the classification would impact unfavourably on its economic interests as an exporter. It would be harmful in the sense that it would:

1 lead to reduced demand and substitution by other elements as well as halting further experiments on potential new uses of cobalt;
2 entail prohibitive toxic waste disposal regulations which would curtail demand for cobalt;
3 open a "can of worms" in terms of worldwide litigations where cobalt is present in the workplace, a situation which could ruin cobalt exporters.[79]

Zambia based its claim on the fact that the supposed carcinogenicity of cobalt was not based on sufficient scientific evidence, arguing that most of the medical evidence was based on experiments going back some 27 and 47 years, and that in any case there was no epidemiological proof on which the case could be made.

Zambia won a partial success with its case when the EC Group of Independent Experts disagreed with Germany and relegated cobalt to the group of category 3 substances, i.e. substances which have no conclusive evidence as to their harmfulness to humans. However, Zambia was not satisfied with even this modest concession, preferring that cobalt be deleted altogether from the list of hazardous substances until enough evidence be found from further scientific research. The Embassy took the case to the Sub-Committee on "Industrial Cooperation, Development of Mining Potential and Sysmin", which it hoped would prevail on the ACP Committee of Ambassadors to pressure the EC Commission to drop cobalt from the list of carcinogens pending the results of further scientific investigation in which the ACP states should also participate.[80]

The ACP solicited the support of an EC mining pressure group, Euromines, to put additional pressure on the Commission regarding the issue.

Euromines' lobbying strategy was to appeal to the self-interest of the Community, arguing not only that producers such as Zambia and Zaire would be harmed but also that many Western strategic industrial concerns would be affected. Although no final decision has been made, the cobalt case is an illustration of astute Zambian diplomacy. The Embassy used available platforms within the Lomé system as well as bargaining resources from an industrial pressure group to advance its case. However, its modest success indicates the limits of Zambian diplomatic bargaining in relation to Germany and the European Commission. It is also curious that Zambia did not work more closely with the other major African cobalt producer, Zaire. As they control between them more than 60 per cent of world production, their combined bargaining power would have been considerably enhanced. Zaire might have also made use of its French and Belgian connections within the Community to put additional pressure on the Commission's DGXI to reverse its decision. This is perhaps indicative of the rift which exists between the so-called "Francophone" and "Anglophone" Africans within the ACP Group in Brussels.

PROBLEMS OF DEVELOPMENT AID MANAGEMENT

Under the first three Lomé Conventions a total of ECU 195 million was earmarked for Zambia's National Indicative Programmes. The figure comes down to 193 million when we subtract the operating costs of the EC Delegation, which under Lomé I and II had been borne by the EDF. By December 1990 about ECU 180.7 million had been allocated to specific projects, out of which 114.7 million had already been spent, leaving a balance of unutilized funds amounting to ECU 79.6 million.[81] Table 8.5 indicates a total disbursement rate of 58 per cent for EDF funds in Zambia, a percentage which is far from satisfactory. Delays in financial disbursements by the EDF have become proverbial. The situation is not applicable to Zambia alone. Most ACP countries have had to complain at one point or another about such bureaucratic delays. For its part the Commission has raised issues ranging from the "absorptive capacity" of some ACP countries to their lack of technical know-how in preparing fundable projects or

Table 8.5 Utilization of EDF funds from Lomé I to Lomé III (in ECU million)

	Lomé I	*Lomé II*	*Lomé III*	*Total*
NIP	42.3	58.0	92.7	193.0
Commitments	42.3	57.3	80.1	179.7
Payments	42.3	42.1	29.0	113.4
P as % of NIP	100.0	72.6	31.3	58.8

Source: National Commission for Development Planning, Lusaka, 1992

their slowness to understand EC financing operations and administrative procedures. Most ACP countries would complain about the "Brussels bureaucracy" or about EC "delay tactics", which they often interpret as a form of creeping conditionality.[82]

In the particular case of Zambia, the problem seems to rest partly with the Zambian authorities and partly with the Community. Given the weaknesses in the Zambian bureaucracy and the lack of technical expertise, project planning has been a rather difficult process. It has therefore been hard for GRZ to submit good project proposals for consideration under the framework of national indicative programming. It would seem that some of the projects proposed by the erstwhile Kaunda administration were inspired by ideological and political considerations rather than by technical consideration for the long-term requirements of the Zambian economy. During the early stages of the food dialogue, as may be recalled, Commissioner Pisani rejected most of the projects which President Kaunda had submitted.

The weaknesses of Zambia's foreign missions

Some of these weaknesses were reflected in the organizational set-up of the Zambian Embassy in Brussels. Although the outgoing Zambian Ambassador to Brussels was evidently a man of ability, one got the impression that the Embassy was not well organized to cope with the diplomatic and technical work expected of it. It seemed that previous ambassadorial postings to Brussels were based on political patronage which had been widespread under the Kaunda regime.[83] It was indeed instructive that the Personal Secretary to the Ambassador also happened to be President Kaunda's own daughter. She had her own official chauffeur-driven car and was said to enjoy as many privileges and perhaps even more powers, than the Ambassador himself.[84] It was perhaps not merely coincidental that as soon as President Kaunda lost the elections and a new leader was sworn in, these privileges were withdrawn. In terms of personnel, there was only one trained economist to assist the Ambassador in dealing with Lomé affairs. This also reflects the fact that Zambia does not have an effective economic service in its foreign missions.[85]

Between "eurocracy" and the "soft state"

It is the contention of this study that the problems of aid management and project performance in Zambia can be reduced to the twin questions of bureaucratic red-tape in Brussels on the one hand, and the bureaucratic and structural incapacity of the Zambian state and administration (Myrdal's "soft state"), on the other.

On the EC side, it seems justified to say that its funding procedures remain complex, cumbersome and slow-moving. It is also evident that the Commission has applied conditionality by holding back funds whenever irreconcilable differences of policy emerged between itself and the Zambian authorities. The problem has been only partly assuaged under Lomé III with the initiation of quick-disbursing financing programmes. It goes without saying that such delays have contributed to deterioration of diplomatic relations and to problems of project performance under the Lomé aid regime. This conclusion is confirmed in a study by the Centre d'Étude et de Documentations Africaines (CEDAF), in Brussels:

> *De délais trop longs sont générateurs de malentendus avec les pays bénéficiaires et parfois de gaspillage ou de choix erronés au niveau de l'exécution dans la mesure ou les données d'un projet ont pu être modifiées entre la conception initiale et la mise en route.*[86]
>
> [Lengthy delays cause friction with recipient countries and can sometimes lead to financial waste or to mistakes at the level of execution, in that the ideas behind a project may become modified between initial conception and eventual implementation.]

Apart from the problem of slowness of fund disbursements, there have been other bottlenecks relating to programme performance. These have ranged from project-level problems (such as mismanagement, fraud, procurement and personnel) to macroeconomic and institutional constraints deriving from the wider society and polity.

In 1978 the Commission undertook an internal evaluation study of Lomé aid operations. The evaluation was based on case-studies from integrated rural development projects in nine African countries.[87] Although Zambia was not on the list of the countries studied, the findings of the report could be said to be reflective of the general trend in Lomé project aid operations. The report was an interesting exercise in self-criticism by the Commission. Although the report maintained that EC aid projects had a positive effect on African agriculture, it also conceded that in most cases the initial objectives were only partially accomplished.[88] In as many as a third of all the projects, results were only 50 per cent successful. The report attributed this weak performance to three factors:

1 The initial conceptualization of projects, which was not based on adequate planning;
2 the implementation approach, which was said to be rather technocratic and "authoritarian", and failed to take into account societal factors, particularly the psychological and cultural attributes of the local populace;
3 the constraint of the wider macroeconomic framework, particularly pricing policies, which tended to defeat the objectives of rural development assistance.

Susan Gitelson's model of *generative* and *low-yield* projects may be usefully employed in giving a general assessment of EC project performance in Zambia.[89] A *generative* project, in contrast to the *low-yield* type, is one that contributes to national development and self-reliance in the following ways:

- It is well integrated into the country's national development plan.
- It possesses a central, practicable goal mutually accepted by both donor and recipient,
- Its project manager offers leadership, with an *esprit de corps* amongst all staff in an efficient work environment.
- It enjoys continuous and strong support throughout the project cycle from donor as well as recipient.
- It produces positive effects in terms of improved technical and manpower skills and innovative ideas.

Judged by this yardstick, there is little evidence to show that EC projects have yielded positive generative effects in Zambia. In fact, it would seem that most were of the low-yield variety. Even the Mpongwe agricultural project, which was considered by President Kaunda as a show-case of EC–Zambia cooperation, has not been without its fair share of problems.[90] Our preceding discussion on sectoral aid reveals only rare instances where EC assistance was based on a complete meeting of minds between Lusaka and Brussels. The Zambian authorities "capitulated" in most instances not out of conviction but out of a desperate need for financial resources.

In January 1989, following the first meeting in 1988, the Commission sent in a technical mission headed by Mr G. Bonnaci, Head of Division for East Africa. The purpose of the mission was to discuss with the Zambian administration how to improve EC aid implementation in the country.[91] The mission diagnosed the problem of aid management, especially in the Zambian agricultural sector, in terms of the failure to undertake structural reforms. They urged the Zambian authorities to re-open dialogue with the international finance institutions as the prerequisite for a macroeconomic environment which would also be conducive to improved EC project performance. Decision was reached to appoint an EC Technical Coordinator to oversee EC projects and set up a coordinating framework to enhance renewed dialogue with donors.[92]

In October 1989, the EC Coordinator was posted to the office of the National Authorizing Officer. This has improved to some extent the monitoring of EC projects. The use of computers in the office of the Expert has led to greater efficiency in the tracking down of projects and in the preparation of technical papers for donor meetings and other important policy matters. Officials of the EC Delegation also felt that it had led to better working relations with the Zambian authorities.[93]

However, there was some discernible conflict with regard to routine working relations between the Office of the EC Expert and counterparts in the National Commission for Development Planning. The former and his support staff (all of them expatriates) were in an annexe somewhat slightly removed from the Planning Commission main building. Although they were expected to work together, staff in the Planning Commission's Economic and Technical Cooperation (ETC) Division appeared to have had little or no knowledge of the goings-on in the Expert's Office. There was no indication that a meaningful working rapport had been established between them, and one came away with the impression that they were even hoarding information from each other.[94]

The decision to hold regular consultations between the Delegation and the Zambian government has not been able to take off. The planned meetings for coordination of agricultural policies have also never been held. During the preparation of the Lomé III Indicative Programme the EC had underlined the holding of such meetings as one of the "corresponding actions" which devolved on the Zambian administration. It was envisaged that regular quarterly review meetings would be held with the Commission to ensure "rapid and effective preparation and implementation of programmes and projects".[95] Failure to hold such meetings has led to conflicting policy perspectives between the GRZ, the Delegation in Lusaka and the Commission in Brussels, which, according to DGVIII Zambia Desk Officer, has led to the submission of "disparate project proposals which have been neither fitted into the Lomé . . . indicative programme framework nor at project level do they take account of [required guidelines]".[96]

As a consequence, it has been difficult for Zambia and the Community to evolve a common understanding of development priorities. In the particular case of Lomé III indicative programming, the Desk Officer wrote disapprovingly about the situation whereby the Development Assistance Programme was characterized by "at least three different understandings . . . those of DGVIII, the Delegation and the Government of Zambia".[97] On the Zambian side, their reluctance to be involved in regular consultations with the EC can only be interpreted in terms of a desire to preserve a sphere of autonomy and control over national economic decision-making.

A major factor inhibiting the effectiveness of Lomé aid may be attributable to the fact that the Delegation has very little autonomy in decision-making. Sometimes even routine matters have to be approved from Brussels, with the inevitable delays which such referrals may entail. Although the granting of diplomatic status to the EC Delegation has endowed it with greater authority than it had in the past, it has neither the requisite staff nor the autonomy to be able to play a more effective role in the implementation of Lomé aid.[98] Apart from the Delegate who acts as Ambassador and chief spokesman on behalf of the Commission in the host country, the entire Delegation consists of only four key experts: two for agriculture, one for the economy and another for mining. These specialists have neither technical support staff nor a firm research base on which to undertake their duties. This perhaps partly explains the heavy reliance by the Commission on expensive foreign consultants, who may have little or no understanding of the cultural milieu in which the projects are operating. The EC relies very little on independent studies, in contrast with agencies such as NORAD and SIDA, which have funded some notable independent studies which have enriched the economic policy debate in Zambia.[99]

Owing to the frequent changes in personnel within the civil service, there was no single official within the ETC Division who appeared to have specialist knowledge of the workings of Lomé aid programmes.[100] It seemed as if all aspects relating to the monitoring of EC aid projects had been simply handed over to the foreign "experts" without secondment of a competent Zambian counterpart to work with them. Such an approach to technical assistance implies that when the foreign experts eventually leave, there would simply be no Zambian professional who could continue the project.

At a broader level these problems reflect the general weaknesses of aid management and coordination in Zambia. Up to 1989 no clearly defined framework existed for the utilization of external financial resources. Perhaps the "softness" of the Zambian state, to use again Myrdal's enigmatic phrase, required that no such institutional framework existed, so that foreign aid resources could be just another avenue for private accumulation. Zambia is no exception to this syndrome which seems quite widespread in some African countries, notably Kenya and Zaire. A cursory examination of the many evaluation reports on EC projects would reveal that mismanagement and fraudulent practices, although not the norm, are known to happen in Zambia.[101]

The Fourth National Development Plan has sought to alleviate these problems by creating a more coherent strategy for external resource mobilization.[102] The government has also formally subscribed to the National Technical Coordination Action Programming (NATCAP) approach. This involves joint programming of aid resources on a multilateral basis, with the UN agencies and the UNDP in particular playing a central coordinating function.[103] Although these initiatives have resulted in some improvement in the management of aid, it is evident that within such a framework, the EC is just one amongst several multilateral donors, without a particularly distinctive identity of its own.

CONCLUSION

This chapter has examined the evolving pattern of EC aid diplomacy in Zambia. We saw how Zambia's declining economic position has made her increasingly dependent on aid from external donors, including the EC.

Agriculture and mining have been the dominant sectors for Lomé aid in Zambia. EC aid has evolved from the "integrated projects" approach to conditionality-oriented sectoral strategies. The EC's aid diplomacy is guided as much by political motives as by economic interests. It seeks to use aid to gain influence within the Zambian system while attempting to change the policy direction of Zambia's economic management through the "food dialogue" strategy. To what extent it has succeeded remains unclear, given the involvement of other important actors such as the World Bank. What is obvious is that the state and its bureaucrats have attempted to preserve national autonomy while safeguarding the financial advantages of closer cooperation with Europe.

The economic impact of EC aid has been at best ambiguous. Its effectiveness has been hampered by bureaucratic inefficiency and political bottlenecks within the Zambian state on the one hand, and over-centralization of EC decision-making and the poor planning and management of projects, on the other. EC aid diplomacy has succeeded to the extent that the Community evidently enjoys a high profile as an aid donor in Zambia.[104] The EC has gained considerable influence and reputation with the Zambian public as an aid donor, even though there is a discernible "capability gap"[105] in terms of its power to affect and to transform positively the fundamental pillars of the Zambian economy and polity.

9

THE EC AND ECONOMIC REFORM IN ZAMBIA

This chapter extends the analysis of EC–Zambian diplomacy in the previous chapter to the specific question of adjustment and macroeconomic reform. We shall analyse EC responses to Zambia's adjustment programme between 1985 and 1987 and EC attitudes to Zambia's rift with the IFIs. We shall consider, first, the responses to the 1987 rift with the IFIs, and then the aid programmes which the EC has launched in support of Zambia's structural reform programme.

The decision to suspend relations with the IFIs in May 1987 was greeted with widespread public support within the country. The *Times* of Zambia likened the euphoria in the streets of Lusaka to a "carnival atmosphere".[1] From his headquarters in Addis Ababa, OAU Secretary-General Idé Oumarou expressed solidarity with the decision, saying that Zambia, like other adjusting countries, was experiencing:

> weariness and dissatisfaction with IMF-backed programmes which called for sacrifices but resulted in no positive gains. Its prescription of financial austerity and economic liberalization had failed to solve the economic woes of Africa . . . such IMF programmes, devoid of economic recovery, often result in revolts and upheavals.[2]

Such views were certainly not shared by the creditor-countries. According to the London-based *Africa Confidential*,

> Western diplomats and some bankers [were] . . . rather scornful of the Zambian decision . . . [asking why] they should finance Zambia while other African countries need the money rather more and are more pliable to IMF conditions.[3]

The influential weekly *The Economist* was even more trenchant in its criticism, asserting that Kaunda, "like most other African leaders, has never known the first thing about economics":

> he still prefers to talk vaguely of African socialism while his people get steadily poorer. In economic terms, he has put his country beyond the

> pale. If Western governments want to save the rest of Africa from similar impoverishment, they should leave him there.[4]

On 5 May, four days after the break in relations, Dr Kaunda convened a meeting of international donors to explain to them the circumstances which had led to the rift with the IMF. Prime Minister Musokotwane then outlined the five areas of disagreement between the government and the Fund:

1 The Fund wanted abolition of the two-tier exchange rate regime within a period of eighteen months, so that the official rate would level up to the auction rate.
2 The Fund wanted elimination of the budget deficit through a 70 per cent rise in fuel prices and a more than 100 per cent rise in the price of fertilizers.
3 The Fund wanted a complete withdrawal of the subsidies on mealie (maize) meal so that consumers would shoulder the full costs of production and marketing.
4 The Fund was of the view that interest rates should be raised to attain parity with the inflation rate (which in 1986 was 60 per cent), while salary increases in the public sector should not exceed 10 per cent.
5 The Fund was insisting that the mineral export tax applicable to ZCCM, a major source of budget revenue, should be further reduced.[5]

The Prime Minister emphasized that although the government was ready to make sacrifices in line with IMF demands, the implementation of these measures would have entailed unacceptable economic and social consequences.[6]

Kaunda's next diplomatic move was to attempt to dissuade the IMF from blocking alternative sources of finance for Zambia, whilst exploring various international contacts to secure external financing outside the framework of the Fund. He made diplomatic overtures to the Middle East, Western Europe as well as the then Soviet bloc and China. He wrote personal letters to President Ronald Reagan, Prime Minister Margaret Thatcher and Chancellor Helmut Kohl, imploring them to prevail on the IMF for more congenial terms.[7] Musokotwane toured a number of European capitals, notably London, Stockholm, Brussels, Copenhagen and the Hague, in an attempt to convince Western leaders of Zambia's good intentions. However, these diplomatic initiatives did not seem to yield much success. Even the Scandinavian countries, Zambia's traditionally sympathetic and generous friends, were insisting that they would grant a promised US$60 million loan only if Zambia were prepared to accede to IMF conditions.[8]

LIBERALS, MODERATES AND HARD-LINERS

Donor responses ranged from the two extremes of outright hostility to the Zambian decision on the one hand, to that of benign empathy with the government's political predicament, on the other. In the middle were those who maintained an open-minded disposition, being neither absolutely hostile nor wholly sympathetic. I have classified these attitudinal responses as "liberals", "moderates" and "hard-liners".

"Liberals" are donors who express complete sympathy for Zambia's decision. They tend to be appreciative of the social and political constraints and the threats to the regime's legitimacy which the adjustment programme seemed to entail. They would not only continue their aid programmes but may actually decide to increase the volume of financial assistance. They may officially have their programmes linked to fulfilment of IMF agreements, but in practice they remain flexible.

"Moderates" are those who may be appreciative of the social and political constraints, but will see no alternative to IMF conditions. They will continue with existing aid projects but may suspend others, normally balance of payments support, and may decide to stay action on the financing of future programmes pending a rapprochement with the IFIs. They will also continue to work behind the scenes to bring about normalization of relations with the IFIs.

The "hard-liners" not only are hostile to the breach of relations with the IFIs, but may actually attempt to convert sceptics to their hard-line perspective. They see nothing short of complete acceptance of IMF conditions as the basis for both continuation of their aid programmes as well as of all future financial support.

The "liberals" in the Zambian case were Denmark, Sweden, Belgium, Italy and Ireland. They all tended to express understanding of the political constraints and the social costs of adjustment in Zambia. Both Sweden and Denmark have linked their aid programmes to agreements with the Fund, but in practice, have been flexible in their responses. All the four pledged to continue their programmes, while Sweden and Italy announced an increase in the volume of their financial commitments. Italy reportedly expressed indifference to the rift between Zambia and the Fund and announced increased aid amounting to US$180 million over the three-year period to 1990, most of it in form of commodity aid.[9]

Denmark and Sweden belong to the Nordic group, who are prominent donors to Zambia, sharing also some affinity to Kaunda's "humanism". Denmark has a double identity in being both a Nordic country as well as a member of the European Community.[10] Their aid orientation has its roots in their traditions, norms and interests as small or medium powers in the international system. This status leads them to an orientation which Olav Stokke has termed "humane internationalism".[11] Nordic governments would therefore tend to see aid as a moral imperative, a duty on the part of the rich to work towards the alleviation of world poverty. They would tend to discountenance the realist pursuit of national ambition through use of aid, to which other donors seem less averse. Having had a relatively long social democratic tradition, we may conclude that they are not likely to be dogmatically attached to market solutions which underlie most of IMF conditionalities.

The position of Italy, Belgium and Ireland as "sympathizers" is somewhat harder to explain. It is also interesting that they are EC member states and therefore signatories to the Lomé Conventions. With the exception of Italy, which has become a significant donor in recent times, the two others are minor European economic powers and therefore relatively insignificant as global donors or creditors. It is therefore reasonable to surmise that they are likely to have far less to lose in the event of Zambia's or other LDCs' inability to service their debts. It is perhaps significant that they are also predominantly Catholic European states.[12]

Among the "moderates" were the Netherlands, Norway and Japan. All three decided to continue with their normal programmes, although they also tended to support the IFIs and to criticize Zambia's actions. Prime Minister Musokotwane visited the Hague during 2–3 June 1987, as part of his shuttle aid diplomacy. Although the Dutch government were critical of Zambia's actions, they pledged to continue their aid programme and particularly to provide finished fertilizer import support.[13] In the case of Norway, although they continued with their aid programmes, they withdrew from discussions on debt relief which had been in progress with the Zambian government. A senior economist in the NORAD office in Lusaka felt that Zambia's behaviour at this particular time was not only unimaginative, it was also "irrational", because the diplomatic costs were considered to have far outweighed the benefits.[14] The Japanese response was somewhat more ambiguous in this regard. Whilst the Ministry of Foreign Affairs and the Ambassador in Lusaka expressed sympathy and understanding for Zambia's action, the Ministry of Finance took a more hard-line stance.

The Netherlands and Norway basically conform to the tradition of middle power "humane internationalism". The Dutch position is also influenced by strong commercial and private-sector orientation in aid policy, especially after the centre-right coalition came to power in the 1980s.[15] Norway seems to have departed somewhat from the more liberal Nordic tradition because it was among the first of the Nordic countries to embrace neo-conservative attitudes in its domestic and foreign aid policies. Norway has also apparently been more active than the others in putting a high premium on economic as well as political liberalization in its aid diplomacy.

The ambivalence in the Japanese reaction was perhaps a reflection of both its interests as a major economic and financial power as well as of her pragmatism in aid matters. Although Japan follows the United States and the great powers in rallying behind the IFIs, she prefers to tow a pragmatic line in her aid orientation.[16] Another level of explanation may be related to the Japanese tradition of political pragmatism as represented by its foreign-policy establishment on the one hand, and the technocratic conservatism by the powerful Finance Ministry, on the other. This ambiguity partly explains why Japan's economic and financial clout remains largely unmatched by her leadership performance in the international system.[17]

The "hard-liners" were West Germany, France, the United Kingdom and the United States. They belong amongst the elite G7 club of the richest nations. There is a more pronounced tendency for them to use aid as an instrument of foreign policy. They also have more vested interests in structural reform programmes, being dominant share-holders in the IFIs as well as the main creditors to the highly indebted countries in Africa and Latin America. When Finance Minister Gibson Chigaga visited Bonn, for example, he was bluntly informed that the aid funds which were blocked would not be released until Zambia agreed, at least in part, to the IMF conditions. In May 1987 the Germans had even threatened to distribute aid allocations for Zambia to other "more needy" countries.[18]

This marked a turning point in the general deterioration of relations between the two countries. According to the Zambian interpretation, West Germany, which had chosen Zambia as a model country for its development aid policy, was now shifting its attention to its southern neighbour, Zimbabwe. The Germans were said to have been impressed by President Robert Mugabe's policy of racial reconciliation and were therefore anxious to prop him up as the leader of the "front-line" states. Their long-term objective was to use Mugabe as a positive influence on SWAPO's Sam Nujoma when Namibia eventually became independent, given the fact that a sizeable proportion of the European settlers in Namibia are of German descent.[19] Friedrich Bunke, Director of the Lusaka office of the Friedrich Ebert Foundation,[20] one of the prominent German "development foundations" sponsored by the West German Social Democratic Party, was ordered out of the country after he was accused of sponsoring the ZCTU, which was at the time under the chairmanship of Frederick Chiluba.[21]

Although Zambia is not a priority country for French aid, France also followed the hard-line position. In the case of the United Kingdom, although Kaunda did write personally to Mrs Thatcher, perhaps in the hope of exploiting the "Commonwealth connection", the British government was generally unsympathetic. Although Britain had committed a substantial part of its aid to financing the foreign exchange auction, after the break with the IFIs, about UK£9.3 million was frozen. Britain also declared it would stop all future aid funding until an agreement was reached with the IFIs.[22] The American attitude was very close to the British one. Both countries were said to have worked closely behind the scenes in attempting to persuade other donors to freeze all financial support in order to "force the Zambians back into the IMF/World Bank discussions".[23] Since De Gaulle's famous veto in the 1960s, the Anglo-American relationship has been seen as a factor in the EC's inability to evolve a common external political orientation.

EUROPEAN COMMUNITY RESPONSES

The preceding review of donor attitudes sets in perspective our subsequent discussion on the EC's own responses. It is important to note that the biggest EC member states have also been prominent bilateral donors in Zambia, apart from their individual contributions to Lomé funds. Our analysis so far has shown that the most influential EC member states were "hard-liners", although overall responses were often a mixture of both extremes. Only the Netherlands assumed the posture of a "moderate". Considering the status of the big three, Germany, France and Britain, all of whom were "hard-liners", it is not unreasonable to assume that their influence within the EDF Committee would be decisive in tilting the pendulum in favour of the "hard-line" conservative tendency. At a broader level, it is essential to realize that the majority of donors were either sympathetic or moderate in their attitudes to Zambia. Although most of them regretted the collapse of the IMF programme, they were, according to Tom Roe, DGVIII Zambia Desk Officer, "sensitive to and understanding of the political and social unrest and risks" which beset the Kaunda administration.[24]

In considering EC responses, it is imperative to bear in mind that, though prominent as an aid donor to Zambia, the Community's position as a creditor is a comparatively minor one. This is because the overwhelming part of its financial commitments were in grants, with only a small percentage in the form of repayable loans. During 1987, of the $5,800 million of debts and accumulated arrears totalling US$600 million, Zambia owed only about ECU128 million to the Community and its institutions. These were debts incurred as a result of EIB and Commission lending under Lomé I and II, usually in the form of soft loans or risk capital. On 30 April 1987, Zambia was in arrears on its debt service to the EIB to the tune of ECU770,575, which was a relatively small sum.[25]

After the episode of 1 May, J. M. Filori, the EC Delegate in Lusaka, prepared a confidential report to the Commission on Zambia's economic and political situation.[26] Lack of effective coordination by external donors as well as the inherent weaknesses of the Zambian administrative machinery were seen as the main causes for the failure of the reform programme. The budget deficit was also blamed for fuelling excessive growth in money supply, which in 1986 had grown by 30 per cent and which in the long run was said to have undermined the auction.

Significantly, the Delegate did not question the fundamental principles behind the system itself, or indeed some of the anomalies which emerged during its implementation. The so-called "anti-IMF lobby" within UNIP and the administration was singled out for having allegedly sabotaged the reform programme.[27] They were said to have won the power struggle over the "pro-IMF group", as represented by the appointment of Mr Chivuno, a well-known opponent of the IMF programme, as Bank of Zambia Governor in April 1986. The fundamental cause of the IMF débâcle in Zambia, according to the Delegate, was primarily due to political resistance by privileged elites since the economic reform programme challenged their "vested interests, ideological preferences and fundamental instincts".[28]

Whilst it is true that economic reform undermined some of the sources of rent-seeking by elite groups, there is perhaps even more evidence to suggest that certain sectors of the elites, i.e. the commercial bourgeoisie, including foreign capital, were major beneficiaries of the economic reform programme.[29] The overwhelming cost of adjustment was not borne by the elites but by the urban poor and, in particular, "vulnerable groups" such as the unemployed, women and children.[30] The report also put some of the blame on the technical design of IMF programmes themselves, which have tended to be "overly simple and mechanical", and rarely addressing the intricacies of a country's development predicament:

> Nobody in his right sense should think that Zambia can ever repay a debt whose service would absorb 100 per cent of its export earnings. Similarly, subsidies cannot be abolished overnight and external assistance is needed to cushion the reforms, allowing government a reasonable breathing space.[31]

This is not to say that the EC Delegate approved of the NERP which replaced the IMF programme. On the contrary, he expressed strong scepticism about its efficacy, arguing that it would lead to a return of the regime of controls and rent-seeking activities while stultifying long-term prospects for economic diversification. He viewed the unilateral moratorium on debts as a folly which risked blockage of much-needed financial inflows as well as incurring other possible retaliatory measures by international creditors.

Filori argued the case for a more pragmatic approach to structural reform, whereby donors should be content to pursue "second or third best options" rather than the technically optimal but politically disastrous alternative. As an immediate response, he urged the Commission to provide balance of payments support to avert imminent economic disaster in Zambia. He advised the Commission to continue with all development projects in view of the "contractual nature" of the Lomé aid regime.

This sense of realism was shared by other senior officials within DGVIII, who believed that Zambia deserved to be treated with understanding, if not sympathy. One particular official who had spent some years as an aid worker in the country before joining the services of the Commission expressed unreserved sympathy for the Zambian position. He asserted that it was simply impolitic and unrealistic for the IFIs to insist on such drastic reform measures at such a rapid pace, especially in the wake of an election period, since "no government anywhere" would do that.[32]

Perhaps the most immediate factor determining the EC response was the legal character and contractual obligations underlying the Lomé aid system.[33] The elaborate framework of negotiations, the detailed "*travaux préparatoires*", and the processes of approval and ratification, fulfil the essential requirements of the international law of treaties.[34] Although its legal instruments are of restricted application, the Lomé Conventions possess some of the essential qualities of a multilateral treaty between a group of sovereign states and an international organization, i.e. the European Community and its constituent member states.[35] Once the National Indicative Programmes have been agreed and signed, they assume the character of a legal contract.

Given the contractual nature of Lomé aid, therefore, the EC did not want to withdraw unilaterally all financial and technical assistance on the grounds that Zambia had failed to fulfil IMF conditions.[36] The Commission's position was that since Lomé III was concentrated on the focal area of agriculture and "integrated rural development" (with no explicit reference having been made to structural reforms), the new Zambian Interim National Development Plan could not be regarded as a violation on Zambia's part of its commitments under the Lomé National Indicative Programme. The Commission therefore opined that there was no legal basis to discontinue aid programmes in the country.

There were, however, two issues on which the Commission was prepared to put some diplomatic pressure on Zambia. The first, about which the Commission lodged official complaints, was on the question of producer prices for maize and fertilizers. The EC considered these to be well below their expectations with regard to Zambia's sectoral policy on agriculture. An agreement was reached by both sides whereby the matter would be addressed through "bilateral consultations" in accordance with "Lomé principles and procedures". The second was the question of arrears owed to the EIB, which led the Bank to suspend implementation of ongoing loans and also blocking all new operations.[37]

Legal considerations apart, if the Community wanted to exert pressure on Zambia without appearing to violate the Lomé aid agreements, they had the option of using another effective but more subtle weapon. This is the weapon of slowing down the rate of disbursements of already committed funds, which is firmly within the Commission's discretionary powers. Whether or not this weapon has been used is a matter of speculation.

The rate of EDF financial flows were extremely slow even before May 1987. By April 1987, only 62 per cent of Lomé II funds had been committed at project level, and only 20 per cent of the committed funds had been paid out. A mere 10 per cent of Lomé III allocations had been committed and no single disbursement had yet been made. The fact-finding mission by André Auclert, Deputy Director-General of DGVIII, had led to a Memorandum of Understanding by which an ambitious target of ECU7 million were to be disbursed to Zambia by the end of the year.[38] There was no indication that this target was reached by the end of 1987.

The role of EC Commission diplomacy

The Commission's next move was to pursue a double-pronged diplomacy aimed at pressurizing Zambia to re-establish dialogue with the IMF on the one hand, and persuading the IFIs to agree to a more pragmatic and politically feasible reform package, on the other. This scenario clearly depicted the "triangular diplomacy" to which we referred at the beginning of this study. After the 9 June meeting with Mr Kebby Musokotwane at the Berlaymont, the EDF Committee of EC member states met on 16 June 1987. The Commission was later to release a carefully worded press statement declaring that the EC wanted to "play the difficult game of 'policy dialogue' in a positive way, without being accused of direct conditionality or linkage with a formal IMF/Zambia agreement".[39]

The Commission was obviously treading a diplomatic tightrope, as it was anxious not to alienate the ACP states by appearing to be openly taking sides with the IFIs. Zambia was now being seen as a test-case of the Community's official policy on orthodox adjustment programmes and would confirm or disprove the fears expressed by some ACP diplomats that Lomé aid was becoming linked to a country's readiness to implement IMF conditionalities.

Towards the end of May 1987 two DGVIII officials, Giorgio Bonnaci and Tom Roe, went to Washington to "discuss and coordinate" with the IFIs on their policies and attitudes to the countries of East Africa and particularly to Zambia, after the 1 May break.[40] It was unclear what the exact nature of their briefing was, but we can only surmise from the records of the discussions that transpired that the Commission wanted to act the role of intermediator or catalyst to get both Zambia and the IFIs to resume discussions, and possibly to unblock transfer of much-needed funds to Zambia.[41]

The mission team was told by an IMF Deputy Director, Mr Bhatia, that the Fund was "surprised and dismayed" by Kaunda's public renunciation of their policies, especially after their April mission in Lusaka when they had indicated willingness to agree on a "flexible and reasonable set of policies to be implemented in a phased manner".[42] Two senior Bank officials present at the meeting felt similarly "let down", since they had made efforts to convince their respective boards to be "flexible and considerate" with regard to Zambia.[43] The blockage of funds was said to be exclusively due to the accumulation of "excessive arrears" and had no links with the collapse of the economic recovery programme.[44] They pledged that as soon as the arrears were paid up, they would resume disbursement of project loans. However, all structural adjustment lending would remain frozen until Zambia acceded to their terms. In the end they expressed willingness to resume dialogue with Zambia and to be more flexible and pragmatic along the lines suggested by the EC.

EC diplomacy could be said to have been only partially successful in this instance. The Zambians in the end became convinced of the rationale of resuming dialogue with the IFIs. Although the Fund and Bank could not be prevailed upon to resume immediate funding, they were prepared to be "pragmatic, flexible and phased" in the re-packaging of their programme and also agreeing to phase price liberalization and subsidy removals to be effective only after the 1988 elections.

IMPORT FINANCING AND THE FOREIGN EXCHANGE GAP

During the period of the IMF recovery programme, the primary support provided by the EC was by way of general imports. In December 1986 the EC committed ECU1.54 million from the food aid substitution budget to finance procurement of chemical imports for Nitrogen Chemicals of Zambia (NCZ), a parastatal company. It was the first such action to be financed under Article 188 of Lomé III. As part of the chapter on "Financial and Technical Cooperation", it provided for support in terms of general imports for sectoral development to the productive sector and to social sectors such as education and health.[45] The advantages of import support programmes, from the viewpoint of recipients, is that they tend to be quick-disbursing and contribute to filling the foreign exchange gap for financing of crucial imports. For the donor, on the other hand, it serves to boost the external market for exports, given the strictures of the Rules of Origin, whereby purchases have to be from either the EC or from another ACP state.[46]

Under the EC Special Debt Programme and the Agricultural Input Import Support Programme (AIISP), the sum of ECU40 million was allocated to Zambia. The initial objective was to utilize ECU32.8 million to finance imports of chemicals to NCZ for manufacture of fertilizers at its Kafue plant and the balance of ECU7.2 million for agricultural inputs. EC support for the NCZ project was part of a multilateral aid programme to the parastatal. The Japanese development agency and KFW of Denmark were each to finance rehabilitation of a production line while the World Bank was to support upgrading of management.

The EC and the conditionality game

In July 1987, shortly after the renunciation of the reform programme, the Commission got approval from the EDF Committee to commence financing to Zambia under the AIISP scheme. The conditions laid down by both the EC and KFW for funding the project were that fertilizer prices would be linked to import parity levels; that government and management would ensure that NCZ remained economically viable; and that it would have access to adequate foreign exchange for importation of raw materials, spare parts and other supplies. In March 1988 both the EC and KFW withdrew from the project because they felt Zambia was not meeting the conditions stipulated.[47]

EC conditionality did yield some positive results in this regard. In May 1988, the government announced a number of policy measures aimed at improving the viability of NCZ and the agricultural sector:

- NCZ would be allowed to charge import parity plus 15 per cent for fertilizers;
- producer price increases for maize and other food crops as well as for fertilizers;
- commitment to allocate US$6 million to NCZ through FEMAC;
- continuing support to the World Bank-financed management team and recruitment of an expatriate procurement expert.[48]

These policy measures were accompanied by a plan by NCZ to rehabilitate its German plant by September 1989, with financial resources to be provided by West Germany, Italy and Japan. In August 1989, however, most donors withdrew from the project because they had been informed by the Steering Committee that conditions in the NCZ were worse than had been previously thought, and that an additional DM60 million would be required. The EC transferred most of the funds originally allocated to the programme to the AIISP and the Forex Facility.

Macroeconomic policy inconsistencies as well as internal management problems, which had been quite endemic in the Zambian parastatal sector, were largely responsible for the poor performance of the NCZ. But it was probably also a case of lack of multi-donor coordination. Multi-donor involvement may be a vehicle for maximizing additional financial resources, but such co-financing arrangements can often mean introduction of disparate financing procedures and conflicting managerial perspectives, with the consequent outcome in terms of managerial as well as institutional incoherence. There was also the question of equipment procurement. Donors would expect to benefit from supply of equipment, with the effect that a single industrial subsector would be faced with equipment of differing technical specifications from Japan, Germany, Italy and other EC countries. Indeed, the EC Delegation itself admitted that "equipment supply to NCZ has, in hindsight, proved not to be viable", which was a diplomatic way of saying the co-financing arrangement was technically a failure.[49]

THE EC FOREIGN EXCHANGE FACILITY

One of the most important components of the AIISP was the Foreign Exchange Facility (ECFF) launched by the EC to procure agricultural inputs through the FEMAC which had replaced the auction system. The programme was said to be guided by four principles:

1 It should operate as far as possible within the framework of FEMAC.
2 It should conform to generally accepted practice.
3 It should be well publicized.
4 It should supplement foreign exchange allocation to the agricultural sector provided by FEMAC.[50]

A set of eligibility criteria was outlined whereby interested applicants could apply through their commercial banks to FEMAC. Such proposals had to be specifically for use in the agricultural sector (fertilizers were excluded from the list of eligible supplies); origins of supplies were to be either from an EC member state or from an ACP country; and foreign exchange requested had to be within the range of US$5,000–250,000.[51] Successful applicants were expected to pay the kwacha equivalent through their bank to be deposited in a joint EC–GRZ countervalue account in the Bank of Zambia.

The first ECFF was between July 1987 and March 1988. Two other schemes were implemented during 1989–91. Our main concern however is to give a detailed account of the first one, on which we have some documentary evidence. The first ECFF covered the nine months up to March 1988, and coinciding with 20–24 FEMAC sessions. A firm of private consultants was contracted to assist in implementing the programme, their main task being to screen all applications and to make appropriate recommendations to the Steering Committee for final vetting and approval.[52] Under the first scheme, a total of 393 applications were received, out of which 128 requesting ECU7.16 million (K70.43 million) were approved. The remaining 265 applications were not approved for various reasons relating to eligibility criteria.

A careful examination of the data compiled by Price Waterhouse reveals a number of significant trends about the programme. It was indeed revealing that allocation of foreign exchange tended to favour applicants who had requested large sums more than those who had applied for smaller ones.

Table 9.1 ECFF successful applications by sector and economic agents, 1988

Economic agents/sector	*US$*	*ECU*	*Kwacha*	*% of total*
Commercial farmers	299,113	250,049	2,459,752	3
Small farmers	—	—	—	—
Agricultural holdings	487,681	407,685	4,010,430	6
Traders	282,004	235,746	2,319,052	3
Distributors	3,973,464	3,321,686	32,675,689	46
Agro-services industries	3,486,761	2,914,818	28,673,296	41
Agric. raw materials	35,906	30,016	295,269	1
TOTAL	8,564,929	7,160,000	70,433,488	100

Source: Price Waterhouse, Lusaka, April 1988

The overwhelming beneficiaries were the big-time enterprises, specifically, the agro-services and distribution sectors, who received 65 per cent of total financial allocations, while small farmers received absolutely no loans from the scheme. In relation to the category of economic agents, Table 9.1 shows that 90 per cent of total disbursements went to the private sector while only 10 per cent went to the parastatals. Most of the allocations were overwhelmingly to distributors and agricultural services (46 per cent and 41 per cent respectively). This was indeed a major contradiction in the Community's agricultural policy perspective which ostensibly is based on encouragement of the smallholder and the so-called "emergent farmer".

Price Waterhouse consultants pointed out that the reason for this anomaly was simply because small farmers made no effort to take advantage of the scheme, adding that "lack of finance" and problems of complying with "complex and cumbersome procedures" made it difficult for peasant farmers to benefit from the scheme.[53] But certainly this should have been known from the beginning and appropriate measures taken so that smallholders would benefit. We can only conclude that apart from serving the export interests of European firms, the ECFF was geared mainly to the needs of foreign and indigenous mercantile classes rather than the interests of small-scale producers. The "politics of capture" were clearly at work here, as financial or credit opportunities which claim to give priority to peasant farmers are seized or commandeered by politically dominant social forces.

Table 9.2 presents a summary of successful applications by type of product or import. Tractors and tractor spares together with herbicides and pesticides accounted for nearly a half of all the products imported. Veterinary products as well as equipment, pumps and mills were another important set of products. These allocations indicate what were considered the priority areas, i.e. the needs of agricultural mechanization, which have nothing to do with the small farmer, and agricultural chemicals which are

Table 9.2 Summary of ECFF successful applicants by type of product, 1988

Type of product	*US$*	*ECU*	*Kwacha*	*% of total*
Herbicides & pesticides	1,708,072	1,428,874	14,050,564	20
Veterinary products	1,176,989	978,820	9,639,323	14
Tractors & tractor spares	2,313,312	1,957,647	19,245,793	27
Equipment, pumps & mills	1,275,265	1,061,478	10,429,929	15
Spares & tools	936,258	774,917	7,620,583	11
Irrigation equipment	684,832	568,888	5,618,154	8
Other	470,201	389,370	3,829,141	5
TOTAL	8,564,929	7,159,994	70,433,487	100

Source: Price Waterhouse, April 1988

required as herbicides and pesticides for crops such as maize, soya beans, cotton and tobacco.

To what extent, therefore, was the ECFF successful in meeting input needs in the agricultural sector? Given the paucity of data on sectoral input requirements, only a very general answer can be given to this question. During the first programme, Zambia allocated US$34.19 million to agriculture, with the facility accounting for about US$6.26 million or 18 per cent of the total allocation to the sector. It was therefore a significant contribution, even though there is evidence that it remained far below the input requirements of the agricultural sector.[54]

THE EC STRUCTURAL ADJUSTMENT FACILITY

In March 1990 Commissioner Marin formally declared Zambia eligible for structural adjustment support under Section 3 of the Second Chapter of the Development Finance Corporation provision of Lomé IV. Zambia was adjudged to have fulfilled the conditions stated in the NIP. The Commission was reasonably satisfied that:

1 the country was pursuing a reform programme with the support of the principal donors;
2 the government was adhering to its NIP conditions with regard to public expenditure and the priority sectors of social services, infrastructures, and non-copper exports;
3 some progress was being made with regard to exchange rate adjustment and external trade liberalization.[55]

The EC Structural Adjustment Facility (SAF) provides a grant of ECU25.5 million for procurement of imports under the General Import Programme. The goods to be imported would be those within the list of priorities under the Open General Licensing (OGL) system.

Although the decision was taken while Dr Kaunda was still in power, the

SAF was not implemented until Frederick Chiluba's administration took over in October 1991. Although the SAF represented just an estimated five to six weeks of non-mining import requirements for Zambia, it is significant that the EC got the new administration to commit itself to the following set of policies as the conditions for the financing agreement. The government agreed that it would:

- keep to the guidelines of the 1992–94 Policy Framework Paper;
- honour its implicit commitments in the 1992 budget by keeping the budget deficit within 1.9 per cent;
- maintain and expand the OGL system as well as improving financial control of public expenditures;
- gradually bring down the exchange rate to a "market-clearing" level and inform donors regularly on the economic outlook and progress in implementation of its economic reform programme.[56]

A careful analysis of the EC–SAF shows that it is hardly more than an import aid programme. Its only linkage to structural adjustment is the set of conditions that are formalized in the financing agreement, which bind Zambia to follow the path marked out for it by the IFIs. One looks in vain for any clues to the oft-repeated claim about the Community's "unique" approach to structural adjustment. What it essentially represents is yet another small financial inducement to keep Zambia's economic policy in check while also benefiting EC exporters. Like many of such import programmes, they feed the country's import-dependence syndrome which promotes the interests of foreign exporters much more than it does the development of the importing country's productive capacity.

Countervalue funds and budget control

Import programmes have also generated a huge reserve of countervalue funds which can have a detrimental effect on the economy. Economists are generally agreed that such funds have the potential effect of swelling the money supply and thereby exacerbating inflation.[57] Countervalue funds generated from import support programmes alone were estimated at K877 millions.[58] Utilization of countervalue funds are governed by the 1987 agreements on procedures for allocation and use of local currency generated by EC aid operations. The general understanding is that most of the funds would be utilized on the social sector and on rural development projects. The EC has also utilized some of the funds in the retroactive settlement of Zambia's debt arrears to external creditors, and especially to the IFIs, which was one of the preconditions for resumption of Bank and Fund operations after 1990. Table 9.3 shows utilization of K232,097,624 of EC countervalue funds during 1989–90, most of which were used in productive sectors, notably the NCZ fertilizer company and the Copperbelt

Table 9.3 Disbursement of EC/GRZ countervalue funds in 1989–90

Project title	*Kwacha*
Batoka Ranch	957,386
Palabana Dairy Training Institute	290,708
RTTCP (Trypanosomiasis programme)	16,547,788
Export Development Seminar	183,000
Anti-Aids Programme	500,000
English Teaching Texts Printing	385,600
British Council Book Survey	174,906
Copperbelt Smallholder Credit Scheme	10,000,000
George Compound Pilot Project	11,424,761
TOTAL	40,464,149

Source: EC Delegation, Lusaka, 1991

Smallholder Credit Scheme. During 1992 up to 1994 countervalue funds were projected to increase even more. Table 9.4 indicates a total increase of up to K3.8 billion, which will be expended on social services (particularly education) and for debt-servicing as well as EDF projects.

In June 1991 the EC Delegate and the National Authorizing Officer reached a new and revised agreement on use of countervalue funds. They reaffirmed joint management of the funds which are deposited on Account 552 of the Bank of Zambia and joint decision-making with regard to allocation of funds either to budget headings or to specific projects.[59]

Under the new guidelines, emphasis is placed on ensuring that funds are used in conformity with macroeconomic policies and targets, especially with regard to money supply and the budget deficit. As a precautionary measure against potential negative effects, it was agreed that utilization of funds could be slowed down or suspended altogether. The government, for its part, undertook to inform the Delegation on a regular basis about all movements of funds on the special account as well as on the government's

Table 9.4 Cost estimates for disbursement of EC/GRZ countervalue funds during 1992/3 and 1993/4 (in kwacha million)

Sectoral support	*1992/3*	*1993/4*	*Total*
Education	200	150	350
Health sector	600	550	1,150
Water/sanitation	200	200	400
Food security	200	140	340
SAP institutional support	180	180	360
Debt servicing	400	400	800
EDF projects	200	200	400
TOTAL	1,980	1,820	3,800

Source: Commission of the European Communities, 1992

quarterly fiscal reviews and revenue estimates. Most significantly, the new arrangement has explicitly linked operation of countervalue funds with "the obligations of structural adjustment monitored by the IMF", and that non-compliance with those obligations will lead to an automatic suspension of countervalue funds within the budget until new guidelines can be worked out. A joint account with the Bank of Zambia has been opened for countervalue funds. In principle, they can be used in the state budget, although the EC Delegation is required to give its seal of approval before any such expenditures can be made. This means, in effect, that the EC Delegation has been accorded the right to inspect all budget proposals and to determine which of them can be regarded as priority projects and which should be dropped. Countervalue funds have thus considerably enhanced the potential leverage and influence which the Community can have over the national budget economic decision-making in general.

THE SOCIAL DIMENSIONS OF ADJUSTMENT

The EC response to the "social dimensions of adjustment" can only properly be understood against the background of the debate on the human costs of adjustment programmes in the latter part of the 1980s. Such programmes had provoked criticisms not only from several LDC governments and their articulate publics but also from international agencies such as UNICEF.[60] Much of the critique centred mainly on the adverse effects of adjustment programmes on "vulnerable groups" such as children, women, the infirm, and female-headed households.

Although the debate is far from settled,[61] such criticisms, in particular the UNICEF study, while conceding the necessity for adjustment, were influential in drawing attention to the need for "adjustment with a human face". By 1990, it was becoming increasingly evident that some learning process was taking place within the IFIs in response to the widespread criticisms. The World Bank in its 1990 *Annual Report* was underlining poverty alleviation and distributive strategies as a necessary part of structural adjustment.[62]

As early as 1983 countries such as Costa Rica and Chile, which had fairly well-established social welfare bureaucracies, had already started relief programmes targeted at workers and other under-privileged groups who were adjudged to have suffered the adverse social consequences of adjustment.[63] The Bolivian Emergency Social Fund (ESF) and the Programme of Action to Mitigate the Social Costs of Adjustment (PAMSCAD) in Ghana, launched with the full backing of the IFIs, were to become the models for such relief programmes elsewhere in the developing world. In both Ghana and Bolivia, the programmes were directed mainly at workers laid off as a result of adjustment programmes (Cocoa Board workers in the case of Ghana and tin miners in the case of Bolivia).[64]

The Bolivian ESF was specifically mentioned as the model which inspired the Bank's social rehabilitation programme in Zambia which is being jointly implemented with the EC Micro-Projects Programme (MPP). The Bank's representative at the joint World Bank–EC office in Lusaka joined the institution after graduation from Harvard's Kennedy School of Government and was posted as a programme officer in Bolivia with primary assignment on the ESF. She emphasized that her experiences in Bolivia were important in guiding her and the Bank's approach to the Zambia programme.[65]

The cornerstone of the EC approach to the "social dimensions of adjustment" is its Micro-Projects Programme, whose history dates back to the Lomé I era in 1974–75, long before adjustment was to enter the lexicon of international development. Micro-projects were envisioned as small-scale, community-based projects to be jointly financed by the EC, the recipient ACP state and the local communities concerned. Its inspiration derived from the ideas of grassroots development, rural social mobilization and "appropriate technology" associated with the writings of E. F. Schumacher.[66] Under Articles 14 to 17 of Chapter 7 of the First Convention, a special fund was established to help finance "the needs of local communities with regard to development".

A sum of ECU20 million was allocated to this fund, with the declared objective of fostering active "grassroots participatory development" in the ACP states.[67] For every approved project EC contribution was initially put at a maximum of ECU75,000, and total Community contribution was not to exceed 50 per cent of total project costs. Under Lomé IV EC contribution was revised upwards to a maximum of ECU300,000, and up to 75 per cent of total project costs. Zambia was not amongst the first group of beneficiaries of the Lomé I micro-projects fund. It was as late as 1986 that an agreement was reached for Zambia's first MPP amounting to about ECU2.12 million. Disbursements under this programme continued until 1990, when the second MPP amounting to ECU5 million was approved to cover a period of one year, up to mid-1991. A third programme began in mid-1991 with a relatively large budget of ECU12 million to cover the period up to 1994, as part of the Community's support to the multi-donor Social Action Programme (SAP) for Zambia.[68]

The Social Action Programme

The SAP was begun in 1990 as a "time-bound, prioritized and targeted programme in the social sector designed to mitigate the adverse economic effects of the ERP on the poorest and most vulnerable groups in Zambian society".[69] In light of the deteriorating economic and social conditions, the priority areas were specified as being the following: food security, employment and income-generation, and rehabilitation of basic social infrastructures. Six sectoral areas, each under a Working Group were carved out:

- health;
- education;
- water and sanitation;
- household, food, security and nutrition;
- income generation and employment;
- women in development.

The SAP Secretariat, located at the annexe of the NCDP building, is headed by an expatriate Coordinator who is assisted by four civil servants seconded from the mainstream administration. The main policy guidelines for all its operational activities are to be provided by a Steering Committee consisting of donor representatives as well as some members of the higher administration. The task of implementation will be overseen by a new Social Projects Implementation Department (SPID) in the Office of the President. The Department itself is divided into three major divisions: the SAP Secretariat, the EC Micro-Projects Unit and the GRZ/World Bank Social Recovery Fund.

Given the serious problems of aid management and policy coordination in Zambia, it seems that this heterogeneous structure is unlikely to enhance efficient performance by the various divisions. The presidency evidently provides a vital authoritative cover for all of them, but beyond which the SAP, EC Micro-Projects and the Bank's Social Recovery Fund would operate with relative autonomy, constituting a gigantic social welfare "superstructure" essentially operated by expatriates and running parallel with, and probably even in conflict with, the mainstream bureaucracy.

EC financial involvement covers virtually every aspect of the SAP, with co-financing commitments in each of the twenty-five major projects under the 1992–95 SAP.[70] Although precise figures are yet to be made public, EC funding, which comes both by way of EDF disbursements as well as countervalue funds derived from food aid and various import programmes, constitutes a sizeable part of the estimated total of K14.63 billion of funding so far secured for the five-year programme.[71] EC contributions would probably rank as the highest by any single donor. During the 1992/93 financial year alone, the SAP proposed to spend some K2.6 billion of EC countervalue funds on various projects in health, education, water and sanitation, and food security. The general picture that emerges is that the EC certainly does attach much importance to the "social dimensions of adjustment", although such policy commitment exists as part of a multi-donor effort rather than as a distinctive Community aid programme.

The EC–World Bank Micro-Projects Programme

The EC Micro-Projects Unit (MPU) which operates the MPP was set up in 1985, and began actual operations in 1986 at its annexe buildings at the

NCDP headquarters. The task of running the Unit between 1985 and June 1988, was contracted to Gossner Mission, a West German NGO. Between July 1988 and July 1991 the MPU was headed by an Italian Coordinator. In July 1991, an EC-appointed British Coordinator took over. Two professional staff were recruited from the mainstream administration to assist the head of the Unit, one as Assistant Coordinator and the other as Field Operations Officer.

The signing of the World Bank–GRZ Social Recovery Fund and the appointment of a World Bank programme officer to the MPU has led to the modification of the administrative structure. The World Bank representative became Deputy Coordinator while the local counterpart who was Assistant Coordinator becomes Higher Field Officer, although with the status of counterpart Deputy Coordinator. Two new positions were created but were yet to be staffed at the time this research was being conducted: the post of Technical Officer (to handle the engineering side of projects) and a Regional Officer to be based at Kasama in the Northern Province.

Figure 9.1 illustrates the new administrative structure of the MPU. The MPU Coordinator is a contracted employee who is paid by the EDF. His

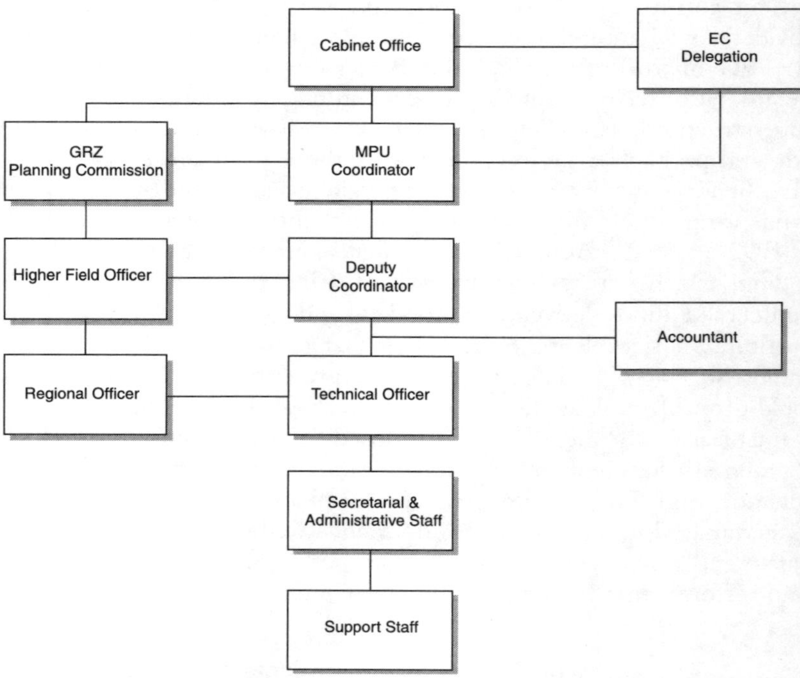

Figure 9.1 Administrative structure of the EC/World Bank Micro-Projects Unit
Source: EC/World Bank Micro-Projects Headquarters, Lusaka, 1991

operations are overseen by both the EC Delegation and the National Authorizing Officer, to whom he is primarily accountable. He is assisted by a Deputy Coordinator, who is seconded from the World Bank. As the latter has full authority over use of World Bank funds under the programme, there can be said to exist an inherently conflictual situation. Local staff are expressly anxious about their career paths and employment conditions. Having been recruited from the mainstream administration, they are on two-year contracts with no firm plans regarding their positions within the MPU and its future work. Although they are better paid than their colleagues in the civil service, there have been complaints about the wide disparities in emoluments between expatriate and local staff, leading to feelings of resentment on the part of local staff.[72]

The MPU exists essentially as a funding rather than an implementing agency, since all initiatives in terms of project identification and funding proposals must come from the local communities themselves or from NGOs that can produce viable projects within the identified priority areas. The initial areas of priority were in rehabilitation of rural schools and rural clinics, although consideration is now extended to such infrastructures as roads, bridges and dams, which are expected to open the path to "productive and income generating projects".[73]

EC intervention was focused on health and education as the two vital social sectors which suffered severe budgetary cutbacks during the 1980s. Figures in Table 9.5 (see also Figure 9.2) show that real expenditure for education fell from K212.3 million in 1981 to K131.5 million in 1991, a fall of about 80 per cent; and for health it fell by almost 30 per cent from K108.5 million in 1981 to K77.3 million in 1991. The sharpest cutbacks

Table 9.5 Real expenditure on health and education in Zambia (at constant 1984 kwacha millions) as a percentage of the total annual budget, 1981–91

Year	*Education*	*Health*	*Education %*	*Health %*	*Total kwacha billion*
1981	1,961.3	212.3	108.5	10.8	5.5
1982	2,189.0	294.6	159.1	13.5	7.3
1983	1,741.0	265.2	127.6	15.2	7.3
1984	1,484.6	249.3	112.3	16.8	7.6
1985	1,525.3	204.8	102.0	13.4	6.7
1986	2,051.4	165.1	85.2	8.0	4.2
1987	1,460.5	150.0	87.7	10.3	6.0
1988	1,328.2	114.9	103.0	8.7	7.8
1989	965.0	83.7	64.5	8.7	6.7
1990	1,124.9	101.9	71.3	9.1	6.3
1991	1,075.3	131.5	77.3	12.2	7.2

Source: G. de Crombrugghe *et al.*, "Evaluation of Microprojects Programmes", Consultancy Report for the EC Commission, Brussels: COTA, 1991

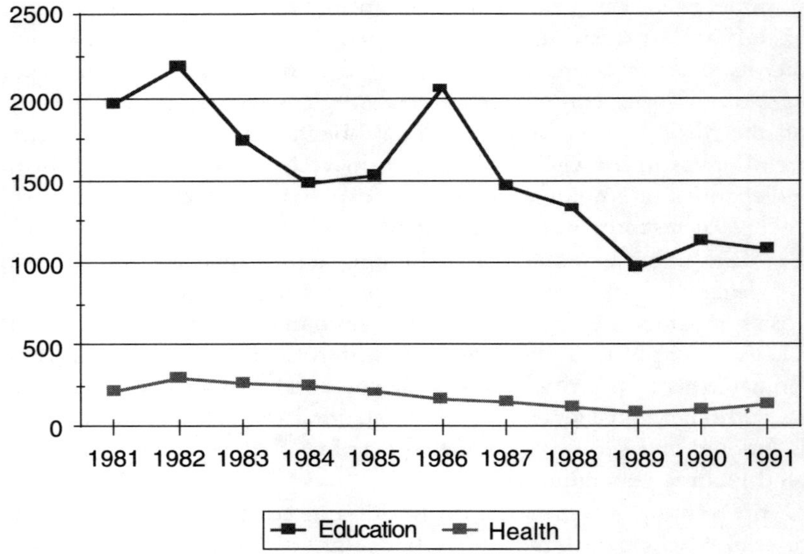

Figure 9.2 Zambia expenditure on health and education, 1981–91 (in kwacha million)
Source: G. de Crombrugghe *et al.*, *The Evaluation of the Micro-Projects Programmes*, Brussels: COTA, 1991

were between 1986 and 1989 when Zambia embarked upon the structural adjustment experiment. In relation to total public spending, budgetary allocations to the two sectors also declined between 1981 and 1991, from 10.8 to 8.0 per cent for education; and from 5.5 to 4.2 per cent for health.

The position appears even more gloomy when it is realized that the population was growing at the rate of 3.2 per cent annually. Moreover, the two sectors' budgetary allocations seemed to go predominantly to recurrent costs, i.e. personnel and emoluments, with very little left for maintenance purposes, such as textbooks for schools and basic drugs for rural clinics. Capital expenditures had become an all but forgotten issue. Personnel emoluments alone were said to have taken 97 per cent of primary school budget spending and 94 per cent of health spending.[74] The Micro-Projects programme was therefore seen as a means of filling an important gap in the

Table 9.6 Sectoral distribution of completed EC micro-projects, 1990

Sector	*Total of completed projects*	*Total expenditure by June 1990 (kwacha)*
Agriculture & irrigation	8	818,715
Education	51	12,135,067
Food processing	2	363,000
Health	21	5,599,861
Rural infrastructure	7	775,600
Water supply/sanitation	7	289,130
Youth training	1	95,600
TOTAL	97	20,076,973

Source: EC/NCDP Micro-Projects Unit, Lusaka, 1990

health and education sectors, particularly with regard to capital spending and rehabilitation of existing infrastructures.

The MPP's operational strategy

The MPP operational strategy is based on the utilization of existing rural administrative structures. It should be borne in mind that since 1980 Zambia had embarked upon a programme of administrative and regional decentralization which was aimed at enhancing "participatory democracy" and rapid rural transformation. Figure 9.3 shows the rural administrative structure of Zambia after the 1980 "decentralization" reforms.

Decentralization proved to have been at best a noble aspiration rather than a practical possibility in the Zambian context, mainly due to the highly centralized political "superstructure" and the conflicting interests between local party apparatchiks and the rural *apamwamba* (rich and powerful men) on the one hand, and the generality of the rural populace, on the other.[75]

At the village or community level, a Project Committee initiates a project proposal which seeks to address a clear need and commits itself to support every stage of the implementation process, either by cash or direct labour, or both. Project proposals are then submitted to the District Council who must confirm that they fall within the District's development priorities. Proposals then go up to the Provincial Planning Unit who appraise them and make recommendations for funding to the MPU in Lusaka. The MPU then finalizes the project selection process in conjunction with the EC Delegation and a committee comprising of NGOs and representatives of the line ministries.

MPP projects span the entire country, with concentrations in the Southern, Eastern, Copperbelt and Central Provinces (Table 9.7). They have proved to be quite popular among rural communities as well as NGOs.[76] About 300 rural projects have so far been undertaken in a number of

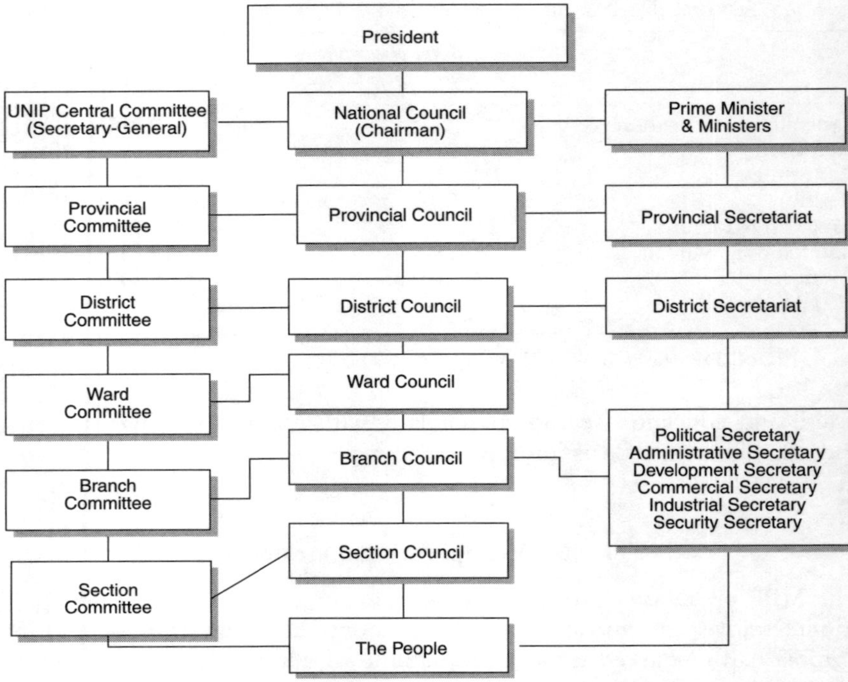

Figure 9.3 Structure of local government in Zambia, December 1990
Source: Office of the President, Lusaka, 1991

Table 9.7 Spatial distribution of completed EC micro-projects

Province	*Total number of completed projects*	*Total expenditure by June 1990 (kwacha)*
Central	13	3,005,716
Copperbelt	13	3,362,292
Eastern	18	3,388,322
Luapula	6	1,123,250
Lusaka	11	3,023,738
Northern	8	2,132,370
North-Western	4	191,290
Southern	19	3,143,914
Western	5	705,901
TOTAL	97	20,076,793

Source: EC–NCDP Micro-Projects Unit, Lusaka, 1990

districts scattered across the country. It would be outside the scope of this study to make a detailed evaluation of the entire programme.[77] What is important for us is the extent to which it serves to illustrate the EC's orientation and involvement in the politics of adjustment in Zambia. While it is true that the programme has been generally well received, there is evidence of conspicuous project failures in several cases.[78] Perhaps three examples may suffice to illustrate the kinds of problems that beset the micro-projects strategy.

The first example is the Katondwana Primary School Project in the Western Province. The project was approved in April 1990 for construction of a three-room classroom block and two staff houses. The cost of the project was estimated at K1.35 million, expected to be completed within a period of twelve months. In June, two months after official approval of the project, the sum of K350,000 had been advanced as initial allocation. A couple of months after receipt of the initial advance, the Project Committee did not submit any progress reports in contravention of the original conditions of financial assistance. Money was spent without any evidence of progress on the building project. Only 500 bricks had been moulded, and in the mean time the costs of materials had escalated well beyond what had been estimated originally. The MPU in the end had to recommend cancellation of the project.

A similar rural project in Mwenyi, with the same cost estimates and technical specifications, ended up with even more problems. Only 3,000 bricks had been moulded, all of which turned out to have been very poorly done (they had very little cement in them and crumbled easily when you walked on them), a clear indication of the questionable integrity of the labour employed on the project. The Committee Chairman reportedly treated the project almost as a private business concern, insisting that he, rather than the Treasurer, should keep the bank book, and also refusing to discuss any aspect of the project with District officials. He also did not send any monthly reports as expected and made it a point of duty to be always absent whenever MPU staff paid field visits to the project site. This project also had to be closed, in this case, owing largely to the grasping proclivities of a single village "strongman".

The third example is the Chikundu Embankment Project in Chilubi District of Northern Province which was approved in 1990. Estimated at a cost of K1.7 million, it was to construct an embankment on the islands of Chilubi and Nsumbu on Lake Bangweulu. About K1.2 million was spent with very little evidence of any substantial progress on the project. Very few accounting records were kept by the Project Committee and no one could account for most of the money spent. Meanwhile the very modest construction that was started had been washed away by the heavy rains. The project clearly would have done better with the benefit of technical supervision by a civil engineer, quite apart from the problem of mismanagement on the part of the Project Committee.

The apparent failure of some of these projects reveal the short-comings of the EC micro-project approach. The first and perhaps the most obvious relates to the technical requirements of project identification. Most project committees, with the exception of foreign NGOs which have some wealth of experience in project management, have little or no familiarity with project identification. Such projects as those of Chikundu Embankment would have required the services of technical experts. The MPP should have liaised with the Ministry of Works to second local experts to assist with such projects. The recent decision to create the position of Higher Technical Officer to advise the MPU on engineering and technical issues is an important decision that will hopefully reduce the gap in project identification.

A second and related problem pertains to the politico-administrative framework of the MPP's strategy. Most District Officers, who are expected to pay regular visits to project sites and advise Committee members, hardly keep up with the duties expected of them.[79] Given the hierarchical structure of regional administration and the UNIP political tradition of "developmental paternalism", District Officers seem unable, and perhaps unwilling, to work with local communities in identifying their real needs. According to de Crombrugghe *et al.*, while paying lip-service to "participatory democracy", they seem more amenable to "telling people how to do things than in listening to people's problems and looking with them for the best way to address these problems".[80]

Underlying this difficulty is the wider political problem which seems to afflict local-level development in many LDCs. It has been aptly described by Joel Migdal as the "Triangle of Accommodation".[81] It refers to the situation whereby even the best thought-out development schemes can end up becoming virtually unrecognizable during implementation at the local level (see Figure 9.4). This is a result of the bargaining process which emerges between the three dominant social forces in rural society: the bureaucrats or "implementors", the partymen or local politicos, and rural "strongmen". These three groups are in a perpetual contest to capture state resources meant for local development. The final outcome of rural development programmes therefore tends to be a result of bargaining and accommodation between these competing social forces. The MPP experience in Zambia shows that elements of the "Triangle of Accommodation" would seem to have been operative there as well.

Another major gap is in the area of project monitoring while they are being implemented.[82] Project Committees are expected to submit regular monthly reports to MPU to help the latter assess the extent of progress in implementation and any reasons which may cause delays. Such reports are supposed to be verified on-site by District Officers while provincial plan-

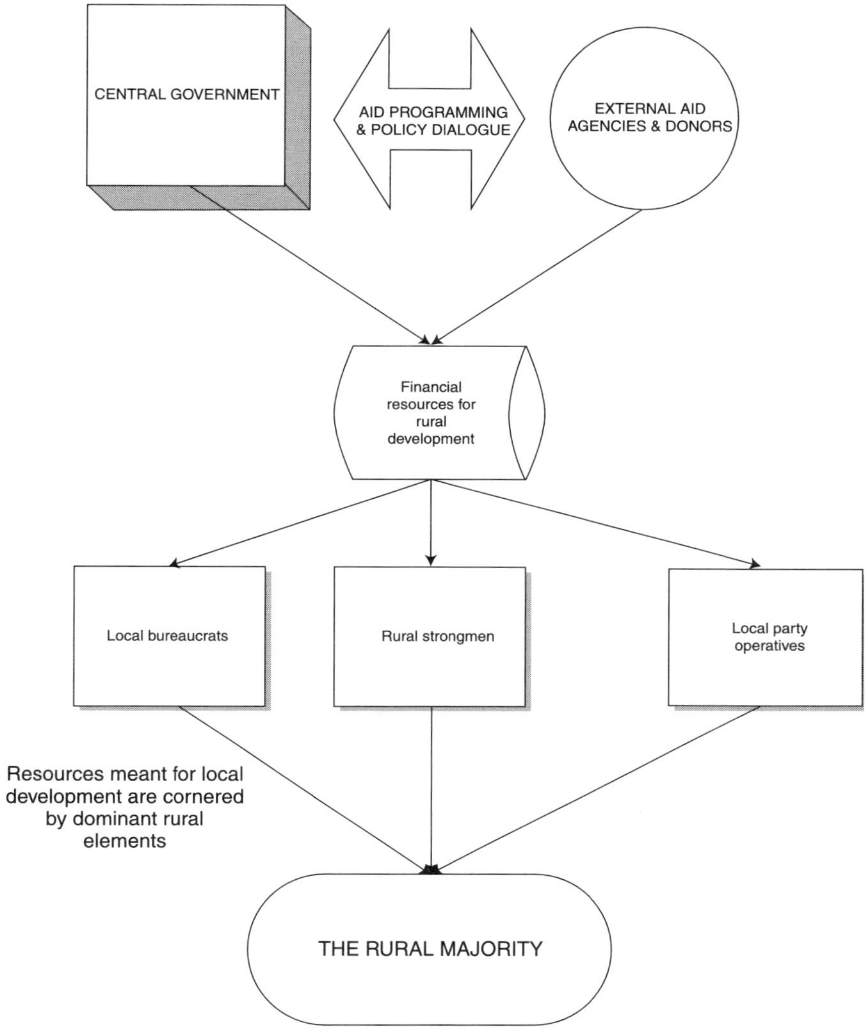

Figure 9.4 Development financing and the mechanisms of rural power in Zambia

ning staff are expected to pay quarterly visits and to send quarterly reports to Lusaka. However, many projects are not properly monitored, as a result either of poor motivation, or of lack of requisite technical skills on the part of those responsible, or of inaccessibility or transport problems.

Staff from the MPU are also expected to visit every project at least three times during its implementation. Given the existence of some 200 projects during the one and half-year period from 1990–91, for example, it represents many working days per annum for an already highly overstretched half a dozen staff members. The problem has been eased somewhat by the newly introduced computerized Micro-Projects Tracking System (MTS), which still cannot be a substitute for on-site inspection. The new position of Regional Officer under the recent reorganization of the MPU hopefully will further improve the situation.[83] Figure 9.3 shows the highly centralized administrative machinery within which the MPP has had to operate.

Ex-post evaluation also does not appear to be one of the strong points of the MPP. Apart from the projects implemented by NGOs, which were generally considered to be of reasonably good standard, most MPP projects have been of a rather poor quality.[84] Apart from shoddy quality of buildings, there have been uncertainties in follow-up services, resulting in some instances of completed classrooms without textbooks for pupils and clinics without beds, mattresses or drugs. As shown in Table 9.8, the MPU does not finance all costs of a project. It finances external materials and transport costs, while the government pays personnel wages and the local communities contribute through direct labour. No firm arrangements exist with regard to supplies, maintenance, drugs and learning materials. Co-financing support is expected from other donors, with the Finnish International Development Agency (FINNIDA) and the Swedish International Development Agency (SIDA) playing a particularly prominent role. Total unconsidered costs amount to 12 per cent of the total costs of Rural Primary Schools (RPS) and 26 per cent for Rural Health Clinics (RHC).

In addition, vandalism and theft are not uncommon, especially if rural

Table 9.8 Existing financial arrangement of the Micro-Projects Programme (in Kwacha)

Financing	*Rural primary schools**						*Rural health clinics*	
	1×2	*%*	*1×3*	*%*	*1×4*	*%*		*%*
MPU	1,812,738	60	2,692,738	60	3,642,050	60	3,205,050	51
Local community	762,500	25	1,117,500	24	1,472,500	24	1,327,500	21
GRZ	106,734	3	160,101	4	213,468	4	133,418	2
Not covered	365,148	12	547,084	12	730,273	12	1,627,921	26
of which:								
Equipment	(160,000)		(240,000)		(320,000)		(1,000,000)	
Maintenance	(45,148)		(67,084)		(90,273)		(151,281)	
Learning/ drugs	(160,000)		(240,000)		(320,000)		(476,640)	
TOTAL	3,047,120		4,517,423		6,058,291		6,293,889	

Note: * The type of rural primary school is differentiated by the number of rooms. 1×2 indicates a two-room block; 1×3 a three-room block; 1×4 a four-room block
Source: De Crombrugghe *et al*., op. cit., p. 20

school buildings, for example, are designed in such a way that they appear different from or "alien" to, the surrounding village architecture.[85] The MPU has not been able to get firm commitment or assurance from local Project Committees regarding availability of services and maintenance once projects have been completed. Quite clearly the MPU could have benefited from closer working relations with the line ministries, especially those of health and education.

The MPP strategy suffers from a basic organizational contradiction. The MPU is essentially a funding rather than an implementing agency. The task of implementation is reserved for local community beneficiaries, while the intermediate task of technical management support rests with regional administrative officials, most of whom have neither the expertise nor the political orientation to perform such a task. The MPP ends up trying to play this intermediary role with a very small group of professional staff, most of whom are overworked and overstretched.

Under the Lomé IV programme, the MPU will work jointly with the World Bank SRF on a larger nation-wide programme in tackling the social problems of adjustment. The EC will provide a grant of ECU12 million (or US$16 million) for the period 1992–95 while the Bank's contribution is by way of an IDA loan of US$20 million over 1992–96. The two agencies will utilize a common administrative core staff and a joint financial tracking and monitoring system.

The World Bank component is in three stages.[86] First, a priority survey is undertaken by the Central Statistical Office based on the Bank's model of the "Social Dimensions of Adjustment Surveys". Such a survey was undertaken with funding support from the Norwegian Government, amounting to US$2.2 million. The next stage is a number of policy studies on five priority areas: women; household/food/security; variations in the price mechanism; poverty analysis; and beneficiary assessment. About sixty such studies are planned to last the duration of the project. They are estimated to cost US$1.6 million and financial support has been provided by the Swedish International Development Agency (SIDA). The aim of the studies component is to strengthen the policy analysis base of development administration and management, which currently is virtually non-existent in Zambia. The third stage is the implementation of the Social Recovery Programme itself.

Policy differences between the World Bank and the EC

Basic differences in approach as well as inter-institutional conflicts between the Bank and the EC are already beginning to emerge even at this early stage. The Bank's conceptual approach is to establish a nation-wide programme with many more professional staff to be posted to remote parts of the country where micro-projects are being implemented. The EC, on the other hand, is reluctant to turn the programme into a large bureaucracy which may appear to be working outside the mainstream administrative-political framework.[87]

Moreover, the EC is content to delegate the task of project monitoring and evaluation to Provincial Planning Units and District Offices, whilst the Bank is insistent that the task should be undertaken by MPU staff. The World Bank insists that each project should be monitored on at least four different occasions by MPU staff before its completion, while the EC is insistent that such a requirement is impracticable owing to a shortage of staff and the size of the country. The EC Delegation which oversees the MPU was anxious to delink its activities from the specific goal of alleviation of the social effects of structural adjustment, whereas for the Bank, this specific objective ought to be its *raison d'être*.

The Bank is less insistent on the requirement of community participation and on 25 per cent contribution to project costs. Indeed, it would much prefer to contract out some of the more technical projects and also would wish to encourage income-generating projects which could be expected to enhance the absorptive capacity of the economy. The EC, for its part, prefers to work with local communities and to utilize existing administrative structures, by which it hopes to enhance capacity-building through training and experiential learning.[88] At the level of project selection, the EC tends to concentrate on building constructions while the Bank emphasizes what it terms "social assistance" projects, such as training for community health and for nutritional education, as well as income-generating schemes, all of which the Community excludes from its list of priorities.

In-depth interviews with both the EC–MPU Coordinator and the World Bank official and Deputy Coordinator of the MPU reveal quite a wide gap in conceptual as well as operational approaches between the two institutions. The Bank official complained that she was being virtually ignored by the EC Delegation with whom she was expected to hold regular consultations. EC–MPU officials, on the other hand, thought that their own approach was less politically risky whilst the Bank's seemed to encourage the creation of additional bureaucracy and a disregard of local community mobilization while harbouring implicit conditionalities in its financing agreement.

These conflicts reflect fundamental differences in philosophy as well as inter-institutional bureaucratic struggles. The EC emphasis is on community self-help and on "visible" projects which might enhance the EC's influence and the prestige of the Lomé aid regime. To this extent it has largely succeeded, in view of the popularity of its projects in the local communities, despite the acknowledged shoddiness of most of the projects and the relatively modest financial commitment involved. The Bank, on the other hand, appears to be less politically sophisticated. Its approach is clearly linked to its wider policy-based lending and support for market solutions and structural adjustment. This leads the Bank to an orientation which may be characterized in terms of "technocratic paternalism", given its insistence on working outside existing administrative structures, while putting less emphasis on community participation. However, the positive side of the Bank's approach is its stress on strengthening policy analysis skills and building a strong data and analytical base for public management in Zambia. From the viewpoint of "social learning", therefore, the Bank's orientation compares more favourably than the Community's.

EXPORT PROMOTION AND ECONOMIC DIVERSIFICATION

The external trade dimension is an essential aspect of all structural adjustment strategies. Trade liberalization and export promotion are seen as vital aspects of the drive towards economic diversification and "outward-oriented" development. The success of the Newly Industrializing Nations (NICs) of South-East Asia, such as South Korea, Hong Kong, Taiwan and Singapore, is often cited as proof of the superiority of the outward- as opposed to the inward-oriented strategy, which most other LDCs and especially those of sub-Saharan Africa, had followed hitherto.[89] The Fourth National Development Plan sought to give a new policy direction for the external trade sector. Amongst its stated objectives were to encourage non-traditional exports, boost exports with particularly high local value-added, encourage private-sector participation in export promotion activities, and improve trade links within the PTA and SADDC regions while diversifying commercial relations with the rest of the world.[90] The basic strategy was to be centred on:

- strengthening the Export Board of Zambia (EBZ) with regard to export promotion, marketing development and research;
- improving upon the incentives provided under the Investment Act No. 5 of 1986;
- rationalizing trading services and eliminating non-transparent practices;
- strengthening the role of trade missions in Zambia's embassies abroad.

In the last chapter we saw that EC support for Zambia's external trade focused mainly on the Sysmin commodity stabilization scheme, whose aim is not necessarily economic diversification, but to ensure continuation of traditional mineral exports to the Community. As part of Lomé II aid, the EC provided technical assistance to the EBZ. An EDF-funded adviser was seconded to the Board between 1987 and 1990. EC assistance did not seem to have gone without major problems. The EC helped to establish an Export–Import (EXIM) bank to operate a revolving fund for exporters, which soon became saddled with massive corruption, and had to be eventually suspended.[91]

Under the Lomé IV Indicative Programme, the EC has made export promotion a major aspect of its development intervention in Zambia, and obviously as a prop to its adjustment strategy under the new Convention. A Lomé IV Export Promotion Programme (LEPP) was launched in November 1990. It is an ECU10 million project which will provide technical assistance as well as an export financing facility for Zambian exporters. Its primary objective is to promote non-copper exports and to improve the country's export supply capability. Its immediate target is to ensure at least US$200 million of non-traditional exports by 1993 while doubling that figure by 1995.[92] Of the 1993 projection of US$1.46 billion of total export earnings, an overwhelming US$1.044 billion is still expected to come from metallic (predominantly copper) exports alone.[93]

The poor performance of the export sector has been attributed to lack of adequate incentives, constraints in the business environment, unreliable sourcing of raw materials, utilization of outdated technologies, expensive transport costs and ineffective management and marketing. However, the diagnosis seems to have omitted the important factor of entrepreneurial culture, which seems lacking in Zambia. In my observations and discussions with Zambians of all walks of life, I almost shared the view expressed by René Dumont, that Zambia is a "nation without ideals". The culture of entrepreneurial creativity and hard work seems lacking, at least when compared to the "trading cultures" of the Igbo and the Hausa of Nigeria, for example.[94]

The LEP aims to boost non-traditional exports which currently operate on a narrow productive base, with only ninety-two companies known to have exported more than US$10,000 worth of goods. Few companies produce predominantly for exports, while most export only between 15 and 20 per cent of their total output.[95]

From Table 9.9 we can see that such non-traditional exports have been growing steadily between 1987 and 1989, with the most important sectors being manufacturing and processing, gemstones, transport and agriculture-

Table 9.9 Zambia: non-traditional exports, 1987–89 (in US$ millions)

Sector	*1987*	*1988*	*1989*
Agriculture based	10.4	20.1	14.3
Manufacturing/processing	49.5	49.4	51.2
Non-metallic minerals	1.9	3.1	1.9
Tourism and hotels	2.9	3.6	6.6
Transport	3.7	10.1	23.7
Services and electricity	1.0	2.4	1.7
Other (including gemstones)	9.0	7.5	20.4
TOTAL	78.4	96.2	119.8

Source: David Jones & Associates, 1991

Table 9.10 Zambia: value of non-traditional exports by sector, 1987–89 (in US$ million)

Sector	*1987*	*1988*	*1989*
Animal products	2.690	2.828	2.613
Building materials	3.154	3.125	2.583
Chemicals	3.730	4.023	3.505
Flowers	0.330	0.502	0.500
Fruits & vegetables	2.127	3.333	1.950*(p)*
Garments	2.426	2.174	3.460*(p)*
Non-copper minerals	1.916	3.088	1.742
Petroleum products	9.282	7.400	5.079
Agricultural commodities	5.240	13.435	10.266
Processed foods	5.522	2.741	2.552
Rough gemstones	7.863	5.232	0.808*(p)*
Textiles, yarn & fabrics	5.945	4.962	8.057
Wood & wood products	0.324	0.392	0.186
Other	0.307	0.392	0.369
TOTAL	50.856	53.627	43.670*(p)*

Note: *(p)* = provisional figure
Source: Export Board of Zambia, 1989

based products. Table 9.10 provides an even more detailed breakdown of non-traditional exports between 1987 and 1989.

Four sectors have been selected for LEP funding: coffee, horticulture and flowers, tobacco, and cotton textiles. One of the major criteria for selecting these four sectors relates to production lead-times for the commodities in question. However, other important sectors such as long-term market risks have not been taken into account. Interestingly, the most important non-copper export commodity, engineering and processed manufactures, has been omitted from the list of priorities. It seems evident therefore, that the LEP is biased in favour of agriculture-based exports and does not wish to encourage development of industrial manufacturing. It will be premature to speculate on the long-term impact of the LEP, but it is safe to conclude that the uncertainties of global markets will continue to be a major constraint while bias towards agriculture exports may not be in the long-term interest of inter-sectoral linkages for balanced growth in the economy. Given also the potentially enormous importance of gemstones, of which illegal smuggling is estimated at more than US$200 million annually, it is a major gap in the EC export promotion policy that it does not assist Zambia to devise a means to curtail such massive losses in potential revenue. Within Zambia itself, EC involvement in export promotion has probably sensitized local business communities to a greater awareness of the potential opportunities offered by the Lomé trade regime, leading to the formation of a kind of EC–Zambia Chamber of Commerce. In January 1990, the then Zambian Ambassador in Brussels, Kapembe

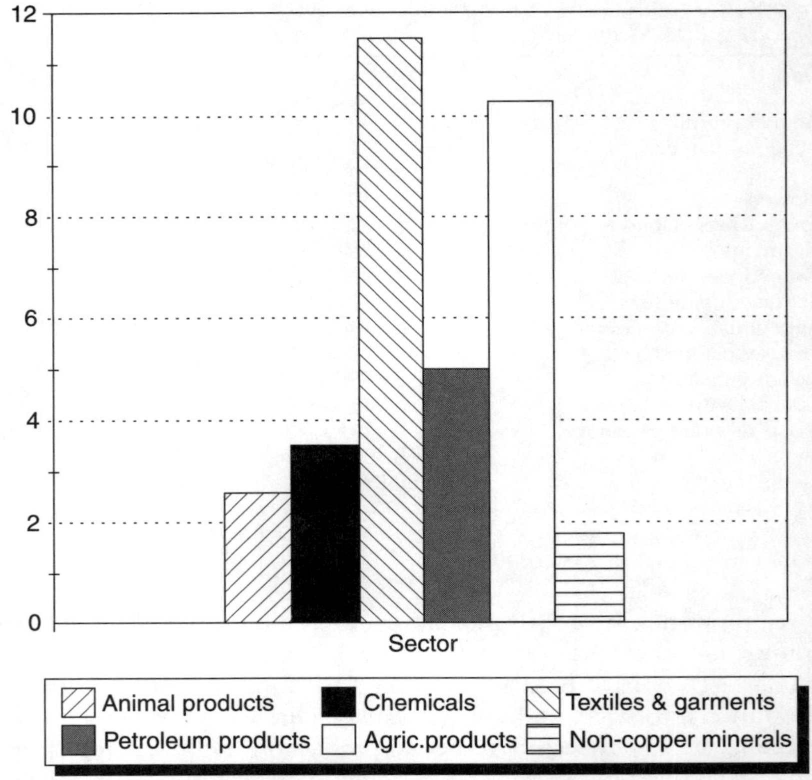

Figure 9.5 Zambia: main non-traditional exports, 1987–89 (in US$ million)
Source: David Jones & Associates, Surrey, 1989

Nsingo, had taken the initiative in organizing a seminar to familiarize the country's businessmen about export opportunities in the EC within the context of Lomé IV.

This initiative inspired the launching of an association of private businessmen and women who are interested in exporting to the Community. The Zambia Business, Industry and Trade Link With the European Economic Community and the African, Caribbean and Pacific Countries (known as the "Zambit-Lomé Group"), was founded to promote trade and investment between Zambia and the Community as well as with other ACP states.[96] The association has about forty registered members and operates an information centre on EC–Lomé affairs and business opportunities. Its Chairman is a highly well-informed and prominent businessman.[97]

The Zambit-Lomé Group has gradually emerged as a trade interest group which seeks to promote its own export interests as well as those of joint partnerships with European investors.[98] It seems to have been relatively successful in influencing the direction of government policy on non-traditional exports such as gemstones (especially aquamarines and emeralds), in which illegal exports have been estimated to be over US$200 million per annum.[99] Although they got the EIB to finance an ECU1.5 million cold storage facility at Lusaka International Airport for the Zambia Export Growers Association, they have been less successful in persuading the EIB to provide smaller loans directly to their members. The Association has established formal links with the government as well as with EC Ambassadors and trade representatives in Lusaka. It is in many ways an important development in EC–Zambia relations, given that Lomé had hitherto been largely the preserve of government and EC officials, with little or no participation by the private sector.[100]

CONCLUSION

The EC response to Zambia's economic reform and its attendant problems manifests a contradictory tendency. The moderate stance of the Commission is in contrast with the "hard-line" attitude taken by dominant EC member states, notably, France, the United Kingdom and Germany. EC aid programmes in support of adjustment are heavily oriented towards general and sectoral import programmes. The accompanying countervalue funds have enhanced EC influence within Zambia's domestic decision-making system, quite apart from their potentially negative impact on the money supply.

Through its micro-projects strategy and its Social Action Programme, the EC clearly accords much importance to the "human dimensions" of adjustment. We have noted the differences which have emerged between the EC and the Bank in the joint Micro-Projects Programme. Such differences reflect inter-institutional competition and bureaucratic conflict between two major international actors rather than fundamental differences in policy or philosophy of development. The EC shows itself to be more sensitive to the social and political constraints faced by Zambia's economic managers. The MPP, with its emphasis on local community participation, could be said to represent an interesting experiment in "people-centred" development. However, the short-term horizon of this strategy and the shoddiness of many of its projects offers no long-term prospects for structural change. The political logic underlying EC intervention seems to aim at forestalling popular revolt while expanding the Community's political asset position in Zambia. Such diplomatic capital was advantageous in the EC's mediating role following the collapse in relations between Lusaka and the Washington institutions. The matrix of triangular diplomacy was clearly operative here, as we have seen, although the lines separating EC and IMF-Bank approaches to adjustment were more apparent than real.

10

EUROPE AND AFRICA IN A CHANGING WORLD

> Nations, like individuals, have . . . a vocation or none at all. Taking possession of the riches of the world by violence, or enslaving other nations is not a vocation; but liberating them, giving them to themselves, enabling them to fulfil the vocation which is theirs, is. Here . . . we meet the blessed paradox that no one can realise himself except by cooperating in the realisation of everyone else.[1]

Reflecting on Africa's contemporary predicament, Professor Dennis Austin recalled Samuel Johnson's tale about Prince Rasselas of the ancient African kingdom of Abyssinia, who, having grown tired of the "gardens of fragrance" and the "fortress of security" in his native land, wandered through Egypt, "where every man was happy".[2] This study has shown that the African condition today is far from being a happy one. The object of this investigation was to analyse EC–African diplomacy in the context of adjustment, debt and macroeconomic reform. Our central question was the claim that the EC has a "unique" approach to adjustment which is different from the orthodox model of the Bretton Woods institutions. We set out to consider EC–African diplomacy from the viewpoint of power, influence and social exchange. We traced the historical origins of Lomé from the colonial era up to the Rome Treaty in 1957.

We saw how EC–African relations metamorphosed from the epoch of colonialism, when concepts of "Eurafrica" were fashioned as ideological tools of Empire, to the postwar era of decolonization, when "association" became the dominant idiom of Euro-African diplomacy. Although taken up at the insistence of France, "association" soon became a major pillar of Europe's international policy, as the nascent Common Market sought to maintain some influence in the emerging African nations. We argued that the colonial model of development under "association" was, to echo von Clausewitz, a continuation of Eurafrica by other means. In the 1970s, EC–African diplomacy entered a new, qualitative phase. The uncertainties following the collapse of the Bretton Woods system, Western anxieties about raw materials shortages following OPEC, and the Southern challenge to the international economic order, all contributed to Europe's willingness to negotiate a new multilateral agreement with the ACP countries. In terms of bargaining power, the South seemed to hold the stakes, even if temporarily. A "social exchange" relationship was evident in Europe's desire to maintain its traditional influence and secure access to ACP raw materials: in exchange for financial and trade political equality, the ultimate levers of power remained firmly within the European Community.

Towards the end of the 1970s, Euro-African relations entered yet another phase. This phase was characterized by a deepening in the asymmetrical relations between North and South. The Southern coalition was in virtual disarray; the world recession following the two oil shocks was taking its toll in terms of indebtedness and economic decline; and in Africa, desertification, famine and civil strife were becoming the dominant images of a ravaged continent. As the region became less relevant as a global trading partner to the EC, in face of new competitors from Asia, Latin America and Eastern Europe, whatever strategic bargaining power she and her Caribbean and Pacific partners once held was becoming increasingly tenuous. Consequently, the Lomé II negotiations reflected a weakening in the bargaining position of the ACP Group. With little by way of bargaining chips, they faced a more confident Europe which could afford to retreat from "interdependence". The beginning of the 1980s marked a turning point in EC development policy. The new politics of adjustment was increasingly becoming the focal point of development thinking. Beginning with the Ferrero Resolution by the European Parliament, the Pisani Memorandum and the "food dialogue" strategy, the EC was shifting decisively towards "policy dialogue". Lomé IV marks the formal introduction of adjustment and macroeconomic conditionality in EC–African aid diplomacy. EC official policy claims to promote an adjustment framework which is sensitive to political constraints, and which takes account of the "human factor" in the development process.

From the available evidence, the EC's claim to have a different or unique approach to structural adjustment cannot be convincingly sustained. Much as the Commission seeks to evolve its own approach to adjustment, it clearly has neither the political resources nor the technical capability to design viable alternative strategies. The dominant member states of the Community are also unlikely to support an EC strategy which conflicts with that of the IFIs, where they have vital interests as major share-holders.[3] On the question of adjustment, therefore, the EC seems relegated to being a player of the second rank. To assert that the EC is a second-order player in the adjustment game is not to say that there are no differentiating elements in the Brussels approach. The EC has been demonstrably more sensitive to the reality of political constraints, and to the human and equity aspects of the adjustment process.

In the particular case of Zambia, as we saw, the Community's role was mainly in the areas of import support, micro-projects and the "social dimensions" of adjustment. The EC has also sought to play a moderating role in the politics of adjustment, as it did during the 1987 rift with the IFIs, when the Commission effectively used its diplomatic influence within the triangular matrix. Although EC initiatives in Zambia clearly confirm its orientation with regard to the "social dimensions" of adjustment, this does not necessarily prove that there is a "unique" Community model of adjustment. As we have seen, EC development interventions have become progressively linked to fulfilment of IMF conditionalities or to encouraging a rapprochement whenever there is a breakdown in relations with the IFIs.

It is safe, therefore, to conclude that the Community does not have a structural adjustment strategy as such. Even its Structural Adjustment Facility is no more than a continuation of commodity import support, which we have pointed out, probably helps EC exporters as much as it does Zambia. What the Community seems to have as a consistent policy is a series of responses – often not very coherent – whose sole motivation appears to be to keep Zambia firmly within the sway of the IFIs and to forestall possibilities of social upheaval within the country. The legal and contractual nature of Lomé has to some extent served to limit EC unilateral actions in response to fulfilment of IMF/World Bank conditionalities, especially under Lomé III. However, most Lomé IV actions and subsequent import programmes have had explicit conditionality clauses, which can be interpreted as increased leverage for the Commission *vis-à-vis* ACP recipients and a subtle but real change in the character of the Lomé aid regime.

The EC Micro-Projects Programme has a number of innovative aspects which cannot be denied: its support for local community efforts, in spite of the practical limitations, could be seen as the beginning of a novel approach to mobilizational and democratic rural participation for development. The EC approach has obvious advantages over that of the Bank. A major limitation of the micro-projects strategy, however, relates to the politics of "capture", the nature of Zambia's rural social structure, and the existence of an over-centralized, politico-administrative system.

The new politics of adjustment has clearly enhanced the influence of the EC as an actor in the international aid regime. What are the bases of EC influence and what power resources does it employ in the exercise of such influence?

The EC enjoys, first and foremost, at least in relation to sub-Saharan Africa, a position of structural dominance in the international political economy. Second, it has the power to set the agenda in terms of the choice of issues which can be considered a legitimate subject for multilateral negotiations. The EC, for example, has succeeded in blocking any major debates on the debt question within Lomé. Third, its control of the decision-making levers of power within the institutional architecture of

Lomé is an additional source of influence. The ACP has never succeeded in its bid to have even observer status within the EDF Committee, for example. The problems of the ACP Secretariat, and its increasing dependence on EDF financial support, is a major constraint on its institutional capacity and independence of judgement. Most importantly, the EC has the influence of the "purse holder". It is able to circumvent the contractual strictures of Lomé by simply delaying financing decisions until such a time as the aid recipient is implementing policies which the Commission prefers. A novel source of power is in the accumulation of countervalue funds which are generated by import programmes. Given that these are normally operated jointly with the EC and the latter has to approve all public expenditures that involve the use of such funds, the EC has potentially considerable influence in ACP countries' budgets. Counterpart funds, most of which derive from balance of payments financing and food aid, will no longer be a one-off operation but will constitute part of the regular EC aid intervention.

THE PROSPECTS OF LOMÉ IN A CHANGING WORLD

In concluding this study, it is important to reflect on the long-term prospects of Lomé as a model of North–South cooperation. There is an obvious gap between "rhetoric and reality" in the EC's role as an international actor. This is what Christopher Hill has termed the Community's "capability-expectations gap".[4] The prominence of the EC as a global actor is not often commensurate with its effectiveness in development project performance or aid programming. While the Lomé trade provisions are generous, the actual record of EC–ACP trade remains rather unsatisfactory.[5] Stabex and Sysmin as commodity stabilization schemes have been quite popular with beneficiaries, but their effectiveness is constrained by insufficient funds. There is also the potential long-term effects of the Single Market which became effective in January 1993. As Loukas Tsoukalis has observed, intra-European trade liberalization is not incompatible with protectionism against the rest of the world.[6] While the Community denies that it is building a "European Fortress", the potential negative effects of "1992" on the African subregion have been well documented.[7] Table 10.1 shows the generalized effects on external developing economies, both negative and positive, while Table 10.2 illustrates the potential negative effects for specific developing regions.[8] For Africa in particular, it has been estimated that "Europe 1992" is likely to result in high levels of trade diversion in the long term, although this may be offset by increased demand for exports such as cocoa, tea, coffee, processed wood, horticultural products, and by a projected increase in the volume of aid. A positive political effect could be said to be the greater urgency being given by African leaders to their own regional economic integration efforts.[9]

Table 10.1 Potential external effects of Europe 1992 on developing countries

Positive	*Negative*
Direct effects:	
Trade creation (from faster EC growth)	Trade diversion (lower costs of EC production)
Investment creation (from faster EC growth)	Investment diversion (increased attractions of EC)
Indirect effects:	
Less protectionism (no national NTBs)	More protectionism (more severe EC NTBs)
More liberal trade policy (majority voting)	Less liberal trade policy (to alleviate social costs)
More cost-effective aid (EC-wide procurement tying)	Lower total aid budget (less commercial incentive) (increased social fund demand)
Easier migration (removal of national barriers)	More restrictive migration (reinforcement of EC barriers)

Source: Christopher Stevens, *Europe 1992 and the Developing Countries*, 1990, p. 13

Table 10.2 Potential dangers of 1992 for different LDCs

Country group	*Potential dangers*	*EC aid levels*
NICs, MICs (e.g. E. Asia, ASEAN)	Increased protectionism	Low
Mediterranean (e.g. Algeria, Morocco, Tunisia)	Trade diversion Investment diversion Restricted migration	Medium
Latin America	Investment diversion Increased protectionism	Low
Africa, Caribbean, Pacific	Trade Diversion	High

Source: Christopher Stevens, *Europe 1992 and the Developing Countries,* 1990, p. 14

Current global trends are also tending to have a negative effect on Lomé and EC interest in Africa in general. With the ending of the Cold War, international marginalization of Africa has become the new threat to the economic security of the region.[10] According to *Newsweek*, the United States has reduced its bilateral aid to the region by half since 1985, to about US$2 billion in 1990.[11] Poles, Hungarians and other Eastern Europeans are expected to receive ten times as much aid per capita from Europe as compared to Africa. According to Chester Crocker, a former US Under-Secretary of State, "Africans could end up paying for the expanding frontiers of freedom everywhere else".[12]

During the EC–ACP joint ministerial meeting in Suva, Fiji, in April 1990

Table 10.3 African and total overseas manufacturing investment by British companies: net earnings and net investment, 1987–92 (in UK£ million)

Year	*Net earnings* *Africa*	*World*	%	*Net investment* *Africa*	*World*	%
1978	55	1,160	4.7	67	1,520	4.5
1979	58	1,466	3.9	62	1,397	4.5
1980	91	1,479	6.1	82	1,427	5.7
1981	81	1,673	4.8	68	2,647	2.5
1982	91	1,762	5.1	92	1,579	5.8
1983	117	2,145	5.4	52	2,120	2.4
1984	1,116	2,425	4.7	79	2,100	3.2
1985	157	3,060	5.0	29	2,984	1.0
1986	1,115	3,326	3.4	27	7,714	0.5
1987	120	4,859	2.4	75	5,663	1.0
1988	123	6,158	2.0	70	7,714	0.6
1989	140	7,477	1.9	112	11,892	0.9
1990	131	7,130	1.8	116	4,303	2.7
1991	134	6,462	2.1	89	5,106	1.7
1992	135	6,378	2.1	108	4,958	2.2

Source: Department of Trade and Industry, Business Monitor M4 Overseas Transactions, 1978–92

only one EC minister, Holland's Development Minister, Piet Dankert, was reportedly in attendance. The EC was said to have brought with it little or no prepared documents for discussion. It not only refused to discuss the debt question, it continued to press for Senegal, Gabon and Liberia to pay back their outstanding Stabex loans. Commissioner Marin declared to the assembly that the ACP countries would have to rise to the challenge of international competitiveness, since their problems are "beyond the objectives and instruments of the Convention".[13] During the April 1990 summit of *La Francophonie*, President Mitterrand warned delegates that regimes that failed to reform their political systems should not expect automatic protection from Paris, and that "liberty could not be separated from development".[14]

Perhaps the case of British investment in Commonwealth Africa provides a good indication of the current trends in disinvestment by the companies of OECD countries. A recent economic study reveals that more than half of British manufacturing companies have disinvested from sub-Saharan Africa within the last five years.[15] Table 10.3 shows trends in British manufacturing investment and investment earnings in Africa and the rest of the world. In 1978 British investments in Africa were 4.5 per cent of its world total. In 1991, however, it had fallen to as low as 1.7 per cent. Prominent among the disinvesting companies have been such corporate giants as Leyland Trucks, Unilever, Courtaulds and UAC. Among the factors accounting for this trend are low profitability, foreign exchange constraints and the negative effect of devaluation in terms of the rising costs of raw material inputs.

There is also evidence that French and other European companies have been rapidly disinvesting from Africa.[16] Given the crucial French factor in Lomé, this would mean an even further erosion of the political foundations of the Euro-African partnership.[17] Africa's global marginality is already evident in the area of portfolio equity flows to LDCs, which between 1989 and 1992 recorded nought for the entire SSA region, as compared to US$13 billion for Latin America and the Caribbean, and US$467 million for South Asia (see Table 10.4).[18]

Are we then witnessing what amounts to the gradual demise of Lomé? Some of the African countries have read the writing on the wall and are currently rethinking their links with the Community. Nigeria, for example, has begun internal discussions on a possible withdrawal from Lomé after the year 2000. She hopes that she could then be in a position to renegotiate her old bilateral agreement with the Community. A report from the Nigerian Foreign Office observes that "the present state of affairs is far from being satisfactory, and if nothing is done urgently, the situation could worsen, affecting Lomé terminally".[19]

This study has brought out some of the inherent limitations of the Lomé model of North–South cooperation. It is evident that Europe will not commit itself to African development indefinitely if African leaders come to the negotiating table with nothing to offer but their traditional mendicancy. The world itself has changed, with an almost Copernican revolution in the structure of world politics and economics. The end of the Cold War may not have brought an end to the notion of the "Third World" as a

Table 10.4 Gross portfolio equity flows to developing countries by region (US$ million)

Region	*1989*	*1990*	*1991*	*1992(E)*	*1989–92*
Sub-Saharan Africa	0.0	0.0	0.0	0.0	0.0
East Asia & the Pacific	2,623.1	2,267.8	1,049.3	2,678.5	8,618.7
South Asia	168.0	105.0	22.6	171.1	466.7
Europe & Central Asia	184.4	266.0	0.0	138.3	588.7
Latin America & the Caribbean	434.0	1,099.1	6,227.7	5,195.3	12,956.1
North Africa & the Middle East	0.0	0.0	0.0	0.0	0.0
Global*	76.4	35.7	252.6	0.0	364.7
All LDCs	3,485.9	3,773.6	7,552.2	8,183.1	22,994.8

Notes:
(E) = Estimated
* Global country funds that invest across regions
Source: World Bank, *World Bank World Debt Tables, 1992–93*, Washington DC, December 1992

political category, but it has certainly eroded the political motivations for aid-giving. A proposition which future research could examine is the argument that the retreat from interdependence increases when one or the other party suffers a depletion in those economic or political assets which it brings to the exchange relationship.[20]

AFRICA FACING THE TWENTY-FIRST CENTURY

African countries have no choice but to rise up to the challenge of competitiveness in a changed international environment.[21] However, as Jacques Delors, outgoing President of the European Commission, has observed, speaking for Europe, "Society's destiny does not depend exclusively on the logic of the market and its invisible hand."[22] Africa's destiny may similarly be said to be far too important to be left in the hands of bankers and international technocrats. The neo-liberal assumption about a perfect market with competitive actors all having equal influence and equal access to information hardly conforms to the facts of the real world. It was the eminent economic historian, Karl Polanyi, who observed that the market mechanism does not belong to the natural order of things; rather, it is a human construct. And like all human artefacts, it is not devoid of entrenched interests and imperfections.[23] Neo-liberalism often ignores the structural constraints and bottlenecks which limit the potential benefits which developing countries could derive from international trade.[24] The theoretical elegance of the neo-classical economics paradigm should not blind us to its practical shortcomings.[25] Successful adaptation requires not only macroeconomic reform; it has to be complemented by responsible leadership, democratic participation, intellectual guidance, sound investment in human and natural resources, and the transformation of national mindsets. But the process of change will inevitably come to grief if it is perceived as being *imposed from outside*, with little regard to the demands of Lockean legitimacy or popular consent.[26] From a neo-realist perspective, it could be argued that the long-term interests of adjusting countries and those of Western creditors will not necessarily be compatible, even if we did not subscribe to the zero-sum view of North–South interactions.[27] Power and interests are still vital factors even in an allegedly emerging post-Westphalian global society.[28]

In all matters of politics, the great Spinoza taught, the most important task is not to weep or to laugh, but to understand. Facing the end of our century of upheavals, we see what was proclaimed as a "New World Order" being overtaken by the incubi of hatred, fanaticism and lawless greed. Where is Africa's place under the *nouveau désordre* of which Alain Minc has written with such elegant lucidity?[29] To quote John Maynard Keynes, "Who can say how much is endurable, or in what direction men will seek at last to escape from their misfortunes?"[30]

Social science provides little or no scope for idle prophecy. Those who entertain the gloomiest prospects for Africa should not forget the role of Providence in history.[31] As the Roman statesman, the Elder Pliny famously remarked, Africa does often turn up with surprises. The extraordinary political rebirth of South Africa following the release of Nelson Mandela in February 1990, and the prospects of peace in the region may be regarded as a positive augury for the rest of the continent. In an age bereft of the historical imagination, it is easily forgotten that no group of people in the entire history of humanity has endured such unspeakable crimes as the African peoples have done for centuries.[32] But Africans cannot continue to blame Europe and external powers for all their misfortunes. They have to make their own choices and assume responsibility for their own destiny. The post-independence paradigm of state and civil society has largely failed to deliver its promise. Unlike in Asia, where the state has been an agent of stability and progress, the state in Africa is the classic Leviathan, a rapacious beast which saps the creative energy of its peoples.[33]

Africa's cruel fate threatens to banish her from the civility of international society.[34] The challenge of renewal will require no less than a new generation of leaders who are imbued with a new public philosophy founded on the norms of selfless service, transparency, democratic accountability and the rule of law.[35] Of crucial importance is also the need for the strengthening of technical capacity. This calls for the reform of civil service systems and the building of a *cadre administratif* consisting of highly skilled and competent professionals who have a sense of national mission and destiny.[36] Alternative development strategies will have to be designed, free of the strictures of dogma and the tyranny of received economic models, and taking full account of the lessons of past development experience and the realities of a dynamic and competitive global economy. The new discourse on "governance" and democracy opens up new possibilities of dialogue for constructive political change. Africans should welcome this reversal in Western policy, because only yesterday the major powers had propped up murderous tyrannies under the pretext of defending Cold War allies. But it will be absurd to imagine that democracy is a finished product which can be imported from outside. Ever since Aristotle, history has shown that free and stable republics have evolved according to the inner logic of historical development of the societies in question. Africa's development trajectory will have to be rooted in its own historical experience and cultural milieu, as William Abraham, the Ghanaian scholar and quondam Fellow of All Souls, has warned.[37]

In the area of foreign policy, African states will need to reassess their place in the post-Cold War order and their relations with Europe in particular.[38] Given the disappointing results of Lomé, and the fortress-like architecture of the New Europe, with its decidedly insular temper, African countries should diversify their external relations by establishing alternative trade and diplomatic linkages with an emergent Asia.[39] The search for effective policy responses to the new regional mercantilism will also be a major task for economic and political planning.[40] Africans may never escape from the chains of serfdom until they revisit the failed project of regional and continental integration. Lessons can be learned from postwar Europe, where statesmen such as Jean Monnet, Konrad Adenauer and Charles de Gaulle understood that the dream of *la Grande Europe* could be realized only through the functionalist road. The mistake of leaders such as Nkrumah and Pan-Africanists in general was to have emphasized the political objectives of integration at the expense of economic and functionalist solutions.[41] From the lessons of the Franc Zone in French-speaking Africa, the formation of regional currencies is clearly a viable option.[42] Such currencies could form the basis of a single African currency which may eventually attain the status of international convertibility.[43] This will ensure monetary stability while shielding African countries from easy economic manipulation and political pressure from external actors.[44] Perhaps the idea of an African Payment Union, which was considered and abandoned a few years ago (under pressure from the GATT and the OECD countries) should be re-considered. Such a union would serve the practical needs of intra-African trade without the burden of having to use dollars, francs, marks, pounds or even a future European monetary unit. This could also from the basis for future monetary integration in the region.

From a global perspective, it is evident that the emerging tripolar system of competitive regional economic power blocs is unlikely to ensure a just international equilibrium.[45] As Dame Margery Perham once observed (in a different context) a tripod is, by definition, an unstable structure. The developed world will need to rethink its current retreat from interdependence.[46] A tacit policy of international social Darwinism may hold short-term gains, but it will amount to a denial of the *Civitas Humana,* and certainly cannot be the foundation of a lasting peace.[47] Much will depend on the sense of enlightened self-interest on the part of the leaders of the New Europe, whether they will seek to incarnate their ideals of civilized existence in a renewed international amity or will prefer to pursue the old game of power politics.[48] Ultimately, Africans will have to assume responsibility for their own future, whether or not the Euro-African model of cooperation endures into the next century, and whether or not the IMF and the World Bank remain in business. The observations once made by Nobel laureate Sir Arthur Lewis merit being quoted at length:

> It is true that the prosperity of underdeveloped countries has in the past depended on what they could sell to the industrial countries, but there is no reason why this should continue. The underdeveloped countries have all the resources needed for their own development.

> Taken together they have a surplus of fuel, fibres, iron ore, copper, bauxite, and practically every other raw material. In agriculture they are perfectly capable of feeding themselves. . . . [They] are short of skills, but these can be learnt, so they could do all their own manufacturing. Apart from skills, the development of Asia, Africa and Latin America could continue even if all the rest of the world were to sink under the sea.[49]

Sir Arthur was, of course, not suggesting that the rest of the world should be sunk under the sea. Rather, he was underlining the requisites for economic development which he saw as already available in the LDCs. Dependence on external aid is clearly not a viable option for long-term economic emancipation. While there may be a place for charity in the politics of nations, the statesman who is guided by what the Florentines termed *virtù* will not place his hope in moral abstractions or in the axiomatic goodwill of foreign powers.

NOTES

1 INTRODUCTION

1 Robert Reich, *The Work of Nations: Preparing Ourselves for 21st Century Capitalism*, London: Simon & Schuster, 1991, p. 306. On the phenomenon of polarization in international economic relations, see Marie Lavigne, *International Political Economy and Socialism*, trans. by David Lambert. Cambridge: Cambridge University Press, 1991, pp. 53–86.

2 Maurice Duverger, *Modern Democracies: Economic Power Versus Political Participation*, Hinsdale, Ill.: Dryden Press, 1974, p. 2.

3 Cf. Claude Ake, "The Unique Case of African Democracy", *International Affairs*, 69 (2), 1993, pp. 239–244.

4 This optimism was shared by modernization theorists in the social sciences, who believed that rapid economic development could be achieved through the adoption of Western values and the imitation of Western political institutions. Cf. Walt W. Rostow, *The Stages of Economic Growth: a Non-Communist Manifesto*, Cambridge: Cambridge University Press, 1971; Samuel P. Huntington, *Political Order in Changing Societies*, New Haven: Yale University Press, 1968. For an analysis of the impact of modernization on international relations, see Edward L. Morse, *Modernisation and the Transformation of International Relations*, New York: The Free Press, 1976.

5 The French agronomist René Dumont was quite prescient in his prediction in the 1960s that the "false start" that characterized African development strategies was bound to lead to famine and socioeconomic disaster. See his *False Start in Africa*, London: Deutsch, 1966. Some scholars have underlined the nature of the African state and the constraints that limit its developmental capability. Cf. Jean-François Médard, "L'État sous-développé en Afrique Noire: clientèlisme politique ou néo-patrimonialisme?", Bordeaux: *Centre d'Étude d'Afrique Noire*, 1982 (mimeo); Richard Sandbrook, "The State and Economic Stagnation in Tropical Africa", *World Development*, 14 (3), March 1986, and his (with J. Parker), *The Politics of Africa's Economic Stagnation*, Cambridge: Cambridge University Press, 1987; Zaki Ergas, "In Search of Development in Africa", in Zaki Ergas (ed.), *The African State in Transition*, London: Macmillan 1987, pp. 295–329; and Nelson Kasfir, "Relating State to Class in Africa", in Nelson Kasfir (ed.), *State and Class in Africa*, London: Frank Cass, 1984, pp. 1–20; Piotr Dutkiewicz and Gavin Williams, "All the King's Horses and All the King's Men Couldn't Put Humpty-Dumpty Together Again", *IDS Bulletin*, 17 (1), 1986, pp. 39–43; E. A. Brett, "State Power and Economic Inefficiency: Explaining Political Failure in Africa", *IDS Bulletin*, 17 (1), 1986, pp. 22–29; Björn Beckman, "The Post-colonial State:

Crisis and Reconstruction", *IDS Bulletin*, 19 (4), 1988, pp. 26–34. For a concise summary of this debate, see Martin Doornbos, "The African State in Academic Debate: Retrospect and Prospect", *The Journal of Modern African Studies*, 28 (2), 1990, pp. 179–198.

6 The "North–South dialogue", short-lived as it was, opened up an important debate on the role of moral norms in international relations. The work of the philosopher John Rawls seemed to have anticipated the debate. See his *A Theory of Justice*, Cambridge, Mass.: Harvard University Press, 1971. Cf. Robert Amdur, "Rawls' Theory of Justice: Domestic and International Perspectives", *World Politics*, 29 (3), April 1977, pp. 438–461; Terry Nardin, "Distributive Justice and the Criticism of International Law", *Political Studies*, 29 (2), September 1981, pp. 232–244; Robert W. Tucker, *The Inequality of Nations*, London: Robertson, 1977. On the relationship between ethics and economic development, see Amartya Sen, *On Ethics and Economics*, Oxford: Blackwell, 1987.

7 Carol C. Twitchett, *Europe and Africa: From Association to Partnership*, Farnborough: Teakfield/Saxon House, 1978, p. vi.

8 As recently as 1991 one American scholar was describing it as a model which the United States could emulate in Latin America, while encouraging Japan to do the same for the Asia-Pacific region. See Robert A. Isaak, *International Political Economy: Managing World Economic Change*, Englewood Cliffs, NJ: Prentice-Hall International, 1991, p. 218.

9 S.K.B. Asante, "Africa and Europe: Collective Dependence or Interdependence?" in Amadu Sesay (ed.), *Africa and Europe: From Partition to Interdependence or Dependence?*, London: Croom Helm, 1986.

10 Cf. Samir Amin, *Maldevelopment: Anatomy of a Global Failure*, London: Zed Books, 1990, p. 121; Guy Martin, "Africa and the Ideology of Eurafrica: Neo-Colonialism or Pan-Africanism?", *The Journal of Modern African Studies*, 20 (2), 1982, pp. 221–38; Daniel W. Nabudere, *Essays on the Theories and Practice of Imperialism*, London: Onyx Press, 1979; Jyrki Käkonen and Ilka Vaura, "The Strategy of Neo-Colonialism and Associated African Member-States", in J. Käkonen (ed.) *The Mechanisms of Neo-Colonialism: Proceedings of a Nordic Seminar*, Mannta: Swedish Peace Research Association, 1974, pp. 39–68; J. Käkonen, *Effects of the EEC Association on Foreign Trade and Diplomatic Relations of the African States*, Turku: University Institute of Sociology and Political Science, 1976; Vidar Svensson, *Essays on the EEC–African Association*, Lund: Lund University Press, 1979.

11 Shridath Ramphal, "The ACP Years", *The Courier*, September–October 1985.

12 Pius Okigbo, "Africa and a Changing Europe: Hopes and Fears": text of a lecture delivered at the Royal Institute of International Affairs (Chatham House), London, 19 June, 1990, p. 7 (mimeo).

13 World Bank, *World Development Report 1993*, Oxford: Oxford University Press, 1993.

14 On the utility of the case-study method, see Alexander L. George, "Case Studies and Theory Development: The Method of Structured, Focused Comparison", in Paul G. Lauren (ed.), *Diplomacy: New Approaches in History, Theory and Policy*, London: Macmillan, 1979, pp. 43–65.

15 Stephen D. Krasner, *Structural Conflict: The Third World Against Global Liberalism*, Berkeley: University of California Press, 1985.

16 Cf. Björn Hettne, *Development Thinking and the Three Worlds*, Harlow, Essex: Longman, 1990; Hans W. Singer, *Lessons of the Post-War Development Experience: 1945–1988*, Sussex: IDS, April 1989.

17 The "global liberalization project" which was launched under the tutelage of

the IMF and the World Bank, may be interpreted in part as a means of dealing with the so-called "adjustment problem" under advanced capitalism and in part as a way of shifting the burdens or costs of indebtedness and economic recession to the dispossessed classes in the periphery. Cf. Joyce Kolko, *Restructuring the World Economy*, New York: Pantheon Books, 1988. See also Henk Overbeek and Kees van der Pijl, "Restructuring Capital and Restructuring Hegemony", in Henk Overbeek (ed.), *Restructuring Hegemony in the Global Economy: The Rise of Transnational Neo-Liberalism*, London and New York: Routledge, 1993, pp. 1–27.

18 On "political economy" approaches to adjustment, see Paul Mosley, Jane Harrigan and John Toye, *Aid and Power: The World Bank and Policy-Based Lending, vols 1* & 2, London and New York: Routledge, 1991; Barbara Stallings, "International Influence on Economic Policy: Debt, Stabilisation and Structural Reform", in Stephan Haggard and Robert R. Kaufman (eds), *The Politics of Economic Adjustment: International Constraints, Distributive Conflicts and the State*, Princeton, NJ: Princeton University Press, 1992, pp. 41–88; Joan M. Nelson, *Economic Crisis and Policy Choice: The Politics of Adjustment in the Third World*, Princeton, NJ: Princeton University Press, 1990; Robert Bates and Anne O. Krueger (eds), *Political and Economic Interactions in Economic Policy Reform*, Oxford: Basil Blackwell, 1993; Luigi Manzetti, *The IMF and Economic Stabilisation: The Argentinian Case*, New York: Praeger, 1991.

19 Cf. Loukas Tsoukalis, *The New European Economy: The Politics and Economics of Integration*, Oxford: Oxford University Press, 1991.

20 This is not intended to be a "regime analysis" of the Lomé process. Robert E. Wood has attempted to apply regime analysis to the study of foreign aid. See his *From Marshall Plan to Debt Crisis: Foreign Aid and Development Choices in the World Economy*, Berkeley: University of California Press, 1986.

21 In the area of aid and development cooperation, diplomacy may be seen as the instrument by which donors as well as recipients attempt to maximize outcomes within a cooperative framework. While there is a well-established tradition of academic writing on diplomacy, works on "aid diplomacy" are comparatively few. For a good summary of the main elements of traditional diplomacy, see K. J. Holsti, *International Politics: A Framework of Analysis*, 6th edn, Englewood Cliffs, NJ: Prentice-Hall, 1992, pp. 132–156; see also the recent magisterial work by Henry A. Kissinger, *Diplomacy*, New York: Simon & Schuster, 1994. For a "post-modernist" critique of traditional diplomacy, see James Der Derian, *On Diplomacy: A Genealogy of Western Estrangement*, Oxford: Blackwell, 1987.

22 On the "level of analysis problem", see Kenneth N. Waltz, *Theory of International Politics*, New York: Random House, 1979; and also his *Man, the State, and War: A Theoretical Analysis*, New York: Columbia University Press, 1959.

23 George Ball, quoted in Wood, op. cit., p. 5.

24 On the radical critique of aid, see Teresa Hayter, *Aid as Imperialism*, Harmondsworth: Penguin, 1971; Teresa Hayter and C. Watson, *Aid Rhetoric and Reality*, London and Sydney: Pluto, 1985; Susan George, *A Fate Worse than Debt*, Harmondsworth: Penguin, 1988. The neo-conservative critique of aid is perhaps best expressed in the work of Lord Bauer. Cf. Peter T. Bauer, *Equality, the Third World and Economic Delusion*, Cambridge, MA: Harvard University Press, 1983. And by the same author, *Dissent on Development*, London: Weidenfeld & Nicolson, 1972; and Bauer and B. S. Yamey, *The Economics of Underdeveloped Countries*, Cambridge: Cambridge University Press, 1957. A more liberal approach has been taken by writers such as: Paul Mosley, *Overseas Aid: Its*

Defence and Reform, Brighton: Harvester Wheatsheaf, 1987; J. R. Parkinson, *Poverty and Aid*, Oxford: Basil Blackwell, 1983; and James Morton, *The Aid Dilemma at the Heart of Africa*, London: Academic Press, 1994.

25 Quoted in Robert Cassen & Associates, *Does Aid Work? Report to an Intergovernmental Task Force*, Oxford: Clarendon Press, 1987, p. 2.

26 Ibid.

27 The World Bank, *Africa's Adjustment and Growth in the 1980s*, Washington, DC: The World Bank, 1989.

28 Tony Killick, "The Sound of Cautious Optimism: Developing Country Adjustments in the 1980s and 1990s", in Graham Bird (ed.), *The International Financial Regime*, Guildford: University of Surrey Press, 1990, pp. 197–224.

29 Ibid., pp. 206–207.

30 Paul Streeten, "A Survey of the Issues", in Simon Commander (ed.), *Structural Adjustment and Agriculture: Theory and Practice in Africa and Latin America*, London: Overseas Development Institute (ODI), 1989, pp. 3–18.

31 Robert Gilpin, *War and Change in World Politics*, Cambridge: Cambridge University Press, 1981, p. 13.

32 James N. Rosenau, *The Study of Political Adaptation: Essays in the Analysis of World Politics*, London: Frances Pinter, 1981.

33 Ibid., p. 9.

34 We have identified four theoretical approaches in the existing literature on EC–African diplomacy:

- **the neo-liberal approach**, e.g., Joanna Moss, *The Lomé Conventions and Their Implications for the United States*, Boulder, Col.: Westview Press, 1982; Enzo R. Grilli, *The European Community and the Developing Countries*, Cambridge: Cambridge University Press, 1993.
- **structuralist and dependency approaches**, such as those of Lynn Mytelka, "The Lomé Conventions and a New International Division of Labour", *Journal of Common Market Studies*, 18, 1979, pp. 135–158; Henrik S. Marcussen and Jens E. Torp, *Internationalisation of Capital: The Prospects for the Third World*, London: Zed Books, 1982; Ellen Frey-Wouters, *The European Community and the Third World: The Lomé Convention and Its Impact*, New York: Praeger Publishers, 1980.
- **clientelist analysis**, such as in the work of John Ravenhill, *Collective Clientelism: The Lomé Conventions and North–South Relations*, New York: Columbia University Press, 1985.
- **bargaining and decision-making analysis**, e.g., I. William Zartman, *The Politics of Trade Negotiations between Africa and the European Economic Community*, Princeton, NJ: Princeton University Press, 1971; Zartman (ed.) *Positive-Sum: Improving North–South Relations*, New Brunswick and Oxford: Transactions Books, 1987; Christopher Stevens, *Negotiating Lomé III: An Example of North–South Bargaining*, Sussex: IDS Discussion Paper no. 215, May 1986.

35 For a "post-modernist" critique of realism, see R. B. J. Walker, *Inside/Outside: International Relations as Political Theory*, Cambridge: Cambridge University Press, 1993.

36 Hans J. Morgenthau, *Politics among Nations: The Struggle for Power and Peace*, New York: McGraw-Hill, revised edn, 1993, p. 30.

37 A. F. Kenneth Organski, *World Politics*, 2nd edn, New York: Alfred Knopf, 1968, p. 104; Karl W. Deutsch, *The Analysis of International Relations*, Englewood Cliffs, NJ: Prentice-Hall, 1967, p. 22.

38 Steven Lukes, "Introduction", in Steven Lukes (ed.), *Power*, Oxford: Blackwell, 1986, pp. 4–5.

39 Steven Lukes, *Power: A Radical View*, London and Basingstoke: 1974, p. 27. Felix Oppenheim has rightly observed that such an understanding of power may be rather too restrictive, since not all power relations necessarily involve conflicts of interest. See his *Political Concepts: A Reconstruction*, Oxford: Basil Blackwell, 1981, pp. 50–51.
40 Lukes, ibid., p. 5.
41 Oppenheim, op. cit., p. 52.
42 Cf. Michael P. Sullivan, *Power in Contemporary International Politics*, Columbia, SC: University of South Carolina Press, 1990.
43 Joseph S. Nye, *Bound to Lead: The Changing Nature of American Power*, New York: Basic Books, 1990, pp. 25–26.
44 Some observers, notably Henry A. Kissinger, have argued that the traditional realist understanding of power is being replaced by the primacy of economic performance and national competitiveness. Kissinger, quoted in Waltz, *Theory of International Politics*, op. cit., p. 130.
45 Stephen Gill and David Law, *The Global Political Economy: Perspectives, Problems and Policies*, New York: Harvester Wheatsheaf, 1988, p. 71.
46 Klaus Knorr, *Power and Wealth*, New York: Basic Books, 1973, pp. 13–14.
47 Ibid., pp. 82–90.
48 Much of the academic debate in IPE in recent times has centred on the role of hegemony and international regimes in the world economy. Central to this debate is the relationship between power distribution (hegemonic leadership) and the construction of liberal world economic orders. Cf. Charles P. Kindleberger, *The World in Depression, 1929-1939*, Berkeley: University of California Press, 1973; Robert O. Keohane, *After Hegemony: Cooperation and Discord in the World Political Economy*, Princeton, NJ: Princeton University Press, 1984; Stephen D. Krasner (ed.), *International Regimes*, Ithaca and London: Cornell University Press, 1991. Andrew Walter's seminal study has challenged the prevailing notion that hegemonic powers provide stability to international monetary relations. See his *World Power and World Money: The Role of Hegemony and the International Monetary Order*, New York: Harvester Wheatsheaf, 1993.
49 Stephen D. Krasner, *Structural Conflict: the Third World against Global Liberalism*, Berkeley: University of California Press, 1985, p. 28.
50 Marchal, quoted in Robert Gilpin, *The Political Economy of International Relations*, Princeton, NJ: Princeton University Press, 1987, p. 81.
51 Following Polanyi and Hirschman, Robert Gilpin sees relations of power as being inherent in the market system itself, as its existence "creates economic power which one actor can use against another". Given this reality, states would normally seek to "enhance their own independence and to increase the dependence of other states". (Gilpin, op. cit., p. 23).
52 Interest in the role of power in economic life is quite recent in the development economics literature. Cf. Jean-Marie Baland and Jean-Philippe Platteau, "Are Economists Concerned with Power?", *IDS Bulletin*, 24 (3), July 1993, pp. 12–20; Jock Cameron, "Power as Central in Economic Exchange: Can Keynes Help?", *IDS Bulletin*, 24 (3), July 1993, pp. 31–35. For an interesting survey of the evolving literature, see Pranab Bardhan, "Some Reflections on the Use of the Concept of Power in Economics", in Kaushik Basu and Pulin Nayak (eds), *Development Policy and Economic Theory*, Oxford: Oxford University Press, 1992, pp. 64–77.
53 His own approach seems to be largely influenced by Antonio Gramsci, on the one hand, and Max Weber, on the other. Stephen Gill, *American Hegemony and the Trilateral Commission*, Cambridge: Cambridge University Press, 1990, p. 55.

Pierre Grou has applied the concept of structural power in his analysis of international finance. See his *The Financial Structure of Multinational Capitalism*, Leamington Spa: Berg Publishers, 1985. Cf. Beth Mintz and Michael Schwartz, *The Power Structure of American Business*, Chicago and London: University of Chicago Press, 1985.

54 Robert W. Cox, *Power, Production and World Order: Social Forces in the Making of History*, New York: Columbia University Press, 1987. See also the following works by Robert Cox, "Social Forces, States and World Orders: Beyond International Relations theory", in R. O. Keohane (ed.), *Neorealism and Its Critics*, New York: Columbia University, 1986, pp. 204–254; and "Gramsci, Hegemony and International Relations: An Essay in Method", *Millennium* (12), 1983, pp. 162–175.

55 Cox, op. cit., p. 75.

56 Stephen Gill and David Law, *The Global Political Economy: Perspectives, Problems and Policies*, New York and London: Harvester Wheatsheaf, 1988, p. 73.

57 Ibid., p. 78.

58 Caroline Thomas, *In Search of Security: The Third World in International Relations*, Boulder, Col.: Lynne Rienner, 1987, p. 4. On the economic aspects of the "security dilemma" in international relations, see Barry Buzan, *People, States and Fear: The National Security Problem in International Relations*, Chapel Hill: The University of North Carolina, 1983, pp. 128–155.

59 Bruce Russett and Harvey Starr, *World Politics: The Menu for Choice*, New York: W. H. Freeman & Co., 1981, p. 127.

60 Ibid., p. 130.

61 *The Dictionary of World Politics*, New York: Harvester Wheatsheaf, 1992, p. 142.

62 Jeffrey Hart, quoted in Sullivan, op. cit.

63 See Sullivan, op. cit., p. 98. Peter Morriss has argued that both influence and power have completely different Latin derivatives – *influere* and *potere* – and therefore ought to be kept analytically distinct. See his *Power: A Philosophical Analysis*, Manchester: Manchester University Press, 1987, p. 9.

64 Paul R. Kauppi and Mark Viotti, *International Relations Theory: Realism, Pluralism, Globalism*, New York: Macmillan, 1987, p. 44.

65 Ernst B. Haas, *When Knowledge Is Power: Three Models of Change in International Organisations*, Berkeley: University of California Press, 1990.

66 Cheryl Payer, *The World Bank: A Critical Analysis*, New York and London: Monthly Review Press, 1982, pp. 15-52. Bruno S. Frey has undertaken an econometric analysis of the World Bank's external policy behaviour, testing four competing models of the Bank:

- the "needs model", in which the Bank extends loans to countries that need them most;
- the "deserts model", in which loans are given to countries that are most "deserving" of them;
- the "benevolence model", where Bank policies are guided by pure altruism;
- the "politico-economic model", in which political and economic factors are both influential variables, including the utilitarian calculations of Bank employees.

Frey concludes that the latter model comes closest to explaining as well as yielding reliable predictions of future Bank behaviour. See his *International Political Economics*, Oxford: Basil Blackwell, 1984, pp. 143–164.

67 Russett and Starr, op. cit., p. 127.

68 Razaq Adefulu has utilized Peter Blau's theory of "exchange and power in social life" in his study of Lomé diplomacy. See his "The Lomé Conventions

and the NIEO: A Study of the Political Economy of North–South Relations", unpublished PhD thesis, University of Lancaster, 1988.

69 David A. Baldwin, *Economic Statecraft*, Princeton, NJ: Princeton University Press, 1985, p. 292.

70 Ibid., p. 293.

71 Werner J. Feld has undertaken a similar analysis with regard to the European Community in the international system. His approach, however, emphasizes influence but does not include social exchange. See his *The European Community in World Affairs: Economic Power and Political Influence*, Boulder, Col.: Westview Press, 1983.

72 Marc Williams, *International Economic Organisations and the Third World*, New York and London: Harvester Wheatsheaf, 1994, p. 46.

73 Ibid., p. 47.

74 IMF, *Annual Report, 1992*.

75 See Krasner, op. cit. On the critique of this approach, see Richard K. Ashley, "The Poverty of Neorealism", in Robert O. Keohane (ed.) *Neorealism and Its Critics*, New York: Columbia University Press, 1986, pp. 255–300.

76 There has been an interesting debate among scholars as to whether or not the state is still the dominant actor in world politics. Cf. Fred Halliday, "State and Society in International Relations", in Michael Banks and Martin Shaw (eds) *State and Society in International Relations*, New York: Harvester Wheatsheaf, 1991, pp. 191–209.

77 Krasner, op. cit., p. 28. This approach presupposes a utility-maximizing rational-actor model, in which key actors are presumed to be pursuing various and often conflicting interests and goals. Jeffry Frieden specifies four elements in this methodological tradition: "defining the actors and their goals, specifying actors' policy preferences, determining how they group themselves, and following their interaction with other social institutions". See his *Modern Political Economy and Latin America, 1965–1985*, Princeton, NJ: Princeton University Press, p. 16. For a general survey of the evolution of theory and method in International Political Economy, see William C. Olson and A. J. R. Groom, *International Relations Then and Now*, London: Harper Collins, 1991, pp. 222–305. In the analysis of domestic economics and politics, the most important advances have been made in "public choice" theory and the so-called new "political economy". Cf. James M. Buchanan, *Constitutional Economics*, Oxford: Basil Blackwell, 1991. Moncur Olson's work has been influential in focusing attention on the role of domestic structures and interest groups in policy-making and economic growth. See his *The Logic of Collective Action*, Cambridge, Mass.: Harvard University Press, 1971; and *The Rise and Decline of Nations*, New Haven and London: Yale University Press, 1982.

2 AFRICA AND THE NEW INTERNATIONAL AID REGIME

1 The development consensus was perhaps best expressed in the Pearson report on development cooperation. See Lester B. Pearson, *Partners in Development*, Report of the Commission on International Development, New York: Praeger, 1969.

2 Susan Strange has analysed the international aid as a global welfare system. See her *States and Markets: An Introduction to International Political Economy*, London: Pinter Publishers, 1988, pp. 207–227.

3 On the evolution of North–South relations, see Joan A. Spero, *The Politics of International Economic Relations*, London: Routledge, 1994, 4th edn, pp. 147–304.

4 Organization of African Unity, *The Lagos Plan of Action for the Economic Development of Africa 1980–2000*, Geneva: International Institute for Labour Studies, 1979.

5 The World Bank, *Accelerated Development in Sub-Saharan Africa: An Agenda for Action*, Washington, DC: The World Bank, 1981.

6 For a good summary of the debate on the merits and demerits of the Berg report, see Sheila Smith and John Sender, *What's Right with the Berg Report and What's Left of its Critics?*, Sussex: IDS Discussion Paper no. 192, June 1984.

7 David F. Luke and Timothy M. Shaw (eds), *The Lagos Plan of Action and Africa's Economic Future*, Lanham: University Press of America, 1984.

8 Robert R. Brown and Robert J. Cummings, *The Lagos Plan of Action vs. the Berg Report: Contemporary Issues in African Development*, Washington: Howard University, 1983, p. 32.

9 Adebayo Adedeji, "African Alternative Framework to Structural Adjustment", text of a speech delivered at the University of Ottawa, 23 October 1989 (mimeo), p. 4.

10 UN Resolution 39/29, New York, 3 December 1984.

11 The first chairperson of the Committee was Edgard Pisani, former EC Development Commissioner. Monsieur Pisani urged the international community to take a fresh look at Africa's problems and to develop a new "solidarity contract" with the continent. See Henricus Gajentaan, "Conference Diplomacy at the 1986 United Nations General Assembly's Special Session on the Critical Economic Situation in Africa", in Johan Kaufman (ed.), *Effective Negotiation: Case-Studies in Conference Diplomacy*, Dodrecht: Martinus Nijhoff Publishers, 1989, pp. 109–135.

12 United Nations, *Programme of Action for African Economic Recovery and Development 1986–1990*, New York, 1986.

13 But perhaps this was also a double-edged sword to the extent that it signalled a certain level of exasperation within the international community with regard to the long-term prospects for Africa, thereby justifying extreme and increasingly desperate economic panaceas.

14 Javier Perez de Cuellar, "Progress in the Implementation of the United Nations Programme of Action for African Economic Recovery", *Development Seeds of Change*, 2 (3), 1987, pp. 42–43.

15 H. M. A. Onitiri, "African Recovery and Development", in Sidney Dell (ed.), *Policies for Development: Essays in Honour of Gamani Corea*, London: Macmillan, 1988, pp. 33–34.

16 Interview with a senior Zambian official who attended the review meeting in New York (Lusaka, March 1992). He told me that the tone of the entire meeting was unprecedented, with the American Ambassador resorting to undiplomatic language to describe what he regarded as the irresponsibility of African governments.

17 For a comprehensive overview of World Bank/IMF involvement in Africa, see John Loxley, "The IMF, the World Bank, and Sub-Saharan Africa: Policies and Politics", in Kjell Havnevik, *IMF and World Bank Policies in Africa*, Uppsala: Scandinavian Institute for African Studies, 1987, pp. 47–63.

18 On the evolution of IMF financing policies in developing countries, see Graham Bird, *IMF Lending to Developing Countries: Issues and Evidence*, London and New York: Routledge, 1995; Margaret G. de Vries, *The IMF in a Changing*

World, 1945–85, Washington, DC: IMF, 1986; Graham Bird, *International Financial Policy and Economic Development*, London: Macmillan, 1989, pp. 42–107.

19 Laurence Harris, "The Bretton Woods System and Africa", in Bade Onimode (ed.), *The IMF, the World Bank and the African Debt, vol. 1 and 2: The Social and Economic Impact*, London: Zed Books, 1989, pp. 19–24.

20 Edward Mason and Robert Asher, *The World Bank since Bretton Woods*, Washington, DC: Brookings, 1973. On the role of the World Bank in developing countries as perceived by a former insider, see Stanley Please, *The Hobbled Giant: Essays on the World Bank*, Boulder, Col., and London: Westview Press, 1984. For a general appraisal of Bank policies among the rural poor, see Robert L. Ayres, *Banking on the Rural Poor: The World Bank and World Poverty*, Cambridge, Mass.: The MIT Press, 1983.

21 For a critical appraisal of World Bank rural development projects in Africa, see Gavin Williams, "The Contradictions of the World Bank and the Crisis of the State in Africa", Paris Conference, December 1985 (mimeo).

22 Cf. Kenneth W. Dam, *The Rules of the Game: Reform and Evolution in the International Monetary System*, Chicago and London: The University of Chicago Press, 1982; Robert Solomon, *The International Monetary System, 1945–1976*, New York: Harper & Row, 1977.

23 The Peterson Commission appointed by President Richard Nixon in the 1960s had recommended that the United States should concentrate on project lending and should leave policy-reform aspects of aid to the Washington institutions, who were supposed to have a "comparative advantage" in that area.

24 Loxley, "The IMF, the World Bank and Sub-Saharan Africa", op. cit.

25 Thomas Biersteker (ed.), *Dealing with Debt: Financial Negotiations and Adjustment Bargaining*, Boulder, Col.: Westview Press, 1993, pp. 1–20.

26 Cf. Oxfam Policy Department, *A Case for Reform: Fifty Years of the IMF and the World Bank*, Oxford: Oxfam Publications, 1995.

27 Cf. Oxfam Policy Department, *Structural Adjustment and Inequality in Latin America: How IMF and World Bank Policies Have Failed the Poor*, Oxford: Oxfam, 1994; Oxfam Policy Department, *Africa Make or Break*, Oxford: Oxfam, 1993; John Clarkee, *Zambia: Debt and Poverty*, Oxford: Oxfam, 1989.

28 Andrea Cornia, Richard Jolly and Frances Stewart (eds), *Adjustment with a Human Face*, Oxford: Clarendon Press, 1987.

29 Ibid., p. 7.

30 John Williamson, "Introduction", in John Williamson (ed.), *IMF Conditionality*, Washington, DC: Institute for International Economics, 1983, p. xiv.

31 George M. von Furstenberg, "The IMF as Market-Maker for Official Business between Nations", in Robert J. Myers (ed.), *The Political Morality of the International Monetary Fund*, New Brunswick and Oxford: Transaction Books, 1987, pp. 111–126.

32 Robert H. Cassen, "Structural Adjustment in Sub-Saharan Africa", opening address for the workshop on "The Management of Structural Adjustment Negotiations", organized and sponsored by the Structural Adjustment Advisory Team for Africa (SAATA) at Harare, Zimbabwe, 1991 (mimeo).

33 Tony Killick, *A Reaction Too Far: Economic Theory and the Role of the State in Developing Countries*, London: ODI, 1989.

34 Tony Killick, "Twenty-Five Years in Development: The Rise and Impending Decline of Market Solutions", *Development Policy Review*, 4, 1986, pp. 99–116.

35 Among the lessons learned, according to Killick, are:

- greater circumspection about the traditional assumption that governments always serve the public interest;

- the ineffectiveness of medium-term planning;
- the mistake of emphasizing industrialization at the expense of agriculture;
- the shortcomings of import-substitution and inward-oriented development strategies;
- the positive role of foreign investment;
- the importance of market incentives and relative prices (Killick, op. cit.).

36 Lance Taylor, *Varieties of Stabilisation Experience: Towards a Sensible Macroeconomics in the Third World*, Oxford: Clarendon Press, 1988, pp. 148–149. See also his earlier book, *Structuralist Macroeconomics*, New York: Basic Books, 1983.

37 The WIDER Group is a group of economists who have researched on stabilization and adjustment policies under the aegis of the Helsinki-based World Institute for Development Economics Research, an arm of the United Nations University. Prominent among them are Lance Taylor, Amartya K. Sen, Kaushik Basu and Reginald H. Green.

38 An American lawyer, Andrew Schoenholtz, has referred to the case of Zaire – the paradigm of the corrupt state in Africa – where IMF policies were derailed because the Fund failed to take into account the elaborate structures of private accumulation established by the power elite. See his "The IMF in Africa: Unnecessary and Undesirable Western Restraints on Development", *The Journal of Modern African Studies*, 25 (3), 1987, pp. 403–433. Cf. Laurence Whitehead, "Political Explanations of Macroeconomic Management: A Survey", *World Development*, 18 (8), 1990, pp. 1133–1146.

39 Christopher Colclough and James Manor (eds), *States or Markets: Neo-Liberalism and the Development Policy Debate*, Oxford: Clarendon Press, 1991.

40 David Evans, "Visible and Invisible Hands in Trade Policy Reform", in Colclough and Manor, op. cit., pp. 48–77.

41 John Toye, "Is There a New Political Economy of Development?", in Colclough and Manor, op. cit., pp. 321–378.

42 Samir Amin, in the Preface to Azzam Mahjoub (ed.), *Adjustment or Delinking? The African Experience*, Tokyo, UNU and London: Zed Books, 1990, p. x.

43 Cf. Kwame A. Ninsin, "Ghana under the PNDC: Delinking or Structural Adjustment?" in Mahjoub, op. cit., pp. 131–156.

44 In the *Austro-German Customs Union Case 1931*, Judge Anzilotti of the Permanent Court of International Justice defined sovereignty as being synonymous with political independence. According to him: "Independence . . . is really no more than the normal condition of States according to international law; it may also be described as *sovereignty (suprema potestas)*, or *external sovereignty*, by which is meant that the State has over it no other authority than that of international law." *Advisory Opinion P.C.I.J. Reports, Series A/B, No. 41 (1931),* reproduced in D. J. Harris, *Cases and Materials on International Law*, London: Sweet & Maxwell, 4th edn, 1993, pp. 105–108. Cf. Ian Brownlie, *Principles of Public International Law*, Oxford: Clarendon, 3rd edn, 1985, pp. 81–82.

45 Cf. Alan James, *Sovereign Statehood: The Basis of International Society*, London: Allen & Unwin, 1986.

46 On the historical evolution of the concept of sovereignty, see F. H. Hinsley, *Sovereignty*, London: C. A. Watts, 1966. On the concept of sovereignty in Western political thought, see Bertrand de Jouvenal, *Sovereignty*, Cambridge: Cambridge University Press, 1957.

47 The IFIs would disagree with this criticism, arguing that the essence of "policy dialogue" is precisely to seek an exchange of views between donors and recipients. Evidence from fieldwork in Zambia indicates that there was indeed some collaboration between Bank/Fund officials and technocrats in the

Zambian Finance Ministry and the Planning Commission in the formulation of Zambia's Structural Adjustment Programme. However, it is debatable as to what extent this was a collaboration between equals.

48 Marguerite Michaels, "Retreat from Africa", *Foreign Affairs*, 27 (1), 1992/3, pp. 93–108.

49 Kendall W. Stiles, "IMF Conditionality: Coercion or Compromise?", *World Development*, 18 (7), 1990, pp. 959–974.

50 A major fault with a study of this nature is that it assumes little or no difference in the bargaining capabilities of Sudan, for example, and the United Kingdom, or even between Burkina Faso and the Fund. Second, having interviewed Fund staff, there was no indication that Stiles took up the logically necessary step of interviewing some negotiators from developing countries to hear their side of the story. But it would be misleading to suggest that African governments are always the pliant victims of IMF-imposed programmes. Some of the agreements were reached only after long, drawn-out negotiations in the case of countries such as Nigeria, Tanzania and Zambia. In such instances the IFIs were compelled to modify some of their positions in order to reach a compromise.

51 Marie-France L'Hériteau, *Le Fonds Monétaire International et Les Pays du Tiers-Monde*, Paris: Presses Universitaires, 1986. On the fate of sovereignty in an integrated world economy, see Joseph A. Camilleri and Jim Falk, *The End of Sovereignty? The Politics of a Shrinking and Fragmenting World*, Aldershot, Hants: Gower, 1992, pp. 69–103.

52 Eboe Hutchful, "From 'Revolution' to Monetarism: The Economics and Politics of the Adjustment Programme in Ghana", in Bonnie Campbell and John Loxley (eds), *Structural Adjustment in Africa*, London: Macmillan, 1989, pp. 92–131.

53 Edward V. K. Jaycox, in an interview with Margaret A. Novicki, *Africa Report*, November–December 1989, p. 18.

54 For a critical assessment of the World Bank's role, see Teresa Hayter and C. Watson, *Aid Rhetoric and Reality*, London and Sydney: Pluto, 1985; Susan George, *Food Strategies for Tomorrow*, San Francisco: The Global Hunger Project, 1987; Susan George, *A Fate Worse than Debt*, Harmondsworth: Penguin, 1988.

55 The SSA recipients were: Benin, Burkina Faso, Burundi, Central African Republic, Chad, Comoros, Gambia, Ghana, Guinea, Guinea Bissau, Haiti, Kenya, Lesotho, Madagascar, Mali, Mauritania, Mozambique, Niger, Rwanda, Sao Tome & Principe, Senegal, Sierra Leone, Somalia, Tanzania, Togo, Uganda, Zaire. The highest SSA recipients were: Zaire (SDR146 million) and Ghana (SDR143 million).

56 The SSA recipients were: Burundi, Gambia, Ghana, Guinea, Kenya, Lesotho, Madagascar, Malawi, Mauritania, Mozambique, Niger, Senegal, Tanzania, Togo and Uganda. The highest SSA recipients were Ghana (with the highest overall total of SDR389 million), Kenya (SDR261 million) and Uganda (SDR179 million).

57 Cf. Tyrone Ferguson, *The Third World and Decision-Making in the International Monetary Fund: The Quest for Full and Effective Participation*, London and New York: Pinter, 1988.

58 J. K. Nyerere, "An Address", in *Development and Change*, 17 (3), July 1986.

59 The South Commission Report, released in 1990, seemed to mirror many of Nyerere's ideas. However, it has been largely ignored by the rest of the international community. See *The Challenge to the South*, the Report of the South Commission, Oxford: Oxford University Press, 1990.

60 Bade Onimode (ed.), (1989) *The IMF, the World Bank and the African Debt, vol. 1 and 2: The Social and Political Impact*, London: Zed Books, p. 31.
61 Thandika Mkandawire, "The Road to Crisis, Adjustment and De-industrialisation: The African Case", *African Development*, 12 (1), 1988, pp. 5–31.
62 von Furstenberg, op. cit.
63 The Dakar-based Council for Development, Economic and Social Research in Africa is the main body which brings together African social scientists and coordinates social science research in Africa.
64 Thandika Mkandawire, "Crisis and Adjustment in Sub-Saharan Africa", in Dharam Ghai (edn), *The IMF and the South: The Social Impact of Crisis and Adjustment*, London: Zed Books, 1991, pp. 80–94.
65 For a concise account of the role of the ECA in African development, see Isebill Gruhn, *Regionalism and the Economic Commission for Africa*, Boulder, Col.: Lynne Rienner, 1980.
66 For some insight into Adedeji's period at the ECA, see his collection of speeches and papers: Adebayo Adedeji (ed.) *Towards a Dynamic African Economy: Speeches and Lectures* (with the assistance of Jeggan Senghor), London: Frank Cass, 1989.
67 Economic Commission for Africa, "The Abuja Statement", *African Journal of Political Economy*, 2 (1), 1988, pp. 132–147.
68 Ibid.
69 United Nations Economic Commission for Africa, "The Khartoum Declaration: Towards a Human-Focused Approach to Socio-Economic Recovery and Development in Africa", in ECA *Annual Report*, New York: The United Nations, 1988.
70 Quoted in *Africa Recovery*, 2 (2), June 1988, p. 23.
71 The World Bank, *Africa's Adjustment and Growth in the 1980s*, Washington, DC: The World Bank, 1989.
72 See the Economic Commission for Africa, *Statistics and Policies: ECA Preliminary Observations on the World Bank Report, "Africa's Adjustment and Growth in the 1980s"*, Addis Ababa (undated).
73 The United Nations Economic Commission for Africa, *African Alternative Framework to Structural Adjustment for Socio-Economic Recovery and Transformation*, Addis Ababa (undated).
74 Adebayo Adedeji, "Press Statement on the Occasion of the Launching of AAF-SAP", London, 6 July 1989 (mimeo).
75 Ibid.
76 *Africa News*, 25, 1989, p. 2.
77 Ibid.
78 Ibid.
79 Ibid., p. 6.
80 The World Bank, *Sub-Saharan Africa: From Crisis to Sustainable Development*, Oxford: Oxford University Press, 1989.
81 Quoted in "Aid and Political Reform", ODI Briefing Paper, January 1992, p. 1.
82 On the evolution of US political conditionality, see Thomas Carothers, "Recent US Experience with Democracy Promotion", *IDS Bulletin*, 26 (2), 1995, pp. 62–69.
83 Ibid.
84 Ibid.
85 Quoted in *IDS Bulletin*, 24 (1), 1993, p. 7.
86 Angola, Benin, Burkina Faso, Cameroon, Cape Verde, Chad, Congo, Côte d'Ivoire, Gabon, Ghana, Guinea, Guinea-Bissau, Kenya, Liberia, Madagascar,

Mozambique, Niger, Nigeria, Rwanda, Sao Tome & Principe, Sierra Leone, Somalia, Tanzania, Togo, Zaire, Zambia, Zimbabwe. Whilst political reforms in many of them have been implemented, in some others, notably Nigeria, Sierra Leone, Zaire and Togo, the changes have been effectively reversed.

87 Cf. Samuel Decalo, "The Process, Prospects and Constraints of Democratisation in Africa", *African Affairs*, 91, 1992, pp. 7–35.

88 See "The European Bank for Reconstruction", ODI Briefing Paper, September 1990.

89 World Bank, *Sub-Saharan Africa: From Crisis to Sustainable Growth*, op. cit.

90 Peter Anyang Nyong'o (ed.), *Popular Struggles for Democracy in Africa*, London: Zed Books, 1987. For an interesting African debate on the democratization process, see also Anyang Nyong'o, "Political Instability and the Prospects for Democracy in Africa", *African Development*, XIII (1), 1988, pp. 71–86; Thandika Mkandawire, "Debates: Comments on Democracy and Political Instability", *African Development*, XIII (3), 1988, pp. 77–87; and Shedrack Gutto, "Debates: Social Revolutions – the Preconditions for Sustainable Development and People's Democracies in Africa", *African Development*, VIII (4), 1988, pp. 89–103.

91 *Africa Recovery*, October–December 1990, p. 8.

92 Björn Beckman, "Empowerment or Repression? The World Bank and the Politics of African Adjustment". Paper to a Symposium on the Social and Political Context of Structural Adjustment in sub-Saharan Africa at Bergen, Norway, 17–19 October 1990 (mimeo).

93 An opposite view has been expressed by Jeffrey Herbst, who argues that certain aspects of economic liberalization, such as privatization of public enterprises, reduce the clientelist-patrimonial character of the state and therefore contribute towards a new style of governance and accountability from leaders. See his "The Structural Adjustment of Politics in Africa", *World Development*, 18 (7), 1990, pp. 949–958.

94 Cf. Eboe Hutchful, "The Crisis of the New International Division of Labour, Authoritarianism and the Transition to Free Market Economies in Africa", *African Development*, XII (2), 1983, pp. 35–53.

95 For a study of organized labour responses to the Nigerian reform programme, see Yusuf Bangura and Björn Beckman, "African Workers and Structural Adjustment: the Nigerian Case", in Ghai, op. cit., pp. 139–165.

96 ODI Briefing Paper, January 1992, p. 4.

97 John-Jean B. Barya, "The New Political Conditionalities of Aid: An Independent View From Africa", *IDS Bulletin*, 24 (1), 1993, pp. 16–23.

98 One study suggests some evidence in support of this proposition. See Mark Robinson, "Will Political Conditionality Work?", *IDS Bulletin*, 24 (1), 1993, pp. 58–66. In the case of Algeria, for example, Western support for democracy ceased when it was evident that the Muslim fundamentalists were on their way to winning the general elections. In the more recent case of Nigeria, the country's commercial importance was a factor in determining the West's relatively moderate responses to the country's human rights problems under the military regime of General Sani Abacha.

3 THE ORIGINS OF EC–AFRICAN DIPLOMACY, 1957–71

1 Cf. Alexander A. Kwapong, *The Role of Classical Studies in Africa Today*, Lagos: University of Lagos Press, 1969. For a concise account of the historical evolution of Euro-African relations, see Norman R. Bennett, *Africa and Europe:*

From Roman Times to National Independence, New York and London: Holmes & Meier Publishers, 1984.

2 On the economics and politics of empire, the magisterial work by Eric Hobsbawm remains a classic. See his *Industry and Empire, 1875–1914*, London: Weidenfeld & Nicolson, 2nd edn, 1995.

3 Cf. Terence Ranger, "The Invention of Tradition in Colonial Africa", in Eric Hobsbawm and Terence Ranger (eds), *The Invention of Tradition*, Cambridge: Cambridge University Press, 1983, pp. 211–262.

4 Michel Foucault, *Madness and Civilisation: A History of Insanity in the Age of Reason*, trans. by R. Howard, London: Routledge, 1989. On the ideological and cultural basis of the imperial idea, see Edward Said, *Culture and Imperialism*, London: Chatto & Windus, 1993. The social sciences, as Pierre Bourdieu has shown, shared in the ethnocentric paradigms which dominated European studies of non-Western societies in the colonial era. See his *The Logic of Practice*, trans. by Richard Nice, Oxford: Polity Press, 1990, pp. 1–5.

5 On the historical incorporation of Africa into the European international system, see Hedley Bull, "European States and African Political Communities", in Hedley Bull and Adam Watson (eds), *The Expansion of International Society*, Oxford: Oxford University Press, 1989, pp. 99–114.

6 On the concept of "informal empire", see Ronald Robinson and J. Gallagher, "The Imperialism of Free Trade", *Economic History Review*, 6, 1953, pp. 1–15.

7 Gérard Chaliand and Jean-Pierre Rageau, *Strategic Atlas*, Harmondsworth: Penguin, 1985, p. 20.

8 Guy Martin, "Africa and the Ideology of Eurafrica: Neo-Colonialism or Pan-Africanism?" *The Journal of Modern African Studies*, 20 (2), 1982, pp. 221–238.

9 John Chipman, *French Power in Black Africa*, Oxford: Basil Blackwell, 1989, p. 64.

10 Ibid.

11 Cf. Georges Duhamel, *Civilisation Française*, Paris: Librairie Hatchette, 1944.

12 Quoted in Theodore Zeldin, *France 1848–1945*, Oxford and New York: Oxford University Press, 1984, p. 266. Ferry and a few fellow colonialists were the force behind the French acquisitions of Tunisia (1881), Tonkin (1885), Madagascar (1885) and the French Congo (1885).

13 Cf. Michael Howard, *The Franco-Prussian War: The German Invasion of France 1870–1871*, London: Hart-Davis, 1961.

14 Immanuel Wallerstein, *Africa: The Politics of Independence*, New York: Vintage Books, 1961, p. 63.

15 Quoted in Maurice Liniger-Goumaz, *L'Eurafrique: utopie ou réalité?*, Yaoundé: Presses de Yaoundé, 1972, p. 27.

16 Quoted in Chipman, op. cit., p. 71.

17 It is a moot question as to how "African" Senghor's views were. Hailing from the Serer ethnic group, the former Senegalese President, Leopold Sedar Senghor (b. 1906) is the quintessential example of French colonial assimilation. Widely regarded as one of the greatest living poets writing in the French language, he is a product of the most elitist of French education. A graduate of the Sorbonne and a *professeur agrégé*, he was also a classmate of President Georges Pompidou at the École Normale Supérieure. He fought for the French in the Second World War and was a prisoner in a Nazi concentration camp. He later married into an aristocratic family in Normandy and was appointed official grammarian during the drafting of the Constitution of the Fifth Republic. He was later to become Senegalese Deputy at the Assemblée Nationale (1946–58). In 1980 he retired from the Presidency of Senegal after

twenty years in office, to the exalted status of Membre de l'Académie Française.

18 Chipman, op. cit., p. 80.

19 Cf. Jack Hayward, *The One and Indivisible French Republic*, London: Weidenfeld & Nicolson, 1973, pp. 248–254.

20 Martin, op. cit., p. 231.

21 Carol C. Twitchett, *Europe and Africa: From Association to Partnership*, Westmead, Hants: Saxon House, 1987, p. 1.

22 The Treaty of Rome, 1957.

23 Ibid.

24 Twitchett, op. cit., p. 3.

25 *The Strasbourg Plan,* Strasbourg: Council of Europe, 1952.

26 Walter Hallstein, *Europe in the Making*, trans. by Charles Roetter, London: Allen & Unwin, 1972, p. 257. Coming from Germany, it is reasonable to assume that Hallstein's views on this question were coloured by the scepticism which his country felt about "association".

27 Cf. Alan S. Milward, *The European Rescue of the Nation State*, London: Routledge, 1992, pp. 218–221.

28 On the international economic crisis of the interwar years, see Charles Kindleberger, *The World in Depression 1929–1939*, Berkeley: University of California Press, 1986.

29 Cf. Maurice Viand, "La Caisse centrale de coopération economique et les nouvelles orientations de la politique française d'aide au développement", *Afrique Contemporaine*, 126, April–June 1984, pp. 3–20.

30 Quoted in Virginia Thompson and Richard Adloff, "French Economic Policy in Tropical Africa", in Peter Duignan and L. H. Gann (eds), *Colonialism in Africa, vol. IV: the Economics of Colonialism*, Cambridge: Cambridge University Press, 1975, pp. 127–164.

31 Henrik S. Marcussen and Jens E. Torp, *The Internationalisation of Capital*, London: Zed Books, p. 50.

32 Ibid.

33 D. K. Fieldhouse, *Black Africa 1945–1980: Economic Decolonisation and Arrested Development*, London: Allen & Unwin, 1986, p. 13.

34 Ibid.

35 Thompson and Adloff, op. cit., p. 51.

36 Fieldhouse, op. cit., p. 13.

37 Henri Grimal, *Decolonisation: The French, Dutch and Belgian Empires 1919–1963*, trans. by Stephen de Vos, London: Routledge & Kegan Paul, 1965, pp. 363–369. Cf. Dorothy Pickles, *The Fifth French Republic: Institutions and Politics*, London: Methuen, 1962, pp. 159–167.

38 In 1958 when de Gaulle returned to power, he proposed a new French Community which would include France and the colonies. A referendum was organized in which the colonies were offered the choice of whether or not to remain in the Community. All voted in favour of the Community with the exception of Sékou Touré's Guinea. Although this decision implied that Guinea was no longer a member of the AASM, the EEC continued to treat her in its aid programmes as though she still were. France's response to Guinea's decision was infamously harsh. See R. F. Holland, *European Decolonisation: An Introductory Survey*, London: Macmillan, 1975, pp. 153–162.

39 Milward, op. cit., pp. 219–220.

40 John Ravenhill, *Collective Clientelism: The Lomé Conventions and North–South Relations*, New York: Columbia University, 1985, p. 50.

41 Quoted in Twitchett, op. cit., p. 11.
42 Hallstein, op. cit., pp. 258–259.
43 Neil Malcolm, "The Soviet Union and Europe", in Jonathan Story (ed.), *The New Europe: Politics, Government and Economy since 1945*, Oxford and Cambridge: Blackwell, 1993, pp. 91–114.
44 Hallstein, op. cit., p. 260.
45 Ibid.
46 Ibid., p. 258.
47 Pius N. C. Okigbo, *Africa and the Common Market*, London: Longman, 1967, pp. 38–49.
48 Peter Duignan and L. H. Gann, "Economic Achievements of the Colonisers: An Assessment", in Duignan and Gann, op. cit., pp. 673–696.
49 J. A. Fralon, *The Lomé Convention: Renegotiation and Renewal*, Brussels: Agence Européenne d'Informations, 1978, p. 18.
50 Joanna Moss, *The Lomé Conventions and their Implications for the United States*, Boulder, Col.: Westview, 1982, p. 7.
51 Quoted in Mwesiga Baregu, "The Lomé Convention Viewed from the South", in Kimmo Kiljunen (ed.), *MINI-NEO*, Uppsala: Scandinavian Institute for African Studies, 1989, p. 164.
52 *Africa Confidential*, 23, 22 November 1968, p. 6.
53 UNCTAD had calculated that the price index for European agricultural products had risen from 100 in 1958 to 111 in 1965 whilst coffee and cotton prices from the Eighteen had fallen from 100 in 1958 to 75.66 in 1965. See UNCTAD, op. cit.
54 Ibid.
55 For an exhaustive analysis of the early phase of EC–African negotiations, see I. William Zartman, *The Politics of Trade Negotiations between Africa and the European Economic Community*, Princeton, NJ: Princeton University Press, 1971.
56 *Africa Confidential*, 15 July 1969, p. 2.
57 Ibid.
58 Moss, op. cit.
59 Ibid.
60 Among Caribbean leaders, Dr Eric Williams of Trinidad & Tobago had declared that his country was prepared to consider the offer. See Dennis Austin, "Britain, Commonwealth Africa and the EEC", in Pierre Uri (ed.), *From Commonwealth to Common Market*, London: Penguin/Atlantic Institute, 1968, pp. 141–142.
61 Ibid., p. 142.
62 Quoted in Baregu, op. cit., p. 163.
63 Kwame Nkrumah, *Africa Must Unite*, London: Heinemann, 1964, p. 162.
64 Quoted in S. R. de la Mahotière, *The Common Market: A Comprehensive Guide*, London: Hodder & Stoughton, 1961, p. 98.
65 Ahmed Sékou Touré, "Africa's Destiny", in J. Duffy and R. A. Manners (eds), *Africa Speaks*, Princeton, NJ: Van Nostrand, 1960, p. 37.
66 Cf. Ali A. Mazrui, *Towards a Pax Africana*, London: Heinemann, 1967.
67 United Nations Economic and Social Council, DOCE/CN.14/72, December 1960.
68 Okigbo, *Africa and the Common Market*, op. cit.
69 Ibid.
70 Moss, op. cit., p. 9.
71 *Africa Confidential*, 22 November 1968, p. 7.

72 Tom Soper, "European Trade with Africa", *Africa Contemporary Record*, 1968–69, pp. 787–797.
73 Ibid., p. 797.
74 On the major trends in Nigeria's economy and macroeconomic policy, see Pius N. C. Okigbo, *National Development Planning in Nigeria*, London: James Currey, 1989, pp. 162–163. For an account of the transformation of Nigerian foreign policy after 1970 see Olajide Aluko, *Essays on Nigerian Foreign Policy*, London: Allen & Unwin, 1981.
75 Moss, op. cit., p. 9.
76 On Britain's role under the Commonwealth Preference Area and the Sterling Zone, see Susan Strange, *Sterling and British Policy*, London: Oxford University Press/RIIA, 1971.
77 For a number of selected countries, for example, exports to Britain were: Nigeria (37%), Ghana (13%), Uganda (14%), and Tanzania (25%); whereas imports from Britain constituted for Nigeria (32%), Ghana (25%), Kenya (25%), Uganda (27%), and Tanzania (24%). See Soper, op. cit., p. 790.
78 Moss, op. cit.
79 *Africa Confidential*, 13 (5), 3 March 1972, p. 4.
80 1 ua = US$ 1.21 in 1975.
81 Moss, op. cit., p. 13.
82 Ravenhill, op. cit., p. 67.
83 *Africa Confidential*, 9, 26 April 1968, p. 8.
84 Quoted in Ravenhill, op. cit., p. 68.
85 The EDF was allowed to supplement EIB resources through provision of risk capital by way of temporary purchase of shares in AASM industrial projects (ibid).
86 *Africa Confidential*, 6, 17 March 1967, p. 8.
87 Ibid.

4 THE EMERGENCE OF LOMÉ AND ITS INSTITUTIONS, 1973–78

1 *The Courier*, 31, March 1975, p. 4.
2 On Britain's first application and the Gaullist veto see Miriam Camps, *European Unification in the Sixties: From Veto to Crisis*, Oxford: Oxford University Press, 1967. A detailed account of the second round of negotiations in the 1970s is in Simon Z. Young, *Terms of Entry: Negotiations with the European Community 1970–72*, London: Heinemann, 1973.
3 *Keesing's Contemporary Archives*, 27 February–6 March 1971, p. 24461.
4 The "Economic Assessment" White Paper was published on 10 February 1970, quoted in *Keesing's Contemporary Archives*, 27 Feb.–6 March 1971, pp. 24463–4.
5 *Keesing's Contemporary Archives*, 27 Feb.–6 March 1971, p. 24466.
6 HMSO, "The United Kingdom and the European Communities", presented to Parliament by the Prime Minister, July 1971, p. 29.
7 Cf. Susan Strange, *Sterling and British Policy*, London: Oxford University Press/RIIA, 1971.
8 On the formation of the postwar international economic regime, see the classic study by Richard N. Gardner, *Sterling–Dollar Diplomacy in Current Perspective: The Origins of Our International Economic Order*, New York: Columbia University, 1980. Cf. Andrew Walter, *World Power and World Money: The Role of Hegemony*

and International Monetary Order, New York and London: Harvester Wheatsheaf, 1993.

9 John Ravenhill, *Collective Clientelism: The Lomé Conventions and North–South Relations*, New York: Columbia University Press, p. 5.

10 *Africa Confidential*, 11 (12), 12 June 1970, p. 2.

11 Cf. Graham Bird and Tony Killick, "Balance of Payments Management: The IMF and the Third World", in Loukas Tsoukalis (ed.), *The Political Economy of International Money*, London: London: Sage/RIIA, 1985, pp. 233–259.

12 *Africa Confidential*, 12 June 1970, p. 2.

13 *Africa Confidential*, 12 June 1970, p. 2.

14 On the evolution of Nigerian foreign policy, see Olajide Aluko, *Essays on Nigerian Foreign Policy*, London: Allen & Unwin, 1981.

15 *The Courier*, 31, March 1975, p. 4.

16 Ravenhill, op. cit., p. 82.

17 *The Courier*, 32, March 1975, p. 5.

18 *Africa Contemporary Record*, 1974–75, pp. A15–A21.

19 *Africa Confidential*, 14 (18), 7 September 1973, p. 8.

20 It is not clear why Senegal took such a strong position on the question of reciprocity. It could be assumed that she was most probably acting under the influence of France, which within the EC had stood strongly against its abrogation.

21 Ruth Weiss, "Africa and the EEC", *African Contemporary Record*, 1974–75, p. A17.

22 *The Courier*, 31, March 1975, p. 5.

23 The forty-six states comprised the original eighteen, with Mauritius, and twenty-seven other countries: The Bahamas, Barbados, Botswana, Burundi, Cameroon, Côte d'Ivoire, Equatorial Guinea, Ethiopia, Fiji, Gabon, Gambia, Ghana, Guinea, Guinea Bissau, Grenada, Guyana, Jamaica, Kenya, Lesotho, Liberia, Madagascar, Malawi, Mali, Mauritania, Mauritius, Niger, Nigeria, Rwanda, Senegal, Sierra Leone, Somalia, Sudan, Swaziland, Tanzania, Togo, Tonga, Trinidad & Tobago, Uganda, Upper Volta (now Burkina Faso), Western Samoa, Zaire, Zambia and four French Overseas Territories.

24 The Centre for Industrial Development, with its headquarters in Brussels, is best known by its French abbreviation. With several regional antennae or links in the ACP states, it has operated chiefly as an information centre for European investors.

25 *The Courier*, 31, March 1975, p. 22.

26 Ibid., p. 23.

27 Ibid.

28 *The Courier*, 32, March 1975, p. 25.

29 EC Commission, *The European Community and Rural Development*, Brussels, DE 62, January 1990, p. 6.

30 Ibid.

31 *The Courier*, 31, March 1975, p. 37.

32 Comité des Représentants Permanents.

33 Altiero Spinelli, quoted in Werner J. Feld, *The European Community in World Affairs: Economic Power and Political Influence*, Boulder, Col.: Westview Press, 1983, p. 42.

34 Juliet Lodge, "EC Policymaking: Institutional Considerations", in Juliet Lodge (edn), *The European Community and the Challenge of the Future*, London: Pinter Publishers, 1989, pp. 26–57.

35 Sources in Brussels say that Commissioner Marin never really wanted the DGVIII post, as he had his eyes on a more prestigious department.
36 Philip Raikes, *Modernising Hunger: Famine, Food Surplus and Farm Policy in the EEC and Africa*, London: James Currey and Heinemann, 1988, pp. 170–202.
37 André Staner, "The EDF Committee: Twelve Years' Work", *The Courier*, 36, March–April 1976, pp. 38–43.
38 Ibid., pp. 38–39.
39 Ibid.
40 Ibid.
41 EC Commission, *Ten Years of Lomé: A Record of EEC–ACP Partnership, 1976 to 1985*, Brussels, September 1986, p. 63.
42 ACP Secretariat, "Interim Report on the Review of the Georgetown Agreement", internal doc. ACP/27/036/91, Brussels, November 1991.
43 The Caribbean and Pacific states have always complained of a pro-African EC bias.
44 Edwin W. Carrington, "The ACP Secretariat", *The Courier*, 102, March–April, 1987, pp. 12–16.
45 Until February 1985 there was also a Deputy Secretary-General, a post which was abolished to cut down costs.
46 ACP Secretariat, *Groupe D'États de l'Afrique, des Caraïbes et du Pacifique (ACP): Quinze Années de Coopération ACP–CEE et Intra ACP*, Brussels, 6 June 1990.
47 Feld, op. cit., p. 36. The ECSC had a representative of ambassadorial rank in London until 1972 when Britain became a member of the Community. President Charles de Gaulle was known to have been opposed to the ceremonies and pageantry which the Commission President, Walter Hallstein, encouraged when receiving the credentials of new envoys to the Community.
48 ACP Secretariat, "Report of the ad hoc Committee to Examine Matters Relating to the Strength and Operation of the ACP Secretariat", internal doc. ACP/2641/82, Brussels, 31 March 1982.
49 Ibid., p. 15.
50 ACP Secretariat, Brussels, internal doc. ACP/41/051/88, 1988.
51 ACP Secretariat, "Recommendations from the Establishment and Finance Sub-Committee on the Strengthening of the Manpower of the Secretariat in the Framework of the Negotiations of the Next Convention", internal doc. ACP/41/051/88/ Rev. 2, Brussels, 18 November 1988, p. 3.
52 ACP Secretariat, "A Suggested Approach to the Negotiations for a Successor Convention to Lomé", Brussels, internal doc. 003/82/NEG, 11 October 1982. As a guide to EC it was thoroughly inadequate.
53 ACP sources, Brussels.
54 *The Courier*, 97, May–June 1986, p. iv.
55 Stevens, op. cit., p. 36.
56 For a general overview of the performance of Lomé II, see Michael Dolan, "Lomé II: The Evolution of Relations between the European Community and the ACP Countries", in Werner J. Feld (ed.), *Western Europe's Global Reach: Regional Cooperation and Worldwide Aspirations*, New York and Oxford: Pergamon Press, 1979, pp. 54–79.
57 Christopher Stevens and Ann Weston, "Trade Diversification: Has Lomé Helped?" in Christopher Stevens (ed.) *The EEC and The Third World*, ODI, 1984, pp. 27–61.
58 Ibid., p. 41.
59 Stevens and Weston (op. cit., p. 55), maintain that neither problem has proved to be a major constraint. Their argument that the application of protectionism

bilaterally is of lesser consequence than if it were applied on an EC-wide basis remains unconvincing. International trade practices show that the threat of protectionism is often almost as effective as its actual imposition.

60 Ibid., p. 54.

61 Sandy Bullock, "Structural Adjustment and Conditionality in European Community Aid to Sub-Saharan Africa: The Record of Lomé III and the Prospects of Lomé IV", MA thesis, School of Development Studies, University of East Anglia, 1989, quoted in Trevor W. Parfitt and Sandy Bullock, "The Prospects for a New Lomé Convention: Structural Adjustment or Structural Transformation?", *Review of African Political Economy*, July–August 1992, pp. 105–116.

62 Marjorie Lister, *The European Community and the Developing World*, Aldershot: Avebury, 1988, p. 138.

63 The Court of Auditors' Reports, 1981 and 1982 quoted in Lister, op. cit., p. 148.

64 Isebill V. Gruhn, "Lomé Convention Renegotiations: Litmus Test for North–South Discussions", in Robert Boardman, *et al.* (eds) *Europe, Africa, and Lomé III*, Lanham: University Press of America, 1985, pp. 23–42.

65 Adrian Hewitt, "The Lomé Conventions: Myth and Substance of the 'Partnership of Equals'", in Margaret Cornell (ed.), *Europe and Africa: Issues in Post-Colonial Relations*, London: ODI: 1981, pp. 21–45.

66 John Ravenhill, "Europe and Africa: An Essential Continuity", in Robert Boardman *et al.* (eds), *Europe, Africa and Lomé III*, Lanham: University Press of America, 1985, pp. 35–57.

5 LOMÉ, POLICY DIALOGUE AND STRUCTURAL ADJUSTMENT

1 On the role of the EC Parliament in European policy-making, see Francis Jacobs and Richard Corbett, *The European Parliament*, London: Longmans, 1990.

2 ODI\IDS, *EEC and the Third World: A Survey 2,*, London: Hodder & Stoughton, 1982, p. 10.

3 European Commission, *European Parliament Resolution on Hunger in the World*, Brussels, September 1980.

4 Cf. Margaret P. Karns and K. A. Mingst (eds), *The United States and Multilateral Institutions: Patterns of Changing Instrumentality and Influence*, New York: Routledge, 1992.

5 EC *Resolution on Hunger in the World.*

6 For a concise account of the relationship between agricultural policy failure and African underdevelopment, see Uma Lele, "Comparative Advantage and Structural Transformation: A Review of Africa's Development Experience", in Gustav Ranis and T. Paul Schultz (eds), *The State of Development Economics: Progress and Perspectives*, Oxford: Basil Blackwell, 1990, pp. 187–221.

7 Cf. Teresa Hayter and Catherine Watson, *Aid: Rhetoric and Reality*, London and Sydney: Pluto, 1985.

8 On the problem of surplus capacity in OECD countries in the early 1980s, see Susan Strange and Roger Tooze (eds), *The Politics of International Surplus Capacity*, London: Allen & Unwin, 1982.

9 ODI\IDS, *EEC and the Third World: A Survey 2*, London: Hodder & Stoughton, 1982, pp. 3–4.

10 European Commission, *Towards a Plan of Action to Combat World Hunger*, COM (81) 560 final, Brussels, 5 October 1981.

11 Ibid.
12 This appeared to have been an "open-ended" approach to conditionality, as it did not provide precise criteria against which reforms in ACP countries could measured.
13 This phrase was used perhaps in reference to the Basilica of Our Lady of Peace at Yamossoukrou, constructed at the cost of over US$300 million by late President Houphouet Boigny of Côte d'Ivoire.
14 Quoted in Christopher Stevens "Renegotiating Lomé", in Christopher Stevens (ed.), *The EEC and the Third World*, London: ODI, 1984, p. 19.
15 Cf. Ernst B. Haas, *The Uniting of Europe*, London: Stevens, 1958.
16 Pisani, op. cit.
17 Ibid.
18 ODI, "Prospects for the Next Convention", op. cit., p. 10.
19 For an insider account of the evolution of EC food aid policy, see Walter Kennes, "The European Community and Food Security", *IDS Bulletin*, 21 (3), 1990, pp. 67–71.
20 Michael Lipton, "African Agricultural Development: The EEC's New Role", *Development Policy Review*, 1, 1983, pp. 1–21.
21 Cf. Philip Raikes, *Modernising Hunger: Famine, Food Surplus and Farm Policy in the EEC and Africa*, London: James Currey & Heinemann,1988.
22 Adrian Hewitt, "Export Earning: the Fostering of the Development of the ACP States through the Stabilisation of their Import Capacity." Report to the Commonwealth Secretariat (mimeo), Overseas Development Institute, London, February 1984, p. 15.
23 Christopher Stevens, "The EEC's Year, 1984", *Africa Contemporary Record*, xviii, 1984–85, p. B167.
24 Tony Hill, "Whither Lomé? A Review of Lomé III Negotiations", *Third World Quarterly*, 7 (3), July 1985, pp. 661–681.
25 European Commission, "Commission Communication to the Council on Guidelines for the Forthcoming ACP–EEC Negotiations", COM (83) 153 final, Brussels, 1983, p. v.
26 Christopher Stevens, *Negotiating Lomé III: An Example of North–South Bargaining*, IDS Discussion Paper, 215, May 1986, pp. 6–7.
27 ACP Committee of Ambassadors, "Memorandum on the Position of the ACP Group in Its Future Negotiations with the European Communities", ACP Secretariat, Brussels, ACP/0023/83/ NEG (Rev. 2), August 1983.
28 ACP Committee of Ambassadors, op. cit., p. 39.
29 The OAU/ECA, *Lagos Plan of Action for the Economic Development of Africa, 1980–2000*, Geneva: International Institute for Labour Studies, 1979.
30 ACP Committee of Ambassadors, op. cit., pp. 48–50.
31 Claudine Déschouwer *et al.*, *Lomé III: 1985–1990*, Brussels: Bureau d'Informations Européennes, July 1988, p. 20.
32 Christopher Stevens, "The Lessons of Lomé III", *Lomé Briefing*, 2, September 1988.
33 "The Adjustment Process in Africa: A European Council Resolution", *The Courier*, 111, September–October 1988, p. 73.
34 Ibid.
35 Ibid.
36 Trevor Parfitt and Sandy Bullock, "The Prospects for a New Lomé Convention: Structural Adjustment or Structural Transformation?", *Review of African Political Economy*, August 1989.

37 Dieter Frisch, "Adjustment, Development and Equity", *The Courier*, 111, September–October 1988, pp. 67–72.
38 Ibid.
39 Ibid.
40 For a detailed analysis of the Lomé IV negotiations, see John Ravenhill, "When Weakness Is Strength: The Lomé IV Negotiations", (mimeo), to appear in I. William Zartman (ed.), *Europe and Africa: the New Phase*, Princeton, NJ: University of Princeton Press, chapter 4.
41 Myriam Vander Stichele, *Lomé Briefing*, 14, January–February 1990.
42 Ibid.
43 Ravenhill, op. cit., p. 2.
44 Ibid., p. 5.
45 Juliet Lodge, "The Single European Act and the New Legislative Cooperation Procedure: A Critical Analysis", *Journal of European Integration*, 11, 1987, pp. 5–28.
46 Ibid., p. 7.
47 Ibid., p. 9.
48 Edgard Pisani, "Warning", *Lomé Briefing*, 2, September 1988.
49 ACP Secretariat, "Memorandum on ACP Guidelines for the Negotiations for a Fourth ACP/EEC Convention", ACP internal doc. 00/012/88/ NEG Rev. 2, Brussels, 4 October 1988.
50 *Financial Times*, 29 November 1989.
51 ACP Secretariat, *Memorandum on Guidelines for the Negotiations for a Fourth ACP/EEC Convention*, Brussels, 4 October 1988.
52 Ibid., p. 170.
53 Ibid.
54 ACP Secretariat, "The Framework for Negotiations: Debt and Structural Adjustment and Investment", ACP Negotiating Group 6, internal doc. ACP/81/006/89, Brussels, 17 May 1989, p. 6.
55 Ibid.
56 Ibid., p. 1.
57 *Financial Times*, 28 November 1989.
58 Financial resources under previous Conventions:
Lomé I (1975–80) ECU3,450 million
Lomé II (1980–85) ECU5,600 million
Lomé III (1985–90) ECU8,500 million, of which ECU7,400 million through the EDF
59 The debt question is discussed in the next chapter.
60 EC Commission, "Progress Report on the Community's Involvement in the Structural Adjustment Process in ACP states", Communication of the Commission to the Council, internal doc. CAB IV/259/91 EN, Brussels, 1991, p. 6.
61 EC Commission (1991), op. cit.
62 Ibid., p. 3.
63 Peter Landymore, "Structural Adjustment: the European Community's Approach", *The Crown Agents' Review*, April 1990.
64 Moore (untitled notes of a speech), p. 5.
65 Standard Bank and Fund programmes have tended to neglect this aspect, with the resultant effect of leakages such as smuggling of petroleum products from Nigeria and of maize from Zambia to neighbouring countries.
66 EC Commission (1991), op. cit.
67 Ibid., p. 15.

68 Cf. Paul Collier, "Africa's External Economic Relations: 1960–90", *African Affairs*, 90, 1991, pp. 339–356.
69 ACP Council of Ministers, "Report of the Commission on the Implementation of Programming and Structural Adjustment Provisions of the Fourth Lomé Convention". Report of the Article 193 Committee, Brussels, 3 May 1991, doc. ACP/81/047/91, p. 35.
70 Christopher Stevens and Tony Killick, "The EC and Structural Adjustment", in Renée Prendergast and Hans W. Singer (eds), *Development Perspectives for the 1990s*, London: Macmillan, 1991, pp. 91–116.
71 EC Commission sources.
72 Ibid.
73 *The Courier*, 121, May–June 1990, p. xii.
74 Manuel Marin quoted in *The Courier*, 128, July–August 1991, p. 7.
75 Ibid.
76 EC Commission (1991) op. cit., p. 9.
77 Based on an analysis of fifty-one Structural Adjustment Loans (SALs) and Sectoral Adjustment Loans (SECALs) in fifteen LDCs, of which the SSA countries were: Cote d'Ivoire, Ghana, Kenya, Malawi and Zambia. There were a total of 504 legal conditions in the fifty-one loans that were analysed.
78 Interview, DGVIII, Berlaymont, January 1992.
79 Michael Laidler, "Programming Lomé IV", *The Courier*, 128, July–August 1991, pp. 8–10.
80 See Christopher Stevens and Tony Killick, "Development Co-operation and Structural Adjustment: The Issues for Lomé IV", London and Dublin: ODI and Trocaire, Centre for Development Research, 1989.
81 *The Courier*, 128, July–August 1991, pp. 6–7.
82 Parfitt and Bullock, op. cit., p. 111.
83 Ibid.
84 Article 245 of Lomé IV.
85 EC Commission, 1991, p. 13.
86 EC Commission, 1991, p. 14.
87 Representatives of ACP/EEC Economic and Social Interest Groups, "Final Declaration on Structural Adjustment: Its Economic, Social and Regional Dimensions and the Role of the Economic and Social Interest Groups", under the auspices of the EC Economic and Social Committee, Brussels, 4 December 1991, ACP internal doc. D/OU/ET/mg/vh, 9 December 1991.
88 World Bank, *Sub-Saharan Africa: From Crisis to Sustainable Growth*, Washington, DC: The World Bank, 1989.
89 The Bank cited the examples of Mauritius and Botswana, where openness and democracy have been correlates of economic growth.
90 Cf. Arturo Israel, *Institutional Development: Incentives and Performance*, Baltimore: Johns Hopkins University Press, 1990.
91 Cf. Peter Anyang' Nyong'o, "Political Instability and the Prospects for Democracy in Africa", *African Development*, XIII (1), 1988, pp. 71–86; Thandika Mkandawire, "Debates: Comments on Democracy and Political Instability", *African Development*, XIII (3), 1988, pp. 77–87.
92 Laidler, op. cit., pp. 8–10.
93 In 1976 the EC found itself in the embarrassing position of having to continue its aid programmes to Uganda and Equatorial Guinea, where there had been gross violations of human rights. The Council, however, issued a special release condemning human rights abuses in both countries and urging re-channelling of aid directly to the population so as not to be seen to be supporting the

regimes in power. Cf. Marjorie Lister, *The European Community and the Developing World*, Aldershot: Avebury, 1988.

94 Cf. Timothy M. Shaw, "EEC–ACP Interactions and Images as Re-definitions of Eurafrica: Exemplary and/or Exploitative?", *Journal of Common Market Studies*, 18 (12), December 1979.

95 Article 5 of the Fourth Lomé Convention.

96 Cf. John Vincent, *Human Rights and International Relations*, Cambridge: Cambridge University Press, 1986.

97 Manuel Marin, "Democracy Cannot Be Imposed From Outside", *The Courier*, 128, July–August 1991, pp. 50–51.

98 Cf. ACP-EEC Joint Assembly, "Motion for a Resolution on Political Detainees in Malawi", by Mrs Ewing *et al.*, Port Moresby, 7 March 1990.

99 Giovanni Bersani, "Human Rights: The Joint Assembly's Experience", *Lomé Briefing*, 13, December 1989.

6 EUROPE AND THE AFRICAN EXTERNAL DEBT BURDEN

1 The International "debt strategy" has been considered a success in terms of having shielded the commercial banks and the global financial system from the catastrophes that had been predicted. Cf. Masood Ahmed and Laurence Summers, "A Tenth Anniversary of the Debt Crisis", *Finance and Development*, September 1990 (29), pp. 2–5; *The Economist*, "The Disaster That Didn't Happen', 12 September 1992, pp. 23–26. On the continuing difficulties of heavily indebted countries in Africa and Latin America, see Stephany Griffith-Jones and Rolph van der Hoeven, *Debt: The Unwanted Heritage of Today's Children*, Sussex: IDS Discussion Paper 280, November 1990.

2 For the Asian and Latin American countries, the path to rapid industrialization in the 1970s was seen in terms of access to foreign capital to finance import-substitution strategies. Consequently, countries such as Mexico, South Korea and Brazil incurred huge foreign debts at commercial and variable rates of interest. On the development strategies of the NICs, see Stephan Haggard, *Pathways from the Periphery: The Politics of Growth in the Newly-Industrialising Countries*, Ithaca and London: Cornell University Press, 1990.

3 On the dynamic of North–South debt and adjustment bargaining, see Thomas Biersteker (ed.), *Dealing with Debt: International Financial Negotiations and Adjustment Bargaining*, Boulder, Col.: Westview Press, 1993.

4 The World Bank, *World Debt Tables 1990–91*, Washington, DC, 1990.

5 SSA debts did not include the debts of countries such as Angola, which at this time did not report their debt data to the World Bank. They were grouped with "Other Developing Countries".

6 World Bank, *World Development Report*, Washington, DC, 1991.

7 Ibid.

8 Philip Ndegwa, "Critical Issues for Africa in the Eighties: External Indebtedness", Uppsala: Scandinavian Institute for African Studies (mimeo) undated, pp. 5–8.

9 For a general analysis of the evolution of the LDC debt crisis, see David F. Lomax, *The Developing Country Debt Crisis*, London: Macmillan, 1986; Peter Nunnenkamp, *The International Debt Crisis of the Third World: Consequences for the World Economy*, Brighton: Harvester Wheatsheaf, 1986; and Miles Kahler, "Politics and International Debt: Explaining the Crisis", in Miles Kahler (ed.),

The Politics of International Debt, Ithaca and London: Cornell University Press, 1986, pp. 11–36. The particular case of Latin America is comprehensively examined in Stephany Griffith-Jones and Osvaldo Sunkel, *Debt and Development Crises in Latin America: The End of an Illusion*, Oxford: Clarendon Press, 1986. For a critical analysis of the African case, see Trevor W. Parfitt and Stephen P. Riley, *The African Debt Crisis*, London and New York: Routledge, 1989.

10 Cf. Manuel Pastor, "Latin America, the Debt Crisis, and the International Monetary Fund", *Latin American Perspectives*, 16 (60), 1989, pp. 790–110.

11 According to them, the "ability to repay interest and capital depends on whether foreign loans are invested productively so that the profits from the projects so financed and growth rate of the GDP enable the country to earn the funds needed to service its debts. . . . Foreign capital ought to be invested so as to earn enough foreign exchange to meet interest and principal payments". Peter Korner *et al.*, *The IMF and the Debt Crisis: A Guide to the Third World's Dilemmas*, London: Zed Books, 1987, p. 26.

12 For an interesting study on the causes of the African debt based on a regression analysis, see Asayehgn Desta, "Africa's External Debt in Perspective", *Journal of African Studies*, Spring/Summer, 15 (1&2), 1988, pp. 23–31.

13 Exchange rates volatility, owing to the collapse of the Bretton Woods system, was also a major source of financial difficulty for LDCs at this time. See Graham Bird and Tony Killick, "Balance of Payments Management: The IMF and the Third World", in Loukas Tsoukalis (ed.), *The Political Economy of International Money: In Search of a New Order*, London: Sage/RIIA, 1985, pp. 233–60.

14 Parfitt and Riley, op. cit., p. 2.

15 Bertrand Schneider (ed.), *Africa Facing Its Priorities*: The Club of Rome Cooperation for Development Series, vol. 7, London: Cassell, 1988, p. 36.

16 See Susan George, *A Fate Worse Than Debt*, London: Penguin Books, 1988, pp. 30–46.

17 Parfitt and Riley, op. cit., p. 3.

18 Schneider, op. cit., p. 38.

19 Ibid., p. 43.

20 Parfitt and Riley, op. cit., pp. 190–191.

21 Those who cite Mobutu's Zaire as an archetype of the corrupt state in Africa often forget that this ignoble regime was almost wholly installed and maintained by Western policy. French and Belgian forces have always been on hand to defend Mobutu each time organized opposition movements have attempted to overthrow him. Cf. Thomas M. Callaghy, *The State–Society Struggle: Zaire in Comparative Perspective*, New York: Columbia University Press, 1984; and Winsome J. Leslie, *The World Bank and Structural Transformation in Developing Countries: The Case of Zaire*, Boulder and London: Lynne Rienner Publishers, 1987.

22 Schneider, op. cit., pp. 45–46.

23 On the issue of a debt repayment ceiling, some countries, notably Zambia and Nigeria, did impose a certain limit on the percentage of their foreign earnings which they were prepared to commit to debt-servicing.

24 Tony Hodges, "OAU Urges 10-Year Debt Moratorium", *Africa Recovery*, December 1987, pp. 2–6.

25 Ibid., p. 2.

26 Ibid., p. 1.

27 On the earlier Extended Fund Facility, see Stephan Haggard, "The Politics of

Adjustment: Lessons from the IMF's Extended Fund Facility", in Kahler, op. cit., pp. 157–186.

28 Some critics would see this as further evidence that the United States influences such arrangements in favour of its allies in the LDCs. It is a well-known fact, for example, that Mobutu's Zaire has been the United States' most reliable ally in the SSA region.

29 Overseas Development Institute, "Recent Initiatives on Developing Country Debt", Briefing Paper, April 1990, p. 4.

30 See Eduard H. Brau, "External Debt Management in the African Context", in Gerald K. Helleiner (ed.), *Africa and the IMF*: Papers at a symposium held in Nairobi, Kenya, 13–15 May 1986, Washington, DC: The IMF, 1986, pp. 160–180.

31 The group of 15–17 highly indebted countries were not formally defined under the Baker Plan. But it is clear that the emphasis was largely on the Latin American countries. Another classification of debtor countries is the group of twenty-eight Low-Income Debt-Distressed sub-Saharan African Countries which are eligible for the loans and which have a debt service to export ratio of at least 25 per cent. This group was the focus of the Toronto Agreement and Special Programme of Assistance. In 1989 the World Bank came out with a new classification based on ratios of debts to exports, GNP, and debt service to exports and interest payments to exports. Two most indebted groups were classified as (a) Severely Indebted Middle-Income Countries (SIMICs), which includes Congo, Côte d'Ivoire and Senegal from the SSA region; and (b) the Severely Indebted Low-Income Countries (SILICs), which include Benin, Burundi, Comoros, Equatorial Guinea, Ghana, Guinea, Guinea-Bissau, Kenya, Liberia, Madagascar, Malawi, Mali, Mauritania, Mozambique, Niger, Nigeria, São Tomé, Sierra Leone, Somalia, Sudan, Tanzania, Togo, Zaire and Zambia.

32 Rainer Erbe, "Has the Baker Plan Failed?", *Intereconomics*, September/October 1986, p. 214.

33 Foreign and Commonwealth Office, "International Debt", Background Brief, London, November 1990.

34 On the shortcomings of the Brady Plan, see Paul Gunther-Schmidt, "How to Pay for the Debt – Coping With the Third World's Crisis", *Intereconomics*, January/February 1990, pp. 6–12. On the attitudes of the commercial banks to the Plan, see Walther Otremba, "New Debt Strategies after the Brady Plan", *Intereconomics*, September/October 1989, pp. 241–245. Cf. Wolfgang Spieles, "Debt-Equity Swaps and the Heavily Indebted Countries", *Intereconomics*, May/June 1987, pp. 120–124.

35 Otremba, op. cit., p. 241.

36 Foreign and Commonwealth Office, op. cit. See also Central Office of Information, *Britain and International Debt Relief*, London, June 1990.

37 The Trinidad Terms were to be applicable to countries with a GNP per capita of less than US$600, and who spend up to 25 per cent of their export earnings on debt-servicing.

38 Overseas Development Institute, "Recent Initiatives on Developing Country Debt", Briefing Paper, London, April 1990.

39 Vincent Cable wrote a position paper on Lomé and the debt issue which represented one of the inputs from the Commonwealth Secretariat to the ACP Secretariat in preparation for the Lomé IV negotiations. See his "ACP Debt and the EC: The Role of the Lomé Convention", Economic Affairs Division, Commonwealth Secretariat, Marlborough House, London, (mimeo) undated.

40 *The Courier*, 89, January–February, 1984, p. 45.

41 Cable, op. cit., p. 15.
42 Ibid.
43 Article 188 of Lomé III did provide for greater flexibility in the use of financial disbursements. It allowed for the reorientation of National Indicative Programmes so that funds could be used for "sector development and import programmes" such as raw materials, spare parts, fertilizers and other vital imports.
44 Overseas Development Institute, "Negotiating the Fourth Lomé Convention", Briefing Paper, London: October 1989, p. 3.
45 EC Commission, *Lomé III: Mid-Term Review, 1986–88*, Brussels, July 1989, pp. 7–10.
46 EC Commission, "Final Report on the Special Community Programme to Help Highly Indebted Low-Income Countries in sub-Saharan Africa", Brussels, internal doc. CABIV/69/91–EN, 16 April 1991, p. 1.
47 France's political interests in Benin may have been a major factor in the decision to give adjustment support even when the country had not reached an agreement with the IFIs.
48 EC Commission, 1991, op. cit., p. 4.
49 Ibid.
50 ACP sources, Brussels.
51 Ibid.
52 The EC Commission was also involved in negotiating with striking workers during the long-drawn out strikes in the country (Commission sources, Brussels, January 1992).
53 EC Commission, "Final Report on the Special Community Programme to Help Highly Indebted Low-Income Countries in Sub-Saharan Africa", op. cit. p. 16.
54 Christopher Stevens, "The Lessons from Lomé III", *Lomé Briefing*, 2, September 1988.
55 *The Courier*, 111, Septemper–October 1988. The summary of the seminar proceedings are to be found in the ACP Secretariat internal doc. ACP/82/002/88, op. cit.
56 See ACP Secretariat, "Memorandum on ACP Guidelines for the Lomé IV Negotiations", internal doc. ACP/00/012/88, Brussels, 4 October 1988.
57 *The Courier*, 120, March–April 1990, p. 15.
58 Ibid., p. 9.
59 Manuel Marin, "Writing off the ACP debt to the EEC", *The Courier* 125, January–February 1991, p. 9.
60 The EIB now rivals the World Bank as an international financial institution. Like the Bank, it borrows considerably from the capital market and is consequently heavily dependent on its revolving loans. It is therefore quite understandable that it could not be part of the ACP debt cancellation arrangement.
61 The EBRD itself seemed to have begun its operations in London under rather inauspicious circumstances, with media reports of improprieties and mismanagement, culminating in the resignation of its first President, Jacques Attali, a former policy advisor to President François Mitterrand. ACP spokesmen have often drawn attention to the proposed ACP Trade and Investment Bank under Lomé II which fell through due to lack of political support from the Community. See United Nations, *Recommendations for the Establishment of a Trade and Investment Bank for the African, Caribbean and Pacific Group of States: Final Report of the Meeting of Experts,* New York and Brussels: United Nations Department of Technical Cooperation for Development, March 1979.

62 He has stated that, "When Lomé IV was signed, I also personally committed myself to looking at new ways of solving the debt problem." See *The Courier*, 120, p. 13.
63 Ibid.
64 This argument is rather tenuous, given that most SSA debts are public and therefore within the powers of the EC Council of Ministers and their governments.

7 ECONOMIC DECLINE AND POLICY CHOICE IN ZAMBIA

1 Arab and Portuguese merchants were already in the area by the late sixteenth century.
2 Marcia M. Burdette, *Zambia between Two Worlds*, Boulder, Col.: Westview Press, 1988. Perhaps the definitive work on the career of Cecil Rhodes is the one by Robert I. Rotberg (with Miles F. Shore), *The Founder: Cecil Rhodes and the Pursuit of Power*, New York: Oxford University Press, 1988.
3 For an account of the activities of mining companies in Zambia, see Simon Cunningham, *The Copper Industry in Zambia: Foreign Mining Companies in a Developing Country*, New York: Praeger, 1981.
4 Burdett, op. cit., p. 23.
5 Robert I. Rotberg, *The Rise of Nationalism in Central Africa: The Making of Malawi and Zambia 1873–1964*, Cambridge, Mass.: Harvard University Press, 1965.
6 It has been estimated that by 1963 Northern Rhodesia did sustain a net loss of UK£97 million to the other two territories of the Federation. Andrew Roberts, *A History of Zambia*, London: Macmillan, 1976, p. 214.
7 Robert H. Bates, *Patterns of Uneven Development: Causes and Consequences in Zambia*, Monograph Series in World Affairs, University of Denver, Colorado, 1974.
8 In colonial times the Lozis were governed under the so-called Protectorate of Barotseland, under their Kings, the *Litungas*. The *Litunga* had a cabinet consisting of a Prime Minister, the *Ngambela*, and advisers who were known as the *Indunas*. During the era of decolonization the Lozi leadership had hoped that they would separate from the rest of the country and would have the Caprivi Strip in South West Africa as part of an independent Barotseland. During constitutional talks with the British government in London in early 1964, Kaunda had made an undertaking in the presence of the Lozi King, Sir Mwana Wina Lewanika, not to interfere with the traditions and customs of the Lozis after independence. Kaunda was later to enrage the Lozi leadership when the Litunga Ilute Yeta was made a member of the UNIP Central Committee, a move which signalled the erosion of their regional political autonomy. See *Africa Confidential*, 31 (22), 9 November 1990.
9 Cherry Gertzel, Caroline Baylies and Morris Szeftel, *The Dynamics of the One-Party State in Zambia*, Manchester: Manchester University Press, 1984, p. 15.
10 Kenneth D. Kaunda, *Towards a Great and Prosperous Zambia,* Address to the 16th National Council of the United National Independence Party, Mulungushi Hall, 14 December 1981, Lusaka: Government Printer, 1981.
11 Henry S. Meebelo, *Main Currents of Zambian Humanist Thought*, Lusaka: Oxford University Press, 1973, p. 39.
12 Cf. Paul A. Mwaipanya, *African Humanism and National Development*, Washington, DC: University Press of America, 1984.

13 Benedict V. Mtshali *et al.*, *Zambia and the World: Essays on Problems Relating to Zambia's Foreign Policy*, Lusaka: University of Zambia School of Humanities and Social Sciences, September 1970.

14 After the Universal Declaration of Independence (UDI) in November 1965, the Rhodesia railway was no longer a reliable route for Zambia. Destabilization from the south involved training and arming of dissident groups in south-western Zambia as well as direct military attacks on bridges, roads and refugee camps. See Republic of Zambia, *Twenty Years of Independence 1964–1984*, Lusaka: State House, 1984, p. 8.

15 Richard Hall, *The High Price of Principles: Kaunda and the White South*, Harmondsworth: Penguin, 1973.

16 John Clarke, *Zambia: Debt and Poverty*, Oxford: Oxfam Publications, 1989, p. 9.

17 The Tazara rail project was executed through an aid agreement between Zambia, Tanzania and the People's Republic of China in 1967, after Britain and other Western countries had declined to support the project on the grounds that it was technically and economically unviable.

18 SADCC emerged out of the group of front-line states comprising Zambia, Angola, Tanzania, Mozambique and Botswana. In April 1980 they were joined by Zimbabwe, Swaziland, Lesotho and Malawi to form the nine SADCC members. Namibia and South Africa have recently become members. Apart from direct bilateral aid to the member states, the EC also gives regional assistance to SADCC.

19 In 1970–71 President Kaunda was OAU Chairman. During his tenure he sought to make the Organization a genuine instrument of African solidarity, which he saw as a necessary precondition in the liberation of the continent from the remaining vestiges of colonialism.

20 Biafra was also recognized by Tanzania and Côte d'Ivoire.

21 Zambia was elected into the Security Council from 1 January to 30 December 1970 and from 1 January 1979 to 31 December 1980.

22 In 1966 Kaunda threatened to pull his country out of the Commonwealth in protest against Britain's reticence to press on the Ian Smith regime in Southern Rhodesia to revoke UDI.

23 Cf. Lionel Cliffe, "Zambia in the Context of Southern Africa", in Centre for African Studies, University of Edinburgh, *The Evolving Structure of Zambian Society*, Proceedings of a Seminar, 30–31 May 1980, pp. 240–261.

24 Burdette, op. cit., p. 157.

25 Muna Ndulo, "Domestic Participation in Mining in Zambia", in Ben Turok (ed.), *Development in Zambia: A Reader*, London: Zed Books, 1979, pp. 49–69.

26 The twenty-five companies that complied were adequately compensated and some of the owners were asked to stay on as managers or consultants. See Burdette, op. cit., p. 85.

27 For a comprehensive account of the Mulungushi reforms and the expansion of state participation in the Zambian economy, see Jonathan H Chileshe, *Third World Countries and Development Options: Zambia*, New Delhi: Vikas Publishing House, 1987, pp. 98–144.

28 The outcome of the takeover was the establishment of two major companies, the Roan Consolidated Mines Ltd (RCM), and the Nchanga Consolidated Copper Mines Ltd (NCCM), with the state controlling 51 per cent of the shares in both companies. In early 1970 the Mining Development Corporation (MINDECO) was set up to manage government shares in NCCM and RCM and to act as a watchdog on the mining sector.

29 Burdette, op. cit., p. 89.

30 Conseil Intergouvernemental des Pays Exportateurs de Cuivre.

31 CIPEC, however, was an ineffective organization. Cf. Dorothea Mezger, *Copper in the World Economy*, London: Heinemann, 1979.

32 For an interesting analysis of the politics and economics of Zambia's economic decline by an insider, see Akashambwata Mbikusita-Lewanika, *Milk in a Basket: The Political-Economic Malaise in Zambia*, Lusaka: Zambia Research Foundation, 1990.

33 Clarke, op. cit., p. 7.

34 Ibid.

35 On Zambia's industrialization, see Igor Karmiloff, *Industrialisation in Sub-Saharan Africa: Country Case Study – Zambia*, WP 26, London: ODI (undated).

36 Tony Hodges, "Zambia's Autonomous Adjustment", *Africa Recovery*, 2(2), December 1988, pp. 6–12.

37 Ravi Gulhati, *Impasse in Zambia: the Economics and Politics of Reform*, EDI Analytical Case Studies no. 2, Washington, DC: the World Bank, 1989, p. 3.

38 The others are Mozambique, Sudan, Guinea-Bissau and Somalia.

39 Hodges, op. cit.

40 Mineral export dependence often entails what economists have termed the "Dutch disease", i.e., the long-term negative effects arising from a mineral export boom. The booming sector tends to attract labour as well as capital to itself, thus leading to resource depletion in other sectors of the economy, particularly agriculture. Increases in export revenues lead to increased demand for imports (tradables) as well as for domestically produced consumer items (non-tradables). Such pressures will tend to fuel domestic inflation while forcing up exchange rates. The "Dutch disease" syndrome in Zambia has been analysed by Fons Meijer. See his "Structural Adjustment and Diversification in Zambia", *Development and Change*, 21, 1990, pp. 657–692.

41 Meijer, op. cit., p. 663. For an account of Zambian agricultural development from independence to the current context of economic reform, see Adrian P. Wood *et al.*, *The Dynamics of Agricultural Policy and Reform in Zambia*, Ames: Iowa State University Press, 1990.

42 Gulhati, op. cit., p. 4.

43 Cf. Uma Lele, "Comparative Advantage and Structural Transformation: A Review of Africa's Development Experience", in Gustav Ranis and T. Paul Schultz (eds), *The State of Development Economics: Progress and Perspectives*, Oxford: Basil Blackwell, 1990, pp. 187–221.

44 Ibid., p. 21.

45 Cf. Robert H. Bates, *States and Markets in Tropical Africa*, Berkeley and Los Angeles: University of California Press, 1981.

46 Cf. William Tordoff (ed.), *Politics in Zambia*, Manchester: Manchester University Press, 1974; and Cherry Gertzel (ed.), *The Dynamics of the One-Party State in Zambia*, Manchester: Manchester University Press, 1984.

47 Cf. Julien Freund, *The Sociology of Max Weber*, Harmondsworth: Penguin, 1965.

48 Robert H. Jackson and Carl Rosberg describe Kaunda's Zambia as an example of the "Princely state", in their book, *Personal Rule in Black Africa*, Princeton, NJ: Princeton University Press, 1986.

49 D. M. Shafer, quoted in Thomas Callaghy, "Lost between State and Market: The Politics of Economic Adjustment in Ghana, Zambia, and Nigeria", in Joan M. Nelson (ed.), *Economic Crisis and Policy Choice: The Politics of Adjustment in the Third World*, Princeton, NJ: Princeton University Press, 1990, p. 289.

50 See Richard L. Sklar, *Corporate Power in an African State*, Berkeley: University of

California Press, 1975; Klaas Wöldring (ed.), *Beyond Political Independence: Zambia's Economic Predicament in the 1980s*, Berlin: Mouton, 1984; and Turok, op. cit.

51 Gatian F. Lungu, *Administrative Decentralisation in the Zambian Bureaucracy: an Analysis of Environmental Constraints*, Zambian Papers no. 8, Gweru, Zimbabwe: Mambo Press, 1985; William Tordoff (ed.), *Administration in Zambia*, Manchester: Manchester University Press, 1980. Jeffrey J. Hawkins, Jr has attempted to develop a historical-institutional model of the Zambian political economy using the concept of the "political economic regime". See his "Understanding the Failure of IMF Reform: the Zambian Case", *World Development*, 19 (7), 1991, pp. 839–849.

52 Patrick E. Ollawa, *Participatory Democracy in Zambia*, Devon: Arthur H. Stockwell, 1979, p. 446.

53 Alex B. Chikwanda, "Governance and Economic Development in Sub-Saharan Africa", at the Conference on Governance and Economic Development in Sub-Saharan Africa, sponsored by the World Bank and Queen Elizabeth House, University of Oxford, held at Queen Elizabeth House, Oxford, 2–4 May, 1991, p. 2 (mimeo).

54 Zambia joined the Fund on 23 September 1965, with an initial quota of SDR50 million which was later augmented to SDR270.3 million. See P. D. Ncube *et al.*, "The International Monetary Fund and the Zambian Economy: A Case-Study", in Kjell Havnevik, (ed.), *The IMF and the World Bank in Africa: Conditionality, Impact and Alternatives*, Uppsala: Scandinavian Institute for African Studies, 1987, pp. 127–148.

55 Ibid., p. 130.

56 Ibid., p. 131.

57 Ibid., p. 134.

58 Ibid.

59 Ibid., p. 137.

60 Ibid.

61 Government of Zambia, "Memorandum on the Economic and Financial Policies of Zambia", letter from the Hon. Nalumino Mundia, Prime Minister/Finance Minister of Zambia, to M. Jacques de la Rosière, IMF Managing Director, Lusaka, 25 February 1983, IMF internal doc. EBS/83/67 Supplement 3, 19 April 1983.

62 Ncube *et al.*, op. cit., p. 140.

63 Robert H. Bates and Paul Collier, "The Politics and Economics of Policy Reform in Zambia", Duke University, Department of Political Science, and Centre for the Study of African Economies, University of Oxford, third draft (mimeo), January 1991, p. 22.

64 Ibid.

65 Ibid.

66 Callaghy, "Lost between State and Market", in J. M. Nelson (ed.) *Economic Crisis and Policy Choice: The Politics of Adjustment in the Third World*, Princeton, NJ: Princeton University Press, pp. 292–293.

67 Christopher Allsopp *et al.*, have noted the limitations of these assumptions with regard to Zambia. Given the place of copper in the country's economy, the distributional effects of devaluation are likely to be limited. See their *Zambia Exchange Rate Policy*, Stockholm: SIDA, 1989, p. 33–41.

68 On the role of the financial sector in Zambia's economic reform programme, see Situmbeko Musokotwane, "Structural Adjustment and Financial Institutions in Zambia", Presentation at the Conference on Structural Adjustment in Zambia, Copperbelt University, Kitwe, March 1992 (mimeo).

69 Clarke, op. cit., p. 15.
70 Callaghy, op. cit., p. 297.
71 Ibid.
72 Clarke, op. cit., p. 16.
73 Meijer, op. cit., pp. 678–680.
74 Cf. Dennis Chiwele and Christopher Colclough, "Economic Crisis, Adjustment and the Effectiveness of the Public Sector in Zambia", in Charles Harvey (ed.), *Constraints on the Success of Structural Adjustment in Africa*, London: Macmillan, 1996, pp. 192–209.
75 Callaghy, op. cit., p. 296.
76 Richard Pearce, *Food Consumption and Adjustment in Zambia*, Working Paper No. 2, Food Studies Group, Queen Elizabeth House, Oxford (undated), p. 2.
77 Callaghy, op. cit., p. 296.
78 Ibid.
79 Ibid., p. 297.
80 Ibid., p. 298.
81 President Kaunda accused him publicly of spreading a "smear campaign" to prevent aid donors from continuing their assistance programmes to Zambia. *Africa Contemporary Record*, xix, 1986–87, p. B870.
82 Ibid.
83 *Keesing's Contemporary Archives*, xxxiii, February 1987, p. 34923.
84 Ibid.
85 Andrew Kamya, "Zambia's Exchange Rate Policy in the 1980s", in F. Sumaili and G. Lungwangwa (eds), *Zambia in the 1990s*, Lusaka: The Professors' World Peace Academy, 1991, p. 150.
86 Cf. Akashambwata K. Lewanika and Andrew Kamya, *A Critique of the Dual Exchange Rate System in Zambia*, Occasional Paper no. 2, Lusaka, 1990.
87 Allsopp *et al.* have argued that the auction was a major factor in the Zambian inflationary spiral. Paul Collier and Robert Bates concede that while it did lead to a rise in price levels for some items, owing to the natural effects of "transition from controlled to market-clearing prices", it was, on the whole, disinflationary. They argue that the money supply increases associated with the budget and increases in expenditures were more to blame. See their "The Zambian Auction and Its Aftermath", op. cit.
88 Hodges, "Zambia's Autonomous Adjustment", op. cit., p. 9.
89 Allsopp *et al.*, pp. 62–63.
90 *Africa Recovery*, 2 (4), December 1988, p. 8.
91 Cf. Clarke, op. cit.
92 Conversation with Owen Ben Sichone, Acting Head of the Centre for African Development Studies, University of Lusaka. A Cambridge-trained anthropologist, Dr Sichone did field research among retired mine workers in the Copperbelt. Lusaka, March 1992. Cf. Dennis Chiwele, "Economic Adjustment, the Mining Sector and the Real Wage in Zambia", in Harvey, op. cit., pp. 210–233.
93 On the social impact of the Zambian reform programme, see Clarke, op. cit., pp. 18–37.
94 *Keesing's Contemporary Archives*, xxxi, October 1985, p. 33901.
95 *Keesing's Contemporary Archives*, xxxiii, February 1987, p. 34923.
96 In 1980 the government claimed to have uncovered a coup plot masterminded by prominent Zambian citizens, amongst them, former Junior Minister and Bank of Zambia Governor, Valentine Musakanya, army Brigadier-General Godfrey Miyanda, and air force Commander Major-General Christopher

Kabwe, all of whom were incarcerated and were later to be granted presidential pardon. For a journalistic account of military coup attempts in Zambia, see Beatwell S. Chisala, *Lt. Luchembe: Coup Attempt*, Lusaka: Multimedia, 1991.

97 I have talked to some people in Lusaka who knew Lt Luchembe. They describe him as a maverick character and habitual drunk who single-handedly decided to announce the overthrow of President Kaunda. This view is shared by others who think the 1990 coup attempt was a single uncoordinated act by a mercurial character seeking to ride on the wave of popular disenchantment.

98 Cf. Tony Killick, "Problems and Sources of Difficulty with Adjustment Conditionality". Paper presented to the National Conference on Zambia's Structural Adjustment Programme, Kitwe, 21–23 March 1992 (mimeo).

99 Cf. Lise Rakner, "Political Transition and Economic Reform: The Role of Labour in Zambian National Politics", *Forum for Development Studies*, 2, 1993, pp. 131–147.

100 For an analysis of class and economic development in Zambia, see Ben Turok, *Mixed Economy in Zambia*, London: Institute for African Alternatives, 1989.

101 Bates and Collier, op. cit., p. 47.

102 Callaghy, op. cit., p. 301.

103 Per-Åke Andersson and Steve Kayizzi-Mugerwa, *Mineral Export Dependence, Goal Attainment and Equity: Zambia's Experience with Structural Adjustment in the 1980s*, Göteborg: School of Economics and Legal Science, April 1989, p. 26.

104 Republic of Zambia, *Social Action Programme for 1990–93* (written with support of the Consultative Group for Zambia), Lusaka: April 1990, p. 2.

105 Republic of Zambia, *Zambia Economic and Financial Policy Framework, 1989–93*, Prepared by the Zambian Authorities in collaboration with the staffs of the Fund and the World Bank, Lusaka, 25 August 1989.

106 Ibid., p. 27.

107 Vol. 4, Chapter 181 of the Laws of Zambia.

108 Republic of Zambia, *Summary of the Main Recommendations of the Constitution Commission of Inquiry together with the Government Reactions to the Recommendations*, Lusaka: Government Paper no. 2, 1991.

109 *Africa Confidential*, 32 (20), 11 October 1991, pp. 6–7.

110 Ibid., p. 6.

111 It seems clear that economic liberalization and multi-party democracy have so far brought very little by way of improved conditions for the majority of Zambia's citizens. On the politics of Zambia under the Chiluba administration, see "The Politics of Poverty and the Poverty of Politics in Zambia's Third Republic", *Third World Quarterly*, 16 (4), December 1995, pp. 675–690.

8 ZAMBIA AND LOMÉ AID DIPLOMACY

1 Charles Elliott (ed.), *Constraints on the Economic Development of Zambia*, London: Oxford University Press, 1971, p. 7.

2 For a political analysis of aid, security and external relations during the first decade of Zambia's independence, see Jan Pettman, *Zambia: Security and Conflict*, Sussex: Julian Friedman, 1974.

3 Ibid. The outcome of the visit was the provision of 5,000 tonnes of wheat by the EEC. Proceeds from the sales by way of countervalue funds were supposed to be used for training truck drivers.

4 EC Commission, "Zambia: Political and Economic Note", December 1975.

5 EC Commission, "Zambia Country Programme Outlines", Brussels, September 1974.

6 This provoked a response from European envoys in Lusaka, whose Chairman, the French Ambassador, wrote in protest to the Zambian Ministry of Foreign Affairs. However, their reaction did not appear to have been effective. EC Commission, Brussels, "Fact-Finding Visit to Zambia", Report by C. Pirzio-Biroli, Directorate-General for Development and Cooperation, 1975, VIII/B/1, 14 February.

7 *The Daily Mail* (Lusaka), 14 February 1975.

8 I have not come across any Zambian official document which sought to present a serious analysis of the policy implications of the country's association with the EEC at the time.

9 Benedict V. Mtshali, "Zambia's Foreign Policy: the Dilemmas of a New State", unpublished PhD thesis, New York University, October 1972.

10 In 1964 there were only 6,000 Africans with two years of secondary education, 1,000 with secondary school certificate, and a mere 103 university graduates.

11 Mtshali, op. cit., p. 9.

12 EC Commission, Brussels, "Zambia: Political and Economic Note", December 1975, p. 14.

13 Embassy of the Republic of Zambia, Brussels (undated), "Brief on Development Co-operation between the European Economic Community and Zambia" (mimeo).

14 *The Courier*, 44, July–August 1977, p. 33.

15 The conference was held at Mulungushi Hall, Lusaka, from 6–10 December 1977. It was the second most important international conference to have been held in the country since the Group of 77 meeting in 1975.

16 EC Commission sources.

17 Republic of Zambia, "Indicative Programme on the Financial and Technical Cooperation Provided under the Lomé II Convention between the Republic of Zambia and the European Economic Community", Lusaka, 11 June 1980.

18 EC Commission.

19 Embassy of Zambia, Brussels, *Report of the Visit to Zambia by the EEC Commissioner for Development Cooperation*, by N. M. Zimba, First Secretary (Political), ZBR/CEC/2 Conf. 3 March 1982.

20 According to Mr N. M. Nzimba, then a First Secretary in the Zambian Embassy in Brussels, the Pisani visit was poorly handled in Lusaka, underlining once again the weaknesses of the Zambian bureaucracy and the inadequacies of the country's diplomatic experience. According to him:

> The protocol arrangements made by the host Ministry did not work well. First, it was not realized until rather late that there was no transport for the Commissioner and his delegation. . . . Both Ministries of Finance and Commerce and Industry which were expected at the meeting at the NCDP Office failed to arrive. . . . The writer [Mr Zimba], who saw the team off, together with another EEC official, had to use their own money to buy refreshments for the delegation. . . . Perhaps in future a different approach could be adopted for such a valuable visitor.
>
> (Ibid.)

21 The Republic of Zambia, "Lomé III National Indicative Programme", Lusaka, 6 December, 1985.

22 Commission of the European Communities, "Pre-Programming Document: Zambia", VIII/970/85–EN, Brussels, October 1985.

23 Commission of the European Communities, "Orientation Note: Zambia", prepared for Lomé III National Indicative Programming (undated).
24 Republic of Zambia, *Lomé III National Indicative Programming*, op. cit., p. 4.
25 EC Commission sources, 1990.
26 Delegation of the Commission of the European Communities, "Lomé IV: Preparation of the National Indicative Programme for Zambia", Lusaka, June 1990.
27 I shall leave the detailed discussion of the paper's position on Zambia's adjustment for the next chapter.
28 The Republic of Zambia, *Zambia – Community Cooperation Framework: National Indicative Programme under the Fourth Lomé Convention*, February 1991.
29 Jos van Gennip and P. M. van Dijk, "Food Strategies, NGOs and Lomé III", *Lomé Briefing*, 20, 1984.
30 "European Parliament Resolution on Hunger in the World" (September 1980), in Christopher Stevens (ed.), *EEC and the Third World: a Survey 2; Hunger in the World*, London: Overseas Development Institute, 1982, pp.153–160.
31 Commission of the European Communities, "Briefing Note: Food Strategy in Zambia", internal doc. VIII/A/2, 2 November 1985.
32 The Royal Tropical Institute, *Food Strategies in Four African Countries: A Study on Food Policy Formulation and Implementation in Kenya, Mali, Rwanda and Zambia*, (Prepared for the EC Commission), Amsterdam, January 1984, p. 21.
33 I was unable to have access to this particular report and therefore cannot assess its contribution to the Zambian food strategy debate.
34 It essential to keep in mind the distinction between food strategy policy and food aid. Whereas the first, which is our primary concern, falls under the Development Division (DGVIII), food aid comes under the Agricultural Division (DGVI) of the Commission, and has been operated with virtually no coordination with DGVIII. On the problems of EC food aid, see Raikes, *Modernising Hunger*, London and Portsmouth: Catholic Institute for International Relations, pp. 170–202.
35 For a general overview of the EC food strategy in the developing countries, see Commission of the European Communities, Brussels, *The European Community and Rural Development*, DE 62, January 1990. See also the Royal Tropical Institute, Amsterdam, op. cit.
36 Jean Gyselinck, "Zambia: Restoring Agriculture to Its Rightful Place", *The Courier*, 84, March–April 1984, p. 61.
37 Ibid.
38 The Commission of the European Communities, "Briefing Note: Food Strategy in Zambia", Brussels, internal doc. VIII/A/2, 25 November 1985, p. 3.
39 Interview with a Commission Administrator at DGVIII, Commission of the European Communities, Brussels.
40 The World Bank, *Zambia Agricultural Rehabilitation Project*, Staff Confidential Report No. 5050–ZA, 24 May 1984.
41 The Bank quotes the reports of the Commercial Farmers' Bureau, which indicated that most of them did not experience any problems in securing commercial bank loans so long as they could provide viable investment proposals. See the World Bank, *Zambia Agricultural Rehabilitation Project*, p. 19.
42 The Bank itself has frankly admitted that many of its Zambian projects were not successful, although most of the blame was apportioned to managerial problems and pricing policies rather to the Bank's approach itself (ibid., p. 23).
43 Government of the Republic of Zambia, *Restructuring in the Midst of Crisis*, Lusaka, May 1984.

44 EC Commission sources, Brussels.
45 Commission of the European Communities, *Food Strategy in Zambia: Issues and Prospects*, DGVIII, Brussels, 1986, p. 8.
46 Wheat and wheat product prices were to be subsequently liberalized in November 1984.
47 Delegation of the Commission of the European Communities, *Report of Activities between 1987 and 1990*, Lusaka, January 1992, p. 167.
48 Ibid.
49 Ibid., p. 168.
50 Siegfried Schultz, "Food Aid: An Effective Instrument of Development Policy?", *Intereconomics*, May/June 1987, pp. 137–144.
51 *The Courier*, 89, January–February 1985, p. 27.
52 These views have been expressed in various interviews with Commission and ACP Secretariat officials in Brussels.
53 Ministry of Foreign Affairs sources, Lusaka.
54 Under Lomé IV Sysmin funds are to be awarded as outright grants.
55 Commission of the European Communities, "Zambia Mining and Energy Sectors", internal doc. VIII-A-3, Brussels, 25 November 1985, p. 1.
56 The Second Lomé Convention, 1980.
57 ACP Secretariat, "Report on Sysmin", internal doc. ACP/89/006/91, Brussels, 23 May 1991.
58 Delegation of the European Communities, *1987 Annual Report*, op. cit., p. 17.
59 Much of what we know about the project can be gleaned from a confidential report prepared for the EC Commission and a financial evaluation prepared by a consultancy firm, Coopers & Lybrand: Olivier Bomsel, *Sysmin I and II Evaluation Study: Executive Summary*, Centre d'Économie des Ressources Naturelles, École Nationale Supérieure des Mines de Paris, Paris, 1991.
60 Commission of the European Communities, Southern Africa Division, "Meeting Between H.E. Mr S. J. Kazunga and Mr Muller, Head of Division", internal memo, 27 May 1983.
61 Quoted in Bomsel, op. cit., p. 5.
62 Ibid., p. 6.
63 Ibid., p. 7.
64 Edwin M. Koloko, "Sysmin and Mining in Zambia", *The Courier*, 94, November–December, 1985, p. 89.
65 Ibid., p. 9.
66 Ibid.
67 I was able to confirm this through personal observations and interviews during my visit to the Copperbelt region.
68 Bomsel, op. cit., p. 9.
69 EC Delegation, Brussels, *Cooperation between Zambia and the European Communities*, (1992 Report), op. cit., p. 27.
70 Bomsel, op. cit.
71 The first was approved in September 1987 and the second in November 1988.
72 Commission of the European Communities, "Zambia Smallholder Project", internal doc. VIII/372/87 -EN, Brussels, 1987.
73 EC Delegation, Lusaka, "Report of Activities 1987 to 1990", op. cit., pp. 94–101.
74 EC Delegation Lusaka, *Annual Report, 1987*, Lusaka, March 1988, p. 105.
75 Ibid., p. 106.
76 I have been reliably informed by Dr Brian Williams of the London School of

Hygiene and Tropical Medicine, who has conducted research in this area, that the tsetse programme was hardly a success.

77 According to the Nigerian geologist, Professor Cornelius Kogbe, there are 1.2 million tons of economically exploitable cobalt reserves in Africa, with Zambia and Zaire accounting for 39 per cent and 58 per cent respectively. See Cornelius A. Kogbe, "Africa: Appreciable Resources of Minerals and Metals", *The Courier*, 94, November–December 1985, p. 74.

78 The Embassy of the Federal Republic of West Germany, "Letter to Ambassador of the Republic of Zambia from the German Mission to the European Community", Brussels (undated).

79 Embassy of the Republic of Zambia, "Submission to the ACP Secretariat General", internal doc. 02/90, ZBR/ZAMB/COB/1 Brussels, June 1990.

80 African, Caribbean and Pacific Group of States, "Draft Summary Record of the Meeting of the Sub-Committee on Industrial Cooperation, Development of Mining Potential and Sysmin, Held on 29 June 1990 in ACP House, Brussels", internal doc. ACP/89/015/90 MC/mp, Brussels, 5 July 1990.

81 Lusaka National Commission for Development Planning sources.

82 Professor Robert Cassen confessed to me that when he was doing research for the report of the United Nations Inter-Governmental Task Force on Development Aid, of which he was Chairman, the European Development Fund proved to be a particularly difficult institution to study. He said most of its operations seemed shrouded in secrecy and most of its officials were rather uncooperative.

83 Lusaka, Ministry of Foreign Affairs sources.

84 This was confirmed through personal observations and informal and discrete interviews during my study visit to the Zambian Embassy in Brussels. Given the prestige with which a diplomatic posting to the EC is held in African circles, a Brussels appointment is often regarded as a plum reward for political loyalists or favourites, and often with little or no regard for competence or suitability.

85 At the Zambian High Commission in London, a substantive Economic Attaché had not been appointed after the previous one had been recalled. The Counsellor for Administrative and Consular Affairs was given the additional responsibility for commercial and trade issues. In Brussels the Economic Attaché is on secondment from the National Commission for Development Planning.

86 Centre d'Étude et de Documentations Africaines, "Synthèse de l'Aide de la CEE en Zambie et au Zaire", Rapport effectué pour la Diréction des Programmes et Méthodes d'Évaluation de la Commission des Communautés Européennes, Brussels, May 1984, p. 1.

87 Niger, Togo, Rwanda, Central Africa, Chad, Côte d'Ivoire, Upper Volta, Benin and Zaire.

88 Commission of the European Communities, "Evaluation ("ex post") of Integrated Rural Development Projects Carried out with EDF Aid in Black Africa", internal doc. VIII/658 (78), Brussels, December 1978, p. 7.

89 Susan Aurelia Gitelson, "Multilateral Aid for National Development and Self-Reliance: A Case-Study of the UNDP in Uganda and Tanzania", Unpublished PhD thesis, Columbia University, New York, 1970, pp. 38–40.

90 A mid-term evaluation report by a team of private consultants blamed both the EC and the Zambian bureaucracy for the failures of the Mpongwe project. The consultants blamed, on the one hand, the EC for its "slow and cumbersome set of financial procedures which are totally unfitted to an agricultural project",

and, on the other, the inefficiencies of public-sector management in Zambia. They concluded that if Zambian project managers had learned any lessons in the art of development management, it was in "attaching small parachutes to projects so that they crash to the ground at a smaller multiple of lethal velocity than previously". Perhaps not surprisingly, the report was rejected by the European Development Fund. See Landell Mills Associates Ltd, "Mpongwe Development Project Phase Two", Financing Agreement 2188/ZAM, Lusaka, August 1980.

91 Delegation of the Commission of the European Communities, "*Cooperation between Zambia and the European Community*", main report vol. I, January 1992, p. 13.

92 The EC also proposed that a Technical Expert be seconded to the Zambian Ministry of Agriculture's Directorate for Planning in order to monitor EC agricultural projects. This was apparently rejected by GRZ.

93 EC Delegation sources, Lusaka.

94 This is based on personal observations made during several visits to the Expert's Office and the Planning Commission and from unstructured interviews with personnel on both sides. It was instructive that both sides were anxious to hear what the other side had told me.

95 Commission of the European Communities, "Briefing Note on Zambia in Preparation for Delegates' Meeting", Brussels, internal doc. VIII/C/3, 9 June 1986.

96 Ibid.

97 Ibid.

98 During my working visit to the Delegation in Lusaka, I was able to discuss with all the key officials and to observe for myself the workings of the Delegation. After visiting other development agencies such as the World Bank, UNDP, SIDA and NORAD, I came away with the impression that the Delegation did not compare favourably with these agencies in terms of numbers of qualified and experienced personnel and in terms of a solid research base which should inform its policy interactions with the Zambian government.

99 Although hardly avoidable, consultants can easily become part of the problem of, rather than the solution to, underdevelopment. As the CEDAF study has stressed, consultants are profit-making entrepreneurs and are therefore unlikely to give advice that would drive them out of business. On the contrary, they tend to give reports suggesting further areas where their services could be required in future. Centre d'Étude et de Documentations Africaines, op. cit., p. 4.

100 I discovered this in the course of my interviews with the Director of the ETC and with planning officials. Most appeared to have been at a loss and simply referred me back to the EC Technical Expert.

101 Interviews with various aid agencies in Zambia.

102 Republic of Zambia, *New Economic Recovery Programme: Fourth National Development Plan, 1989–1993*, vol. I & II, Lusaka, 1989.

103 The United Nations Development Programme, *Development Co-operation: Zambia*, 1989 Report, Lusaka, July 1990, pp. 46–47.

104 Random oral interviews in Lusaka and the Copperbelt.

105 Cf. Christopher Hill, "The Capability-Expectations Gap, or Conceptualizing Europe's International Role", in Simon Bulmer and Andrew Scott (eds), *Economic and Political Integration in Europe: Internal Dynamics and Global Context*, Oxford: Blackwell Publishers, 1994, pp. 103–126.

9 THE EC AND ECONOMIC REFORM IN ZAMBIA

1 Quoted in *Africa Contemporary Record*, xix, 1986–87, pp. B870–71.
2 Ibid.
3 *Africa Confidential*, 28 (29), 23 September 1987, p. 7.
4 *The Economist*, 9 May 1987, p. 15.
5 EC Delegation, "Change of Economic Policy in Zambia", Note to DGVIII, by J. M. Filori, internal doc. C.I. 3/1226, Lusaka, 19 May 1987.
6 Ibid.
7 *Africa Confidential*, 29 (19), 28 September 1988, p. 3.
8 Ibid.
9 EC Commission, "Donor Attitudes to Zambia after Kenneth Kaunda's May 1st Break with the IFIs", by Tom Roe, Zambia Desk Officer, internal doc. DGVIII, Brussels, 5 June 1987.
10 The Zambian Ministry of Foreign Affairs did a special review of Zambia's diplomatic relations in which the Nordic countries were ranked as its closest political allies in Europe. See their report: *The Relations between Zambia and Its Countries of Accreditation*, op. cit.
11 Olav Stokke (ed.), *Western Middle Powers and Global Poverty: The Determinants of the Aid Policies of Canada, Denmark, the Netherlands, Norway and Sweden*, Uppsala and Oslo: Scandinavian Institute for African Studies\Norwegian Institute of International Affairs, 1989.
12 The Catholic Church's teachings regarding debt and development may have had some influence on their liberal attitudes. See the Papal Encyclicals, especially "*Pacem in Terris, Rerum Novarum*" and "*Populorum Progressio*", in Michael Walsh (ed.), *Proclaiming Justice and Peace*, London: Flame, 1991. Some Catholic aid agencies have been quite critical of IMF policies. Cf. The Catholic Institute for International Relations, *The European Community and Southern Africa: Looking towards Lomé IV*, The Hague: AWEPAA, 1989.
13 EC Commission, "Donor Attitudes to Zambia after Kenneth Kaunda's May 1st Break with the IFIs", op. cit.
14 Interview with Dag Aarnes, Senior Economist, NORAD, Lusaka, 3 October 1992.
15 Stokke, op. cit., p. 297.
16 *The Economist* has aptly summed up the "hands-off" Japanese approach to aid: "Japan provides the money, somebody else provides the people." Japan's priority seems to be to secure commercial niches and to win friends rather than to use aid as a lever for effecting economic reforms. See *The Economist*, "Miyazawa's Foreign Mission", 9 January 1993, p. 55.
17 Cf. Takashi Inoguchi, "Four Japanese Scenarios for the Future", in Jeffry A. Frieden and David A. Lake (eds) *International Political Economy: Perspectives on Global Wealth and Power*, London: Unwin Hyman, 1991, pp. 411–422.
18 Ministry of Foreign Affairs, Lusaka, *The Relations between Zambia and Its Countries of Accreditation*, op. cit.
19 Ibid.
20 On the role of the German independent foundations in Lomé diplomacy, see Veronica Forrester, "The German Political Foundations", in Christopher Stevens and J. Verloren van Themaat (eds), *Pressure Groups, Policies and Development: The Private Sector and the Third World*, London: Hodder & Stoughton/ODI, 1985, pp. 40–60. See also the article in same volume by Stevens and van Themaat, "Non-Governmental Influences on Euro-South Relations", pp. 1–19.
21 President Kaunda had accused the American CIA as well as a host of unnamed

Western countries, of having infiltrated the trade unions and trying to build up Frederick Chiluba as an alternative leader. See *Africa Confidential*, 29 (2), 22 January 1988, pp. 4–5.

22 Interview with Niall Coffey, Zambia Desk Officer, Overseas Development Administration, London, January 1992.

23 European Commission sources.

24 EC Commission "Donor Attitudes to Zambia", op. cit. The Anglo-American relationship was central to the making of the postwar liberal international economic order. Cf. Richard N. Gardner, *Sterling–Dollar Diplomacy in Current Perspective: The Origins and the Prospects of our International Economic Order*, New York: Columbia University Press, 1980.

25 EC Commission, "Zambia: Visit of Prime Minister Musokotwane to the Commission on 9 June 1987", op. cit.

26 EC Delegation, Lusaka, "Change of Economic Policy in Zambia", op. cit.

27 Cf. The Economist Intelligence Unit, *Country Report on Zambia*, 3, 1987, p. 10.

28 EC Delegation, "Change of Economic Policy in Zambia", op. cit.

29 Bates and Krueger have argued that political and institutional constraints prevented commercial groups from articulating their interests effectively. See their "Generalisations Arising from the Country Studies", in Robert H. Bates and Anne O. Krueger (eds), *Political and Economic Interactions in Economic Policy Reform*, Oxford: Blackwell, 1993, pp. 444–472.

30 John Clarke, *Zambia: Debt and Poverty*, Oxford: Oxfam Publications, 1989.

31 Ibid.

32 Interview with a senior Commission official at DGVIII, Brussels, January 1992.

33 Writings by academic lawyers on the legal aspects of the Lomé regime are disappointingly scant. One of the few is the rather dated work by E. C. Djamson, *The Dynamics of Euro-African Cooperation*, The Hague: Martin Nijhoff, 1977.

34 Cf. N. M. Shaw, *International Law*, Cambridge: Cambridge University Press, 3rd edn, 1994, pp. 560–603; D. J. Harris, *Cases and Materials on International Law*, London: Sweet & Maxwell, 4th edn, 1991, pp. 729–816.

35 Until recently, the former Soviet Union and its East European satellites had never accorded recognition to the European Community as a subject of International Law. I owe this point to my esteemed teacher at the Université de Paris I (*Panthéon-Sorbonne*), Mme. Aleth Manin. Cf. Neil Malcolm, "The Soviet Union and Europe", in Jonathan Story (ed.) *The New Europe: Politics, Government and Economy since 1945*, Oxford: Blackwell, 1993, pp. 91–114.

36 The Community has occasionally withdrawn its aid programmes when there have been gross abuses of human rights, as in Idi Amin's Uganda and in the Sudan. In Ethiopia under the Dergue, EC aid was also withdrawn when food policies were adjudged to have aggravated a famine.

37 EC Delegation, *1987 Annual Report*.

38 Ibid.

39 EC Commission, Press Release, Brussels, 16 June 1987.

40 EC Commission "Mission Report to IMF/World Bank in Washington, DC", Brussels, internal doc. VIII/C/2, June 1987.

41 After the break the World Bank announced it would continue to finance projects already begun but would suspend disbursement of all new loans. No reference was made to the break but to outstanding arrears of US$20 million. The Fund similarly maintained that its Executive Board had declared

Zambia ineligible to use its general resources due to unpaid arrears of SDR290 million. See *Keesing's Contemporary Archives*, xxxiv, June 1988, p. 35943.

42 EC Commission, "Mission Report to Washington", op. cit.

43 Ibid.

44 The immediate circumstances of the decision cast some doubts on this claim. The decision by the Bank, which was announced on 5 May less than a week after the break, seems too coincidental to be seen as anything other than a retaliatory measure.

45 The Third ACP–EEC Lomé Convention, in a special issue of *The Courier*, 89, January–February 1985, p. 43.

46 The EC did sometimes allow purchases from the Republic of South Africa because of its proximity and growing trade links with Zambia.

47 EC Delegation, Lusaka, *1992 Report.*

48 Ibid.

49 Perhaps the project might have been more viable if NCZ and fertilizer production had been shared out to one or two major donors who would then be prepared to give financial as well as technical assistance over a sustained period of time.

50 Price Waterhouse, *EEC Forex Facility Report on FEMAC 24 Session*, Lusaka, 8 April 1988.

51 Ibid., p. 30.

52 Price Waterhouse signed a Technical Assistance contract with the EC Commission under Contract No. TA/ZAM/85/87. Their detailed reports and statistical compilations have provided a useful pool of information on the operations of the ECFF.

53 Price Waterhouse, op. cit., p. 12.

54 Ibid., p. 14.

55 EC Commission, "Structural Adjustment Facility for Zambia", Draft Financing Proposal, DGVIII internal document (undated), p. 6.

56 Ibid., p. 8.

57 Countervalue funds were first introduced by the United States during the postwar Marshall Plan for Europe, and were later to emerge in the American food aid to India from the late 1950s to the early 1960s. Cf. Michael Roemer, "The Economics of Counterpart Funds Revisited", *World Development*, 17 (6), 1989, pp. 795–807. On the use of such funds in recent development interventions in Africa, see Reginald H. Green, *Macroeconomic Aspects of Commodity Aid and Counterpart Funds in Sub-Saharan Africa*, IDS Bulletin 290, June 1991; Simon Maxwell and Trudy Owens, *Commodity Aid and Counterpart Funds in Africa*, IDS Bulletin 291, June 1991; Henry J. Burton and C. Hill, "The Macroeconomic Effects of Counterpart Funds", *IDS Bulletin*, 23 (2), 1992.

58 Substantial countervalue funds have also been generated from EC food aid. The food aid account with the Bank of Zambia created problems between the EC and the government, as the latter could not provide any information on how the funds generated from EC food aid between 1975 and 1985 were spent.

59 Government of Zambia, *Agreement on the Procedures for the Establishment and Administration of EC/GRZ Countervalue Funds*, Ministry of Finance and Economic Cooperation, Lusaka, 28 June 1991.

60 Cornia, Jolly and Stewart, *Adjustment with a Human Face*. On the African perspective on the "human centred" strategy of adjustment, see "The Khartoum Declaration: Towards a Human-Focused Approach to Socio-Economic

Recovery and Development in Africa", in ECA *Annual Report*, New York: The United Nations, 1988.

61 Joan Nelson has presented a rather casuistical treatment of the issue. See her "Poverty, Equity, and the Politics of Adjustment", in Stephan Haggard and R. Kaufman (eds), *The Politics of Economic Adjustment*, pp. 221–269. Cf. the contributions of Björn Beckman, Yusuf Bangura, Mahmood Mamdani and Marc Wuyts in D. Ghai (ed.), *The IMF and the South*, op. cit.

62 The World Bank, *World Development Report for 1990*, Washington, DC, 1990.

63 Nelson, "Poverty, Equity, and the Politics of Adjustment", op. cit., p. 239.

64 Cf. Carol Graham, *The Politics of Bolivia's Emergency Social Fund*, Washington, DC: the Brookings Institution, 1990.

65 Interview with Ms Mary Barton, World Bank Representative at the joint World Bank–EC Micro-Projects Unit, Lusaka, 9 March 1992.

66 E. F. Schumacher, *Small is Beautiful*, Harmondsworth: Penguin, 1973.

67 Brian O'Neill, "Small is Beautiful: Micro-Projects in the New Convention", *Lomé Briefing*, 21, 1985.

68 Government of Zambia, *The Social Action Programme 1992–1995,* Report to the Consultative Group Meeting, Paris, March 1992.

69 Ibid., p. 1.

70 SAP Secretariat sources, Lusaka.

71 At the time these figures were given, i.e., March 1992, US$1 was equal to K 125.

72 Government of Zambia sources.

73 Geneviève de Crombrugghe *et al.*, "Evaluation of Microprojects Programmes: Zambia Lomé II and III", Consultancy Report for the EC Commission, Brussels: Collectif d'Échanges pour la Technologie Appropriée (COTA), November 1991, p. 2.

74 Ibid., p. 6.

75 See P. M. Manda, "The Decentralization of Government in Zambia Since Independence", unpublished PhD thesis, University of Leeds, 1988.

76 I met a few NGO representatives at the MPU Secretariat who had been involved in implementing MPP-financed projects.

77 The report by De Crombrugghe *et al.*, whilst being quite informative, has some gaps from the viewpoint of rural development social research. Cf. Robert Chambers, *Rural Development: Putting the Last First*, London: Longman, 1983.

78 Micro-projects Unit, Lusaka, *Quarterly Reports*, September and December 1991.

79 Interview with MPU Field Officer, Lusaka, March 1992.

80 De Crombrugghe *et al.*, op. cit., p. 11.

81 Joel S. Migdal, *Strong Societies and Weak States: State–Society Relations and State Capabilities in the Third World*, Princeton, NJ: Princeton University Press, 1988, p. 248.

82 For an excellent exposition of project planning and management in developing countries, see J. A. Mollett, *Planning for Agricultural Development*, Aldershot: Avebury, 1990.

83 Micro-Projects Unit, "Administrative Manual" (Draft), October 1991.

84 The consultants' report is quite unambiguous about the technical shortcomings of the projects. De Crombrugghe *et al.*, op. cit., pp. 26–39.

85 A German NGO innovated with construction of school buildings with "air bricks" in place of windows, and this design proved to be relatively safe from vandalism.

86 Interview with Ms Mary Barton, World Bank Programme Officer and Deputy Coordinator at the MPU in Lusaka, 9 March 1992.

87 Interview with Mr Mel Jones, National Coordinator of EC Micro-Projects Unit, Lusaka, 11 March 1992.

88 Interview with Mr Benny Zulu, Higher Field Officer, EC Micro-Projects Unit, Lusaka, 5 March 1992.

89 There is an interesting debate amongst students of economic history as to whether the NICs strategy can be replicated in the rest of the developing world, especially in the light of growing protectionism in industrialized countries. Cf. Dieter Senghaas, *The European World: A Historical Critique of Development Theory*, Leamington Spa: Berg Publishers, 1985. See the earlier work by Alexander Gerschenkron, *Economic Backwardness in Historical Perspective*, Cambridge, Mass.: Harvard University Press, 1962.

90 Government of Zambia, *National Economic Recovery Programme: Fourth National Development Plan 1989–1993*, Office of the President, National Commission for Development Planning, Lusaka, January 1989, p. 199. Dr Mwanza is currently Governor of the Bank of Zambia.

91 Interview with Dr Jacob Mwanza, former Vice-Chancellor of the University of Zambia and Special United Nations Economic Adviser to the Government of Zambia, Ministry of Finance, Lusaka, 16 March 1992.

92 The planning and coordination of the project has been contracted out to a Surrey-based team of management consultants, who propose to spend up to 14 per cent (ECU1.4 million) of the funds on technical assistance alone. If one includes the ECU600,000 contingency allowance, it means up to 20 per cent of the funds will not be going directly into funding exporters' activities. See David Jones & Associates, *Lomé IV Programming Project for Zambia – Export Development 1991–1995*, Report to the Government of the Republic of Zambia and the Commission of the European Communities (Final Report), prepared by Martin Hogg, Surrey, United Kingdom, August 1991.

93 National Planning Commission sources, Lusaka.

94 This view is shared by the Economic Adviser of the EC Delegation, in Lusaka, Señor João Melo de Sampaìao. I owe a great deal of anecdotal information to various conversations I had with him. In comparing Zambia to Nigeria, I have benefited from the insights of Mr Tom Forrest, Research Associate at Queen Elizabeth House, Oxford, who has undertaken extensive field research on entrepreneurs in Eastern Nigeria, and with whom I have had enlightening discussions on the subject. See also his *Advance of African Capital*, Edinburgh: Edinburgh University Press, 1994. One of the most important works on the relationship between culture and economic development is the historical and comparative study by Everett E. Hagen. See his *On the Theory of Social Change: How Economic Growth Begins*, London: Tavistock, 1962. Cf. Ibn Khaldun, The Muqaddimah: *An Introduction to History*, trans. by Franz Rosenthall, London: Routledge & Kegan Paul, pp. 297–332.

95 Jones & Associates, op. cit., p. 22.

96 The Zambit-Lomé Group, *The Constitution of the Zambit-Lomé Group,* Lusaka, 22 March 1991.

97 I had an extensive discussion with the Chairman, Mr Theo Bull at his offices at Long Acres, Lusaka, on the 26 March 1992. I also talked to Dr Moses Banda of the Bank of Zambia, who has been active in the Zambit-Lomé forum.

98 See for example, Moses Banda and Richard Suba (eds), "Proceedings of a Seminar on Opportunities for EEC Investments in Zambia," held at Garden House Motel, Lusaka, on 17 September 1991, under the auspices of the "Zambit-Lomé Group", November 1991.

99 Interview with Mr Theo Bull, Lusaka.

100 Although we have no firm evidence that this has happened, it can be supposed that the Association as an economic pressure group may have sought to persuade the EC along certain orthodox policy lines. Most Zambian businessmen are known to favour orthodox reform policies which offer them higher margins of profit but which may not necessarily be in the interest of long-term development. One prominent businessman, for example, referred to the drastic devaluation of the kwacha as a matter of "economic justice", because a higher exchange rate had allegedly robbed business of its just desert in profits. See Murray Sanderson, "Zambia's Structural Adjustment: Where Do We Go from Here? – A Business View", paper presented at the National Conference on Zambia's Structural Adjustment held at Kitwe, Zambia, 21–23 March 1992, p. 8.

10 EUROPE AND AFRICA IN A CHANGING WORLD

1 Louis Lavelle, *The Dilemma of Narcissus*, trans. from the French by W. T. Gardner, London: Allen & Unwin, 1971, p. 110.

2 Dennis Austin, "Reflections on African Politics: Prospero, Ariel and Caliban", *International Affairs*, 69 (2), 1993, pp. 203–221.

3 This is no firm evidence of a "*collective Northern hegemony*" in international economic relations. Cf. Stephen Gill, *American Hegemony and the Trilateral Commission*, Cambridge: Cambridge University Press, 1990; Kees Van der Pijl, *The Making of an Atlantic Ruling Class*, London: Verso, 1984.

4 Christopher Hill, "The Capability-Expectations Gap, or Conceptualizing Europe's International Role", in Simon Bulmer and Andrew Scott (eds), *Economic and Political Integration in Europe: International Dynamics in Global Context*, Oxford: Blackwell Publishers, 1994, pp. 103–126. Cf. Miles Kahler, "Europe and its 'Privileged Partners' in Africa and the Middle East", in Loukas Tsoukalis (ed.), *The European Community: Past, Present and Future*, Oxford: Basil Blackwell, 1983, pp. 199–218.

5 Cf. Martin McQueen, "Developmental Constraints of the Rules of Origin of the Lomé Convention", University of Reading (undated), mimeo.

6 Tsoukalis, *The New European Economy: Past, Present and Future*, Oxford: Oxford University Press, 1991, p. 48.

7 Cf. Michael Davenport (with Sheila Page), *Europe: 1992 and the Developing World*, London: ODI, 1991. See also Sheila Page, "The Effects of 1992 on the World Trading System: A Preliminary Overview", Developing Studies Association 1990 Annual Conference, Glasgow, 5–7 September 1990 (mimeo); Africa Leadership Forum, *The Impact of Europe in 1992 on West Africa*, Proceedings and Results of a High Level Seminar, Abeoukuta and New York: Africa Leadership Forum, April 1989. On the processes leading to the European Single Act itself, see Richard Corbett, "The 1985 Intergovernmental Conference and the Single European Act", in Roy Pryce (ed.), *The Dynamics of European Union*, London and New York: Routledge, 1990, pp. 238–272. Amongst Caribbean countries there is much pessimism about the long-term implications of the Single Market for their exports. See Anthony P. Gonzales, "World Restructuring and Caribbean Diplomacy", in Lloyd Searward (ed.), *Diplomacy for Survival: CARICOM States in a World of Change*, Kingston, Jamaica: Friedrich Ebert Stiftung, 1991, pp. 1–18.

8 On the global effects of the EC Single Market, see David G. Mayes (ed.), *The*

External Implications of European Integration, New York: Harvester Wheatsheaf, 1993.

9 Eddie Momoh, "ECOWAS Summit: West Africa Responds to 1992", *African Economic Digest*, 4 June 1990, pp. 3–9. Cf. Peter da Costa, "Unite or Die: Review of Resolutions at the Banjul Summit", *West Africa*, 11–17 June 1990, pp. 980–981.

10 Ali A. Mazrui, "Global Apartheid? Race and Religion in the New World Order", in Geir Lundestad and O. A. Westad (eds) *Beyond the Cold War: New Dimensions in International Relations*, 90th Anniversary Nobel Jubilee Symposium, Oslo and Oxford: Scandinavian University Press, 1993, pp. 85–98.

11 *Newsweek*, July 24, 1990, p. 65.

12 Ibid.

13 *West Africa*, 16–22 April 1990, p. 636.

14 *West Africa*, 2–8 July, 1990, pp. 2010–2011.

15 Paul Bennell, *British Manufacturing Investment in sub-Saharan Africa: Corporate Response during Structural Adjustment*, Sussex: IDS Working Paper no. 13, December 1994.

16 *Newsweek*, op. cit.

17 On France's African policy during the Mitterrand era, see Jean-Paul Bénoit, *Indispensable Afrique*, Nancy: Berger-Lerrault, 1986.

18 World Bank, *World Bank Tables, 1992–93*, Washington, DC, December 1992.

19 Ministry of Foreign Affairs, Abuja (Nigeria), "ACP–EEC Cooperation after the Year 2000" (internal memo), December, 1991.

20 The emerging world order poses a major theoretical challenge to students of International Relations and International Political Economy. Amongst the most important theoretical discourse in recent times are: William C. Olson and A. J. R. Groom, *International Relations Then and Now: Origins and Trends in Interpretation*, London: Harper Collins, 1991; Charles Reynolds, *The World of States: An Introduction to Explanation and Theory*, Aldershot, Hants: Edward Elgar, 1992; Torbjön L. Knutsen, *A History of International Relations Theory: An Introduction*, Manchester and New York: Manchester University Press, 1992; Martin Hollis and Steve Smith, *Explaining and Understanding International Relations*, Oxford: Clarendon Press, 1991; James N. Rosenau and Ernst-Otto Czempiel (eds), *Governance without Government: Order and Change in World Politics*, Cambridge: Cambridge University Press, 1992. In the area of security and grand strategy, Alvin and Heidi Toffler have argued that new doctrines will have to be constructed to cope with what they regard as a fundamentally new era in world politics. See their *War and Anti-War: Survival at the Dawn of the 21st Century*, London: Little, Brown & Co., 1994.

21 Cf. John Stopford and Susan Strange, *Rival States, Rival Firms: Competition for World Markets*, Cambridge: Cambridge University Press, 1991.

22 Jacques Delors, *Our Europe: The Community and National Development*, London: Verso, 1990, p. 146. The economic historian, Karl Polanyi, long ago warned against the dogmatic belief in the automatic efficiency and equity of the self-regulated market system. See Polanyi, *The Great Transformation*, Boston: Beacon Press, 1957.

23 Karl Polanyi, *The Great Transformation*, United States of America: Rhinehart & Co, 1944. Cf. Robert Gilpin, *The Political Economy of International Relations*, Princeton, NJ: Princeton University Press, pp. 263–305.

24 Cf. Michael Hudson, *Trade, Development and Foreign Debt*, vol. I & II, London: Pluto Press, 1992.

25 The failure of development policy in Africa could be said to be partly attri-

butable to the lack of an authentic African social-scientific tradition which is rooted in the region's historical experience. Cf. Peter P. Ekeh, "Development Theory and the African Predicament", *African Development*, ix (4), 1986, pp. 1–39. There is now a virtual library of critical works against orthodox IMF and World Bank adjustment strategies in Africa and other developing economies. Cf. Tony Killick, *A Reaction Too Far: Economic Theory and the Role of the State in Developing Countries*, London: ODI, 1989; see also his "Twenty-Five Years in Development: The Rise and Impending Decline of Market Solutions", *Development Policy Review*, 4, 1986, pp. 99–116; John Spraos, *IMF Conditionality: Ineffectual, Inefficient, and Mistargeted*, Princeton Essays in International Finance, 166, December 1986; Andrew Schoenholtz, "The IMF in Africa: Unnecessary and Undesirable Western Restraints on Development", *The Journal of Modern African Studies*, 25 (3), 1987, pp. 403–433; Christopher Colclough and James Manor (eds), *States or Markets: Neo-Liberalism and the Development Policy Debate*, Oxford: Clarendon Press, 1991; Azzam Mahjoub (ed.), *Adjustment or Delinking? The African Experience*, London: Zed Books, 1990; Eboe Hutchful, "The Crisis of the New International Division of Labour, Authoritarianism and the Transition to Free Market Economies in Africa", *African Development*, xii (2), 1987, pp. 35–53; Thandika Mkandawire, "Crisis and Adjustment in Sub-Saharan Africa", in Dharam Ghai (ed.), *The IMF and the South: The Social Impact of Crisis and Adjustment*, London: Zed Books, 1991, pp. 80–94; Bade Onimode (ed.), *The IMF, the World Bank and the African Debt*, vols 1 & 2, London: Zed Books, 1989; ECA/OAU, "The Khartoum Declaration: Towards a Human-Focused Approach to Socio-Economic Recovery and Development in Africa", in *ECA Annual Report*, New York: the United Nations, 1988; The ECA, *African Alternative Programme to Structural Adjustment Programmes for Socio-Economic Recovery and Transformation*, Addis Ababa (undated).

26 On the implications of adjustment programmes for the national sovereignty question, see Marie-France L'Hériteau, *Les Fonds monétaires et les pays du Tiers-Monde*, Paris: *Presses Universitaires*, 1986; and Joseph A. Camilleri and Jim Falk, *The End of Sovereignty: The Politics of a Shrinking and Fragmented World*, Aldershot, Hants: Gower House, 1992, pp. 69–103. Cf. Robert Shams, "Adjustment Constraints in Developing Countries: A Comparative Study", *Intereconomics*, March/April 1989, pp. 71–8; Lawrence Whitehead, "Political Explanations of Macroeconomic Management: A Survey", *World Development*, 18 (80), 1990, pp. 1133–1146; James Morton, *The Poverty of Nations: The Aid Dilemma at the Heart of Africa*, London and New York: British Academic Press, 1994, p. 26. On the role of legitimacy in the international political economy, see Constantine Vaitsos, *Intercountry Income Distribution and Transnational Enterprises*, Oxford: Clarendon Press, 1974, pp. 143–144.

27 Cf. Robert L. Rothstein, "Limits and Possibilities of Weak Theory: Interpreting North–South Relations", in Rothstein (ed.), *The Evolution of Theory in International Relations*, Columbia, SC: University of South Carolina Press, 1991, pp. 139–162.

28 Mark W. Zacher, "The Decaying Pillars of the Westphalian Temple: Implications for International Order and Governance", in Rosenau and Czempiel, op. cit., pp. 58–101. Cf. Richard Falk, *The End of World Order: Essays on Normative International Relations*, New York: Holmes & Meier, 1983; Andrew Linklater, *Men and Citizens in the Theory of International Relations*, London: Macmillan, 1982; Lynn H. Miller, *Global Order: Values and Power in International Politics*, Boulder, Col., and London: Westview Press, 1985.

29 Alain Minc, *Le Nouveau Moyen Age*, Paris: *Éditions Gallimard*, 1993. Cf. Samuel P.

Huntington, "The Clash of Civilizations?", *Foreign Affairs*, 72 (3), Summer 1993, pp. 22–49.

30 John Maynard Keynes, *The Economic Consequences of the Peace*, New York: Harcourt, Brace & Howe, 1920, p. 251.

31 The historian Paul Kennedy puts forward a very pessimistic scenario for Africa in the coming century. See his *Preparing for the Twenty-First Century*, London: Harper Collins, 1993, pp. 211–227. On the role of Providence in history, see Herbert Butterfield, *Christianity and History*, London: Bell & Sons, 1950, pp. 93–112.

32 Cf. C. L. R. James, *The Black Jacobins: Toussaint L"Ouverture and the San Domingo Revolution*, London: Allison & Busby, 1980.

33 For a recent account of the debate on the state and underdevelopment, see Alan Carter, "The Nation State and Underdevelopment", *Third World Quarterly*, 16 (4), December 1995, pp. 595–618. On the role of the state in Asian economic development, see Haggard, *Pathways from the Periphery*, Ithaca and London: Cornell University Press, pp. 254–270; Robert Wade, *Governing the Market: Economic Theory and the Role of Government in East Asian Industrialisation*, Princeton, NJ: Princeton University Press, 1990. Cf. Tun-jen Cheng, "Political Regimes and Development Strategies: South Korea and Taiwan", in Gary Gereffi and Donald A. Wyman (eds), *Manufacturing Miracles: Paths of Industrialisation in Latin America and East Asia*, Princeton, NJ: Princeton University Press, 1990, pp. 139–178.

34 On the "Standard of Civilisation", see G. W. Gong, *The Standard of "Civilisation" in International Society*, Oxford: Oxford University Press, 1984.

35 Contrary to the popular prejudices of our age, autocracy and arbitrary rule were not the predominant hallmarks of political power in traditional Africa. Cf. Basil Davidson, *The Black Man's Burden: Africa and the Curse of the Nation State*, London: James Currey: 1992; Isaac Schapera, *A Handbook of Tswana Law and Custom*, Oxford: OUP/International African Institute, 2nd edn, 1955; Taslim O. Elias, *The Nature of African Customary Law*, Manchester: Manchester University Press, 1956; Max Gluckman, *The Ideas in Barotse Jurisprudence*, New Haven: Yale University Press, 1965.

36 I have in mind the French model which was initiated by President de Gaulle with the establishment of the *École Nationale d'Administration* (ENA). Although the alleged existence of an "*Énarchy*" in French public life has led to some criticisms, it is clear that this highly efficient and dedicated corps of administrators has been a contributing factor in France's economic transformation since 1945. During the 1980s I did express my disagreement with Professor Dotun Philips, Chairman of the Philips Commission on Civil Service Reform in Nigeria. I believe that the weakening and removal of tenure for the higher civil service was a grave mistake. During the 1966–70 Nigerian crisis the higher civil service was a critical factor in ensuring economic and political stability. Having a *cadre administratif* which is above politics and which has a sense of national mission can be a positive rather than a negative thing.

37 William E. Abraham, *The Mind of Africa*, London: Methuen, 1967; Cf. V. Y. Mudimbe, *The Invention of Africa: Gnosis, Philosophy and the Order of Knowledge*, Bloomington: University of Indiana Press, 1988; Cheikh Anta Diop, *Civilisation or Barbarism: An Authentic Anthropology*, trans. by Y. Ngemi, Chicago, Ill.: Lawrence Hill Books, 1981.

38 Such paradigmatic reassessments will have to take into account the retreat from internationalism and the growing illiberalism in Western societies. In the field of philosophy, the new "communitarians", for example, deny the exis-

tence of universal values which have been at the foundation of Western culture since the Enlightenment. Cf. Will Kymlicka, *Contemporary Political Philosophy: An Introduction*, Oxford: Clarendon Press, 1990, pp. 199–237. Those who uphold a Grotian or neo-Kantian universalism are becoming lone voices in the wilderness. Cf. Onora O'Neil, *Constructions of Reason: Explorations of Kant's Practical Philosophy*, Cambridge: Cambridge University Press, 1989; See also her "Kantian Ethics", in Peter Singer (ed.), *A Companion to Ethics*, Oxford: Blackwell, 1993, pp. 175–185. On the "Grotian view" of international relations, see Hedley Bull, Benedict Kingsbury and Adam Roberts (eds), *Hugo Grotius and International Relations*, Oxford: Clarendon Press, 1993. Cf. Jeffrey C. Isaac, "A New Guarantee on Earth: Hannah Arendt on Human Dignity and the Politics of Human Rights", *American Political Science Review*, 90 (1), March 1996, pp. 61–73.

39 Most recent forecasts indicate an increasingly dominant role for Asian economies in the twenty-first century. See Kennedy, *The Rise and Fall of the Great Powers*, pp. 565–698; Yoichi Funabashi, "The Asianization of Asia", *Foreign Affairs*, 72 (5), Nov./Dec. 1993, pp. 59–74.

40 On recent developments in the international trading system, see Bernard Hoekman and Michel Kostecki, *The Political Economy of the World Trading System: From GATT to WTO*, Oxford: Oxford University Press, 1995; John H. Jackson, "The World Trade Organization: Watershed Innovation or Cautious Small Step Forward?", in Sven Arndt and Chris Milner (eds), *The World Economy: Global Trade Policy 1995*, Oxford: Blackwell, 1995, pp. 11–32.

41 It may be observed that European and Western attitudes towards African integration efforts have been at best lukewarm. In the case of West Africa, France's role in the formation of the rival Communauté des États d'Afrique de l'Ouest (CDEAO) was seen by many in Africa as an attempt by a neo-imperial power to weaken the nascent Economic Community of West African States (ECOWAS).

42 On recent developments within the Franc Zone, see James M. Boughton, "The CFA Franc: Zone of Fragile Stability in Africa", *Finance and Development*, December 1992, pp. 34–36.

43 Cf. Lawrence J. Brainard, "Eastern Europe: Creating a Capital Market", in Robert O'Brien and Sarah Hewin (eds), *Finance and the International Economy*, The AMEX Bank Review Prize Essays in Memory of Robert Marjolin, Oxford: Oxford University Press, 1991, pp. 7–22.

44 Perhaps a single African currency could be pegged to a single European currency (the "*Euro*") if the latter were to become a reality. In Africa as elsewhere, successful monetary integration will be dependent on the general level of regional economic interdependence and on the existence of political consensus among the major constituent powers. Evidence for this proposition clearly exists in the case of European monetary integration. Cf. Christopher Taylor, *EMU 2000? Prospects for European Monetary Union*, London: Royal Institute of International Affairs, 1995; Peter B. Kennen, *Economic and Monetary Union: Moving beyond Maastricht*, Cambridge: Cambridge University Press, 1995. On the political foundations of international finance, see Andrew W. Walter, *World Power and World Money: The Role of Hegemony and International Monetary Order*, New York and London: Harvester Wheatsheaf, 2nd edn, 1993; Robert Z. Aliber, *The International Monetary Game*, London: Macmillan, 1997; Robert Solomon, *The International Monetary System, 1945–1976*, New York: Harper & Row, 1975.

45 On the emerging tripolar global economic system, see Nicholas Hopkinson, *Trading Blocs and the Future GATT Agenda*, Wilton Park Paper 76, London:

HMSO, 1993. Cf. Paul Krugman, "Competitiveness: A Dangerous Obsession", *Foreign Affairs*, 73 (2), March/April 1994, pp. 28–44. A keen advocate of a new global tripolar hegemony is the Japanese management consultant, Kenichi Ohmae. See his *Triad Power: The Coming Shape of Global Competition*, New York: The Free Press, 1985. On mercantilist attitudes within Europe, see Martin Wolff, "Cooperation or Conflict? The European Union in a Liberal Global Economy", *International Affairs*, 71 (2), April 1995, pp. 325–338.

46 Stanley Hoffmann, *Janus and Minerva: Essays in the Theory and Practice of International Politics*, Boulder and London: Westview Press, 1987, pp. 394–417.

47 For an analysis of world politics from the perspective of the *Civitas Humana*, see Raghavan Iyer, *Parapolitics: Towards the City of Man*, New York and Oxford: Oxford University Press, 1979.

48 On the problems of governance in the emerging international system, see James N. Rosenau, "Governance, Order, and Change in World Politics", in James N. Rosenau and Ernst-Otto Czempiel (eds), *Governance without Government: Order and Change in World Politics*, Cambridge: Cambridge University Press, 1992, pp. 1–30.

49 Quoted in Dieter Senghaas, *The European Experience: A Historical Critique of Development Theory*, Leamington Spa: Berg Publishers, 1985, p. 223.

REFERENCES

EUROPEAN COMMUNITY OFFICIAL DOCUMENTS

EC Commission (1974), *Zambia Country Programme Outlines,* Brussels, September.

—— (1975), *Zambia: Political and Social Development*, Brussels, December.

—— (1975), "Fact-Finding Visit to Zambia", Report by C. Birzio-Piroli, Directorate-General for Development and Cooperation, VIII/B/1 14 February.

—— (1978), "Evaluation ('Ex Post') of Integrated Rural Development Projects Carried out with EDF Aid in Black Africa", internal doc. VIII/658/78, Brussels, December.

—— (1981), "Towards a Plan of Action to Combat Hunger in the World", COM (81) 560 final, Brussels, 5 October.

——, Southern Africa Division (1983), "Meeting between Mr S. J. Kazunga (Zambian Ambassador) and Mr Muller, Head of Division", internal memo, Brussels, 27 May.

—— (1985), "'Pre-Programming Document: Zambia", internal doc. VIII/970/85/ Brussels, October.

—— (1985), "Briefing Note: Food Strategy in Zambia", Brussels, internal doc. VIII/A/2, 25 November.

—— (1985), "Second Special Action for the Fight against Hunger in the World", Brussels, doc. 958/84/ZAM/2,12 December.

—— (1985), "Zambia Mining and Energy Sectors", Brussels, internal doc. VII/A/3, 25 November.

—— (1986), "Ten Years of Lomé: A Record of EEC–ACP Partnership, 1976–1985", Brussels, September.

—— (1986), "Food Strategy in Zambia: Issues and Prospects", Brussels, internal doc. DGVIII.

—— (1986), "Briefing Note on Zambia", in preparation for Delegates' Meeting, Brussels, internal doc. VIII/C/3, 9 June.

—— (1987), "Donor Attitudes to Zambia after Kenneth Kaunda's May 1st Break with the IFIs", by T. Roe, Zambia Desk Officer, internal doc. DGVIII, Brussels, 5 June.

—— (1987), "Zambia Smallholder Project", VIII/372/87-EN, Brussels.

—— (1987), "Mission Report to IMF/World Bank in Washington, DC", Brussels, internal doc. VIII/C/2, June.

—— (1987), "Zambia: Visit of Prime Minister Musokotwane to the Commission on 9 June 1987", internal doc., Brussels, 1987.

—— (1989), *Lomé III: Mid-Term Review, 1986–1988.*

—— (1990), "The European Community and Rural Development", DE 62, January.
—— (1991), "Final Report on the Special Programme to Highly Indebted Low-Income Countries in Sub-Saharan Africa", Brussels, internal doc. VIII/3.
—— (1991), "Draft Financing Proposal Adjustment Facility For Zambia", Brussels, internal doc. ZA/.
—— (1991), "Progress Report on the Community's Involvement in the Structural Adjustment Process in the ACP States", Communication of the Commission to the Council, internal doc. CAB IV/259/91 EN, Brussels.
—— (Undated) "Orientation Note: Zambia", Prepared for Lomé III Indicative Programming, Brussels (internal doc.)
EC Delegation, Lusaka (1987), "Change of Economic Policy in Zambia", Note to DGVIII by J. M. Filori (EC Delegate), internal doc. C.I. 3/1226, 19 May.
—— Lusaka (1988), *Annual Report, 1987*, March.
—— Lusaka (1990), *Lomé IV: Preparation of the National Indicative Programme for Zambia,* (June).
—— Lusaka (1992), *Report of Activities between 1987 and 1990,* January.
—— (1992), "Cooperation between Zambia and the European Communities", *1992 Annual Report*, Lusaka.
EC Parliament (1980), *Resolution on Hunger in the World,* Strasbourg, September.

ACP DOCUMENTS AND OFFICIAL RELEASES

ACP Committee of Ambassadors (1983), "Memorandum on the Position of the ACP Group in its Future Negotiations with the European Communities", ACP Secretariat, Brussels, ACP/0023/83/ NEG (Rev. 2) August.
ACP Council of Ministers (1991), "Report of the Development Finance Committee to the ACP Council of Ministers", Brussels, 3 May, internal doc. ACP/81/047/91.
—— (1991), "Report of the Commission on the Implementation of Programming and Structural Provisions of the Fourth Lomé Convention", Brussels, 3 May, internal doc. ACP/81/047/91.
ACP Group of States, (1988), "Memorandum on ACP Guidelines for the Lomé IV Negotiations", Brussels, internal doc. ACP/00/012/88, 4 October.
—— (1990), "Draft Summary Record of the Meeting of the Sub-Committee on Industrial Cooperation, Development of Mining Potential and Sysmin", held on 29 June 1990 in ACP House, Brussels, internal doc. ACP/89/015/90/MC/mp, 5 July.
ACP Secretariat (1982), "Report of the ad hoc Committee to Examine Matters Relating to the Strength and Operation of the ACP Secretariat", internal doc. ACP/264/82, Brussels, 31 March.
— (1982), "A Suggested Approach to the Negotiations for a Successor Convention to Lomé", Brussels, internal doc. 003/82/NEG/ Rev. 2, Brussels, 18 November.
—— (1988), "Recommendations from the Establishment and Finance Sub-Committee on the Strengthening of the Manpower of the Secretariat in the Framework of the Negotiations of the Next Convention", internal doc. ACP/41/051/88/ Rev. 2, Brussels, 18 November.
—— (1990), "Group d'États de l'Afrique, des Caraïbes et du Pacifique: Quinze Années de Coopération ACP et Intra-ACP", Brussels, 6 June.
—— (1991), *Interim Report on the Georgetown Agreement,* Brussels, November.

—— (1991), "Report on Sysmin", Brussels, internal doc. ACP/89/006/91, 23 May.

GOVERNMENT OF ZAMBIA OFFICIAL PUBLICATIONS AND DOCUMENTS

Embassy of Zambia, Brussels (1982), "Report of the Visit to Zambia by the EEC Commissioner for Development Cooperation", N. M. Zimba, First Secretary (Political), internal doc. ZBR/CEC/2 Conf., March.

—— (1990), "Address to the ACP-EEC Council in Fiji on the Development of Mining Potential and the Sysmin Mechanism", (by the Zambian Minister for Industries) internal doc. Or: Fr:Tr: Ahm/Rev:SB/mjb.

—— (1990), "Submission to the ACP Secretariat General", Brussels, internal note no. 02/90/ ZBR/ZAMB/COB1, June.

—— (undated), "Brief on Development Cooperation between the European Economic Community and Zambia".

—— (undated), "Letter to Ambassador of the Republic of Zambia from the German Mission to the European Community", internal memo.

Government of Zambia (1983), "Letter from the Hon. Nalumino Mundia, Prime Minister and Finance Minister, to M. Jacques de la Rosière, IMF Managing Director", 25 February also in IMF Document EBS/83/67 (Supplement 3 April 1983).

Republic of Zambia (1980), *Indicative Programme on the Financial and Technical Cooperation Provided under the Lomé II Convention between the Republic of Zambia and the European Economic Community*, Lusaka.

—— (1984), *Twenty Years of Independence*, Lusaka, State House.

—— (1984), *Restructuring in the Midst of Crisis*, Government Printer, Lusaka, May.

—— (1985), *Lomé III National Indicative Programming*, Lusaka, 6 December.

—— (1989), *New Economic Recovery Programme: Fourth National Development Plan 1989–93*, vols I and II, Lusaka, Government Printer.

—— (1989), *Zambia Economic and Financial Policy Framework, 1989–93*, prepared by the Zambian authorities with the collaboration of the staffs of the Fund and the World Bank, Lusaka, 25 August.

—— (1990), *Social Action Programme for 1990–1993*, (written with the support of the Consultative Group for Zambia), Lusaka, April.

—— (1991), *Zambia – Community Cooperation Framework: National Indicative Programme under the Fourth Lomé Convention*, Lusaka, February.

— (1991), *Agreement on the Procedures for the Establishment and Administration of EC/GRZ Countervalue Funds*, Ministry of Finance and Economic Cooperation, Lusaka, 28 June.

—— (undated), *Summary of the Main Recommendations of the Constitution Commission of Inquiry together with the Government Reactions to the Recommendations*, Lusaka, Government Paper no. 2.

BOOKS AND ARTICLES CONSULTED

Abraham, William E. (1967), *The Mind of Africa*, London: Methuen.

Adedeji, Adebayo (1989a), "African Alternative Framework to Structural Adjustment", text of a speech delivered at the University of Ottawa, 23 October (mimeo).

—— (1989b), *Towards a Dynamic African Economy: Speeches and Lectures* (with the assistance of Jeggan Senghor), London: Frank Cass.

—— (1989c), "Press Statement on the Occasion of the Launching of AAF-SAP", London, 6 July.

Africa Leadership Forum, *The Impact of Europe in 1992 on West Africa*, Proceedings and Results of a High Level Seminar, Abeokuta and New York: Africa Leadership Forum, April 1989.

Ahmed, Massoud and L. Summers (1990), "A Tenth Anniversary on the Debt Crisis", *Finance and Development*, September (29), pp. 2–5.

Ake, Claude (1993), "The Unique Case of African Democracy", *International Affairs*, 69 (2), pp. 239–44.

Akinrinade, O. and J. K. Barling, (eds) (1987), *Economic Development in Africa: International Efforts, Issues and Prospects*, London: Pinter.

Aliber, Robert Z. (1977), *The International Money Game*, London: Macmillan, 2nd edn.

Allsopp, Christopher *et al.* (1989), *Zambia Exchange Rate Policy*, Stockholm: The Swedish International Development Agency.

Aluko, Olajide (1981), *Essays in Nigerian Foreign Policy*, London: Allen & Unwin.

Amdur, Robert (1977), "Rawls's Theory of Justice: Domestic and International Perspectives", *World Politics*, 29 (3), April, pp. 438–461.

Amin, Samir (1976), *Imperialism and Unequal Development*, Brighton, Sussex: Harvester.

—— (1990), "Preface", in A. Mahjoub (ed.), *Adjustment or Delinking? The African Experience*, London: Zed Books.

Andersson, Per-Åke and S. Kayizzi-Mugerwa (1989), *Mineral Dependence, Goal Attainment and Equity: Zambia's Experience with Structural Adjustment in the 1980s*, Göteberg: School of Economics and Legal Science.

Asante, Samuel (1986), "Africa and Europe: Collective Interdependence?" in A. Sesay (ed.), *Africa and Europe: From Partition to Interdependence or Dependence?*", London: Croom Helm, pp. 1–28.

Austin, Dennis (1968), "Britain, Commonwealth Africa and the EEC", in P. Uri (ed.), *From Commonwealth to Common Market*, Harmondsworth: Penguin, pp. 130–156.

—— (1993), "Reflections on African Politics: Prospero, Ariel and Caliban", *International Affairs*, 69 (2), pp. 203–221.

Ayres, Robert L. (1983), *Banking on the Poor: The World Bank and World Poverty*, Cambridge, Mass.: The MIT Press.

Baland, Jean-Marie and Jean-Philippe Platteau (1993), "Are Economists Concerned with Power?", *IDS Bulletin*, 24 (3), July, pp. 12–20.

Baldwin, David A. (1985), *Economic Statecraft*, Princeton, NJ: Princeton University Press.

Banda, Moses and R. Suba (eds), (1991) "Proceedings of a Seminar on Opportunities for EEC Investments in Zambia", held at the Garden House Hotel on 17 September 1991, under the auspices of the "Zambit-Lomé Group", Lusaka, November.

Bangura, Yusuf and Björn Beckman (1991), "African Workers and Structural Adjustment: The Nigerian Case", in Dharam Ghai (ed.) (1991), *The IMF and the South: The South Impact of Crisis and Adjustment*, London: Zed Books and the United Nations Research Institute for Social Development, pp. 139–165.

Bardhan, Pranab (1994), "Some Reflections on the Use of the Concept of Power in Economics", in Basu and Nayak, *Development Theory and Policy*, pp. 64–77.

Baregu, Mwesiga (1989), "The Lomé Convention View South", in Kimmo Kiljunen (ed.), *MINI-NIEO: The Potential for Regional South–South Cooperation*, Helsinki: Institute for Development Studies, pp. 158–170.

Barya, John-Jean (1993), "The New Political Conditionalities of Aid: An Independent View from Africa", *IDS Bulletin*, 24 (1), pp. 16–23.

Basu, Kaushik (1989), *The International Debt Problem: Could Someone Explain It to Me?*, Helsinki: WIDER.

—— and Pulin Nayak (eds) (1994), *Development Policy and Economic Theory*, Oxford: Oxford University Press.

Bates, Robert H. (1974), *Patterns of Uneven Development: Causes and Consequences in Zambia*, Monograph Series in World Affairs, University of Colorado Press.

—— (1981), *Markets and States in Tropical Africa*, Berkeley and Los Angeles: University of California Press.

—— (1983), *Essays on the Political Economy of Rural Africa*, Cambridge: Cambridge University Press.

—— and P. Collier (1991), "The Politics and Economics of Policy Reform in Zambia", Duke University, Department of Political Science and Centre for the Study of African Economies, University of Oxford (third draft), January (mimeo).

—— and A. O. Krueger (eds) (1993), *Political and Economic Interactions in Economic Policy Reform* Oxford: Basil Blackwell.

Bauer, Peter T. (1981), *Equality, the Third World and Economic Delusion*, London: Methuen.

Beckman, Björn (1988), "The Post-Colonial State: Crisis and Reconstruction", *IDS Bulletin*, 19 (4), pp. 26–34.

—— (1990), "Empowerment or Repression? The World Bank and the Politics of Structural Adjustment", paper submitted to a symposium on the Social and Political Context of Structural Adjustment in sub-Saharan Africa, organized jointly by the UN Research Institute for Social Development (UNRISD), the Scandinavian Institute for African Studies (SIAS) and the Chr. Michelsen Institute (CMI) in Bergen, Norway, 17–19 October (mimeo).

Bennell, Paul (1994), *British Manufacturing Investment in sub-Saharan Africa: Corporate Response during Structural Adjustment*, Sussex: IDS Working Paper (13), December.

Bennett, Norman R. (1984), *Africa and Europe: From Roman Times to National Independence*, New York and London: Holmes & Meier Publishers, 2nd edn.

Bénoit, Jean-Paul (1986), *Indispensable Afrique*, Nancy: Berger-Lerrault.

Bersani, Giovanni (1989), "Human Rights: The Joint Assembly's Experience", *Lomé Briefing*, 13, December.

Best, Michael H. (1990), *The New Competition: Institutions of Industrial Restructuring*, Oxford: The Polity Press.

Bhagwati, Jagdish and J. N. Ruggie (eds) (1984), *Power, Passions and Purpose: Prospects for North–South Negotiations*, Cambridge, Mass.: MIT Press.

Biersteker, Thomas (ed.) (1993), *Dealing with Debt: Financial Negotiations and Adjustment Bargaining*, Boulder, Col.: Westview Press.

Bird, Graham (1987), *International Financial Policy and Development: A Disaggregated Approach*, London: Macmillan.

—— (ed.) (1990), *The International Financial Regime*, Guildford, Surrey: University of Surrey Press.

—— (1995), *IMF Lending to Developing Countries: Issues and Evidence*, London and New York: Routledge.

—— and T. Killick (1985), "Balance of Payments Management: The IMF and the Third World", in Loukas Tsoukalis (ed.) *The Political Economy of International Money*, London: Sage/RIIA, pp. 233–59.

Boardman, Robert, *et al.* (eds) (1985), *Europe, Africa and Lomé III*, New York: University Press of America.

Bomsel, Olivier (1991), *Sysmin I and Sysmin II Evaluation: Executive Summary*, Centre d'Économie des Ressources Naturelles, École Nationale Supérieure des Mines, Paris.

Bourdieu, Pierre (1990) *The Logic of Practice*, trans. Richard Nice, Oxford: Polity Press.

Braillade, Philippe and M.-R. Djalili, *The Third World and International Relations*, London and Boulder, Col.: Pinter/Rienner Publishers, 1984.

Brainard, Lawrence J. (1991), "Reform in Eastern Europe: Creating a Capital Market", in Richard O'Brien and Sarah Hewin (eds), *Finance and the International Economy 4*, The AMEX Bank Review Prize Essays in Memory of Robert Marjolin, Oxford: Oxford University Press, pp. 1–22.

Brau, Edwin (1986), "External Debt Management in the African Context", in G. K. Helleiner (ed.) *Africa and the IMF*, a symposium held in Nairobi, Kenya, 13-15 May, Washington DC: The IMF, pp. 160–180.

Brett, E. A. (1986), "State Power and Economic Inefficiency: Explaining Political Failure in Africa", *IDS Bulletin*, 17 (1), pp. 22–29.

Brown, Robert R. and Robert J. Cummings (1983), *The Lagos Plan of Action vs. the Berg Report: Contemporary Issues in African Development*, Washington, DC: Howard University Press.

Brownlie, Ian (1987), *Principles of Public International Law*, 3rd edn, Oxford: Clarendon Press.

Bull, Hedley (1989), "European States and Africa Communities", in H. Bull and A. Watson (eds) *The Expansion of International Society*, Oxford: Oxford University Press.

Bull, Hedley, B. Kingsbury and A. Roberts (eds) (1992), *Hugo Grotius and International Relations*, Oxford: Clarendon Press.

Burdette, Marcia (1988), *Zambia Between Two Worlds*, Boulder, Col.: Westview Press.

Burnell, Peter (1995), "The Politics of Poverty and the Poverty of Politics in Zambia's Third Republic", *Third World Quarterly*, 26 (4), December, pp. 675–690.

Burton, H. J. and C. Hill (1992), "The Macroeconomics of Counterpart Funds", *IDS Bulletin*, 23 (2), pp. 7–12.

Buzan, Barry (1983), *People, States and Fear: The National Security Problem in International Relations*, Chapel Hill: University of North Carolina Press.

Cable, Vincent (1988) "ACP Debt and the EC: the Role of the Lomé Convention", Economic Affairs Division, Commonwealth Secretariat, Marlborough House, London (mimeo).

Callaghy, Thomas M. (1984), *The State–Society Struggle: Zaire in Comparative Perfective*, New York: Columbia University Press.

—— (1989), "Toward State Capability and Embedded Liberalism in the Third World", in J. M. Nelson, (ed.), *Fragile Coalitions: The Politics of Economic Adjustment*, Washington, DC: Overseas Development Council, pp. 115–138.

—— (1990), "Lost between State and Market: the Politics of Economic Adjustment in Ghana, Zambia, and Nigeria", in J. M. Nelson (ed.) *Economic Crisis and Policy Choice: The Politics of Adjustment in the Third World*, Princeton, NJ: Princeton University Press, pp. 57–320.

Cameron, Jock (1993), "Power as Central in Economic Exchange: Can Keynes Help?", *IDS Bulletin*, 24 (3), July, pp. 31–35.

Camilleri, Joseph A. and J. Falk, (1992), *The End of Sovereignty? The Politics of a Shrinking and Fragmented World*, Aldershot, Hants: Gower House.

Campbell, Bonnie and J. Loxley (eds) (1989), *Structural Adjustment in Africa*, London: Macmillan.

Camps, Miriam (1967), *European Unification in the Sixties: From Veto to Crisis*, Oxford: Oxford University Press.

Carrington, Edwin (1987), "The ACP Secretariat", *The Courier*, March–April, pp. 12–16.

Carrothers, Thomas (1995), "Recent US Experience with Democracy Promotion", *IDS Bulletin*, 26 (2), pp. 62–69.

Carter, Alan (1995), "The Nation State and Underdevelopment", *Third World Quarterly*, 16 (4), December, pp. 595–618.

Cassen, Robert & Associates (1986), *Does Aid Work? Report to an Intergovernmental Task Force*, Oxford: Clarendon.

—— (1991), "Structural Adjustment in Sub-Saharan Africa", opening address for the workshop on "The Management of Structural Adjustment Negotiations", organized and sponsored by Structural Adjustment Advisory Team for Africa (SAATA) at Harare, Zimbabwe (mimeo).

Catholic Institute for International Relations (1989), *The European Community and Southern Africa: Looking towards Lomé IV*, The Hague: AWEPAA.

Central Office of Information (1990), *Britain and International Debt Relief*, London, June.

Centre d'Étude et de Documentations Africaines (1984), *Synthèse de l'aide de la CEE en Zambie*, report carried out under the direction of the Programmes et Méthodes d'Évaluation de la Commission des Communautés Européennes, Brussels, May.

Chaliand, Gérard and J.-P. Rageau (1985), *Strategic Atlas*, Harmondsworth: Penguin.

Chambers, Robert (1983), *Rural Development: Putting the Last First*, London: Longman.

Chase-Dunn, Christopher (1991), *Global Formation: Structures of the World Economy*, Oxford: Basil Blackwell.

Chazan, Naomi *et al.* (1988), *Politics and Society in Contemporary Africa*, London: Macmillan.

Cheng, Tun-Jen (1990), "Political Regimes and Development Strategies: South Korea and Taiwan", in Gary Gereffi and Donald A. Wyman (eds), *Manufacturing Miracles: Paths of Industrialisation in Latin America and East Asia*, Princeton, NJ: Princeton University Press, pp. 139–178.

Chikwanda, Alex (1991), "Governance and Economic Development in sub-Saharan Africa". Statement by Chairman of Zambia Confederation of Industries and Chambers of Commerce, at a Conference on Governance and Economic Development in sub-Saharan Africa sponsored by the World Bank and Queen Elizabeth House, University of Oxford, and held at Queen Elizabeth House, Oxford, 2–4 May (mimeo).

Chileshe, Jonathan H. (1987), *Third World Countries and Development Options: Zambia*, New Delhi: Vikas Publishing House.

Chipman, John (1989) *French Power in Black Africa*, Oxford: Basil Blackwell.

Chipungu, Samuel N. (1988), *The State, Technology and Peasant Differentiation in Zambia: A Case Study of the Southern Province, 1930–1936*, Lusaka: Historical Association of Zambia.

Chisala, Beatwell S. (1991), *Lt. Luchembe: Coup Attempt*, Lusaka: Multimedia.

Chiwele, Dennis (1996), "Economic Adjustment, the Mining Sector and the Real Wage in Zambia", in C. Harvey, *Constraints on the Success of Structural Adjustment Programmes in Africa*, London: Macmillan pp. 210–234.

—— and Christopher Colclough (1996), "Economic Crisis, Adjustment and the

Effectiveness of the Public Sector in Zambia", in Harvey, *Constraints on the Success of Structural Adjustment Programmes in Africa*, pp. 192–209.

Clarke, John (1989), *Zambia: Debt and Poverty*, London: Oxfam.

Cliffe, Lionel (1980), "Zambia in the Context of Southern Africa", in Centre for African Studies, University of Edinburgh, *The Evolving Structure of Zambian Society*, Proceedings of a Seminar, 30–31 May, pp. 240–261.

Colclough, Christopher and J. Manor (eds) (1991), *States or Markets: Neo-Liberalism and the Development Policy Debate*, Oxford: Clarendon Press, 1991.

Collier, Paul (1991), "Africa's External Economic Relations: 1960–90", *African Affairs*, 90, pp. 339–356.

Corbett, Richard (1990), "The 1985 Intergovernmental Conference and the Single European Act", in Roy Pryce (ed.), *The Dynamics of European Union*, London and New York: Routledge, pp. 238–272.

Cosgrove, Carol (1978), *Europe and Africa: From Association to Partnership*, Farnborough, Teakfield: Saxon House.

da Costa, Peter (1990), "Unite or Die: Review of the Resolutions at the Banjul Summit", *West Africa*, 11–17 June, pp. 980–981.

Council of Europe (1952) *The Strasbourg Plan*, Strasbourg: Council of Europe.

Cox, Robert W. (1983), "Gramsci, Hegemony and International Relations: An Essay in Method", *Millennium*, 12, pp. 162–175.

—— (1986), "Social Forces, States and World Orders: Beyond International Relations Theory", in R. O. Keohane (ed.), *Neorealism and Its Critics*, New York: Columbia University Press, pp. 204–254.

—— (1987), *Production, Power, and World Order: Social Forces in the Making of History*, vol. I, New York: Columbia University Press.

Crowder, Michael (1987), "Whose Dream Was It Anyway? Twenty- Five Years of African Independence", *African Affairs*, 86 (342), January, pp. 7–23.

Cunningham, Simon (1981), *The Copper Industry in Zambia: Foreign Mining Companies in a Developing Country*, New York: Praeger.

Dam, Kenneth W. (1982), *The Rules of the Game: Reform and Evolution in the International Monetary System*, Chicago and London: The University of Chicago Press.

Daniel, Philip (1986), "Structural Adjustment and Policy Dialogue", *IDS Bulletin*, 17 (2), pp. 46–57.

Davenport, Michael and S. Page (1991), *Europe 1992 and the Developing Countries*, London: ODI.

Davidson, Basil (1992), *The Black Man's Dilemma: Africa and the Curse of the Nation State*, London: James Currey.

Decalo, Samuel (1992), "The Process, Prospects and Constraints of Democratization in Africa", *African Affairs*, 91, pp. 7–35.

De Crombrugghe, Géneviève (1991), "Evaluation of Microprojects Programmes: Zambia Lomé II and III", Consultancy Report for the EC Commission, Brussels: Collectif d'Échanges pour la Technologie Appropriée (COTA), November.

De Cuellar, Javier Perez (1987), "Progress in the Implementation of the United Nations Programme of Action for African Economic Recovery", *Development Seeds of Change*, 2 (3), pp. 42–43.

De Jouvenal, Bertrand (1957), *Sovereignty*, Cambridge: Cambridge University Press.

De la Mahotière, Stuart R. (1961), *The Common Market: A Comprehensive Guide*, London: Hodder & Stoughton.

De Lupis, Ingrid D. (1987), *International Law and the Independent State*, Aldershot, Hants: Gower.

De Vries, Margaret (1986), *The IMF in a Changing World, 1945–85*, Washington, DC: International Monetary Fund.

Dell, Sidney (ed.) (1988), *Policies for Development: Essays in Honour of Gamani Corea*, London: Macmillan.

Delors, Jacques (1990), *Our Europe: The Community and National Development*, London: Verso.

Demery, L. and T. Addison, (1987), "Food Security and Adjustment Policies in Sub-Saharan Africa: a Review of the Evidence", *Development Policy Review*, 5, pp. 177–196.

Der Derian, James (1987), *On Diplomacy: A Genealogy of Western Estrangement*, Oxford: Blackwell.

Deschouwer, Claudine *et al.* (1988), *Lomé III: 1985–1990*, Brussels: Bureau d'Informations Européennes, July.

Desta, Asayehgn (1988), "Africa's External Debt in Perspective", *Journal of African Studies*, Spring/Summer, 15 (1&2), pp. 23–31.

Dictionary of World Politics (1992), New York: Harvester Wheatsheaf.

Diop, Cheikh Anta (1981) *Civilization or Barbarism: An Authentic Anthropology*, trans. Y. Ngemi, Chicago, Ill.: Lawrence Hill Books.

Dolan, Michael (1979), "Lomé II: The Evolution of the Relations Between the European Community and the ACP Countries", in Werner Feld (ed.), *Western Europe's Global Reach: Regional Cooperation and Worldwide Aspirations*, New York and Oxford: Pergamon Press.

Doornbos, Martin (1990), "The African State in Academic Debate: Retrospect and Prospect", *The Journal of Modern African Studies*, 28 (2), pp. 179–198.

Dore, Ronald (1990), "Reflections on Culture and Social Change", in G. Gereffi and D. L. Wyman (eds), *Manufacturing Miracles: The Paths of Industrialisation in Latin America and East Asia*, Princeton, NJ: Princeton University Press, pp. 353–367.

Dornbusch, Rudiger (1985), "Dealing with Debt in the 1980s", *Third World Quarterly*, 7 (3), July, pp. 532–575.

Drèze, Jean and Amartya Sen (1989), *Hunger and Public Action*, Oxford: Clarendon Press.

Drucker, Peter (1986), "The Changed World Economy", *Foreign Affairs*, 64, Spring, pp. 768–769.

Duhamel, Georges (1944), *Civilisation Française*, Paris: Librairie Hatchette.

Dumont, René (1966), *False Start in Africa*, London: Deutsch.

Dutkiewicz, Peter and G. P. Williams (1987), "All the King's Horses and All the King's Men Couldn't Put Humpty-Dumpty Together Again", *IDS Bulletin*, 18 (3), pp. 39–43.

Duverger, Maurice (1974), *Modern Democracies: Economic Power Versus Political Participation*, Hinsdale, Ill.: Dryden Press.

ECA (1984), *Special Memorandum by the ECA Conference of Ministers on Africa's Economic and Social Crisis*, Addis Ababa: ECA.

—— (1988a) "The Abuja Statement", *African Journal of Political Economy*, 2 (1), pp. 132–147.

—— (1988b), "The Khartoum Declaration: Towards a Human-Focused Approach to Socio-Economic Recovery in Africa", *ECA Annual Report*, New York: The United Nations.

—— (1988c) *Annual Report*, New York: The United Nations.

—— (undated) *Statistics and Policies: ECA Preliminary Observations on the World Bank Report, "Africa's Adjustment and Growth in the 1980s"*, Addis Ababa: ECA.

—— (1989) *African Alternative Programme to Structural Adjustment Programmes for Socio-Economic Recovery and Transformation (AAF-SAP)*, Addis Ababa: ECA.

—— and OAU (1981), *Lagos Plan of Action for Economic Development of Africa*, Addis Ababa: ECA and OAU.

The Economist (1993), "Miyazawa's Foreign Mission", 9 January, p. 55.

The Economist Intelligence Unit (1987), *Country Report on Zambia*, vol. 3, London: *The Economist*.

Ekeh, Peter P. (1986), "Development Theory and the African Predicament", *African Development*, ix (4), pp. 1–39.

Elias, Taslim O. (1956), *The Nature of African Customary Law*, Manchester: Manchester University Press.

Elliot, Charles (ed.), (1971) *Constraints on the Economic Development of Zambia*, Oxford: Oxford University Press.

Embassy of the Federal Republic of West Germany, "Letter to the Ambassador of the Republic of Zambia from the German Mission to the European Community", Brussels, internal doc. (undated).

Erbe, Rainer (1986) "Has the Baker Plan Failed?", *Intereconomics*, September–October, pp. 214–223.

Ergas, Zaki (1987), "In Search of Development in Africa", in Z. Ergas (ed.) *The African State in Transition*, London: Macmillan.

European Council Resolution (1988), "The Adjustment Process in Africa", *The Courier*, 111, p. 73.

Evans, David (1986), "Reverse Dutch Disease and Mineral Exporting Developing Countries", *IDS Bulletin*, 17 (4), pp. 10–13.

—— (1991), "Visible and Invisible Hands in Trade Policy Reform", in Christopher Colclough and J. Manor (eds), *States or Markets: Neo-Liberalism and the Development Policy Debate*, Oxford: Clarendon Press, pp. 48–77.

Falk, Richard (1983), *The End of World Order: Essays on Normative International Relations*, New York and London: Holmes & Meier.

Feld, Werner (1983), *The European Community in World Affairs: Economic Power and Political Influence*, Boulder, Col.: Westview Press.

—— (ed.) (1979), *Western Europe's Global Reach: Regional Cooperation and Worldwide Aspirations*, New York and Oxford: Pergamon Press.

Ferguson, Tyrone (1988), *The Third World and Decision-Making in the International Monetary Fund: The Quest for Full and Effective Participation*, London and New York: Pinter Publishers.

Fieldhouse, D. K. (1986), *Black Africa 1945–80: Economic Decolonization and Arrested Development*, London: Allen & Unwin.

Foreign and Commonwealth Office (1990), "International Debt", *Background Briefing*, London, November.

—— (1990) "Recent Initiatives on Developing Country Debt", Briefing Paper, November.

Forrest, Tom (1994), *The Advance of African Capital*, Edinburgh: Edinburgh University Press.

Forrester, Veronica (1985), "The German Political Foundations", in C. Stevens and J. V. van Themaat, *Pressure Groups, Policies and Development*, London: Hodder & Stoughton, pp. 1–19.

Foucault, Michel (1989), *Madness and Civilisation: A History of Insanity in the Age of Reason*, London: Routledge.

Fralon, J. A. (1978), *The Lomé Convention: Renegotiation and Renewal*, Brussels: Agence Européennes d'Informations.

François, Jean (1987), *De Lomé I à Lomé III*, Paris: Médicins Sans Frontières.

Frey, Bruno (1984), *International Political Economics*, Oxford: Basil Blackwell.

Frey-Wouters, Ellen (1980), *The European Community and the Third World: The Lomé Convention and its Impact*, New York: Praeger.

Frieden, Jeffry (1991), *Modern Political Economy and Latin America, 1965–1985: Debt, Development and Democracy*, Princeton, NJ: Princeton University Press.

—— and D. A. Lake (eds) (1991), *International Political Economy: Perspectives on Global Power and Wealth*, 2nd edn, London: Unwin & Hyman.

Frisch, Dieter (1988), "Adjustment: Development and Equity", *The Courier*, 111, pp. 67–72.

Fruling, P. (1988), *Recovery in Africa: A Challenge for Development Cooperation in the 1990s*, Stockholm: Swedish Ministry for Foreign Affairs.

Funabashi, Yoichi (1993), "The Asianization of Asia", *Foreign Affairs*, 72 (5), November/December, pp. 59–74.

Galtung, Johann (1973), *The European Community: A Super-Power in the Making*, London: Allen & Unwin.

Gardner, Richard N. (1980), *Sterling–Dollar Diplomacy in Current Perspective: the Origins and the Prospects of Our International Economic Order,* New York: Columbia University Press.

George, Alexander (1979), "Case Studies and Theory Development: The Method of Structured, Focused Comparison", in P. G. Lauren (ed.), *Diplomacy: New Approaches in History, Theory and Policy*, London: Macmillan, pp. 43–65.

George, Susan (1987), *Food Strategies for Tomorrow*, San Francisco: The Global Hunger Project.

—— (1988), *A Fate Worse Than Debt*, Harmondsworth: Penguin.

Gerschenkron, Alexander (1962), *Economic Backwardness in Historical Perspective*, Cambridge, Mass.: Harvard University Press.

Gertzel, Cherry *et al.* (1984), *The Dynamics of the One-Party State in Zambia*, Manchester: Manchester University Press.

Ghai, Dharam (ed.) (1991), *The IMF and the South: The South Impact of Crisis and Adjustment*, London: Zed and UNRISD.

Gill, Stephen (1991), *American Hegemony and the Trilateral Commission*, Cambridge: Cambridge University Press.

—— and David Law (1988), *The Global Political Economy: Perspectives, Problems and Policies*, New York: Harvester Wheatsheaf.

Gilpin, Robert (1981), *War and Change in World Politics*, Cambridge: Cambridge University Press.

—— (1987), *The Political Economy of International Relations*, Princeton, NJ: Princeton University Press.

Gitelson, Aurelia (1970), "Multilateral Aid for National Development and Self-Reliance: A Case-Study of the UNDP in Uganda and Tanzania", unpublished PhD thesis, Columbia University, New York.

Gluckman, Max (1965), *The Ideas in Barotse Jurisprudence*, New Haven: Yale University Press.

Gong, G. W. (1984), *The Standard of "Civilisation" in International Society*, Oxford: Oxford University Press.

Graham, Carol (1990), *The Politics of Bolivia's Emergency Social Fund*, Washington, DC: The Brookings Institution.

Green, Reginald H. (1991), *Macroeconomic Aspects of Commodity Aid and Counterpart Funds in sub-Saharan Africa*, Sussex: IDS.

Griffith-Jones, Stephany (1986), *The International Debt Problem: Prospects and Solutions*, Helsinki: WIDER.

——— and O. Sunkel (1986), *Debt and Development Crises America: The End of an Illusion*, Oxford: Clarendon.

Grilli, Enzo R. (1994), *The European Community and the Developing Countries*, Cambridge: Cambridge University Press.

Grimal, Henri (1965), *Decolonisation: The French, Dutch and Belgian Empires, 1919–1963*, London: Routledge & Kegan Paul.

Grou, Pierre (1985), *The Financial Structure of Multinational Capitalism*, Leamington Spa: Berg Publishers.

Gruhn, Isebill (1976), "The Lomé Convention: Inching Towards Interdependence", *International Organisation*, 30, pp. 241–262.

—— (1980), *Regionalism and the Economic Commission for Africa*, Boulder, Col.: Lynne Rienner.

Gulhati, Ravi (1989), *Impasse in Zambia: The Economics and Politics of Reform*, Washington, DC: the World Bank.

Gunther-Schmidt, Paul (1990), "How to Pay for the Debt: Coping with the Third World's Crisis", *Intereconomics*, Jan./February, pp. 6–12.

Gutto, Shedrack (1988), "Debates: Social Revolutions – the Preconditions for Sustainable Development and People's Democracies in Africa", *African Development*, XIII (3), pp. 77–87.

Gyselinck, Jean (1984), "Zambia: Restoring Agriculture to Its Rightful Place", *The Courier*, 84, March–April 1984.

Haas, Ernst B. (1958), *The Uniting of Europe*, London: Stevens.

—— (1990), *When Knowledge Is Power: Three Models of Change in International Organisations*, Berkeley: University of California Press.

Hagen, Everett (1962), *On the Theory of Social Change: How Economic Growth Begins*, London: Tavistock.

Haggard, Stephan (1990), *Pathways From the Periphery: The Politics of Growth in the Newly-Industrialising Countries*, Ithaca and London: Cornell University Press.

—— and R. Kaufman (eds) (1992), *The Politics of Economic Adjustment: International Constraints, Distributive Conflicts and the State*, Princeton, NJ: Princeton University Press.

Hall, Richard (1973), *The High Price of Principles: Kaunda and the White South*, Harmondsworth: Penguin.

Halliday, Fred (1991), "State and Society in International Relations", in Michael Banks and M. Shaw (eds), *State and Society in International Relations*, New York: Harvester Wheatsheaf.

Hallstein, Walter (1972), *Europe in the Making*, trans. by Charles Roetter, London: Allen & Unwin.

Harris, David J. (1991), *Cases and Materials on International Law*, 4th edn, London: Sweet & Maxwell.

Harris, Lawrence (1989), "The Bretton Woods System in Africa", in B. Onimode, (ed.), *The IMF, the World Bank and the African Debt: The Economic Impact*, London: Zed Books, pp. 19–24.

Harvey, Charles (ed.) (1996), *Constraints on the Success of Structural Adjustment Programmes in Africa*, London: Macmillan.

Havnevik, Kjell (ed.) (1987) *The IMF and the World Bank in Africa: Conditionality, Impact, and Alternatives*, Uppsala: Scandinavian Institute for African Studies.

Hawkins, J. J. (1991), "Understanding the Failure of IMF Reform: the Zambian Case", *World Development*, 19 (7), pp. 839–849.

Hayter, Teresa and C. Watson (1985), *Aid Rhetoric and Reality*, London and Sydney: Pluto.

Hayward, Jack (1973) *The One and Indivisible French Republic*, London: Weidenfeld & Nicolson.

Helleiner, Gerald K. (ed.) (1986), *Africa and the International Monetary Fund*, Washington, DC: IMF.

Herbst, Jeffrey (1990), "The Structural Adjustment of Politics in Africa", *World Development*, 18 (7), pp. 949–958.

L'Hériteau, Marie-France (1986), *Le Fonds Monétaire International et Les Pays du Tiers-Monde*, Paris: Presses Universitaires.

Hettne, Bjørn (1990), *Development Thinking and the Three Worlds*, Harlow, Essex: Longman.

Hewitt, Adrian (1981), "The Lomé Conventions: Myth and Substance of the 'Partnership of Equals'", in Margaret Cornell (ed.), *Europe and Africa: Issues in Post-Colonial Relations*, London: ODI, pp. 21–45.

—— (1984) "Export Earning: the Fostering of the Development of the ACP states through the Stabilization of Their Import Capacity", Report to the Commonwealth Secretariat, London: ODI, February (mimeo).

Hill, Christopher (1994), "The Capability-Expectations Gap: Conceptualizing Europe's International Role", in Simon Bulmer and Andrew Scott (eds), *Economic and Political Integration in Europe: International Dynamics in Global Context*, Oxford: Blackwell Publishers, pp. 103–126.

Hill, Tony (1985), "Whither Lomé? A Review of the Lomé III Negotiations", *Third World Quarterly*, 7 (3), July, pp. 661–81.

Hine, Robert C. (1985), *The Political Economy of European Trade: An Introduction to the Trade Policies of the EEC*, Brighton, Sussex: Wheatsheaf.

Hinsley, F. H. (1966), *Sovereignty*, London: C. A. Watts.

Hobsbawm, Eric (1987) *The Age of Empire, 1875–1914*, London: Weidenfeld & Nicolson.

—— (1994) *Age of Extremes: The Short Twentieth Century, 1914–1991*, London: Michael Joseph.

—— and T. Ranger (eds) (1983), *The Invention of Tradition*, Cambridge: Cambridge University Press.

Hodd, Martin (1987), "Africa, the IMF and the World Bank", *African Affairs*, 86 (344), July, pp. 331–342.

Hodges, Tony (1987), "OAU Urges Ten-Year Moratorium", *African Recovery*, December, pp. 2–6.

—— (1988), "Zambia's Autonomous Adjustment", *Africa Recovery*, 2 (2), December, pp. 6–12.

Hoekman, Bernard and Michel Kostecki (1995), *The Political Economy of the World Trading System: From GATT to WTO*, Oxford: Oxford University Press.

Hoffmann, Stanley (1987), *Janus and Minerva: Essays in the Theory and Practice of International Politics*, Boulder, Col., and London: Westview Press.

—— (1995), *The European Sisyphus: Essays on Europe*, Boulder, Col.: Westview Press.

Holland, R. F. (1975), *European Decolonisation: An Introductory Survey*, London: Macmillan.

Hollis, Martin and S. Smith (1991), *Explaining and Understanding International Relations*, Oxford: Clarendon Press.

Holsti, Karl J. (1992), *International Politics: A Framework of Analysis*, 6th edn, Englewood Cliffs, NJ: Prentice-Hall.

Hopkinson, Nicholas (1993), *Trading Blocs and the Future GATT Agenda*, Wilton Park Paper 76, London: HMSO.

Howard, Michael (1961), *The Franco-Prussian War: The German Invasion of France*, London: Hart-Davis.

Hudson, Michael (1992), *Trade, Development and Foreign Debt, vols I & II*, London: Pluto Press.

Huntington, Samuel P. (1968), *Political Order in Changing Societies*, New Haven: Yale University Press.

Hutchful, Eboe (1987), "The Crisis of the New International Division of Labour, Authoritarianism and the Transition to Free Market Economies in Africa", *African Development,* XII (2), pp. 35–53.

——— (1989) "From 'Revolution' to Monetarism: The Economics and Politics of the Adjustment Programme in Ghana", in Bonnie Campbell and J. Loxley (eds), *Structural Adjustment in Africa*, London: Macmillan, pp. 92–131.

IMF (1992), *Annual Report*, Washington, DC: The International Monetary Fund.

Inoguchi, Takashi (1991), "Four Japanese Scenarios for the Future", in J. A. Frieden, and D. A. Lake (eds), *International Political Economy: Perspectives on Global Wealth and Power*, London: Unwin Hyman, pp. 411–422.

Isaac, Jeffrey C. (1996) "A New Guarantee on Earth: Hannah Arendt on Human Dignity and the Politics of Human Rights", *American Political Science Review*, 90 (1), March, pp. 61–73.

Isaak, Robert A. (1991), *International Political Economy: Managing World Economic Change*, Englewood Cliffs, NJ: Prentice-Hall International.

Israel, Arturo (1990), *Institutional Development: Incentives and Performance*, Baltimore and London: Johns Hopkins University Press.

Iyer, Raghavan (1976) *The Moral and Political Thought of Mahatma Gandhi*, Oxford: Oxford University Press.

—— (1979), *Parapolitics: Toward the City of Man*, Oxford and New York: Oxford University Press.

Jackson, John H. (1995), "The World Trade Organization: Watershed Innovation or Cautious Small Step Forward?", in Sven Arndt and Chris Milner (eds), *The World Economy: Global Trade Policy 1995*, Oxford: Blackwell Publishers, pp. 11–32.

Jackson, Robert H. and C. G. Rosberg (1986), "Sovereignty and Underdevelopment: Juridical Statehood and the African Crisis", *The Journal of Modern African Studies*, 24 (1), pp. 1–31.

Jacobs, Francis and R. Corbett (1990), *The European Parliament*, London: Longman.

James, Alan (1986), *Sovereign Statehood: The Basis of International Society*, London: Allen & Unwin.

James, C. L. R. (1980), *The Black Jacobins: Toussaint L'Ouverture and the San Domingo Revolution*, London: Allison & Busby.

Jolly, Richard H. and R. van der Hoeven, (1989) *Protecting the Poor and Vulnerable during Adjustment: The Case of Ghana*, New York: UNICEF Staff Paper.

Jones, David & Associates (1991), *Lomé IV Programming Project For Zambia: Export Development 1991–1995*, Surrey: Martin Hogg.

Kahler, Miles (1992), "The United States and the International Monetary Fund", in M. P. Karns and K. A. Mingst (eds), *The United States and Multilateral Institutions: Patterns of Changing Instrumentality and Influence*, London: Routledge.

—— (1983), "Europe and its 'Privileged Partners' in Africa and the Middle East", in L. Tsoukalis, *The European Community: Past, Present and Future*, Oxford: Blackwell, pp. 199–224.

Käkonen, Jyrkki (1976), *Effects of the EEC Association on Foreign Trade and Diplomatic Relations of the African States*, Turku: University of Turku Institute of Social and Political Science, Studies in Political Science No. 5.

—— and I. Vaura (1974), "The Strategy of Neo-Colonialism and Associated African member states", in J. Kakonen (ed.) *The Mechanisms of Neo-Colonialism: Proceedings of a Nordic Seminar*, Mannta: Finnish Peace Research Association, pp. 39–68.

Kamya, Andrew (1991), "Zambia's Exchange Rate in the 1980s", in K. S. Sumaili, and G. Lungwangwa (eds), *Zambia in the World Economy*, Proceedings of the 11th PWPA Conference Held at Livingstone, Lusaka: The Professors World Peace Academy.

Kaplinsky, Raphael (1989), "Technological Revolution and the International Division of Labour in Manufacturing: A Place for the Third World?", *The European Journal of Development Research*, 1 (1), June, pp. 5–37.

Karmiloff, Igor G. (1987), "The Changing Pattern of European Community Trade with the Third World", *Development Policy Review*, 5, pp. 3–34.

—— (undated), *Industrialisation in sub-Saharan Africa: Country Case Study – Zambia*, Working Paper No. 26, London: ODI.

Karns, Margaret and K. A. Mingst (eds) (1992), *The United States and Multilateral Institutions: Patterns of Changing Instrumentality and Influence*, New York: Routledge.

Kasfir, Nelson (1984), "Relating State to Class in Africa", in N. Kasfir (ed.), *State and Class in Africa*, London: Frank Cass, pp. 1–20.

Kaufman, Johan (ed.) (1989), *Effective Negotiation; Case-Studies in Conference Diplomacy*, Dordrecht: Martinus Nijhoff.

Kaunda, Kenneth D. (1981), "Towards a Great and Prosperous Zambia", Address to the 16th National Council of the United National Independence Party, Mulungushi Hall, 14 December, Lusaka: Government Printer.

Kauppi, Paul R. and M. Viotti (1987), *International Relations Theory: Realism, Pluralism and Globalism*, New York: Macmillan.

Kenen, Peter B. (1995), *Economic and Monetary Union in Europe: Moving beyond Maastricht*, Cambridge: Cambridge University Press.

Kennedy, Ellen (1991), *The Bundesbank: Germany's Central Bank in the International Monetary System*, London: Pinter/Royal Institute of International Affairs.

Kennedy, Paul (1988), *The Rise and Fall of the Great Powers: Economic Change and Military Conflict from 1500 to 2000*, London: Fontana Press.

—— (1993), *Preparing for the Twenty-First Century*, London: Harper Collins.

Kennes, Walter (1990), "The European Community and Food Security", *IDS Bulletin*, 21 (3), pp. 67–71.

Keohane, Robert O. (1984), *After Hegemony: Cooperation and Discord in the World Economy*, Princeton, NJ: Princeton University.

—— (ed.) (1986), *Neorealism and its Critics*, New York: Columbia University Press.

Keynes, John Maynard (1920), *The Economic Consequences of the Peace*, New York: Harcourt, Brace & Howe, p. 251.

Khaldun, Ibn Abd-ar-Rahman (1978), *The Muqadimmah: An Introduction to History*, trans. by F. Rosenthal, London: Routledge & Kegan Paul.

Kiljunen, Kimmo (ed.) (1989), *MINI-NIEO: The Potential for Regional North–South Cooperation*, Helsinki: Institute for Development Studies.

Killick, Tony (1986), "Twenty-Five Years in Development: The Rise and Impending Decline of Market Solutions", *Development Policy Review*, 4, pp. 99–116.

—— (1989), *A Reaction Too Far: Economic Theory and the Role of the State in Developing Countries*, London: ODI.

—— (1990), "The Sound of Cautious Optimism: Developing Country Adjustments in the 1980s and 1990s", in G. Bird (ed.) *The International Financial Regime*, Surrey: University of Surrey Press, pp. 197–207.

—— (1992), "Problems and Sources of Difficulty with Adjustment Conditionality", paper presented to the National Conference on Zambia's Structural Adjustment at Kitwe, 21–23 March (mimeo).

—— and Christopher Stevens (1989), *Development Cooperation and Structural Adjustment: the Issues for Lomé IV*, London: HMSO.

Kindleberger, Charles (1986), *The World in Depression, 1929–1939*, Berkeley: University of California Press.

Kissinger, Henry A. (1994), *Diplomacy*, New York: Simon & Schuster.

Knorr, Klaus (1973), *Power and Wealth*, New York: Basic Books.

Knutsen, Torbjön L. (1992), *A History of International Relations Theory: an Introduction*, Manchester and New York: Manchester University Press.

Kogbe, Cornelius (1985), "Africa: Appreciable Resources of Minerals and Metals", *The Courier*, November–December.

Kolko, Joyce (1988), *Restructuring the World Economy*, New York: Pantheon Books.

Koloko, Edwin (1985), "Sysmin and Mining in Zambia", *The Courier*, 94, November–December.

Korner, P. *et al.* (1986), *The IMF and the Debt Crisis: A Guide to the Third World's Dilemma*, London: Zed Books.

Krasner, Stephen D. (1985), *Structural Conflict: The Third World against Global Liberalism*, Berkeley: University of California Press.

Krugman, Paul (1994), "Competitiveness: A Global Obsession", *Foreign Affairs*, 73 (2), March/April, pp. 28–44.

Kubalkova, V. and A. A. Kruickshank (1980), *Marxism-Leninism and the Theory of International Relations*, London: Routledge & Kegan Paul.

Kwapong, Alexander Adum (1969), *The Role of Classical Studies in Africa Today*, Lagos: University of Lagos Press.

Kymlicka, Will (1990), *Contemporary Political Philosophy: An Introduction*, Oxford: Clarendon Press.

Laidler, Michael (1991), "Programming Lomé IV", *Lomé Briefing*, 128, July–August, pp. 8–10.

Landymore, Peter (1990), "Structural Adjustment: The European Community's Approach", *The Crown Agents' Review*, April.

Lavelle, Louis (1971), *The Dilemma of Narcissus*, trans. W. T. Gardner, London: Allen & Unwin.

Lavigne, Marie (1985), *International Political Economy and Socialism*, Cambridge: Cambridge University Press.

Lawrence, Peter (ed.) (1986), *World Recession and the Food Crisis in Africa*, London: James Currey.

Lele, Uma (1990), "Comparative Advantage and Structural Transformation: A Review of Africa's Development Experience", in Gustav Ranis and T. P. Schultz (eds), *The State of Development Economics: Progress and Perspectives*, Oxford: Basil Blackwell, pp. 187–221.

Lewanika, Akashambwata M. (1990), "A Critique of the Dual Exchange Rate in Zambia", Lusaka: University of Zambia, Occasional Paper no. 2.

—— (1990), *Milk in a Basket: The Political-Economic Malaise in Zambia*, Lusaka: Zambia Research Foundation.

Leys, Colin (1975), *Underdevelopment in Kenya: The Political Economy of Neo-Colonialism*, London: Heinemann.

—— (1996), *The Rise and Fall of Development Theory*, London: James Currey.

Liniger-Goumaz, Maurice (1972), *L'Afrique: Utopie ou Réalité?* Yaoundé: Presses de Yaoundé.

Linklater, Andrew (1982), *Men and Citizens in the Theory of International Relations*, London: Macmillan.

Lipton, Michael (1983), "African Agricultural Development: The EEC's New Role", *Development Policy Review*, (1), pp. 1–21.

Lodge, Juliet (1989), "EC Policymaking: Institutional Considerations", in Juliet

Lodge (ed.) *The European Community and the Challenge of the Future*, London: Pinter Publishers, pp. 26–57.

Lomax, David F. (1986), *The Developing Country Debt Crisis*, London: Macmillan.

Long, Frank (ed.) (1980), *The Political Economy of EEC Relations with the African, Caribbean and Pacific States*, Oxford: Pergamon.

Loxley, John (1987), "The IMF, the World Bank and sub-Saharan Africa: Policies and Politics", in K. J. Havnevik, (ed.), *The IMF and the World Bank in Africa: Conditionality, Impact and Alternatives*, Uppsala: Scandinavian Institute for African Studies, pp. 47–63.

Lipton, Michael (1983), "African Agricultural Development: the EEC's New Role", *Development Policy Review*, 1, pp. 1–21.

Lister, Marjorie (1988), *The European Community and the Developing World*, Aldershot: Avebury.

Luke, David F. and Timothy M. Shaw (eds), *The Lagos Plan of Action and Africa's Economic Future*, Lanham: University Press of America.

Lukes, Steven (1974), *Power: A Radical View*, London and Basingstoke: Macmillan.

—— (ed.) (1986), *Power*, Oxford: Blackwell.

Lungu, Gatian F. (1985), *Administrative Decentralisation: An Analysis of Environmental Constraints*, Zambian Papers no. 8, Gweru, Zimbabwe: Mambo Press.

Mahjoub, Azzam (ed.) (1990), *Adjustment or Delinking? The African Experience*, Tokyo: UNU/London: Zed Books.

Malcolm, Neil (1993), "The Soviet Union and Europe", in Jonathan Story (ed.) *The New Europe: Politics, Government and the Economy since 1945*, Oxford: Basil Blackwell.

Manda, Paul M. (1988), "The Decentralisation of Government in Zambia since Independence", unpublished PhD thesis, University of Leeds.

Manzetti, Luigi (1991), *The IMF and Economic Stabilisation: The Argentinian Case*, New York: Praeger.

Marcussen, Henrik S. and Torp, J. E. (1982), *The Internationalisation of Capital: The Prospects for the Third World*, London: Zed Books.

Marin, Manuel (1991), "Writing off the ACP Debt", *Lomé Briefing*, January–February, p. 9.

—— (1991), "Democracy Cannot Be Imposed from Outside", *The Courier*, 128, July–August, pp. 50–51.

Martin, Guy (1982), "Africa and the Ideology of Eurafrica: Neo-Colonialism or Pan-Africanism?", *The Journal of Modern African Studies*, 20 (2), pp. 221–238.

—— (1986), "The Franc Zone, Underdevelopment and Dependency in Francophone Africa", *Third World Quarterly*, 8 (1), January, pp. 205–235.

Mason, Edward and Robert Asher (1973), *The World Bank since Bretton Woods*, Washington, DC: The Brookings Institution.

Maxwell, Simon and T. Owens (1991), *Commodity Aid and Counterpart Funds in Africa*, Sussex: IDS.

Mayall, James (1979), "The Implications for Africa of the Enlarged European Economic Community", in T. M. Shaw and S. Heard (eds), *The Politics of Africa: Dependence and Underdevelopment*, London: Longman, pp. 286–317.

Mayes, David G. (ed.) (1993), *The External Implications of European Integration*, New York: Harvester Wheatsheaf.

Mazrui, Ali A. (1967) *Towards a Pax Africana*, London: Methuen.

—— (1993), "Global Apartheid? Race and Religion in the New World Order", in Geir Lundestad and O. Westad (eds), *Beyond the Cold War: New Dimensions in International Relations*, 90th Anniversary Nobel Jubilee Symposium, Oslo and Oxford: Scandinavian University Press.

McQueen, Martin (undated), "Developmental Constraints of the Rules of Origin of the Lomé Convention", University of Reading (mimeo).
Médard, Jean.-François (1982), "L'État Sous-Développé en Afrique Noire: Clientélisme Politique ou Néo-Patrimonialisme?", Bordeaux: Centre d'Étude d'Afrique Noire, no. 1 (mimeo).
Meebelo, Henry S. (1973), *Main Currents of Zambian Humanist Thought*, Lusaka: Oxford University Press.
Meier, Gerald M. (1982), *Problems of a World Monetary Order*, 2nd edn, New York and Oxford: Oxford University Press.
Meijer, Fons (1990), "Structural Adjustment and Diversification in Zambia", *Development and Change*, 21, pp. 657–692.
Mezger, Dorothea (1979), *Copper in the World Economy*, London: Heinemann.
Michaels, Marguerite (1992/3), "Retreat from Africa", *Foreign Affairs* 27 (1), pp. 93–108.
Migdal, Joel S. (1988), *Strong Societies and Weak States: State–Society Relations and State Capabilities in the Third World*, Princeton, NJ: Princeton University Press.
Miller, Lynn H. (1985), *Global Order: Values and Power in International Politics*, Boulder and London: Westview Press.
Milward, Alan S. (1994), *The European Rescue of the Nation-State*, London: Routledge.
Minc, Alain (1993), *Le Nouveau moyen age*, Paris: Éditions Gallimard.
Ministry of Foreign Affairs (1991), "ACP–EEC Cooperation after the Year 2000", (internal memorandum), Abuja, Nigeria, December.
Mintz, Beth and Michael Schwatz (1985), *The Power Structure of American Business*, Chicago and London: The University of Chicago Press.
Mistry, Percy (1993), *The African Debt Revisited*, The Hague: AWEPAA.
Mkandawire, Thandika (1988a), "The Road to Crisis, Adjustment and de-Industrialisation: The African Case", *African Development*, XIII (1), pp. 5–31.
—— (1988b), "Debates: Comments on Democracy and Political Stability", *African Development*, XIII (3), pp. 77–87.
—— (1991) "Crisis and Adjustment in Sub-Saharan Africa", in Dharam Ghai (ed.), *The IMF and the South: The Social Impact of Crisis and Adjustment*, London: Zed Books, pp. 80-94.
Mollet, John A. (1990), *Planning for Agricultural Development*, Aldershot: Avebury.
Momoh, Eddie (1990), "ECOWAS Summit: West Africa Responds to Europe 1992", *African Economic Digest*, 4 June, pp. 3–9.
Morel, E. D. (1917), *Africa and the Peace of Europe*, London: National Labour Press.
Morgenthau, Hans J. (1993), *Politics among Nations*, rev. edn, New York: McGraw-Hill.
Morriss, Peter (1987), *Power: A Philosophical Analysis*, Manchester: Manchester University Press.
Morse, Edward L. (1976), *Modernisation and the Transformation of International Relations*, New York: The Free Press.
Mortimer, Robert E. (1980), *The Third World Coalition in International Politics*, New York: Praeger.
Morton, James (1994), *The Poverty of Nations: The Aid Dilemma at the Heart of Africa*, London and New York: Academic Press.
Mosley, Paul (1987), *Conditionality as a Bargaining Process: Structural Adjustment Lending, 1980–1986*, Princeton, NJ: Princeton Essays International Finance, no. 168.
Mosley, Paul, J. Harrigan and J. Toye (1991), *Aid and Power: The World Bank and Policy-Based Lending*, vols 1 & 2, London and New York: Routledge.
Moss, Joanna (1982), *The Lomé Conventions and Their Implications for the United States*, Boulder, Co.: Westview.

Mtshali, Benedict V. (1972) "Zambia's Foreign Policy: The Dilemmas of a New State", unpublished PhD thesis, New York University.

—— *et al.* (1970) *Zambia and the World: Essays on Problems Relating to Zambia's Foreign Policy*, Lusaka: University of Zambia School of Humanities and Social Sciences, September.

Mudimbe, Victor Y. (1988), *The Invention of Africa: Gnosis, Philosophy and the Order of Knowledge*, Bloomington, Ind.: University of Indiana Press.

Musokotwane, Situmbeko (1992), "Structural Adjustment and Financial Institutions in Zambia", presentation at the conference on Structural Adjustment in Zambia, Kitwe, March (mimeo).

Mwaipanya, P. A. (1984), *African Humanism and National Development*, Washington, DC: University Press of America.

Myers, Robert J. (ed.) (1987), *The Political Morality of the International Monetary Fund*, New Brunswick and Oxford: Transaction Books.

Mytelka, Lynne K. (1978), "The Lomé Convention and a New International Division of Labour", *Journal of European Integration*, 1(1), pp. 63–76.

Nabudere, Daniel W. (1979), *Essays on the Theory and Practice of Imperialism*, London: Onyx.

Nagle, Sean Colman (1985), "Agricultural Finance and Economic Development with Particular Reference to Zambia", unpublished PhD thesis, National University of Ireland, Cork.

Nardin, Terry (1981), "Distributive Justice and the Criticism of International Law", *Political Studies*, 29 (2), September, pp. 232–244.

Ncube, M. *et al.* (1987), "The International Monetary Fund and Zambian Economy", in K. J. Havnevik (ed.), *The IMF and the World Bank in Africa*, Uppsala: Scandinavian Institute for African Studies, pp. 127–148.

Ndegwa, Philip (1987), "Critical Issues for Africa in the Eighties: External Indebtedness" (mimeo).

Ndulo, Muna (1979), "Domestic Participation in Mining in Zambia", in B. Turok (ed.), *Development in Zambia: A Reader*, London: Zed Books, pp. 49–69.

Nelson, Joan M. (1992), "Poverty, Equity and the Politics of Adjustment", in S. Haggard and R. Kaufman (eds) *The Politics of Economic Adjustment*, Princeton, NJ: Princeton University Press, pp. 221–269.

—— (ed.) (1992), *Economic Crisis and Policy Choice: The Politics of Adjustment in the Third World*, Princeton, NJ: Princeton University Press.

Ninsin, Kwame A. (1990), "Ghana under the PNDC: Delinking or Structural Adjustment?", in Azzam Mahjoub (ed.), *Adjustment or Delinking? The African Experience*, London: Zed Books, pp. 131–156.

Nkrumah, Kwame (1964), *Africa Must Unite*, London: Heinemann.

Nölling, Wilhelm (1993), *Monetary Policy in Europe after Maastricht*, London: Macmillan.

Nowzad, B. (1990), "Lessons of the Debt Decade", *Finance and Development*, March, pp. 9–13.

Nsouli, Saleh M. (1989), "Structural Adjustment in Sub-Saharan Africa: the Policy Issues and Challenges for the 1990s", *Finance and Development*, September.

Nyang'oro, Julius E. (1988), "The Politics of International Debts: The Case of Africa", *Africa Quarterly*, XXVI (1), pp. 17–41.

Nye, Joseph S. (1990), *Bound to Lead: The Changing Nature of American Power*, New York: Basic Books.

Nyerere, Julius K. (1986), "An Address", in *Development and Change*, 17 (3), pp. 1–18.

Ohmae, Kenichi (1985), *Triad Power: The Coming Shape of Global Competition*, New York: The Free Press.

—— (1990) *The Borderless World: Power and Strategy in the Interlinked Economy*, London: Fontana.

Okigbo, P. N. C. (1967), *Africa and the Common Market*, London: Longman.

—— (1989), *National Development Planning in Nigeria*, London: James Currey.

—— (1990), "Africa and a Changing Europe: Hopes and Fears", lecture delivered at the Royal Institute of International Affairs, Chatham House, and published in (London) *Nigeria Homenews*, 28 June–4 July, p. 4.

Ollawa, Patrick E. (1979), *Participatory Democracy in Zambia*, Devon: Arthur H. Stockwell.

Olson, William C. and A. J. R. Groom (1991), *International Relations Then and Now: Origins and Trends in Interpretation*, London: Harper Collins.

O'Neill, Helen (1985) "Small is Beautiful: Micro-Projects in the New Convention", *Lomé Briefing*, 21.

O'Neill, Onora (1989), *Constructions of Reason: Explorations of Kant's Practical Philosophy*, Cambridge: Cambridge University Press.

—— (1993), "Kantian Ethics", in Peter Singer (ed.) *A Companion to Ethics*, Oxford: Blackwell.

Onimode, Bade (ed.) (1989), *The IMF, the World Bank and the African Debt vol. 1 & 2: The Social and Political Impact*, London: Zed Books.

Onitiri, H. M. A. (1988), "African Recovery and Development", in Sidney Dell, *Policies for Development: Essays in Honour of Gamani Corea*, London: Macmillan.

Oppenheim, Felix (1981), *Political Concepts: A Reconstruction*, Oxford: Basil Blackwell.

Organization of African Unity (1979), *The Lagos Plan of Action for the Economic Development of Africa, 1980–2000*, Geneva: International Institute for Labour Studies.

Organski, A. F. Kenneth (1968), *World Politics*, 2nd edn, New York: Alfred Knopf.

Ortega y Gasset, José (1961) *The Revolt of the Masses*, London: Allen & Unwin.

Otremba, Walther (1989), "New Debt Strategies after the Brady Plan", *Intereconomics*, Sept./October, p. 241.

Overbeek, Henk and K. van der Pijl (1993), "Restructuring Capital and Restructuring Hegemony", in H. Overbeek (ed.), *Restructuring Hegemony in the Global Economy: The Rise of Transnational Neo-Liberalism*, London and New York: Routledge.

Overseas Development Institute (1989), "Negotiating the Fourth Lomé Convention", *ODI Briefing Paper*, London, October.

—— (1990a), "Recent Initiatives on Developing Country Debt", *ODI Briefing Paper*, London, April.

—— (1990b) "The European Bank for Reconstruction", *ODI Briefing Paper*, London, September.

—— (1992), "Aid and Political Reform", *ODI Briefing Paper*, London, January.

Oxfam Policy Department (1993), *Africa Make or Break*, Oxford: Oxfam Publications.

—— (1994), *Structural Adjustment and Inequality in Latin America: How IMF and World Bank Policies Have Failed the Poor*, Oxford: Oxfam Publications.

—— (1995), *A Case for Reform: Fifty Years of the IMF and the World Bank*, Oxford: Oxfam Publications.

Page, Sheila (1990), "The Effects of 1992 on the World Trading System: A Preliminary Overview", Development Studies Association Annual Conference, Glasgow, 5–7 September (mimeo).

Parfitt, Trevor W. and Stephen P. Riley (1989), *The African Debt Crisis*, London: Routledge.

Parfitt, Trevor W. and Sandy Bullock (1990), "The Prospects for a New Lomé Convention: Structural Adjustment or Structural Transformation?", *Review of African Political Economy*, August, pp. 104–116.

Pastor, Manuel (1989), "Latin America, the Debt Crisis, and the International Monetary Fund", *Latin American Perspectives*, 16 (60), pp. 790–810.

Payer, Cheryl (1982), *The World Bank: A Critical Analysis*, New York and London: Macmillan.

Pearce, Richard (undated), *Food Consumption and Adjustment in Zambia*, Oxford: Food Studies Group, Queen Elizabeth House.

Pettman, Jan (1974), *Zambia: Security and Conflict*, Sussex: Julian Friedman.

Pickles, Dorothy (1962), *The Fifth French Republic Institutions and Politics*, London: Methuen.

Pinder, John (1984), "Western Europe and the South: A Question of Political Economy", *Third World Quarterly*, 6 (1), January, pp. 117–144.

Pisani, Edgard (1988), "A Warning", *Lomé Briefing*, 2, September.

Please, Stanley (1984), *The Hobbled Giant: Essays on the World Bank*, Boulder, Col., and London: Westview Press.

Polanyi, Karl (1957), *The Great Transformation*, Boston: Beacon Press.

Porter, Michael (1990) *The Competitive Advantage of Nations*, London: Macmillan.

Prendergast, Renée and H. W. Singer (eds) (1994), *Development Policy Perspectives for the 1990s*, London: Macmillan.

Raikes, Philip (1988), *Modernising Hunger: Famine, Food Surplus and Farm Policy in the EEC and Africa*, London and Portsmouth: Catholic Institute for International Relations.

Rakner, Lise (1993), "Political Transition and Economic Reform: The Politics of Labour in Zambian National Politics", *Forum for Development Studies*, 2, pp. 131-147.

Ramphal, Shridath (1985), "The ACP Years", *The Courier*, September–October.

Ravenhill, John (1985), *Collective Clientelism: The Lomé Conventions and North–South Relations*, New York: Columbia University Press.

Rawls, John (1971), *A Theory of Justice*, Cambridge, Mass.: Harvard University Press.

Reich, Robert (1991), *The Work of Nations: Preparing Ourselves for 21st Century Capitalism*, London: Simon & Schuster.

Reynolds, Charles (1992), *The World of States: An Introduction to Explanation and Theory*, Aldershot, Hants: Edward Elgar.

Rimmer, Douglas (1989), "Africa's Economic Future", *African Affairs*, 88 (351), pp. 173–185.

Roberts, Andrew (1976), *A History of Zambia*, London: Heinemann.

Robinson, Ronald and J. Gallagher (1953), "The Imperialism of Free Trade", *Economic History Review*, 6, pp. 1–15.

Roemer, Michael (1985), "Dutch Disease in Developing Countries: Swallowing Bitter Medicine", in M. Lundahl (ed.), *The Primary Sector in Economic Development*, London: Croom Helm, pp. 234–252.

—— (1989), "The Economics of Counterpart Funds Revisited", *World Development*, 17 (6), pp. 795–807.

Rosenau, James N. (1981), *The Study of Political Adaptation: Essays in the Analysis of World Politics*, London and New York: Frances Pinter.

—— (1990), *Turbulence in World Politics: A Theory of Change and Continuity*, New York: Harvester Wheatsheaf.

—— and Ernst-Otto Czempiel (eds) (1992), *Governance without Government: Order and Change in World Politics*, Cambridge: Cambridge University Press.

Rostow, Walt W. (1971), *The Stages of Economic Growth: A Non-Communist Manifesto*, London and New York: Frances Pinter.

Rotberg, Robert. I. (1965), *The Rise of Nationalism in Central Africa: The Making of Malawi and Zambia, 1873–1964*, Cambridge, Mass.: Harvard University Press.

—— (1988), *The Founder: Cecil Rhodes and the Pursuit of Power*, New York: Oxford University Press.

Rothchild, Donald and Chazan, N. (eds) (1988), *The Precarious Balance: State and Society in Africa*, Boulder, Col., and London: Westview Press.

Rothstein, Robert L. (ed.) (1988), *Africa in the 1990s and Beyond: US Policy Opportunities and Choices*, Algonac, Michigan: World Peace Foundation.

—— (1991), "Limits and Possibilities of Weak Theory: Interpreting North–South Relations", in Rothstein, *The Evolution of Theory in International Relations*, Essays in Honour of William T. R. Fox, Columbia, SC: University of Southern Carolina Press.

Royal Tropical Institute (1984), *Food Strategies in Four Africa Countries: A Study on Food Policy Formulation and Implementation in Kenya, Mali, Rwanda and Zambia*, (prepared for the EC Commission), Amsterdam, January.

Russett, Bruce and Harvey Starr (1981), *World Politics: The Menu For Choice*, New York: W. H. Freeman and Co.

Said, Edward (1993), *Culture and Imperialism*, London: Chatto & Windus.

Sandbrook, Richard (1986), "The State and Economic Stagnation in Tropical Africa", *World Development*, 14 (3), March.

—— (with J. Parker) (1987), *The Politics of Africa's Economic Stagnation*, Cambridge: Cambridge University Press.

Sanderson, Murray (1992), "Zambia's Structural Adjustment: Where Do We Go from Here? – A Business View", paper presented at the National Conference on Zambia"s Structural Adjustment Programme, Kitwe, Zambia, 21–23 March (mimeo).

Sauvant, Karl P. (1981), *The Group of 77: Evolution, Structure, Organization*, New York: Oceana.

Schapera, Isaac (1955), *A Handbook of Tswana Law and Custom*, Oxford: Oxford University Press, for the International African Institute.

Schneider, Bertrand (ed.) (1988), *Africa Facing Its Priorities*, The Club of Rome Cooperation for Development Series, vol. 7, London: Cassell.

Schoenholtz, Andrew I. (1987), "The IMF in Africa: Unnecessary and Undesirable Western Restraints on Development", *Journal of Modern African Studies*, pp. 400–433.

Schultz, Siegfried (1987), "Food Aid: An Effective Instrument of Development Policy?", *Intereconomics*, May/June, pp. 137–144.

Schumacher, E. F. (1973), *Small is Beautiful*, Harmondsworth: Penguin.

Sen, Amartya (1987), *On Ethics and Economics*, Oxford: Blackwell.

Senghaas, Dieter (1985), *The European Experience: A Historical Analysis of Development Theory*, Lexington, New Hampshire: Berg Press.

Sesay, Amadu (ed.) (1986), *Africa and Europe: From Partition to Interdependence or Dependence?*, London: Croom Helm.

Sewell, John W. and I. W. Zartman, (1984), "Global Negotiations: Path to the Future or Dead-End Street?", *Third World Quarterly*, 6, April.

Shafer, D.M. (1986), "Undermined: The Implications of Mineral Export Dependence for State Formation in Africa", *Third World Quarterly*, 8 (3), pp. 917–951.

Shams, Robert (1989), "Adjustment Constraints in Developing Countries: A Comparative Study", *Intereconomics*, March/April, pp. 71–78.
Shaw, Timothy M. (1979), "EEC–ACP Interactions and Images as Redefinitions of Eurafrica: Exemplary, Exclusive and/or Exploitive?", *Journal of Common Market Studies*, 18, pp. 1351–1358.
Singer, Hans W. (1989), *Lessons of the Post-War Development Experience: 1945–1988*, Sussex: IDS Discussion Paper no. 260, April.
Sklar, Richard L. (1975), *Corporate Power in an African State*, Berkeley: University of California Press.
Smith, David (1987), *The Rise and Fall of Monetarism*, Harmondsworth: Penguin.
Smith, Sheila and John Sender (1984), *What's Right with the Berg Report and What's Left of Its Critics?*, Sussex: IDS Discussion Paper no. 192, June.
Solomon, Robert (1977), *The International Monetary System, 1945–1976*, New York: Harper & Row.
Soper, Tom (1969), "European Trade with Africa", *Africa Contemporary Record*, pp. 787–797.
South Commission, *The Challenge to the South*, Report of the South Commission, Oxford: Oxford University Press, 1992.
Spero, Joan E. (1993), *The Politics of International Economic Relations*, 4th edn, London: Routledge.
Spieles, Wolfgang (1987), "Debt-Equity Swaps and the Heavily Indebted Countries", *Intereconomics*, Sept./October, pp. 120–124.
Spraos, John (1986) *IMF Conditionality: Ineffectual, Inefficient, and Mistargeted*, Princeton Essays in International Finance, 166, December.
Stallings, Barbara (1992), "International Influence on Economic Development: Debt, Stabilisation and Structural Reform", in Haggard and Kaufman, *The Politics of Economic Adjustment*, pp. 41–88.
Staner, André (1976), "The EDF Committee: Twelve Years' Work", *The Courier*, 36, March–April, pp. 38–43.
Staudt, Karin (1991), *Managing Development: State, Society, and International Contexts*, Newbury Park: Sage.
Stevens, Christopher (1979), *Food Aid and the Developing World: Four Studies*, London: Croom Helm.
—— (ed.) (1981), *The EEC and the Third World: A Survey*, vol. 1, London: ODI.
—— (ed.) (1982), *The EEC and the Third World: A Survey*, vol. 2, London: ODI.
—— (ed.) (1983), *The EEC and the Third World: A Survey*, vol. 3, London: ODI.
—— (ed.) (1984a), *The EEC and the Third World: A Survey*, vol. 4, London: ODI.
—— (1984b), "The EEC's Year", *Africa Contemporary Record*, xviii, p. B167.
—— (1986), *The Lomé III Negotiations*, Sussex: IDS Discussion Paper.
—— (1988), "The Lessons of Lomé III", *Lomé Briefing*, 2, September.
—— (1990), "The Impact of Europe 1992 on the South", *IDS Bulletin*, 21 (1), pp. 50–56.
—— and T. Killick (1989), "Development Cooperation and Structural Adjustment: the Issues for Lomé IV", report prepared for discussion at the Conference on Structural Adjustment and Lomé IV, April (mimeo).
—— and T. Killick (1991), "The EC and Structural Adjustment", in Prendergast and Singer, *Development Policy Perspectives for the 1990s*, London: Macmillan.
—— and J. V. van Themaat (eds) (1985), *Pressure Groups, Policies and Development: The Private Sector and the Third World*, London: Hodder & Stoughton/ODI.
Stiles, Kendall and Takashi Akaha (eds) (1991), *International Political Economy: A Reader*, New York: Harper Collins.
Stokke, Olav (ed.) (1989), *Western Middle Powers and Global Poverty: the Determinants of*

the Aid Policies of Canada, Denmark, the Netherlands, Norway and Sweden, Uppsala: Scandinavian Institute of African Studies and the Norwegian Institute for International Affairs.

Stopford, John and S. Strange (1991), *Rival States, Rival Competition for World Market Shares*, Cambridge: Cambridge University Press.

Strange, Susan (1971), *Sterling and British Policy*, London: University Press/Royal Institute for International Affairs.

—— (1988), *States and Markets: An Introduction to International Political Economy*, London: Pinter Publishers.

—— and R. Tooze (eds) (1982), *The Politics of International Surplus Capacity*, London: Allen & Unwin.

Streeten, Paul (1989), "A Survey of the Issues", in S. Commander (ed.), *Structural Adjustment and Agriculture: Theory and Practice in Africa and Latin America*, London: James Currey, pp. 3–18.

Sullivan, Michael P. (1990), *Power in Contemporary International Politics*, Columbia, SC: University of South Carolina Press.

Svendsen, Karl E. (1987), "The Failure of the International Debt Strategy", Copenhagen: Centre for Development Research.

Svensson, Vidar (1979), *Essays on the EEC African Association*, Uppsala: Lund University.

Taylor, Christopher (1995), *EMU 2000? Prospects for European Monetary Union*, London: Royal Institute of International Affairs.

Taylor, Lance (1983), *Structuralist Macroeconomics*, New York: Basic Books.

—— (1988), *Varieties of Stabilisation Experience: Towards a Sensible Macroeconomics in the Third World*, Oxford: Clarendon.

Thomas, Caroline (1987), *In Search of Security: The Third World in International Relations*, Boulder, Col.: Lynne Rienner.

Thompson, Virginia and R. Adloff (1975), "French Economic Policy in Tropical Africa", in P. Duignan and L. H. Gann (eds), *Colonialism in Africa, vol. IV: The Economics of Colonialism*, Cambridge: Cambridge University Press, pp. 127–164.

Toffler, Alvin and H. Toffler (1994), *War and Anti-War: Survival at the Dawn of the 21st Century*, London: Little, Brown & Co.

Tordoff, William (ed.) (1974), *Politics in Zambia*, Manchester: Manchester University Press.

—— (ed.) (1980), *Administration in Zambia*, Manchester: Manchester University Press.

Touré, Ahmed Sékou (1960), "Africa's Destiny", in J. Duffy, and R. A. Manners (eds), *Africa Speaks*, Princeton, NJ: Van Nostrand.

Toye, John (1989), "Can the World Bank Resolve the Crisis of Developing Countries?", *Journal of International Development*, 1 (2), pp. 261–272.

—— (1991), "Is There a New Political Economy of Development?" in Christopher Colclough and J. Manor (eds), *States or Markets: Neo-Liberalism and the Development Policy Debate*, Oxford: Clarendon Press, pp. 321–378.

—— (1993), *Dilemmas of Development: Reflections on the Counter-Revolution in Development Economics*, 2nd edn, Oxford: Blackwell.

Tsoukalis, Loukas (ed.) (1986), *Europe, America and the World Economy*, Oxford: Basil Blackwell.

—— (ed.) (1983), *The European Community: Past, Present and Future*, Oxford: Basil Blackwell.

—— (1991), *The New European Economy: The Politics and Economics of Integration*, Oxford: Oxford University Press.

Tucker, Robert W. (1977), *The Inequality of Nations*, London: Robertson.

Turok, Ben (ed.) (1989), *Mixed Economy in Zambia*, London: Institute for African Alternatives.

Twitchett, Carol C. (1978), *Europe and Africa: From Association to Partnership*, Westmead, Hants: Saxon House.

—— (1981), *A Framework for Development: the EEC and the ACP*, London: Allen & Unwin.

Underwood, John (1988), "The Debt Problem in Sub-Saharan Africa: Causes, Consequences and Possible Solutions", in R. I. Rotberg (ed.), *Africa in the 1990s and Beyond*, Algonac, Michigan: World Peace Foundation, pp. 73–111.

United Nations (1986) *Programme of Action for African Recovery and Development 1986–1990 (UNPAAERD)*, New York: United Nations.

United Nations Development Programme (1990) *Development Cooperation: Zambia*, 1989 Report, July.

Vaitsos, Constantine (1974), *Intercountry Income Distribution and Transnational Enterprises*, Oxford: Clarendon Press.

—— (1989), "Radical Technological Changes and the New Order in the World Economy", *The European Journal of Development Research*, 1 (1), June.

van der Hoeven, Rolph (1990), *Debt: The Unwanted Heritage of Today's Children*, Sussex: IDS, November.

van der Pijl, Kees (1984), *The Making of an Atlantic Ruling Class*, London: Verso.

Vander Stichele, Myriam (1990), "The Lost Spirit of Lomé", *Lomé Briefing*, January–February.

van Gennip, Jos (1984) and P. M. van Dijk, "Food Strategies, NGOs and Lomé III", *Lomé Briefing*, no. 20.

Viand, Maurice (1984), "La Caisse Centrale de coopération economique et les nouvelles orientations de la politique française d'aide au développement", *Afrique Contemporaine*, 126, April–June, pp. 3–20.

Vincent, John (1986), *Human Rights and International Relations*, Cambridge: Cambridge University Press.

von Furstenberg, George M. (1987), "The IMF as Market-Maker for Official Business between Nations", in Robert J. Myers (ed.) *The Political Morality of the International Monetary Fund*, New Brunswick and Oxford: Transaction Books.

Wade, Robert (1990), *Governing the Market: Economic Theory and the Role of Government in East Asian Industrialisation*, Princeton, NJ: Princeton University Press.

Walker, R. B. J. (1993), *Inside/Outside: International Relations as Political Theory*, Cambridge: Cambridge University Press.

Wallerstein, Immanuel (1961), *Africa: The Politics of Independence*, New York: Vantage.

Walsh, Michael (ed.) (1991) *Proclaiming Justice and Peace*, London: Flame.

Walter, Andrew (1993), *Money and Power: The Role of Hegemony and International Monetary Order*, New York and London: Harvester Wheatsheaf.

Waltz, Kenneth N. (1959), *Man, the State and War: A Theoretical Analysis*, New York: Columbia University Press, 1959.

—— (1979) *Theory of International Politics*, New York: Random House.

Waterhouse, Price (1988), *EEC Forex Facility Report on FEMAC 24 Session*, Lusaka, 8 April.

Weiss, Ruth (1975), "Africa and the EEC", *African Contemporary Record*, p. A17.

Whitehead, Lawrence (1990), "Political Explanations of Macroeconomic Management: A Survey", *World Development*, 18 (80), pp. 1133–1146.

Williams, Gavin P. (1985), "The Contradictions of the World Bank and the Crisis of the State in Africa", Paris Conference, December (mimeo).

Williams, Marc (1994), *International Economic Organisations and the Third World*, New York and London: Harvester Wheatsheaf.

Williamson, John (ed.) (1983), *IMF Conditionality*, Washington, DC: Institute for International Economics.
Winsome, Leslie J. (1987) *The World Bank and Structural Transformation in Developing Countries: The Case of Zaire*, Boulder, Col.: Lynne Rienner.
Wöldring, Klaus (ed.) (1979), *Beyond Political Independence: Zambia's Economic Predicament in the 1980s*, Berlin: Mouton.
Wolf, Martin (1995), "Cooperation or Conflict? The EU in a Liberal Global Economy", *International Affairs*, 71 (2) April, pp. 325–337.
Wood, Adrian *et al.* (1990), *The Dynamics of Agricultural Policy and Reform in Zambia*, Ames: Iowa State University Press.
Wood, Robert E. (1986), *From Marshall Plan to Debt Crisis: Foreign Aid and Development Choices in the World Economy*, Berkeley: University of California Press.
World Bank (1981), *Accelerated Development in Sub-Saharan Africa: An Agenda for Action*, Washington, DC: The World Bank.
—— (1984a), *Towards Sustainable Development in Sub-Saharan Africa*, Washington, DC: The World Bank.
—— (1984b), *Zambia Agricultural Rehabilitation Project*, A Staff Confidential Report, May 24, Washington, DC: The World Bank.
—— (1989a), *Africa's Adjustment and Growth in the 1980s*, Washington, DC: The World Bank.
—— (1989b), *Sub-Saharan Africa from Crisis to Sustainable Growth: A Long-Term Perspective Study*, Washington, DC: The World Bank.
—— (1990), *World Development Report, 1990*, Washington, DC: The World Bank.
—— (1991), *World Debt Tables 1990–91*, Washington, DC: The World Bank.
—— (1992), *World Bank World Debt Tables*, Washington, DC: The World Bank.
—— (1993), *World Development Report,* Oxford: Oxford University Press.
Young, Simon Z. (1973) *Terms of Entry: Negotiations with the European Community 1970–72*, London: Heinemann.
Zacher, Mark W. (1992), "The Decaying Pillars of the Westphalian Temple: Implications for International Order and Governance", in Rosenau and Czempiel (eds) *Governance Without Government*, Cambridge: Cambridge University Press, pp. 58–101.
Zambit-Lomé Group (1991), *The Constitution of the Zambit-Lomé Group*, Lusaka, 22 March.
Zartman, William I. (1971), *The Politics of Trade Negotiations Between Africa and the EEC: The Weak Confront the Strong*, Princeton, NJ: Princeton University Press.
—— (1976), "Europe and Africa: Decolonization or Dependency?", *Foreign Affairs*, January.
—— (ed.) (1987), *Positive-Sum: Improving North–South Negotiations*, New Brunswick and Oxford: Transaction.
Zeldin, Theodore (1984), *France, 1848–1945*, Oxford and New York: Oxford University Press.

INDEX

AAF-SAP ('African Alternative') 28–30
Abraham, W. 260
'accommodation, triangle of' 242, 243
accounting anomalies 203–4
accumulation, capital 21
ACP Committee of Ambassadors 77, 79, 90–2
ACP Council 77, 186
ACP Secretariat-General 77–9
adaptation 5, 190
Addis Ababa memorandum 1984 124–5
Adedeji, A. 15, 25–6, 27
adjustment 3, 5; 'African Alternative' 28–30; autonomous programmes 104–5, 109; EC approach 102–3, 253–4; EC responses to Zambia's 217–51; ECA and politics of 25–8; growth-oriented strategy 128; regional dimension 103; social dimensions 96, 103, 233–47, 253–4; *see also* structural adjustment
administration 157–8, 183–4
Africa Confidential 217
'African Alternative' to adjustment 28–30
African, Caribbean and Pacific (ACP) Group 253; debt to EC 130–3; EC influence and power 255; expansion 101; institutions for Lomé 76–9; Lomé III negotiating position 90–3; Lomé IV negotiations 98–100 (debt question 140–1; position on structural adjustment 99–100); triangle of development diplomacy 12–13
African National Congress 148
African Priority Programme for Economic Recovery (APPER) 15, 16
Agricultural Input Import Support Programme (AIISP) 191, 226, 227
Agricultural Rehabilitation Project 196
agriculture: Lomé (and agricultural products 65–6, 68–9; concentration principle 92–3); World Bank 1989 report 27; Zambia 156, 159, 160, 174, 197, 197–8 (differences with EC 195–6; ECFF 228–30; export promotion 249, 250, 251; Lomé I 184; Lomé III 189–91; policy bias against 156–7; Smallholder Project 207–8; World Bank 196); *see also* food strategy
aid: 'African Alternative' 28–30; African attitudes to IFI programmes 23–33; critique of SAPs 17–23; donor attitudes 219–22; EC influence 254–5; ECA and politics of adjustment 25–8; Ferrero Resolution 85–6; IFI involvement in Africa 16–17; Lomé Convention 111–12 (aid programming 69–71; concentration principle 92–3; EU aid management 101–3; evaluation 82; implementation cycle 83; Lomé III negotiations 89–90; Lomé IV 97–8, 100, 101, 107–9); Monrovia Strategy to the Berg Report 14–16; new international aid regime 14–34; objective of association 45–6; performance of association regime 55–60; Pisani Memorandum 87–8; political conditionality 30–3; potential effects of Europe 1992 255–6; social exchange theory 10–11; structural adjustment, international economic relations and 4–5; UN Special Session on Africa 15–16; Yaoundé system 49–50, 51; to Zambia 150, 166, 181–216 (donors 181; evaluation criteria 173, 174; Fourth National Development Plan 175; INDP 173–4; Lomé I programming 183–6; Lomé II programming 186–9; Lomé III programming 189–91; Lomé IV programming 191–2; problems of management 210–15); *see also* under individual funds and projects
AMAX 150
Amin, S. 21
Anglo-African Commonwealth 51–4, 62, 63–4, 149
Anglo-American Corporation of South Africa 150
anti-colonial nationalism 35–6, 42–4
Arap Moi, D. 31
Article, 108 Committee 76
Arusha Convention 54
Asia 260–1; debt 113, 114; NICs 247
association 35–60, 252; Anglo-African Commonwealth 51–4; French colonial interests and 40–5; objectives 45–6; performance of association regime 54–60; Rome Treaty and emergence of 38–46; Yaoundé Conventions 46–51
Auclert, A. 225
auction 162–6, 169, 170–1, 197
Austin, D. 51–2, 252
autonomous adjustment programmes 104–5, 109

Ba, B. 65, 66
Baker Plan 128–9

balance of payments 158, 159, 162, 162–3
Baldwin, D. 10
Ball, G. 4
Bangladesh 87
bargaining 22–3, 273
Bates, R. H. 162, 163, 173
Bauer, P. T. 4
Beckman, B. 32
Bedié, K. 51
Belgium 44, 50, 219, 220
Benin 107, 136, 137
Berg Report 15
Berlin Conference 1884–85 36–7
Bersani, G. 112
Bhatia, Mr 225
Biafra 53, 149
Biersteker, T, 17, 18
Bolivian Emergency Social Fund (ESF) 233, 234
Bonnaci, G. 213, 225
Botswana 32
Boussac, M. 42
Brady Plan 129
Brazil 114, 117, 188
Bretton Woods institutions *see* international finance institutions
Bretton Woods regime 62–3
Britain 87, 95, 109; membership of EC 61–2; political conditionality 30–1, 31; Zambia 146, 147 (disinvestment 257–8; hard line 221, 221–2; trainees 205)
British South Africa Company (BSAC) 146
budget control 231–3
budget deficits 123; Zambia 161, 162, 170
Bullock, S. 109
Bunke, F. 221
bureaucracy 211–15
Burkina Faso 107
Burundi 136

Cable, V. 131, 134
cadre administratif 260, 309
Caisse Centrale 41
capability-expectations gap 255
capital, international 21
capital accumulation 21
capitalist development model 24–5
capture, politics of 229
Carrington, E. 79
cash-flow problem 188
Cassen, R. 4, 19–20
Central African Federation 147
Central/Eastern Europe 31–2, 99, 256
Central Province Smallholder Project 207
Centre d'Etudes et de Documentations Africaines (CEDAF) 212
centre and periphery 21
Chalker, L. 30–1
Chase-Dunn, C. 8
Cheysson, C. 98
Chigaga, G. 192, 221
Chikundu Embankment Project 241–2
Chikwanda, A. 157–8, 183
Chile 151, 233
Chiluba, F. 172, 177, 221, 231
China 44
Chipman, J. 37, 38
Chivuno, L. 165, 223
Chona, M. 182
CIPEC 151, 155–6
Clarke, J. 166
cobalt 201, 202; Germany and cobalt question 208–10
coercive association 39
collective self-reliance 91
Collier, P. 162, 163, 173
colonialism 35, 36–46; France 40–5; and underdevelopment in Zambia 146–7
commercial banks 121–2, 128, 129
commercial (private) debts 115, 116, 117, 118, 119, 120
Committee of Ambassadors (COREPER) 73
'Committee of Wise Men' 79
commodity exports 47–8
commodity prices 89, 96; collapse and external debt 122–3
commodity stabilization fund *see* Stabex
common African front 65–8
Common Agricultural Policy (CAP) 68–9
Common External Tariff (CET) 45, 47–8, 50
Commonwealth, Anglo-African 51–4, 62, 63–4, 149
community participation 246
Comoros 136
compellence 9
concentration, principle of 92–3
conditionality, macroeconomic 88, 98, 254; critique of structural adjustment programmes 22–3; EC and 109–10, 227–8; structure of World Bank conditionality 106
conditionality, political 30–3, 34, 110–12
copper 202; exports 151–2, 206; prices 151, 155–6, 161, 201, 206; production 151, 158, 161, 201, 206; *see also* mining sector
Copperbelt Smallholder Credit Scheme 207, 231–2
Copperbelt University Training Programme 191
Cornia, A. 18–19
Costa Rica 233
Côte d'Ivoire 117, 122, 129
Cotton Development Project 184, 185
countervalue funds (CVFs) 103–4, 188, 205, 255; and budget control 231–3
Cox, R. 7–8
Crocker, C. 256

Dahrendorf, Lord 31
Dakar seminar 138–40
DANAGRO 207
Dankert, P. 257
De Crombrugghe, G. 242
debt, external 2, 89, 96, 113–45; EC responses 130–44 (special debt programme for Africa 134, 135–44); international perspective 113–24; international responses 124–30 (Baker Plan) 128–9; Brady Plan 129; Lawson Plan 130; Toronto principles 127–8, 130; Trinidad Terms 130); Lomé Convention *see* Lomé Convention/relationship; nature 115–21; origins 121–4; volume 113–15;

Zambia 122, 152–3, 161, 162–3, 166, 178 (arrears 170, 177, 179, 222; 10 per cent ceiling on payments 174–5)
debt cancellation 129, 130, 143–4
debt-exports ratio 120
debt-GNP ratio 118–20
debt management 141–2
debt rescheduling 126–7
decentralized cooperation 110
decentralized development 111
'Declaration of Intent' 1963 61
decolonization 35–6, 42–4
defence budgets 29
delays 202–3, 210–11, 212
Delors, J. 259
democracy, 260; multi-party democracy in Zambia 176–8; political conditionality 30–3, 111–12
Déniau Memorandum 64
Denmark 219
dependence 261–2
deterrence 9
Deutsch, K. W. 6
devaluation 156, 164–5, 170–1, 197
development goals 96
Development Assistance Committee (DAC) 4
development diplomacy, triangle of 12–13
development policy: Lomé and 80–4 (conflict within EC 89–90); Pisani Memorandum 87–8; post-colonial 48–50; Zambia 150–3
Diori, H. 49
Diouf, A. 139–40
disinvestment 257–8
District Officers 242
diversification, economic 247–51
donor attitudes 219–22
Dumont, R. 248
'Dutch disease' 292
Duverger, M. 1

Eastern/Central Europe 31–2, 99, 256
Eastern Cooperative Union 199
EC-ACP Committee of Ambassadors 72
EC-ACP Joint Consultative Assembly 72–3, 112
EC-ACP Joint Council 71–2, 76, 82, 109, 256–7
EC Commission 74, 75–6; coordination with IFIs 105; CVFs and budgetary process 103–4; debt cancellation 143, 144; diplomacy with Zambia 224, 225–6; food strategy 86; Lomé IV negotiations 97–8; Zambia's planning problems 183–4
EC Committee of Ambassadors (COREPER) 73
EC Council 73; resolution on structural adjustment 94–6
EC Delegation 74, 214–15, 232–3
EC Expert's Office 213–14
EC Foreign Exchange Facility (ECFF) 228–30
EC Parliament 73–4, 86–7; debt cancellation 143, 144; Lomé IV negotiations 97; Resolution on Hunger in the World 192
EC Structural Adjustment Facility (SAF) 230–3, 254
EC Technical Coordinator 213
EC-Zambia Joint Committee 194, 195–6, 196–7
Economic Commission for Africa (ECA) 25–30, 52; Alternative Framework 28–30; and politics of adjustment 25–8
economic diversification 247–51
economic growth 128; democracy and 32; development, stabilization and 96
economic security 9
Economist, The 217–18
EDF Committee 75, 107, 109
education/training 188, 191; Micro-Projects Programme 237–9, 244–5; Multi-annual Training Programme 184–5, 187; Sysmin 205
elections 169, 177
eligibility for finance 104–5, 109, 134
Emergency Fund 50–1
energy sector 187
equipment purchasing 203, 204–5
Erbe, R. 128
Eurafrica 36–8, 252
'eurocracy' 211–15
Euromines 209–10
European Bank for Reconstruction and Development 31–2, 289
European Community/Union (EC) 2–3, 3; approach to adjustment 102–3, 253–4; British membership 61–2; coordination with IFIs 105–7; influence 10–11, 254–5; institutions for Lomé cooperation 73–6; Lomé III negotiating position 89–90; Lomé IV (aid management 101–3; negotiating position 96–8); macroeconomic conditionality 109–10, 227–8; Mediterranean enlargement 90–1; potential effects of Europe 1992, 255–6; responses to African debt, 130–44 (special debt programme for Africa 134, 135–44); Single Market 96, 99, 255–6; triangle of development diplomacy 12–13; Zambia (conditionality 227–8; first mission to Zambia 182–3; policy differences with World Bank 245–7; relations 181–2; responses to Zambia's reforms 222–6; *see also* Zambia)
European Court of Auditors 82
European Development Fund (EDF) 74–5; and ACP Secretariat 79, 255; African debt 131–2, 143; association 44, 45–6, 47, 48, 51, 55–60; 'boomerang effect' 60; bureaucratic delays 210–11; Lomé Conventions 66 (I and II compared 67; III 92); Pisani Memorandum 88; Zambia 184, 210, 225; *see also* EDF Committee
European Investment Bank (EIB) 45–6, 75, 289; African debt 131–2, 142, 143; Lomé III 92; Pisani Memorandum 88; Zambia 184, 224, 251
exchange rate 156, 164–5, 166, 169
experts: foreign 23, 25, 207–8, 214–15; technical 207–8, 214–15, 242
Export Board of Zambia (EBZ) 247
export earnings/debt repayment obligations 117
Export-Import (EXIM) bank 247
export promotion 247–51
exports: African commodity exports 47–8; copper 151–2, 206; and external debt 118–20; Zambia's mineral dependence 150–3, 155–6, 292; Zambia's non-traditional exports 248–51; *see also* trade
Extended Structural Adjustment Facility (ESAF) 24, 126, 176

external borrowing 152–3; *see also* debt, external

Federal Reserve 113
Ferrero Resolution 85–6
Ferry, J. 37
fertilizers 198, 224
Filori, J. M. 222–3
Final Act of Lagos (FAL) 14
financial misjudgement 59–60
Finnish International Development Agency (FINNIDA) 244
Foley, M. 183; 1980 programming mission 186–7
Fonds d'Investissement pour le Développement Economique et Social (FIDES) 40, 41
food: growth rate in production 2; imports in Zambia 159, 192–3; Lomé aid to Zambia 188, 189–91; *see also* agriculture
food strategy 85–7, 88; Zambia 192–200 (dialogue 192–8)
foreign exchange: auction 162–6, 169, 170–1, 197; ECFF 228–30; gap in Zambia 226–8
Foreign Exchange Management Committee (FEMAC) 173, 228
foreign experts 23, 25, 207–8, 214–15
foreign missions: Zambia's weaknesses 211
Forum for the Restoration of Democracy (FORD) (Kenya) 31
Franc Zone 40–1, 136
France: and 'African alternative' 29, 30; British membership of EC 61; colonialism 37–8 (and association 40–5; independence 46); disinvestment 258; Lagos Agreement 53; Mannesmann scheme 60; Strasbourg Plan 40; Yaoundé Conventions 50, 63; and Zambia 183, 221
France Afrique 37
Frisch, D. 95–6, 189

Galtung, J. 49
Gardiner, R. K. 25
Gebray, B. 79
gemstones 249, 251
General Agreement on Tariffs and Trade (GATT) 64, 68, 97; and association 45; Uruguay Round 96
General Import Programmes (GIPs) 102, 135, 136, 138, 230
Generalized System of Preferences (GSP) 55, 186
generative projects 213
George, S. 122
Georgetown Agreement 1975 76, 77
Germany 55, 183; and association 44, 50; and cobalt question 208–10; hard line on Zambia 221; Mannesmann scheme 59–60; SIP for Tanzania 109
Ghana 63; PAMSCAD 233; parallel government 23
Ghana–Guinea–Mali Union 52
Gill, S. 7, 8
Gilpin, R. 5
Gitelson, S. 213
'good government' *see* governance
Gossner Mission 236
governance 30–3, 110–12, 260
grain stores 198–9
Greece 97
gross domestic product (GDP): Zambia 152, 154, 155, 161, 174
gross national product (GNP) 118–20
growth-oriented adjustment strategy 128
Gruhn, I. 82–4
Guénier, E. 37, 38
Guinea 52, 136
Guinea-Bissau 136
Gulhati, R. 156
Gyselinck, J. 194

Hague Congress 1948 39
Hallstein, W. 40, 44
Harare Declaration 1985 78
hard-liners 219–22
Hare, Mr 51
Harmel, P. 62
Hart, J. 10
Hayter, T. 4
health centres 187, 237–9, 244
Hill, C. 255
Hill, T. 89
human-centred approach to development 26–7, 29
human rights 31, 111–12, 285
humane internationalism 219–20
humanism 148
humanitarian critique of IFI programmes 18–19
Hurd, D. 30
Hutchful, E. 23

ideology 148
imperialism 35, 36–8
import support 254; EC special debt programme for Africa 135–7, 138, 139; Zambia 198–200, 226–8, 230–1
INDECO 150, 151, 184
industrial sector 59; strangulation 24
inequalities, social 162
inflation 20; Zambia 152, 170, 174, 175
influence: EC 10–11, 254–5; power, social exchange and 6–11
infrastructure 187
Institute of Development Studies (IDS) 20
institutional framework for Lomé 71–9, 82–4
integrated rural development 69–71
integration, regional 261
interest arrears 117–18, 124
interest rates 123
international capital 21
international economic environment: changing 62–3, 259–62
international economic relations 4–5
international finance institutions (IFIs): African attitudes to IFI programmes 23–33; African debt 131, 134, 136 (origins 121; responses 124–30); critique of IFI programmes 17–23; Ferrero Resolution 85–6; impact of World Bank 1989 report 110–11; involvement in Africa 16–17; Lomé Convention and 98, 102–3, 109 (EC coordination with IFIs 105–7); neo-conservative critique 19; 'stop/go syndrome' 110; triangle of development diplomacy 12–13; Zambia 200, 231 (break in

relations 217–18; EC diplomacy 225–6, 254; 1985 reform programme 163–4; policy interventions 161–2; rapprochement 176); *see also* International Monetary Fund, structural adjustment, World Bank
International Monetary Fund (IMF) 96; African attitudes to IMF programmes 23–33; African debt 115, 116; conditionality 22–3; Extended Structural Adjustment Facility (ESAF) 24, 126, 176; involvement in Africa 16–17; Mexican debt 113; neo-conservative critique 19; and SIP for Tanzania 109; stabilization measures 17, 18; Structural Adjustment Facility (SAF) 17, 24; Zambia 152–3, 158–73, 174, 177, 197 (break 169–71, 217–18; EC diplomacy 225–6; extended programme 1981–83 159–61; 1978–80 programme 159; political resistance 223; rapprochement 176); *see also* international finance institutions
investment: disinvestment trends 257–8; French in African colonies 41, 42; promotion as structural weakness of EC 81; rate in Zambia 152; Rome Treaty association clause 45–6
Investment Task Force 197
Ireland 219, 220
Iroha Report 134
Italy 44, 50, 219, 220

Japan 220–1, 226–7, 301
Jaycox, E. 23, 177
Joint Committee (EC–Zambia) 194, 195–6, 196–7
Joint Consultative Assembly (EC–ACP) 72–3, 112
Joint Monitoring Committee (JMC) 197
Jolly, R. 18–19

Kabwe, B. 165
Kapwepwe, S. 147–8
Katondwana Primary School Project 241
Kaunda, K. 149, 194; criticism of 217–18; diplomacy after break with IMF 218; humanism 148; INDP 173; and Lozis 147, 290; Lusaka Manifesto 149; multi-party democracy 176–7; 1985 reform programme 163, 164; political patronage 211; public management 157; and social unrest 168–9, 171; visit to Brussels 185–6
Kawamba Tea Scheme 184, 185
Kazunga, S. J. 200, 203
Kennedy, E. 31
Kenya 107, 136, 137; conditionality 31
Kenyan Consultative Group 31
KFW 226–7
'Khartoum Declaration on Structural Adjustment in Africa' 26
Killick, T. 5, 20, 105, 271–2
Knorr, K. 7
Korner, P. 121
Krasner, S. D. 7, 13
Kunda, R. 182

Lagos Agreement 52–4, 64
Lagos Plan of Action (LPA) 14, 15
Laidler, M. 107
Latin America 49; and African association 45; debt 113, 114, 116, 117, 123, 129; trade with EC 49
Law, D. 8
Lawson Plan 130
Lecomte, B. 87
Lee Kuan Yew 32
legitimation 32
Lemerle, P. 29
leverage 10
Lewis, Sir A. 261–2
L'Hériteau, M.-F. 23
liberals 219–22
Liberia 23
Lipton, M. 88
local currency repayments 142
local government 239, 240
Loi Cadre 43–4
Lomé Convention/relationship 1–2, 4, 61–84, 253; and African debt 131–2, 144–5 (Lomé III 133–4, 135; Lomé IV 101, 137–41); aid programming 69–71; common African front 65–8; contractual obligations in aid system 224; and development policy 80–4; institutional framework 71–9, 82–4 (ACP institutions 76–9; EC institutions 73–6; joint institutions 71–3); Lomé IV and structural adjustment 96–112 (ACP negotiating position 99–100; continuity and change in provisions 100–1; coordination with IFIs 105–7; countervalue funds 103–4; EC aid management 101–3; EC approach to macroeconomic conditionality 109–10; eligibility for finance 104–5; funds available 108–9; governance and political conditionality 110–12; macroeconomic reform and aid programming 107–9; multilateral negotiating framework 97–9); main provisions 68–71; policy dialogue and Lomé III 88–93 (ACP negotiating position 90–3; EC negotiating position 89–90); prospects in a changing world 255–9; social exchange 11; triangle of development diplomacy 12; Zambia 181–216, 245 (EC diplomacy 234; evaluation study 212; Lomé I aid programming 183–6; Lomé II aid programming 186–9; Lomé III aid programming 189–91; Lomé IV aid programming 191–2; Lomé IV Export Promotion Programme (LEPP) 248–51)
London Metal Exchange (LME) 155
Long, O. 45
low-yield projects 213
Loxley, J. 17
Lozis of Western Province 147, 148, 290
Luchembe, M. 172, 295
Lukes, S. 6
Lusaka Manifesto 149

Macmillan, H. 46
macroeconomic conditionality *see* conditionality, macroeconomic
Madagascar 117, 137
maize 171, 224; imports 193; nationalization of mills 168–9; production target 189; subsidies 156, 167, 168, 198

Maize Development Project 187
Major, J. 130
Malawi 137
Mali 52, 137, 199
malnutrition 171
Mannesmann Affair 59–60
manufacturing 160–1
Mapoma, J. 165
Margai, Sir M. 51
marginalization of Africa 256–8
Marin, M. 112, 230, 257; and African debt problem 143, 144; EC coordination with IFIs 105, 106; structural adjustment 109
market access 68–9
market discipline 8
market mechanism 259
Marshall Aid Plan 17
Martin, G. 36
Mauritania 107, 136, 137
Mauritius 32, 80, 81
McNamara, R. 29
Meebelo, H. 188
Mexico: debt 113, 114, 116, 117
Michaels, M. 22
Micro-Projects Programme (MPP) 187, 191, 234, 235–7, 254; operational strategy 239–45; policy differences between World Bank and EC 245–7
Micro-Projects Tracking System (MTS) 244
Micro-Projects Unit (MPU) 235–7, 239, 243–4, 245, 246
Migdal, J. 242
military budgets 29
mineral export dependence 150–3, 155–6, 292
mining sector 150–2, 155–6; Britain 146, 147; Germany and cobalt question 208–10; IMF programme 159, 160, 161; nationalization 150–1; Sysmin 187, 188–9, 200–7; *see also* cobalt, copper
Ministry of Agriculture and Water Development (MAWD) 193
Mitterrand, F. 257
Mkandawire, T. 25
mobilization, political 148
moderates 219–22
modified structural realism 13
Mogadishu Accord 149
monetarism 123
money supply 123, 222–3
Monrovia Strategy 14–15
Morel, E. D. 37
Morgenthau, H. J. 6
Moss, J. 48–9, 54
Movement for Multi-Party Democracy (MMD) 177, 177–8
Mozambique 117, 136
Mpongwe Development Project 184, 185, 195, 213
Mufulira copper mine 158
Mufulira mining hospital 204, 205
Mugabe, R. 221
Mulaisho, D. 164, 165
Multi-annual Training Programme 184–5, 187
multi-party democracy 176–8
Multi-Year Rescheduling Agreement (MYRA) 126
Mundia, N. 161
Mupoma, J. 182
Musokotwane, K. 170, 173, 218, 220
Mvunga Commission 177
Mwaanga, V. 177
Mwananshiku, L. 161, 163, 165, 189
Mwenyi micro-project 241
Mwila, U. G. 186

Namboard 156, 197, 199
Namibia 188, 221
National Commission for Development Planning 213–14
National Technical Coordination Action Programming (NATCAP) 215
nationalizations 150, 151, 168–9, 291
Nchanga Consolidated Copper Mines (NCCM) 201–2, 291
neo-conservative critique of IFI programmes 19
neo-Keynesian critique of IFI programmes 19–20
neo-Marxist critique of IFI programmes 21
Netherlands 44, 50, 109, 220, 222
'New International Economic Order' 2
Newly Industrializing Countries (NICs) 247
Nigeria 63–4, 129, 258; external debt 114, 116, 117, 122; Lagos Agreement 52–4, 64
night aerial spraying 208
Nitrogen Chemicals of Zambia (NCZ) 226–8, 231
Nixon, R. 62, 63
Nkrumah, K. 52
Nkumbula, H. 148
non-concessional debts 127–8
non-tariff barriers 66
non-traditional exports 248–51
Nordic countries 219–20
Norway 220
Nsingo, K. 200, 209, 249–50
Nye, J. S. 6
Nyerere, J. 24

Office for Emergency Operations in Africa (OEOA) 16
oil 170; price shocks 121, 123
Ollawa, P. 157
Onimode, B. 24
OPEC 62–3, 121
Open General Licensing (OGL) system 230
'Operation Food Production' (OFP) Programme 192–3, 193–4
Oppenheim, F. 6
Organization for African Unity (OAU) 14, 31, 33, 64, 149; Lomé negotiating principles 65; Special Summit on Debts 1987 125–6
Organski, A. F. K. 6
Origin, Rules of 69, 81, 226
Otunu, O. 32
Oumaru, I. 217

Pan-African unity 52
parallel government 23
Parfitt, T. 109
Paris Club 126, 127
party-political class 172–3

Payer, C. 10
Pearce, R. 168
Perez de Cuellar, J. 29
periphery and centre 21
personal rule 157
Phiri, D. 163–4, 165
Pirzio-Biroli, C. 182, 183, 184
Pisani, E. 87, 98, 194, 211; 'Plan of Action to Combat World Hunger' 193; visit to Southern Africa 187–9
Pisani Memorandum 87–8, 89
planning 183–4, 211
Polanyi, K. 259
policy bias 156–7
policy dialogue 85–112, 253; EC food strategy in Zambia 192–8; and Lomé III 88–93; Lomé and structural adjustment 96–112
policy failure 121, 140, 156
policy studies 245
political conditionality 30–3, 34, 110–12
political mobilization 148
political resistance 33, 171–3, 223
politicization of North–South relations 62–3
Pooley, P. 191–2
population 154
portfolio equity flows 258
post-colonial development policy 48–50
potential influence 9–10
power: EC power and influence 10–11, 254–5; influence, social exchange and 6–11; modified structural realism 13
Prebisch, R. 25
Preferential Trading Area (PTA) 149
Price Waterhouse 228–9
princely state 157–8
private debts 115, 116, 117, 118, 119, 120
Programme of Action to Mitigate the Social Costs of Adjustment (PAMSCAD) 27, 233
programme approach 184
project aid 69–71; Zambia 184 (evaluation of 212–13)
project appraisal: political manipulation 59–60
project identification 242
project monitoring/evaluation 242–4, 246
project proposals 239
protectionism 80, 81
Provincial Cooperative Unions (PCUs) 156, 197
public expenditure 237–9
public management 157–8, 183–4
public subsidies *see* subsidies
publicly guaranteed debt 115, 116
purchasing of equipment 203, 204–5

Ramphal, Sir S. 2
rate of disbursement of funds 224–5
Ratzel, F. 36
Ravenhill, J. 58, 62, 84, 97
reciprocity: Lomé negotiations 64, 65, 66, 68; subsidies between France and her colonies 41–2; Yaoundé preferences 48, 49
regional currencies 261
regional dimension of adjustment 103
regional insecurity 148–50
regional integration 261
Regional Trypanosomiasis and Tsetse Control Programme (RTTCP) 187, 198, 208
regionalism 50
Reich, R. 1
repression 33
resistance, political 33, 171–3, 223
restructuring 190
Rhodes, C. 146
Rice Development Project 187
risk capital 131–2, 142, 143
Roan Consolidated Mines (RCM) 201–2, 291
Robinson, J. 114
Rochereau, H. 53
Roe, T. 222, 225
Rome Treaty 38–46, 47
Rosenau, J. N. 5
Rules of Origin 69, 81, 226
rural development 92–3; integrated rural development 69–71
rural health clinics 187, 237–9, 244
rural primary schools 237–9, 244–5
Russett, B. 9–10, 10

Sandiford, E. 99
Sâo Tomé and Principe 136
Sauvanargues, J. 66
Schneider, B. 121, 123
Schumacher, E. F. 234
Sectoral Import Programmes (SIPs) 102, 109, 135, 136, 138
Sékou Touré, A. 52
Selection Trust 150
self-interest 21
Senegal 59–60, 137
Senghor, L. S. 38, 44, 65, 276–7
Sierra Leone 63, 136
Single Market 96, 99, 255–6
single-party state 147–50
Smallholder Development Projects 191, 207–8
Social Action Programme (SAP) 175–6, 234–5
Social Development Fund 205
social dimensions of adjustment 96, 103, 233–47, 253–4
social exchange 6–11, 253
social inequalities 162
Social Projects Implementation Department (SPID) 235
social unrest 33, 171–3
social welfare projects 205–6
'soft state' 211–15
South Africa 188, 260
Southern African Development and Co-ordination Committee (SADCC) 149, 188, 291
sovereignty 22–3, 33, 272
Soviet Union 26; and aid debt 130; collapse 31–2; and EC 44–5
Spaak, P.-H. 40, 44
Special Action Programme 198–200
Special Programme of Action against Hunger (SPAH) 194–5, 198
Special Programme of Assistance (SPA) 135–7, 139
Stabex 68, 69, 141, 143, 255; principal exports 70; shortfalls 81–2

stabilization 17, 18, 96; *see also* structural adjustment
Starr, H. 9–10, 10
state 260; parallel government 23; princely state 157–8; 'soft' 211–15; structuralism and 7, 13, 20–1
state farms 193–4, 195, 196–7, 199–200
steel, structural 198, 199
Stevens, C. 80, 93, 105
Stewart, F. 19
Stiles, K. 22–3
Strasbourg Plan 39–40
Streeten, P. 5
strikes 171
structural adjustment: African attitudes to IFI programmes 23–33; aid, international economic relations and 4–5; conditionality and debt relief 130, 134, 135; critique of programmes 17–23; EC approach 102–3, 253–4; EC Council Resolution 94–6; and food dialogue strategy 197–8; Lomé IV and *see* Lomé Convention/relationship; typical measures 17, 18; US support 30; World Bank 1989 report 27–8; Zambia 159–71, 179–80, 191–2, 197–8 (EC responses 217–51); *see also* international finance institutions, International Monetary Fund, World Bank
Structural Adjustment Facility (SAF), EC 230–3, 254
Structural Adjustment Facility (SAF), IMF 17, 24
Structural Adjustment Support Unit 102, 107
structural power 7–9
structural steel 198, 199
structural transformation 26, 28–30, 100
structuralist critique of IFI programmes 20–1
subsidies: France and reciprocal 41–2; Zambia 167–9, 171, 195, 197 (maize 156, 167, 168, 198)
Sudan 33, 117, 122, 136
sugar 66, 69
Sûrprix system 40, 48
Sweden 219
Swedish International Development Agency (SIDA) 244, 245
Sysmin 131, 132, 141, 143, 247, 255; general assessment 206–7; Zambia mining sector 187, 188–9, 200–7

Tanzania 109
Tanzania–Zambia Railway (TAZARA) 149, 291
tariffs 47
Taylor, L. 20
technical assistance 207–8, 214–15
technical capacity 260
technical experts 207–8, 214–15, 242
technical mission 1989 213
Tembo, Lt-Gen. C. 172
tenders restrictions 204–5
terms of trade 123, 152, 153
Thomas, C. 9
Togo 107, 137
Toronto principles/Terms 127–8, 130
Toye, J. 20–1
trade 2, 20, 35; Arusha Convention 54; association 45, 47–8, 48–9, 50–1 (performance under association regime 54–5, 56); France and African colonies 41–2, 43; Lagos Agreement 53–4; Lomé Convention (negotiations 90, 97, 100; prospects for 255–6; trade performance under Lomé 80–2); reciprocity 64; Zambia 151–2, 182 (export promotion 247–51; terms of trade 152, 153); *see also* exports, import support
training *see* education/training
transformation, structural 26, 28–30, 100
'triangle of accommodation' 242, 243
triangle of development diplomacy 12–13
Trinidad Terms 130
Tsetse and Trypanosomiasis Control Project 187, 198, 208
Tsoukalis, L. 255
Twitchett, C. C. 38–9

Uganda 137
underdevelopment 146–7
United Kingdom *see* Britain
United National Independence Party (UNIP) 147, 147–8, 163, 176
United Nations (UN) 1; AAF-SAP debate 29–30; ECA *see* Economic Commission for Africa; Special Session on Africa 15–16; UNDP 215; UNICEF 19, 26, 27, 233; Zambia and 149
United Nations Programme of Action for African Economic Recovery and Development (UNPAAERD) 16
United People's Party (UPP) 148
United States (US) 30, 36; and African debt 113, 128 (commercial banks 120); Agency, for International Aid (USAID) 31; aid to Africa reduced 256; and association, 45, 63; hard line on Zambia 221, 222
universalism 50
urbanization 156
Uruguay Round 96

Vaccine Production Programme 187
Vander Stichele, M. 96–7

water supply project 187
welfare 205–6
Westminster Conference 1949 39
WIDER Group 20, 272
Wilkinson, J. 30
Wilson, H. 62
World Bank 1, 86, 96, 126, 233; adjustment and structural adjustment 5; African attitudes to programmes 23–33; Berg Report 15; competing models of 268; deteriorating African terms of trade 123; EC aid policy and 59; influence 10, 11; integrated rural development 71; involvement in Africa 16–17; 1989 Report on Africa 27, 30, 32, 110–11; 'Special Facility for Sub-Saharan Africa' 16; structural adjustment measures 17, 18; structure of conditionality 106; Zambia, 227, 234 *see also* international finance institutions; Micro-Projects Programme
'World Bank rule' 58
World Food Council 192

Yaoundé Conventions 46–51, 60, 63; Yaoundé I 48–50, 55; Yaoundé II 50–1, 61

Zaire 23, 210, 287, 288; debt rescheduling 126; Sysmin 201, 202
Zambia 3, 23, 146–251, 253–4; and association 63; colonial policy and underdevelopment 146–7; development policy 150–3; donor attitudes 219–22; EC food strategy 192–200; EC Foreign Exchange Facility 228–30; EC responses to economic reforms 222–6; EC Structural Adjustment Facility 230–3; Embassy in Brussels 211; export promotion and economic diversification 247–51; external debt *see* debt; first EC mission 182–3; foreign exchange gap 226–8; Fourth National Development Plan 1989–93 175–6, 215, 247; Germany and the cobalt question 208–10; and IMF *see* International Monetary Fund; import support 198–200, 226–8, 230–1; Interim National Development Programme 173–5, 224; Lomé aid programming 183–92 (Lomé I 183–6; Lomé II and the Foley mission 186–9; Lomé III and the food question 189–91; Lomé IV and the road to adjustment 191–2); Micro-Projects Programme *see* Micro-Projects Programme; mineral export dependence 150–3, 155–6, 292; 1985 reform programme and the auction 162–6; path to economic decline 153–9; policy bias against agriculture 156–7; political resistance 171–3, 223; problems of aid management 210–15; public management and princely state 157–8; rapprochement with IFIs 176; regional insecurity and foreign policy 148–50; return to multi-party democracy 176–8; single-party state 147–50; SIPs, 136, 138; Smallholder Project 191, 207–8; Social Action Programme 175–6, 234–5; social dimensions of adjustment 107, 233–47; social unrest 171–3; 'soft state' and eurocracy 211–15; Special Programme of Assistance (SPA) 135–7, 139; subsidies *see* subsidies; Sysmin and the mining sector 187, 188–9, 200–7; Third National Development Plan 186–7; weaknesses of foreign missions 211
Zambia Centre for Accounting Studies 191
Zambia Congress of Trade Unions (ZCTU) 221
Zambia Consolidated Copper Mines (ZCCM) 201, 201–2, 203, 204–6
Zambia Cooperative Federation (ZCF) 199
Zambia Engineering Company 203
Zambia Export Growers Association 251
Zambia Maths and Science Teacher Education Project 191
Zambit-Lomé Group 249–51
Zimbabwe 221
Zulu, G. 165